The Library of Ancient Wisdom

THE LIBRARY OF ANCIENT WISDOM

Mesopotamia and the Making of the Modern World

SELENA WISNOM

The University of Chicago Press

The University of Chicago Press, Chicago 60637

Published 2025
Printed in the United States of America

34 33 32 31 30 29 28 27 26 25   1 2 3 4 5

ISBN-13: 978-0-226-82255-6 (cloth)
ISBN-13: 978-0-226-82622-6 (e-book)
DOI: https://doi.org/10.7208/chicago/9780226826226.001.0001

First published in the United Kingdom in 2025 by Penguin Books Ltd., London.

Library of Congress Control Number: 2024947003

♾ This paper meets the requirements of ANSI/NISO Z39.48-1992 (Permanence of Paper).

Contents

General Timeline of Mesopotamian History

SOUTHERN MESOPOTAMIA	NORTHERN MESOPOTAMIA
3500–3100 BC Formation of Uruk, the first city	
c. 3400 Invention of proto-cuneiform writing	
c. 2900–2350 Early dynastic period (first kings, expansion of Sumerian city states)	2350–2150 BC Old Akkadian period (Sargon of Akkad accedes 2334 and builds first Mesopotamian empire)
2112–2004 Ur III period (centralised Sumerian state)	
2004–1595 Old Babylonian period (Sumerian dies out, Akkadian takes over)	2000–1600 Old Assyrian period (abundant evidence for international trade, trading outposts established in Turkey)
1792 Accession of Hammurabi (builds first Babylonian empire)	

SOUTHERN MESOPOTAMIA	NORTHERN MESOPOTAMIA
1595–1155 Middle Babylonian period (Hittites sack Babylon and the city is taken over by the Kassites)	1365–1056 Middle Assyrian period (Assyria becomes a substantial territorial state)
c. 1200 Collapse of many states in the eastern Mediterranean; beginning of textual dark age	*c.* 1200 Collapse of many states in the eastern Mediterranean; beginning of textual dark age. Assyria weakened and shrinks to its heartland.
1155 Elamites sack Babylon; the city is ruled by native dynasty once more	911–609 Neo-Assyrian period (Assyria rises again)
626–539 Neo-Babylonian period (Nabopolassar breaks away from Assyria and founds his own dynasty in Babylon)	612 Fall of Nineveh
539–331 Persian rule of Mesopotamia, until Alexander the Great takes Babylon	

Timeline of Events in This Book

Summer 705 BC – death of Sargon in battle

July 705 – chief scribe Nabu-zuqup-kenu copies out Tablet XII of the Epic of Gilgamesh *(see Chapter 7)*

July 705 – accession of Sennacherib (15 days later)

November 689 – Sennacherib's destruction of Babylon

In the years following, Sennacherib rebuilds the Ashur temple in the image of Marduk's temple in Babylon (see Chapter 2)

January 680 – murder of Sennacherib

March 680 – accession of Esarhaddon

May 672 – Ashurbanipal named crown prince of Assyria and Shamash-shum-ukin crown prince of Babylonia

672 or 671 – Ashurbanipal's sister writes to his young wife scolding her for not being good enough at writing cuneiform (see Chapter 1)

Late 671 – conspiracy against Esarhaddon becomes public

March 670 – conspiracy crushed

April–June 670 – Esarhaddon's most serious period of illness

April 670 – the king despairs to his physician Urad-Nanaya, asking why his illness cannot be diagnosed or cured. Early May – the king is at his lowest point; his advisers collectively beg him to stop fasting and come out of isolation; his physician confronts him about his inability to trust anyone (see Chapter 4)

June 670 – the queen mother falls ill

June 670 – the king's exorcist Adad-shumu-utsur performs anti-witchcraft rituals for the queen mother (see Chapter 3)

March 669 – argument among the astrologers over whether Venus or Mercury has risen (see Chapter 6)

November 669 – Esarhaddon dies. In the next month Ashurbanipal ascends the throne of Assyria

March/April 668 – Shamash-shum-ukin ascends the throne of Babylon

664 – Elamites invade Babylonia

Ashurbanipal pushes the Elamites out of Babylonia. Usurpers take control of Elamite throne and the legitimate heirs flee to Nineveh where Ashurbanipal grants them asylum for a decade. Continuing tensions erupt in the battle of Til-Tuba in 653 (see Chapter 8)

September 653 – Ashurbanipal's defeat of the Elamites at Til-Tuba

May 652 – Shamash-shum-ukin rebels against Assyria and war breaks out later that year

20 October 651 – the diviner Dannaya asks the entrails whether Shamash-shum-ukin is fleeing to Elam (see Chapter 5)

Autumn/winter 648 – war ends with the capture of Babylon

In the aftermath Ashurbanipal performs ritual laments in Babylon to appease the gods (see Chapter 9).

Autumn 647 – Ashurbanipal invades Elam and destroys Susa

631 – death of Ashurbanipal?

323 – death of Alexander the Great in Babylon

Babylonian scholars try to save him with the ancient substitute king ritual (see Epilogue)

Dramatis personae

Assyrian names can seem long and complicated, because each name is a miniature sentence – 'Ashurbanipal', for example, is actually a simplification in English of the Assyrian 'Ashur-bani-apli', meaning 'The god Ashur is the creator of the heir'. Many of the names used in modern parlance are based on how they were transcribed in the Hebrew Bible. Though the shorter versions still sound strange to our ears, they are more familiar than the Assyrian ones, so where they exist I have kept them. The scholars, who are less well known, will be called by their Assyrian names.

The Family

Ashurbanipal

The scholar-king who curated the library. Often called the last great king of Assyria, Ashurbanipal ruled 669–631 BC.

Sargon II

Sargon II was Ashurbanipal's great-grandfather and the founder of the dynasty. His death in battle in 705 BC was a disaster for Assyria.

Sennacherib

Sennacherib was Ashurbanipal's grandfather and, like Ashurbanipal himself, had a troubled relationship with Babylon. He suffered personal tragedy after his eldest son was kidnapped from the city and put to death, and reacted by razing Babylon to the ground.

Naqia

Naqia was Ashurbanipal's grandmother, and the wife of Sennacherib. Her name means 'pure' in Aramaic, which betrays the fact that she was not of Assyrian descent but came from the west. Naqia was one of the most important women in Assyrian politics. Astonishingly for the time, she was involved in the daily affairs of government and was the recipient of letters from the scholars about political matters.

Esarhaddon

Esarhaddon was Ashurbanipal's father. He was plagued by ill-health and sedition, had a reputation for being paranoid and constantly wrote to his advisers worrying about the omens, but this same paranoia was what kept him on the throne and could equally be understood as due diligence.

The Scholars

Balasi

Balasi was Ashurbanipal's chief scholar and had been his personal tutor while crown prince. He was primarily an astrologer, but was also well-versed in many different types of omens and rituals. He had a close personal relationship with the king, and this enabled him to speak his mind in a way that few others could.

Adad-shumu-utsur

Esarhaddon's chief exorcist, whose career continued into the reign of Ashurbanipal. He was part of a family of experts who worked at court – his son Urad-Gula was also an exorcist.

Urad-Nanaya

Esarhaddon suffered from a mystery illness that no one else had managed to diagnose or cure; as his chief physician, Urad-Nanaya had the unenviable task of performing the seemingly impossible.

Dannaya

Dannaya was one of many diviners in the palace who specialised in interpreting the omens from sacrificial sheep. He was a eunuch, which was unusual for someone of his position, since only those who were physically perfect were allowed to approach the gods.

Nabu-zuqup-kenu

Sargon's chief scholar, descended from an illustrious line of royal advisors, and father of Adad-shumu-utsur. He reflected on the king's death by copying out Tablet XII of the *Epic of Gilgamesh*.

Nabu-zeru-iddina

A lamentation priest whose job was to sing to the gods in the daily rituals in the temples, as well as lament on special occasions such as when an eclipse was coming. Nabu-zeru-iddina's father had served as chief lamenter under Esarhaddon, and trained his son to follow in his footsteps.

Extent of Assyrian Empire during the reign of Ashurbanipal (669–631?BC)

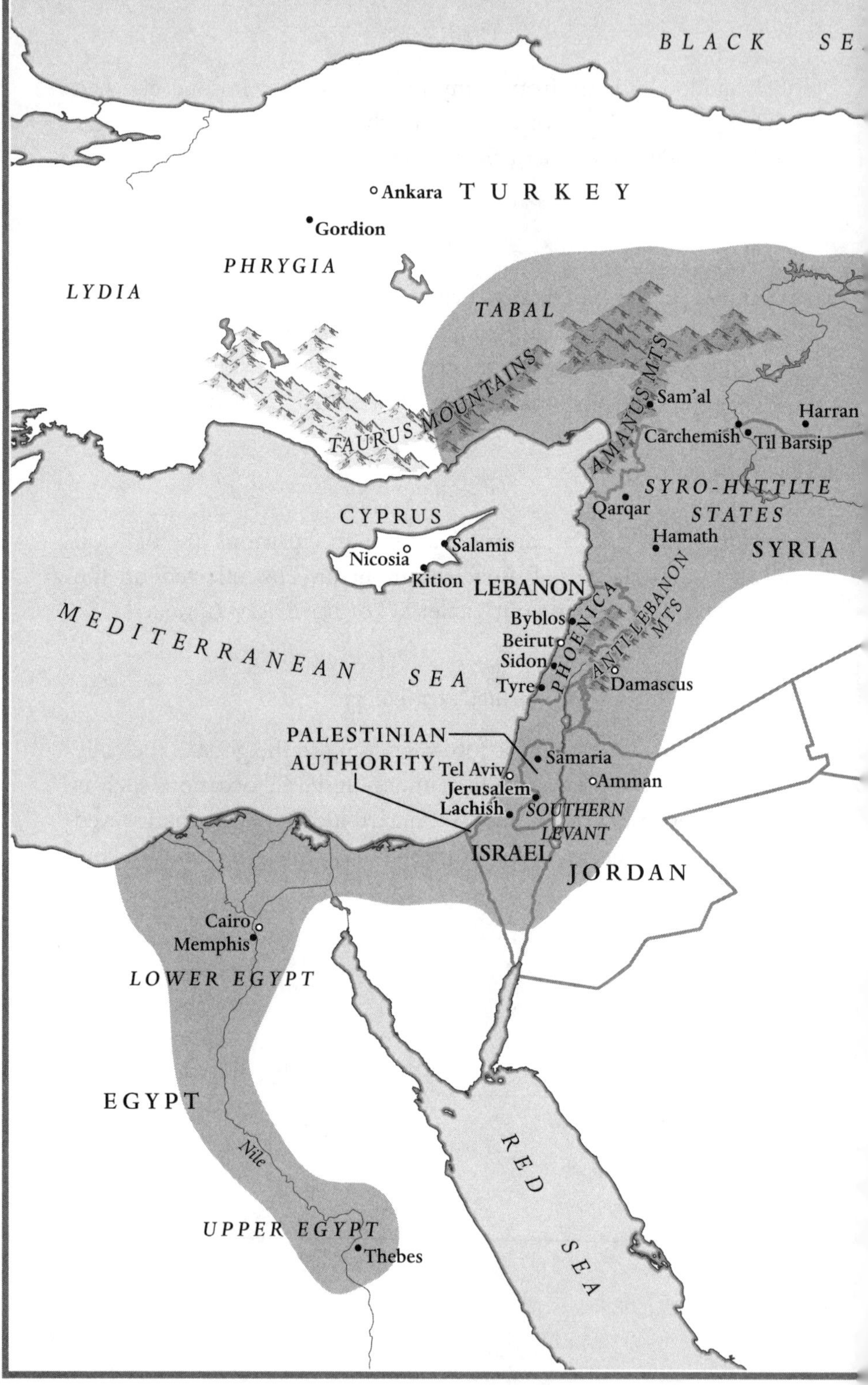

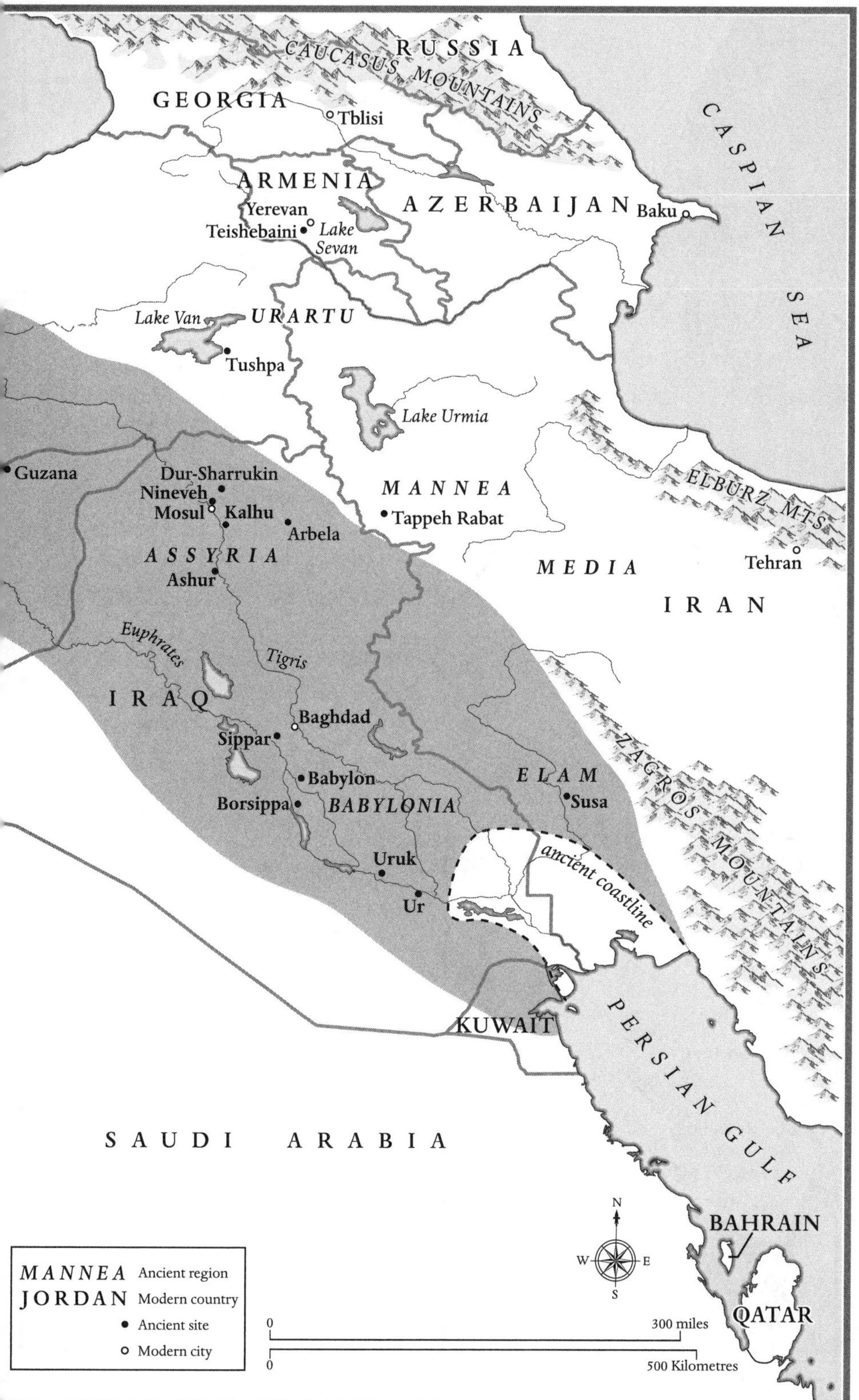
RUSSIA
CAUCASUS MOUNTAINS
GEORGIA
Tblisi
CASPIAN SEA
ARMENIA
AZERBAIJAN
Baku
Yerevan
Teishebaini
Lake Sevan
Lake Van
URARTU
Tushpa
Lake Urmia
Guzana
Dur-Sharrukin
Nineveh
Mosul
Kalhu
Arbela
MANNEA
Tappeh Rabat
ELBURZ MTS
ASSYRIA
Ashur
MEDIA
Tehran
IRAN
Euphrates
Tigris
IRAQ
Baghdad
Sippar
Babylon
ELAM
Susa
Borsippa
BABYLONIA
ZAGROS MOUNTAINS
Uruk
Ur
ancient coastline
KUWAIT
PERSIAN GULF
SAUDI ARABIA
N
W
E
S
BAHRAIN
QATAR
MANNEA Ancient region
JORDAN Modern country
Ancient site
Modern city
0
300 miles
0
500 Kilometres

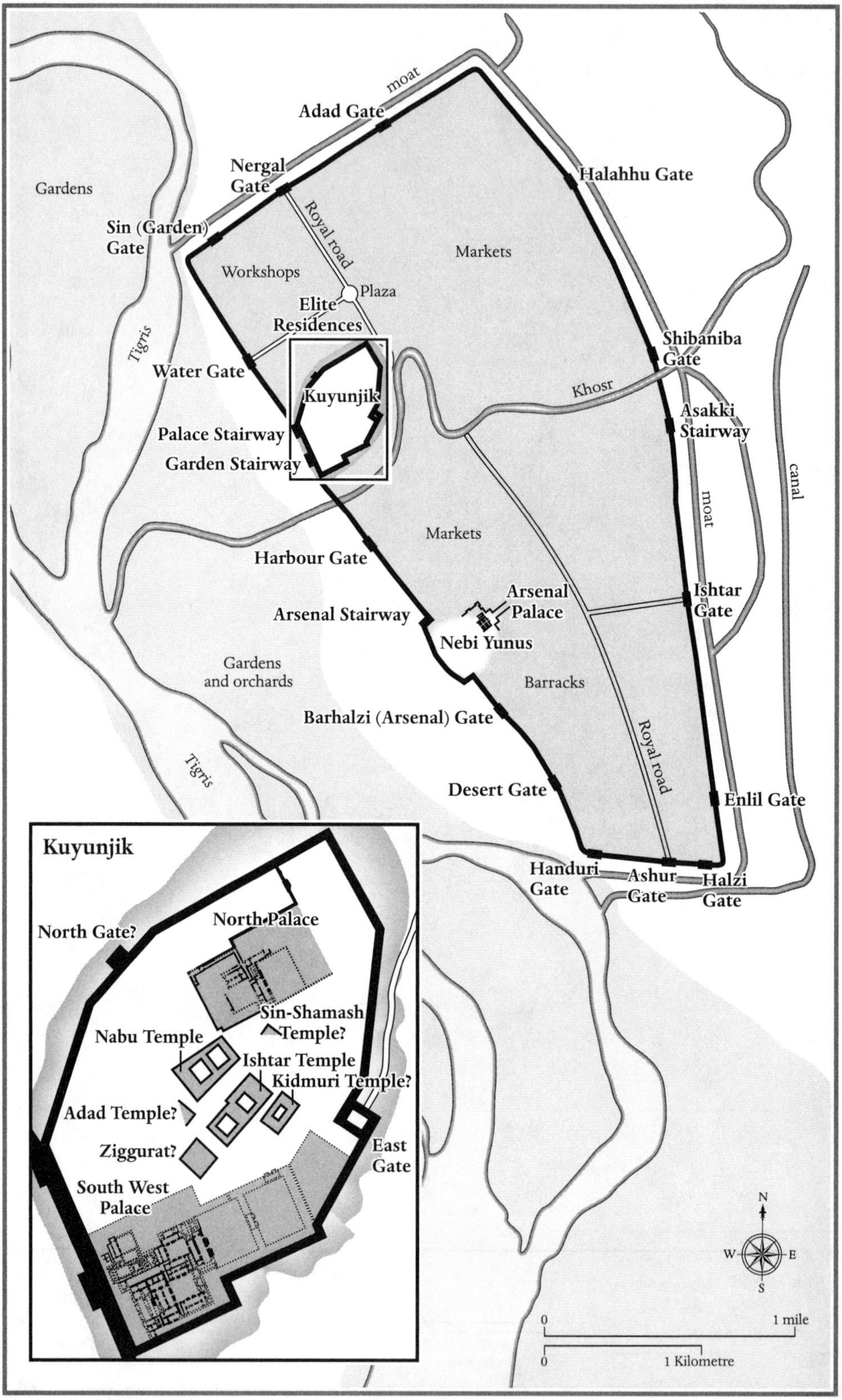
moat
Adad Gate
Nergal Gate
Halahhu Gate
Gardens
Sin (Garden) Gate
Royal road
Markets
Workshops
Plaza
Elite Residences
Tigris
Shibaniba Gate
Water Gate
Kuyunjik
Khosr
Asakki Stairway
Palace Stairway
Garden Stairway
canal
moat
Markets
Harbour Gate
Arsenal Palace
Ishtar Gate
Arsenal Stairway
Nebi Yunus
Gardens and orchards
Barracks
Barhalzi (Arsenal) Gate
Tigris
Royal road
Desert Gate
Enlil Gate
Handuri Gate
Ashur Gate
Halzi Gate
Kuyunjik
North Gate?
North Palace
Sin-Shamash Temple?
Nabu Temple
Ishtar Temple
Kidmuri Temple?
Adad Temple?
Ziggurat?
East Gate
South West Palace
N
W
E
S
0
1 mile
0
1 Kilometre

List of Illustrations

Color images follow page 196.

Preface

Nineveh, 612 BC. The chief scribe looks down from the citadel at the wave of destruction coming towards him like a massive flood. Swarms of troops move through the city, their shields red with blood as they batter down the defenders. Chariots flash through the squares and streets like lightning, aiming for the palace, sweeping towards him up the hill.[1]

The tablets are sitting on their shelves when it happens. They are stacked neatly in rows, as the sound of flames begins to crackle. Smoke seeps under the door as the sound grows louder and louder, from a distant hiss to a mighty roar. Soon the fire breaks down the door; it climbs the walls, and tears through the cedar beams as the roof crashes to the ground; the burning wood leaves a sweet scent mixed with bitter tar in a giant offering as if this were a sacrifice to the gods. The library has become a kiln: as the heat intensifies the clay tablets begin to bake and harden, setting their words almost as if in stone. In places the heat is so extreme that it liquefies the clay, which bubbles and turns to glass.

As all the buildings catch ablaze, the scribe turns and flees. But he has not left his knowledge to die. After the inferno cools, piles of tablets lie in heaps like rubble. Broken like pots and mixed with fractured wreckage, then slowly covered up by the debris of ages, the tablets bide their time. The fire that destroyed their home has ensured their preservation, hardening them to survive in the ground, waiting for the archaeologist's spade.

Nineveh has since fallen into obscurity. Some today might recall it as the place where the Old Testament prophet Jonah was travelling to when he was swallowed by a whale. Many will remember the destruction caused there by the so-called Islamic State of Iraq and Syria (ISIS), who broadcast images of their vandalism across the world. But Nineveh was once the most splendid city on earth, the seat of a powerful empire home to astonishing wealth, art, and culture.

The terrible wars Iraq has suffered in recent decades paint a bleak picture of the current state of its heritage. We have read of the looting of museums and desecration of archaeological sites, and seen videos of cities being bulldozed and blown up with dynamite. Given such dire reports, we might think that the destruction has been total, and that all is lost. Despite the considerable damage, there is much that we can still learn from what remains. Nineveh alone had already been excavated many times by teams from the UK, France, America, and Iraq itself between 1846 and 1990; and in 2019 archaeologists returned to resume conservation work and continue exploring the site. While ISIS did its best to publicise the destruction of the most visible 'idols' in their territory, such as the winged bulls that guarded the gates of Nineveh, Iraq has over ten thousand archaeological sites, many of which were protected by locals who took pride in guarding their heritage. And when ISIS destroyed the tomb of the prophet Jonah on the citadel of Nineveh, they unwittingly uncovered new parts of the Assyrian palace lying underneath it, including a rare frieze depicting Assyrian women. With so much material already excavated, and a tremendous amount of exciting excavation work ongoing, we are better placed than ever to reconstruct this amazing civilisation.

All too often it is destruction that makes the news. Most of us have heard only reports of disaster from this part of the Middle East, but for thousands of years Iraq has been a centre of learning, scholarship, and wisdom. It is time to focus on its achievements rather than its calamities, its wonders instead of its disasters. To do so we will enter the largest library of the ancient world prior to that of Alexandria, a library that has not been lost to history but sits on museum shelves in London as scholars piece it back together; a library that some two and a half millennia ago went up in flames and yet can be accessed today precisely for that reason.

Nineveh is located on the outskirts of Mosul in modern-day northern Iraq. The suburbs of the modern city have grown up around the centre of the ancient one. Today the ancient citadel is not much to look at – a grassy, rubble-littered hill, surrounded by houses and major roads looking out across a modern city. Yet on this site once stood one of the greatest collections of knowledge in history, containing the collected wisdom of the region we call Mesopotamia in ancient Iraq. Holding more than thirty thousand tablets, this library was assembled by King Ashurbanipal, a ruler who aspired to gather all the knowledge of his day under a single roof. Ashurbanipal scoured his empire for texts to add to his collection, obtaining copies from temples in times of peace and confiscating personal libraries in times of war. His library contained everything from the essential documents he would need to govern his lands to the most esoteric lore explaining how to read the future. It had vast stores of medical knowledge, ranging from dentistry to gynaecology, as well as prayers, songs, and great works of literature. There were accounts of victories in battle, and ancient dictionaries that have helped modern scholars to decipher cuneiform, the world's first writing system. In the royal archive there were letters between the king and his advisers, governors of faraway provinces and rulers of other states, and records of the everyday running of the palace and the empire. The library gives us a unique and extraordinary wealth of information about this culture – not only are the highest forms of scholarship of the time found here, but the voices and everyday experiences of the individuals who used it are also preserved in the letters that they wrote to the king.

Ashurbanipal assembled his library in the seventh century BC, but he was part of a much larger story: the Assyrians were conscious of their debt to those who came before them and were just as concerned about safeguarding ancient knowledge as we are today. Therefore, as well as being a snapshot of the state of knowledge in Ashurbanipal's time, the library is a window into the even more remote past. It helps us to understand nearly three millennia of history, preserving all kinds of texts that stretch back to the ancient states of Sumer and Babylonia and giving vital context to the centuries that follow. Ashurbanipal was the ruler of the Neo-Assyrian empire, which was not the first empire in the ancient Middle East. Two millennia earlier the region had been home to Sumerians who developed city states from the south of Iraq to northern Syria. The Babylonians and Assyrians then built their own kingdoms and vied with each other for power. 'Mesopotamia' is a general term that refers to this whole area, inhabited by different peoples at different times. Many developments took place in this vast time span, yet many aspects of the culture were shared and carried on. Its history is significant not just for Ashurbanipal or the Middle East, but for the whole world, as Mesopotamia witnessed numerous developments that have influenced us all in profound and often surprising ways, earning it the title of the 'cradle of civilisation'.

As the birthplace of writing – a revolutionary technology that facilitated the keeping of records, the growth of states, and the preservation of knowledge – Mesopotamia is literally where history begins. Mesopotamian scribes wrote on clay tablets, a simple and cheap medium that has also proved to stand the test of time. Consequently, we have a huge number of sources that give us a fascinating view of the earliest literate societies in the world – the number of tablets excavated so far has been estimated at over half a million. It is often assumed that the contents of these tablets are rather dull; mostly accounts and receipts. Mesopotamia does indeed have many sources of this type, which is how we know so much about its economy and enterprise. But it also has much more: cuneiform tablets document almost every facet of human existence, from the letters of ordinary people to the calculations of advanced mathematics. Mesopotamia, then, was the seat of a rich and complex culture, much of which is represented in Ashurbanipal's library.

Although many languages were used in Mesopotamia, two were dominant: Sumerian, the first attested written language, and Akkadian, which is an umbrella term for Babylonian and Assyrian, slightly different but mutually intelligible dialects. These languages use the same writing system, cuneiform, just as the Latin alphabet is used to write various European languages, regardless of whether they are related. In fact, the cuneiform world is even wider than Mesopotamia, for its writing system was also adapted by its neighbours for Ugaritic on the coast of Syria; Hittite in what is now Turkey; Urartian in modern day Armenia; and Elamite and Old Persian in Iran. This is testament to Mesopotamia's power and influence in the ancient world. Indeed, Akkadian was even used as the international language of diplomacy among the Bronze Age kings of Egypt, Turkey, Syria, and the Levant, such was its international prestige.

Writing is not the only legacy of Mesopotamia. Many concepts indispensable to civilisation originated here, including the city, banking, and law. Our division of hours into sixty minutes is based on the Mesopotamian mathematical system, and the constellations we look for in the sky were first grouped and named by the Babylonians. The Assyrians had aqueducts before the Romans, and the Babylonians had a version of Pythagoras' theorem a thousand years before Pythagoras. Mesopotamia was the cradle of civilisation not just in its very earliest origins but in its ongoing contribution to knowledge over three thousand years.

Yet this 'cradle' metaphor is problematic, predisposing us to view Mesopotamia as primitive. If Mesopotamia is the cradle, by implication it can't be as sophisticated as the civilisations that came after it. In this narrative, the Mesopotamians invented the basics before passing them to Greece and Rome who added the important parts. We regard ourselves as being at the most sophisticated point in this historical timeline, having passed through the Enlightenment and the Industrial Revolution, and having acquired other trophies such as quantum physics, postmodern philosophy, and the internet. However, there is a dangerous tendency for us in modern times to be a little too self-congratulatory, a little too in love with our own achievements, and to see people in the past as somehow lesser beings. We should not underestimate people who lived long ago; when we compare them to ourselves in any real detail what actually emerges is their impressive intelligence. Babylonian astronomers were able to calculate the exact positions of any planet at any time on any day in the future, with no instruments to measure the sky but their bare hands. These intellectuals were versed in not one but two dead languages, which they used for scientific and religious purposes in the same way that Latin and Greek were used in Europe until only a few hundred years ago. For the earliest farmers of the Near East, the invention of irrigation took considerable skill, requiring the development of new techniques to control their challenging environment and manage it to their advantage. The people of Mesopotamia were astonishingly clever, not just in the long view of history, but in ways that we can easily recognise today. Their heritage is a world heritage whose influence has left its mark across the globe.

Despite its importance for world history, scholarly work on Mesopotamia has scarcely reached the popular domain. Most of the books written by academics focus on the grand sweep of history – the development of civilisation, the rise and fall of Mesopotamia's various states and empires, and its rediscovery in the Victorian era. This book will not repeat those stories, though it will cover them where necessary. Instead, it will illuminate Mesopotamian culture through the people who lived it, seeking to understand how they thought and putting their knowledge in its human context. Ashurbanipal's library is extraordinary in that it preserves the voices of the people who used it as well as the knowledge itself, giving us a unique opportunity to see Assyria through Assyrian eyes. Inescapably, this viewpoint is limited to the elite and literary classes who wrote and used the tablets. Much of ordinary Mesopotamian culture would have been oral, but the library still reflects the society's broader traditions and concerns. Our journey will be an adventure that takes us to the heart of what it means to be human: so often we will see that the Assyrians asked similar questions to ours, and even arrived at similar answers, in curious and unexpected ways.

I first discovered Mesopotamia by chance. Browsing in a bookshop one day in my late teens, I saw a new translation of the *Epic of Gilgamesh* and thought it looked like the kind of thing I would like. I bought it and read it in one sitting. I was struck by the familiarity of its themes and the strangeness with which they were expressed. There was something so recognisable and universal in this poem's story of a man's struggle to come to terms with his own mortality after the death of his best friend, and the quest for knowledge that he consequently embarked upon to the ends of the earth. This was a powerful work of literature that had connections with the classical world I knew, yet it was also mysterious and challenging, all the more for its strangeness. I ended up studying both Classics and Assyriology in sequence, journeying into the ever-remoter past.

Above all, it is the strangeness of Mesopotamia that draws me to it, and the desire to make that strangeness understandable once more. Assyriology is a quest to rediscover how the seemingly inexplicable does make sense, and to bring what was once obscure back into the light. To be an Assyriologist is to reconstruct some of the world's most significant ancient cultures, bringing back to life civilisations that have been lost for more than two thousand years. It is a quest as exciting as that of Gilgamesh himself, and one that remains as exhilarating today as when I first began.

Introduction: A World Rediscovered

Ancient Mesopotamia covers the area of modern-day Iraq, and falls within the so-called 'fertile crescent' which also encompasses Syria, the Levant, parts of Turkey, and south-west Iran. 'Mesopotamia' is a Greek word meaning 'between the rivers', referring to the Tigris and Euphrates. Many different peoples lived here over the centuries, beginning with the Sumerians and followed by the Akkadians, the Assyrians, and the Babylonians. The region was a melting pot of cultures but nevertheless was loosely held together by a shared literary and religious tradition, first and foremost the use of cuneiform writing. The cuneiform sources for this culture span from c. 3400 BC up until c. AD 80, a continuum of time so vast that Assyriologists specialise not by decade or century but by millennium. Even after Babylon fell to the Persians, cuneiform culture endured. Under foreign rulers, from the Persians to the Greeks and even the Parthians, priests continued writing calculations in cuneiform and singing to their gods in Sumerian. This culture endured for more than three millennia, meaning that from the Middle East to the West more than half of human history is written in cuneiform.

Mesopotamian culture began with the Sumerians. Sumer is an area in the south of Iraq where the first city states of Uruk and Ur were formed, effectively the first mega-cities and bureaucracies in the world. The Sumerians dominated the region for over a thousand years, but by the second millennium BC their language had fallen out of use and Akkadian had taken over.

Eventually this landscape was inherited by the Babylonians in the south and the Assyrians in the north. The Assyrian people were indebted to the Babylonians much as the Romans were to the Greeks: Assyrian culture owes so much to the Babylonians that the two can be difficult to disentangle. For this reason I will use the term

'Mesopotamian' to refer to aspects of the culture that are shared between the two, as well as with even older Sumerian texts. The fortunes of the two empires rose and fell in more or less alternating patterns over the centuries. The Assyrians traced their ultimate ancestors back to the Old Akkadian empire based in northern Iraq, made great by Sargon of Akkad in the twenty-third century BC. Later, Babylon became a great city and centre of learning in the eighteenth century BC, when King Hammurabi conquered the surrounding territory and the old Sumerian cities to the south and forged the first Babylonian empire. 'Hammurabi's law code' is one of the most iconic monuments of the ancient Near East – carved out of sleek black basalt, it is inscribed with 282 laws that deal with accusations of murder, assault, professional misconduct, misbehaviour of animals, inheritance, and much more. As often happens when any one object from Mesopotamia becomes famous it was labelled as 'the first' law code, even though there were others that preceded it. But Hammurabi's is the most beautiful, and the best preserved, and so justly deserves its limelight. It can be seen today in the Louvre.

Relations between Assyria and Babylon in the first millennium BC were tense. The first few centuries were disastrous for Babylon as it repeatedly suffered from enemy invasion and internal turmoil. This is when Assyria rose to prominence. In the tenth century BC the Neo-Assyrian empire took off, with king after king adding to its territory until, by the time of Ashurbanipal, it was the largest empire the world had ever seen. Babylon was one of the cities conquered by the Assyrians, along with its surrounding regions (known as Babylonia), but the Babylonians resented being under Assyrian domination and frequently rebelled. Babylon was a source of constant trouble to most Assyrian kings, who tried various strategies to pacify it, none of them successful. In fact, it was the Babylonians who eventually brought about Assyria's downfall, teaming up with other tribes to sack Nineveh in 612 BC following centuries of Assyrian rule.

The events of this book take place in a relatively short window of time, in the reigns of the last prominent Assyrian rulers: Sargon II, Sennacherib, Esarhaddon, and Ashurbanipal. These four kings lived dramatic lives, and their library bore witness to some extraordinary events.

Sargon II was the founder of the dynasty, who expanded the empire to limits it had never reached before. Our story begins with his unexpected death in battle in 705 BC, a traumatic event that casts a shadow over the rest of his dynasty. When his son Sennacherib ascended the throne, he did all he could to distance himself from his father, hoping to escape being haunted by his past. But all of the Sargonids would go on to suffer both personal and political crises, which led at least one of them to question whether the source of their troubles was a sin committed by Sargon against the gods.[1]

Like so many Assyrian kings, Sennacherib's reign was marked by conquest. He became famous for his campaign against Judah, which was memorialised in the Bible and in a poem by Byron, 'The Destruction of Sennacherib'. But it was the struggle over Babylon that defined him most of all. The city had been conquered by the Assyrian king Tiglath-Pileser III in 729 BC, but the Babylonians did not come quietly, and continually rebelled against Assyrian rule. Sennacherib tried various strategies to control them, culminating in installing his son and heir Ashur-nadin-shumi as king of Babylon, but this failed spectacularly when his son was kidnapped after six years on the throne and never returned home. Sennacherib's retaliation was brutal, and he destroyed the city in 689 BC. It was a shocking act of violence on Assyria's mother culture that many must have had mixed feelings about, and that his descendants would grapple with for generations, another long shadow over the Sargonid dynasty.

Like his father and son, Sennacherib too had an untimely death. The disappearance of his designated heir caused fatal problems for the line of succession. It seems that an older son, Urdu-Mulissu, had been expecting to succeed Sennacherib, yet it was Esarhaddon who was nominated by their father, a choice that seems to have surprised everyone. Shortly after the announcement was made, Esarhaddon was sent away for his own safety, but he was not the one in danger – Urdu-Mulissu took his anger out on his father, teaming up with another brother and murdering Sennacherib in an attempt to seize the throne. Yet two months then passed while the brothers fought among themselves over which of them should become king. In that time Esarhaddon stormed back to Nineveh and drove his brothers out, taking his place as king of Assyria in 680 BC.[2]

With such a tumultuous start to his reign it is no wonder that Esarhaddon was vigilant about possible threats to his rule, constantly on the look-out for ill omens and portents. He also suffered from a mysterious illness that waxed and waned for years and that none of his physicians could diagnose or cure. This was a serious problem for an Assyrian king, politically as well as personally, since in Assyrian eyes his illness made him look weak. A sick king could not be a legitimate one – regardless of his successes – and when news of his illness got out it sparked a conspiracy to unseat him from the throne.

Esarhaddon ultimately faced down three conspiracies – from a challenger named Sasi, from the chief eunuch, and from the mayor of the city of Ashur – and retaliated by executing much of the top level of his administration. This purge was hugely damaging as it left the country without enough officers to govern it – years in Assyria were named after the top official, and for the first months of 670 no one was in a position to give their name to it.

The crushing of the conspiracies must have made everyone in Esarhaddon's court extremely jumpy, but there were more exhausting events to come. A few months later the king's illness reached its worst crisis and his physicians and exorcists alike became increasingly desperate in their attempts to bring him back to health. As soon as the king recovered, his mother Naqia fell seriously ill, which was thought to be the work of witchcraft. She recovered too, and the entire royal family were exorcised as a precaution. But the next year Esarhaddon died on the way to suppress a rebellion in Egypt, most likely as a result of the illness which finally got the better of him.

Esarhaddon had taken measures to ensure a smooth succession and tried to set things up to spare his sons the troubles he had faced. He divided the kingdom, making Ashurbanipal king of Assyria and his elder brother Shamash-shum-ukin king of Babylonia, hoping that each would be content with their own domain. Unfortunately after their father's death the strategy failed; although the brothers got on at first, eventually hostilities broke out and they went to war in 652 BC. The result was a conflict that lasted four years and ended with the Assyrian defeat of Babylon for a second time in living memory.

Though famed in antiquity for its wealth and sophistication, and remembered in the Bible as the home of Abraham, the tower of Babel, and the whore of Babylon, for millennia Mesopotamia remained as distant as myth. All that people knew of this ancient civilisation came from garbled references by classical authors, passed across continents and down through time like Chinese whispers, and from polemical biblical writers with an axe to grind against the Assyrian and Babylonian kings who had conquered them.

After two thousand years of silence, Mesopotamia emerged again in the nineteenth century AD to speak with its own voice. Sensational archaeological discoveries in the Middle East uncovered the cities of Assyrian kings with their magnificent palaces and extraordinary sculptures and reliefs, which were brought back to the British Museum in London and the Louvre in Paris. Babylon itself was excavated by German archaeologists and its dazzling gate of blue-glazed bricks reconstructed in Berlin. For the first time, readers of the Bible could look upon the faces of the conquerors who appeared in its pages, such as Shalmaneser III and Sennacherib.

Even more exciting were the written sources that were discovered. The decipherment of the cuneiform writing system in 1857 finally allowed us access to the conquest of Judah from Sennacherib's perspective, Nebuchadnezzar's boasting in his own words, and a Babylonian flood story strikingly similar to the one described in Genesis. Later identified as the *Epic of Gilgamesh* that would captivate me as a young adult, the Babylonian account of the deluge caused such a stir that the *Daily Telegraph* funded an expedition to search for the missing pieces of the tablet. It was like looking for a needle in a haystack – small pieces of clay in a site containing thousands – but extraordinarily, another version of the same story was indeed found. George Smith, a self-taught scholar of modest origins, who identified it, was so excited when he read the description of a ship resting on a mountain top and sending out a dove to look for dry land – so uncanny in its echoes of the Bible – that he is said to have started undressing himself and running around the British Museum study room in elation. This story is recorded by E. A. Wallis Budge, a curator who had a long-standing dislike for Smith. Most likely intended to mock him, it had the opposite effect, not only because it is such an eccentric thing to do but for its capturing of the exhilaration of those early days of discovery.

The field of scholarship that covers all this is called 'Assyriology'. The name is misleading, since it encompasses not only Assyrian culture but everything from Sumerian literature to Babylonian economics. The term was coined when the Assyrian palaces were discovered in the nineteenth century, and remained even when excavations continued to unearth older and older states and cultures. As it became clear that the excavators had only scratched the surface of Mesopotamian history, further sub-categorisation developed. The Assyrians were renamed the 'Neo-Assyrians'. There were also Old Assyrians and Middle Assyrians, as well as Old, Middle, Neo-, and Late Babylonians, not to mention the earlier Sumerians and Akkadians. But by then the name 'Assyriology' had stuck.

What had begun as a kind of biblical archaeology seeking to establish the veracity of the Old Testament quickly became an independent field of interest in its own right, with sources reaching much further back in time than any biblical writings. Scholars struggled to keep up as these sources continued to be unearthed at an incredible rate. Many tablets discovered in this era still languish in museum storerooms waiting to be transcribed and published, while archaeologists continue to add new artefacts from fresh excavations.

Put simply, too few people are trained to read cuneiform for us to be able to cope with the demand, simply because not enough people are aware it is possible to study it at university.

It was in this thrilling period of discovery in the nineteenth century that Ashurbanipal's library came to light. The library would prove foundational for the study of Mesopotamia more widely, since it was largely thanks to the tablets held there that its languages were deciphered, and it is those tablets that form the core of our knowledge about Mesopotamian scholarship – Assyrian, Babylonian, and even Sumerian.

The library emerged in stages, as its tablets were found in several places through a series of different excavations. Since Iraq was under Ottoman rule at this time, the site was known by the name of Kuyunjik, a Turkish word meaning 'little sheep' that implies it was then used as a place for grazing. But this great mound of earth covered the ancient citadel of Nineveh and the palaces of the Assyrian kings. French and British expeditions began digging at Kuyunjik in 1842, but the French did not find anything initially, and abandoned the site in favour of other Assyrian cities. The first major discovery at Nineveh was Sennacherib's 'Palace without Rival', found by the British archaeologist Austen Henry Layard and his local assistant Hormuzd Rassam, working for the British Museum, between 1847 and 1851. In 1850 a sensational find was made: while tunnelling through the earth, the excavators reached a room filled with cuneiform tablets, which Layard named 'the chamber of records', describing it as follows:

> The first doorway, guarded by the fish-gods, led into two small chambers opening into each other, and once panelled with bas-reliefs, the greater part of which had been destroyed. On a few fragments, still standing against the walls, could be traced a city on the shore of a sea whose waters were covered with galleys. I shall call these chambers 'the chambers of records', for . . . they appear to have

> contained the decrees of the Assyrian kings as well as the archives of the empire . . . The cuneiform characters on most of them were singularly sharp and well defined, but so minute in some instances as to be almost illegible without magnifying glass.[3]

Spurred on by this discovery, the British Museum continued its work at the site. The next expedition was led by the diplomat Henry Rawlinson, who had a keen interest in the language of the tablets and would play a key role in deciphering cuneiform. The Ottomans divided the rights to excavate Kuyunjik between the British and the French – the French were given the north side, the British the south. It was the local assistant Rassam who made the breakthrough. He had a hunch that the British should work on the north side of the mound, where the French, to his frustration, were not exploiting their right to dig. Rassam decided to take matters into his own hands and excavate on the French side secretly, at night. This hunch proved to be correct, and in 1853 he discovered Ashurbanipal's North Palace, and many more cuneiform tablets. The French conceded their rights to the British in return for some of the reliefs from the palace, which is why Ashurbanipal's library is now housed in the British Museum. Thousands of tablets were uncovered in a series of excavations over the next fifty years. A selection can be seen in gallery 55, while the bulk of the collection is stored in the Arched Room, a study room filled from floor to ceiling with trays of texts.

We do not know what the library looked like, as many of the tablets were not found in their original locations. What Layard grandly named 'the chamber of records', for instance, turned out to be a bathroom next to the throne room – the invading armies who sacked the palace must have dumped the tablets there after taking their pick of what they wanted. To complicate matters further, early excavators often did not record exactly where they found the tablets in the first place. Another large cache was found in Ashurbanipal's North Palace, which is now thought to have been the location of the library proper, and we now know that Nineveh was in fact home to at least two other libraries, belonging to the temples of the goddess

Ishtar and Nabu, god of scribes. All of these have been mixed up under the museum label of 'K', standing for Kuyunjik, making it difficult to always know which tablets came from which building. Thankfully the ancient scribes themselves were often diligent about classifying the works; many tablets were inscribed with the label 'Palace of Ashurbanipal, king of the world, king of Assyria', marking them as his property.

Although the library has not been excavated as a physical place, we can imagine something of its character based on other libraries that have been unearthed elsewhere. In 1986, a library was found in a temple in the city of Sippar, with tablets still on the shelves. The library was a small room with fifty-six rectangular niches built into the walls in a grid-like pattern, the ultimate purpose-built storage. Each niche was 30 cm wide and only 17 cm high, but, perhaps surprisingly to us, 70 cm deep, meaning not all of the tablets could be seen at the same time. The tablets were stacked like books, two or three rows deep, and each niche could hold sixty of them. This small room, only a few metres square, could easily have held 3,360 clay tablets. It does not seem to have been a place for reading like a modern library, but rather was a place for storage, like a closed stack. Cuneiform tablets would be difficult to read indoors in any case, since one needs a bright light to make them easily legible. Most likely the reading and writing of them would have taken place outside in the courtyard.

Assyrian libraries probably had a similar layout. Another temple dedicated to the god of scribes at the Assyrian city of Khorsabad also had these niches, as did an archive at Sennacherib's palace in Nineveh. Another royal archive in the city of Kalhu stored tablets in brick boxes similar to modern filing cabinets. At Nineveh we know that groups of tablets were labelled so that they could be found more easily, perhaps similarly to modern library shelves, since two of these labels for different omen collections have actually been found.

Clay tablets come in various shapes and sizes, depending on how much and what kind of text was written on them. It was easy to make a tablet to fit the occasion. Letters and reports can be quite small – about the size of a mobile phone; smaller if there was less to say. A library tablet would be much larger, perhaps the same size as a modern paperback, but the text would be written in columns only half as wide. The number of columns could be expanded, so that some tablets have as many as four columns across and are more of a landscape format, while others are just a single column, slim and elegant. A work of literature would consist of several different tablets arranged in a numbered series, each one corresponding to one 'chapter' of the story. They range from one tablet long (e.g. *The Descent of Ishtar to the Netherworld*) to twelve (*The Epic of Gilgamesh*). Scholarly works were often much longer – the series describing omens from everyday life is 120 tablets long. When the palace burned and the tablets crashed to the ground they broke into pieces, but the fragments have all been diligently collected, and many have been put back together in what has been described as the world's largest jigsaw puzzle. This work continues today, and finding a missing piece is still one of the great joys of the Assyriologist; artificial intelligence now helps us position the smaller fragments, some of which are the size of a postage stamp. The discovery of new parts of texts is one of the things that makes Assyriology so exciting, and is a regular occurrence – even during the writing of this book, new tablets have become known that could radically change our understanding of the texts they witness, while entirely new compositions also frequently come to light.

As well as clay tablets, the library contained writing boards – wax tablets like those used in the Roman empire, which could be smoothed over and reused. Only a few have survived, but judging from library inventories there must have been thousands in the library in total. Despite the potential for editing in this format, we know that many of the texts we find on tablets were also written on boards – standard reference works on divination, medicine, and ritual. When scholars in the city of Borsippa in northern Babylonia were asked to contribute to the library, they sent writing boards instead of tablets. As well as being easier to carry around than heavy pieces of clay, they could be prestigious items – one that was found in a well in the Assyrian city of Kalhu is made of ivory and has hinges that allow it to be opened and closed like a book. Amazingly, some wax is preserved on the board, with cuneiform signs still visible.

For four decades Ashurbanipal ruled an empire stretching from Iran in the east to Egypt and parts of Turkey in the west. He was the last great king of Assyria, the last of his line to control such a vast territory, and the most powerful Assyrian king who ever lived. He sat on the throne from 669 to 631 BC and during that time crushed Assyria's traditional enemies in Elam (a kingdom in western Iran), put down an Egyptian rebellion, and besieged Babylon. Yet there was more to Ashurbanipal than the list of his victories, as is shown by his vast and varied library.

Every Assyrian king was expected to wage war, and Ashurbanipal was no exception. His own accounts of his conquests of foreign lands portray him as an indomitable warrior who had no rival, who cut down all who were foolish enough to resist him, and who brought breakaway territories back into the fold. But unusually for Assyrian kings, Ashurbanipal was just as much a scholar as a military man. Reliefs in his palace show him spearing lions from his chariot yet carrying a stylus in his belt, as if the instruments of writing are as necessary for him to carry as the instruments of war.

Ashurbanipal even sometimes promotes his scholarly identity above his martial prowess. In a famous inscription where he speaks of the gifts that the gods bestowed on him while he was still in the womb,[4] Ashurbanipal mentions his broad mind, extensive knowledge, and scribal learning before his power and physical strength.[5] It was usual for Assyrian kings to be literate, but Ashurbanipal boasts to have studied to the same level as his scholars, a claim made by no other Assyrian monarch:

> I learned the craft of the sage Adapa, the secret and hidden lore of all the scribal arts. I am able to recognise celestial and terrestrial

> omens and can discuss them in an assembly of scholars. I am capable of arguing with expert diviners about the series called 'If the liver is a mirror image of the heavens'. I can resolve complex mathematical divisions and multiplications that do not have an easy solution. I have read cunningly written texts in obscure Sumerian and Akkadian that are difficult to interpret. I have carefully examined inscriptions on stone from before the Deluge that are sealed, stopped up, and confused.[6]

Here Ashurbanipal lays claim to the totality of Mesopotamian academic wisdom, a secret knowledge accessible only to the highly trained. He claims to be proficient in divination, which was among the most fundamental tools of government – the ability to read the will of the gods, in the sky, on earth, and in the entrails of sacrificial animals, was crucial for navigating difficult situations, both political and personal. Not only could Ashurbanipal interpret these omens in his own right, but he could discuss them with experts and argue about their meaning. Unlike previous rulers, perhaps, this was not a king who could be misled by technical jargon but one who could check it for himself, and who understood the reasoning behind the advice given to him.

Ashurbanipal then claims to be equally proficient in mathematics, a highly sophisticated Mesopotamian art whose achievements would be absorbed by the classical world following Alexander the Great's conquest of Babylon. He is also, we learn, a linguist: many of the texts he mentions were written in dead and difficult languages – Sumerian had died out as a spoken language more than a thousand years before Ashurbanipal's time, and even Akkadian was not easy for everyone to understand, since more and more people were now speaking Aramaic as their mother tongue. Finally, Ashurbanipal claims to have studied inscriptions on stone from before the deluge, the flood – a legendary event that separated myth from history and marked the beginning of historical time. This shows that the Assyrians themselves were conscious of the incredibly long span of their civilisation, and Ashurbanipal's library contains texts that date to at least a thousand years before him, carefully copied and preserved through the ages.

Aside from his scholarly persona, what else do we know about Ashurbanipal? The inscriptions that tell the stories of Ashurbanipal's campaigns preserve something of his own voice, since their tone matches that of his private letters. He sees himself as magnanimous and merciful, as when he declares that 'I Ashurbanipal, king of Assyria, the magnanimous one who performs acts of kindness and repays good deeds, had mercy on [the Egyptian pharaoh] Necho, a servant who belonged to me, and forgave his crime.'[7] Yet he inflicts humiliating punishments on his enemies, justifying them as 'the command of the great gods, my lords', for instance when he places the king of Qedar in a dog collar and makes him guard the city gate.[8] He rewards those who are obedient to him with gifts and kingdoms, the disloyal with obliteration. Nothing riles him more than ingratitude. His bitter complaints about the Elamite king echo those he had made against his own brother when he rebelled against him: 'He forgot the kindness that I had done for him, in having sent aid to him, and constantly sought out evil.'[9] A common theme is his anger when people fail to enquire after his health: 'As for the people living inside it [Bit-Imbi, a royal city of Elam], who had not come out and inquired about the well-being of my royal majesty, I killed them. I cut off their heads, sliced off their lips and took them to Assyria to be a spectacle for the people of my land.'[10] This was not a king you wanted to cross.

Ashurbanipal's library was not open to the public and tablets were not lent out. Instead, it was more of a private collection, made for the use of the king and his scholars. The tablets themselves tell us this, since the labels inscribed at the end of the texts declare they belong to the palace and often contain remarks seemingly from the king, such as: 'I have written, checked and collated this tablet in the assembly of scholars, and placed it in my palace for my royal consultation.'[11]

Whether or not Ashurbanipal really wrote out all of these tablets himself (and this statement appears on a suspiciously high number of tablets for this to be the case) the label attests to his personal interest in their contents and implies he would have consulted them himself, just as he boasts in his inscription. There are some tablets which we can identify as being written in the king's own hand: a letter sent to his father while he must have been still very young,[12] but also a list of medicinal plants, and a technical glassmaking recipe which does indeed belong to the realm of obscure knowledge that he claims to have mastered.[13] The king's writing is twice the size of that on most tablets in the library, which implies that they were written during his training, a subject we will return to in Chapter 1.

Making allowances for his royal hyperbole, Ashurbanipal was still more of an expert than any king who had come before him. This may well be the reason why he emphasises his scholarly interests as much as or more than his military achievements, for they truly did set him apart. He was personally involved in acquiring material for his library, which makes it a collection that reflects his interests. Letters survive that discuss the acquisitions – one astrologer reports that new tablets have arrived and asks for direction about which ones he should copy,[14] and later asks the king to tell him what to remove and what to add from the copies that are to be made.[15] These letters also show us that the king genuinely was interested in safeguarding knowledge: 'The tablets I am speaking about are worth preserving until far-off days,' writes one scholar.[16]

Ashurbanipal actively sought out works for his collection, ordering other libraries to send him copies of what they owned. It was especially important to acquire texts from Babylon, the seat of Mesopotamian learning, and it is common for Assyrian tablets to bear the statement 'written and checked according to an original from Babylon' as testament to their bona fide origins. On one occasion Ashurbanipal wrote to the scholars of the city of Borsippa ordering them to make copies of all the scribal learning in the Nabu temple and send them to him, but the scholars replied that one of the texts he asked for was not available anywhere but in the temple of Marduk in Babylon itself.[17] Ashurbanipal's war against his brother, the king of Babylon, provided opportunities to access these scholarly riches, as tablets were confiscated as war booty. Inventories from the year the city fell record the delivery of tablets and writing boards of all different genres, surrendered by Babylonian scholars. Some of these scholars were brought back to Assyria and forced to work on the copying of texts for the library, kept in chains between jobs.[18]

The library was ultimately a resource to support the workings of government, to be used by both Ashurbanipal and his advisers. A letter from the king to the governor of Borsippa hints at this when it asks him to send texts to the library including 'whatever is good for the kingship' and 'whatever is needed in the palace'.[19] The purpose of the library is reflected by its contents also – uniquely among Mesopotamian collections, it contains more texts on divination than any other genre; this field of study would have been key to making decisions and helping the king run his empire. The collection is also heavy on magic and ritual, important technologies for ensuring the king's safety and keeping the gods onside. In fact everything in the library turns out to be useful in some way, whether for practical or educational purposes. As we will see, even the poems and works of literature communicated important messages about kingship and the gods, and were related to the arts of the ritual practitioners. From an educational standpoint, the library had a role in training the next generation of advisers, since Ashurbanipal also discussed revising the teaching curriculum with his diviners.[20] It seems that apprentices, scholars, and Ashurbanipal himself all benefited from the royal collection.

Ashurbanipal made the library what it was, but it was probably based on a collection that had been started earlier. His great-grandfather Sargon was already assembling a palace reference library, as we know from the ivory writing board mentioned earlier (see page xxxvii), which was labelled 'Palace of Sargon', and many tablets belonging to Sargon's chief scholar ended up in Ashurbanipal's collection. The library also contains other tablets that date to earlier Assyrian periods, and the royal archives preserve letters written by many of Esarhaddon's advisers referring to all sorts of scholarly texts, including requests for their collection and copying. Ashurbanipal may have been the most learned of all Assyrian kings, but he was building on the efforts of others before him, intensifying a process that had started generations earlier. For this reason, we will follow not only Ashurbanipal in these pages, but his father, grandfather, and great-grandfather too.

We will study Ashurbanipal's library thematically, first exploring how the Assyrians viewed the cosmic significance of writing and the all-pervasive influence of the gods. We will then dive into its manuals on magic, medicine, and divination using media from entrails to the stars. Poems and literary works are also found on the library's tablets, as are historical accounts of war and the lamentations that took place in its aftermath. We'll also explore how daily routines could also be shaped by the knowledge found in the library by following a fictional day in the life of Ashurbanipal, showing how these ways of thinking were relevant to all human activity. Finally, we will take a look at the incredible influence Mesopotamian culture has had on the wider world, and its resonance for us today.

Assyrian scholarship was divided into five main branches: astrology, exorcism, medicine, entrail divination, and lamentation. Each of Ashurbanipal's advisers specialised in a particular area, but they often studied other disciplines as well. Marduk-shapik-zeri, a lamentation priest who wrote to the king from prison begging to be reinstated, claims to be qualified in a number of different subjects:

> I fully master my father's profession, the discipline of lamentation; I have studied and chanted the Series. I am competent in . . . 'mouth-washing' and purification of the palace . . . I have examined healthy and sick flesh. I have read the astrological omen series and made astronomical observations. I have read the series of anomalous births, the three physiognomical works, and the terrestrial omen series . . . All this I learned.[21]

Such interdisciplinarity was not unusual. Both lamenters and exorcists knew some divination, while diviners themselves often advised on broader cultic matters. The chief scholars had expertise in all these fields, as Ashurbanipal claims for himself. Therefore, although their responsibilities were divided up, the advisers were part of an interconnected sphere of knowledge.

Ashurbanipal's court was a place of competition and rivalry as well as collaboration – some teams worked together to get results for the king, while others had fierce disagreements. It could be a cut-throat place, too – many surviving letters speak of gross mistreatment at the hands of senior officials and beg the king to intervene. There are complaints from people who have been evicted from their homes by the city governor,[22] from informants about crimes who fear for their lives,[23] and from an astrologer whose field has been seized by a military official and his crops destroyed.[24] One diviner claims to be dying of cold because he has nowhere to live – despite the king saying that he was to be given a house, no one has acted upon his instruction.[25] And one astrologer writes in despair because the king has not summoned him for a long time and he doesn't know why.[26] We do not know whether these pleas were answered, and while those closer to the king must have had more of a chance of having their grievances heard, even they were not immune from abuse. A chief diviner rages that a governor has robbed him of his field, and it is surprising to hear that even Balasi, Ashurbanipal's most senior scholar, was harassed – on one occasion the servants of a military commander snatched his orchards and chased his people away.[27] Scholars may have been indispensable to the king, but this did not ensure their popularity with others.

In these letters to the king, human concerns shine through. Highly skilled professionals complain about being overworked and underpaid, claiming other members of the court are better off.[28] Scholars complain that being forced to do extra work is distracting them from their research and teaching, in a way that is all too familiar to modern-day academics.[29] Likewise, today's medics will empathise with a royal court doctor who is exhausted from working non-stop with no time to himself, and complains that he desperately needs a holiday.[30]

One of the great pleasures of encountering the past is seeing how similar ancient people were to us. In the grand scheme of things, not all that much has changed. Then, as now, people experienced grief, love, anxiety, and joy. They had concerns about job security, disputes with in-laws, jealous rivalries, and profound friendships, and questioned the meaning of life.

It can be deeply moving to recognise our own emotions experienced by a person who lived three thousand years ago. Yet we should not project too much of ourselves on to them. We find many aspects of their culture deeply strange (and the feeling would have been mutual). For instance, the fact that Mesopotamians saw the will of the gods written in the entrails of dead sheep, or blamed dead ancestors for troubling them with illnesses, can make them seem far removed from Western culture. However, anthropological studies show that many of these practices are not at all uncommon and can be found in numerous other cultures across the world. All too often, when we dig deep enough, it emerges that underlying these beliefs is some desire, fear, or other motivation that we also express, but in keeping with the 'rules' of our own culture, which also turn out to be not quite as rational as we first thought. In fact, often it is we who are the strange ones. Our attempts, for instance, to foresee the results of elections are notoriously unreliable, but this does not stop us from trying; during the 2010 football World Cup an octopus in Germany was famously better at predicting the results of matches than professional forecasters (and even received death threats as a result). Whenever we come across an aspect of Mesopotamian culture that seems bizarre, a closer look reveals that it reflects our own society and values, holding up a mirror to our own attempts at rationalisation and certainty.

1.
The Scribal Art

Ashurbanipal's sister Sherua-etirat is irked. She holds a letter from her brother's new wife, Libbali-sharrat, written in sloppy handwriting and simple signs, a tablet full of mistakes that looks like it is from the hand of a child rather than that of the future queen of Assyria. This will simply not do. Ashurbanipal is the crown prince, heir to the greatest kingdom on earth, and needs a wife who is worthy of him in status. His wife's accomplishments reflect not only on her husband but also on the whole royal family, and Sherua-etirat is embarrassed to have a sister-in-law who is not yet proficient in the scribal art. She will have to tell her to step up.

Sherua-etirat picks up her stylus to compose a reply. She unwraps a ready-made clay tablet, taking it out of the damp cloth it has been stored in to keep it moist, and begins to press signs into its soft surface: 'Why don't you write on your tablet and do your homework? For if you don't, they will say: "Can this be the sister of Sherua-etirat, the eldest daughter of the succession palace of Esarhaddon, the great king, mighty king, king of the world, king of Assyria?'[1]

The scene is imagined but the letter is real, written perhaps in 672 or 671, shortly after Ashurbanipal became crown prince, a few years before he ascended to the throne. Sherua-etirat really did admonish her brother's young wife for not working hard enough at her writing, telling her in no uncertain terms. By Ashurbanipal's time in the seventh century BC the cuneiform writing system had been in use for around two and a half thousand years, though change was afoot. More and more people were speaking Aramaic as their mother tongue rather than Akkadian, especially in the countryside, and Aramaic would eventually take over as the dominant language in the Near East and replace the cuneiform writing system with an alphabet. In the cities and at the royal court people continued to speak Akkadian, and many would have been bilingual – in the seventh century we find records in both languages, showing they were used side by side. The Aramaic alphabet was much simpler to learn and to write than Akkadian cuneiform, but it was Akkadian that still stood for power, and Akkadian was the language of letters between the king, his advisers, and his family, as well as the scholarly texts in the library. As the letter shows, learning cuneiform was no easy endeavour and required hard work and persistence that was obviously lacking here, though we only have Sherua-etirat's word for it since no letters from the future queen herself survive.

Cuneiform was far more than a writing system in Mesopotamia. It represented an age-old cultural tradition encoding knowledge that stretched back thousands of years. With knowledge of cuneiform came great prestige, since it was the key not only to communication but to wisdom handed down by the gods themselves. For this reason, the Mesopotamians referred to it as 'the scribal art', a writing system that required great skill to truly master. The scribal art consisted of far more than competence in reading and writing, for the complexities of cuneiform meant that it imparted information beyond the simple sounds and meanings of words. In Mesopotamian philosophy, language bound the world together, and in language the connections between all things could be found. Mastery of writing, then, was the key to understanding the secrets of the universe. For Ashurbanipal, who frequently describes himself as king of the universe, it was a crucial domain to have under his control.

From cuneiform's invention all the way back in the fourth millennium BC to its decipherment in the nineteenth century AD, when Victorian scholars learned to decode it once more, we find scholars grappling with its complexity, a complexity that at times seems baffling to a modern audience. Yet as we will see, for the Mesopotamians this complexity was beautiful, celebrated, almost worshipped. In complexity was strength, making the writing system itself an object of study and of endless fascination, both to Mesopotamian scribes and to those of us who encounter it today.

The Assyrians were well aware of the antiquity of their writing system. The library held tablets that were extremely old, and they were not only treasured but also actively used. One scholar discussing a ritual with the king informs him that he has fetched from Babylon an ancient tablet made by King Hammurabi, who ruled more than a thousand years before Ashurbanipal.[2] In that time much had changed – not only did the signs look very different, but the dialect of the language had changed too. Yet the fact that a tablet so old was not treated as an ancient relic but in fact was understandable and used in contemporary rituals is testament to the extreme longevity of cuneiform culture, and the careful transmission of knowledge through the ages.

Despite the remarkable continuity of the cuneiform tradition, its earliest origins passed into a legend very different from the reality. The Mesopotamians came up with their own myths about the invention of writing, the earliest of which is preserved in the Sumerian poem *Enmerkar and the Lord of Aratta*.[3] This particular poem was not held in Ashurbanipal's library, but modern scholars have reconstructed it from tablets dating to the second millennium BC when the poem was first written down.

Enmerkar was a legendary king of Uruk, Sumer's first great city. He was the grandfather of Gilgamesh, the ultimate Mesopotamian hero. As such, Sumerian rulers in the late twenty-second century BC looked back to Enmerkar and his successors as the inventors and champions of many aspects of Sumerian culture, claiming them as their ancestors in the hope that some of their glory would rub off on them. This is most likely why the stories about Enmerkar and his family were written down and are still with us today.

In the poem, Enmerkar is in a contest with the king of Aratta, to determine which king the goddess Inanna truly favours. Rather than a military contest, it is a battle of wits and ingenuity as the king of

Aratta lays down a series of riddle-like challenges for Enmerkar to solve. The challenges are seemingly impossible: to transport grain in nets, or to make a sceptre out of a completely new material. Enmerkar finds a clever way out of each of them, seemingly inventing a kind of proto-plastic along the way. Caught up in his victories, he wants to send a message to the king of Aratta, reiterating his boasts and threats to destroy the king's city. However, the message that he sends is so long that the messenger who has been running back and forth between these very distant kingdoms cannot remember the whole speech he is supposed to relay. The solution Enmerkar comes up with is the most ingenious of all: he invents writing:

> Because the messenger, whose mouth was tired, was not able to repeat it, the lord of Uruk patted some clay and wrote the message as if on a tablet. Formerly, the writing of messages on clay was not established. Now, under that sun and on that day, it was indeed so.[4]

The messenger takes the tablet back to Aratta and transmits the message. After repeating Enmerkar's words he shows the tablet to the lord of Aratta, who looks at it in incomprehension: to him, the cuneiform signs incised upon it are 'just nails'.[5] Most people today confronted with cuneiform for the first time would sympathise.

After this point the story becomes difficult to interpret, as the tablets are broken in many places, so it is unclear how the contest ends. Yet the Sumerian narrator shortly afterwards refers to Enmerkar as 'the clever champion'[6] – in their eyes he has clearly won.

The invention of writing is presented as the ultimate proof of Sumer's superior culture. It was the cleverest of all Enmerkar's inventions, a technology that gave the Sumerians superior power. While it is a romanticised image, there is a grain of truth in its message, since the invention of writing did indeed take place in Uruk and enable the growth of cities and states, and the spread of Sumerian culture all over the Near East.

Contrary to this story, writing was not invented by a single person at a single time, but evolved over a period of many centuries. One of the great advantages of cuneiform tablets is that they have survived from every stage of that evolution, allowing us to trace these shifts in detail. Cuneiform was not invented to win battles of wit, or write down great stories, but rather more prosaically to aid bureaucracy. Before writing – as early as 8000 BC – people in the Near East used to keep track of transactions with clay tokens. These came in many different shapes and sizes, with one token corresponding to one commodity – a sheep, a goat, a jar of oil, et cetera. Tokens were often enclosed in clay envelopes as a means of storing information about each individual transaction. Sometimes tokens would then be impressed upon these envelopes, so that it was possible to see what was inside without having to break them open. Eventually the tokens themselves were no longer handed over; rather, people made flat clay tablets and impressed the tokens on to those. These numerical tablets represent the first stage of writing's development. Since there were no signs to represent individual numbers yet, one impression stood for one object. For example, if you wanted to record three jars of oil you would impress the relevant token three times on the surface.

Proto-cuneiform emerges at the end of the fourth millennium BC when scribes begin to incise pictographic signs into the clay tablets instead of impressing tokens. Each sign is a drawing or abstract representation of an object, but now we also have signs to represent abstract numbers, with different number systems depending on what you are counting. It is not clear whether these signs are directly based on the tokens that preceded them – there are only a handful of tokens that look like the proto-cuneiform signs for sheep, for example, which is rather odd given that sheep were central to the Mesopotamian economy. Nonetheless, the transition from token to sign is clear, though it takes a few hundred years for the tokens to become obsolete.

The earliest proto-cuneiform tablets were written in Uruk, which by the fourth millennium was a massive city of 250 hectares and home to at least fifty thousand people. At the heart of the city was a monumental precinct boasting temples, great courts, and a ziggurat – a pyramid-like structure that was the main temple of the goddess Inanna, the city's patron. Most of the tablets were discovered in the temple complex, showing that this was the nerve centre of the administration where the scribes were based. The development of proto-cuneiform coincides with the so-called Uruk expansion when the city itself grew and its people founded colonies all over the Near East, taking their culture with them – Uruk-style pottery has been found as far afield as northern Syria and eastwards in Iran, where the legendary land of Aratta was supposedly located. Bureaucracy was well and truly established, and was here to stay.

It can't be shown for certain that proto-cuneiform records the Sumerian language, since these tablets count objects rather than write full sentences. In fact, proto-cuneiform may not record language at all, but may rather convey meaning through symbols in the same way that today a skull and crossbones is a recognisable sign of danger regardless of what language you speak, and the icons on modern road signs can be understood by anyone who has learned to drive. Yet when proto-cuneiform becomes cuneiform proper by around 2800 or 2700 BC, then the words it spells out are distinctly Sumerian. By this time pictorial signs have been replaced by wedge-shaped signs. It is quite difficult to drag a stylus through clay, but cut the reed into a triangular cross-section and one impression of the stylus creates a beautiful, elongated wedge with just one quick tap. Those original pictorial signs are now drawn with wedges and start to look more abstract. At some point in the third millennium the signs rotated 90°, so that by the time the signs are made with wedges the pictures have turned on their side

Imagine you are a Sumerian accountant in the Inanna temple of Uruk. You are quite used to keeping records of commodities going in and out, using tablets that look a bit like modern spreadsheets, divided up into grids with each piece of information in its own square. It's easy enough to draw a stalk of barley to represent grain, a bowl to represent a ration for each worker, and a person's head plus the bowl for the disbursement of that ration, which is after all just giving the bowl to a person in real life.

To write down an individual object you just need to draw it. But how would you write more abstract concepts? How would you draw the word for 'to live'? That is not so easy, but 'to live' in Sumerian is *til*, which sounds similar to the word for 'arrow', *ti*, which is something you can draw. The drawing of the arrow therefore stands for both the noun 'arrow' and the verb 'to live'. Whoever read the tablet would have to work out which one it referred to from the context, but that usually is not as difficult as it sounds.

Similarly, to write the verb 'to stand', pronounced *gub*, you draw a picture of a foot. But then you also need to write the word 'to go', which is *gen*, and a foot seems the most logical way to draw that as well. The verb 'to go' has many forms, so it will be pronounced differently depending on the tense, e.g. whether it means 'went' (also *gen*), or 'will go' (*du*). If multiple people are going anywhere the word sounds different again, and so you write the plural versions *su*, *er*, and *re* with two foot signs on top of each other. In this way one sign can be used to write lots of different sounds.

Sumerian also has words that sound identical when spoken but have very different meanings. In these cases the scribes write these words with completely different signs so there was no confusing them, in the same way that in English 'bear' and 'bare' or 'which' and 'witch' sound the same but look different on the page. When transcribing these signs into Roman characters Assyriologists use numbers to tell them apart – $kiri_3$ meaning 'nose' and $kiri_6$ meaning 'orchard' are easily distinguished in cuneiform, but both are pronounced *kiri*.

Now that sounds are linked to pictures it is possible to write the sounds when they appear in other words that have nothing to do with the original objects. For instance, to write the grammatical element 'of', which is pronounced *a*, you draw a picture of water, also pronounced *a*. This works very well with the Sumerian language, which is agglutinative, meaning that it is mostly made up of single-syllable elements that are stuck together to make bigger words. For example, if you want to say 'the temple of the god of the city' you write 'temple god city of of'. While this is strange from the perspective of most

European and Middle Eastern languages, agglutinative languages make up a quarter of all languages spoken worldwide, including Turkish, Hungarian, Basque, Swahili, and Japanese.

One sign standing for lots of different sounds came in useful when Akkadian speakers came along and adapted cuneiform to their own language. Akkadian is completely unrelated to Sumerian but belongs to the same family as Hebrew and Arabic. The resemblances are still clear today, and speakers of these modern languages can easily recognise the connections with their ancient cousin. Because Akkadian and Sumerian are so different, Akkadian scribes had to be creative to make the writing system work for them. They used the signs to spell out words syllable by syllable rather than using one sign for one concept. But they also retained many Sumerian words as what we call logograms – a single symbol that stands for a whole word. For example, instead of spelling the word 'god' in Akkadian as *i-lum* (necessitating two symbols), the scribes wrote a single symbol representing the Sumerian word for god, DINGIR (which Assyriologists conventionally render in all caps to signal the presence of a Sumerian word in an otherwise Akkadian text). But because one symbol can have many meanings, they also used this same sign for the syllable *an* when writing other words. This proved a major headache for the decipherers of cuneiform in the nineteenth century, since it took a while for them to realise that they were dealing with two different languages in the same text rather than one. It would be like coming across the word 'pain' in an English text and suddenly realising it actually was French for 'bread'. Realising this was a major breakthrough, and the pace of decipherment accelerated soon after.

Akkadian speakers made further changes to the script as well. Over time the signs became simpler to write, with fewer and fewer wedges so that by Ashurbanipal's time the pictorial origins of the script are barely recognisable. Most notably, Akkadian has sounds that Sumerian does not, so signs took on even more values to represent these sounds that had not been needed previously. But over the centuries signs continued to acquire more and more values, even when it was perfectly possible to write words without them. It is as if we are seeing meanings proliferate for the sheer joy of it, exploiting all the possibilities it offered to the max.

For us with our ideals of efficiency and our simple alphabet of twenty-six letters this is the complete opposite to what we would expect – why introduce unnecessary elements into a system that already worked well without them? In fact, this points to a fundamental difference in values between us and the Mesopotamians – efficiency and simplicity are not the point. Complexity is an advantage, as it gives more options to choose from, a freedom of choice that expands possibilities not only in the way the Mesopotamians wrote but also in the way they thought. The Western tradition of analytic philosophy, ultimately based on that of the ancient Greeks, prizes precision and the narrowing down of possibilities in order to find one truth. For the Mesopotamians, truth was not contained in any one definition, and concepts were connected in many different ways, all of which were equally valid. For them flexibility, multiple meanings, and choice were privileged in a way that can be compared to postmodern schools of philosophy – Derrida's theories of language with their emphasis on the written sign may even have been partly inspired by cuneiform. Instead of narrowing down, they expand.

Assyrian scholars believed that connections between signs and sounds in the writing system reflected fundamental connections in the universe. If one sign sounded similar to another, or looked similar to another, this was not merely coincidence but an insight into the nature of reality itself, which was constructed through language. Puns became an important tool for interpreting difficult texts, and a serious object of study. A great many commentaries survive explaining the deeper meanings of well-known works according to these principles. For instance, a court astrologer used one to explain the logic behind the following omen:

> If the moon's horns at its appearance are very dark: it means disbanding of the fortified outposts, retiring of the guards; there will be reconciliation and peace in the land.[7]

We may well wonder what the connection is between the omen and its meaning: why should dark horns of the moon point to peace in the land? The scholar is keen to tell the king exactly why: it is because there are similarities between the sounds and shapes of the words used to write 'dark', 'well', and 'stable', a series of puns that works across both Akkadian and Sumerian. Hence darkness is inherently connected to stability and all things being well, because of similarities between the writings of these concepts. That the astrologer quoted this text when writing to the king shows that this was not only an abstract game, but had a practical application, helping to reassure the king that the omen really was a good one.[8] Here, then, is another difference in values: for us puns are humorous; for the Mesopotamians they are a window into the secrets of the universe.

We can see this in action in the way that Sumerian is translated into Akkadian in the first millennium BC. To take one example, in the Sumerian poem we know as *The Return of Ninurta to Nippur*, found in the library, about the conquests of Mesopotamia's greatest warrior god Ninurta, we find the word 'essences' translated as 'battles'. These two words are written with completely different signs, but they sound the same when pronounced in Sumerian. The unusual rendering is unlikely to be a mistake but rather indicates that to the Akkadian translator both options were possible, and the alternative translation indicated a different way of understanding the text on a deeper level.

Eventually Sumerian faded out of use as Sumerians and Akkadians intermingled and Akkadian took over as the dominant language of Mesopotamia. Although Sumerian was no longer spoken by the early second millennium BC, it retained a high status as a language of learning, religion, and literature, much like Latin in medieval Europe. Mesopotamia held its oldest traditions in high esteem, and the more ancient something was, the more it was valued and considered to be authentic. Hence Sumerian, as the first writing system, was seen as an important source of knowledge because of its antiquity, and Sumerian texts were transmitted and studied for more than a thousand years after they were first written. Ashurbanipal's library contains not only poems in Sumerian but also laments and prayers that were used in the performance of many contemporary rituals. Sumerian technical vocabulary was also the basis of all kinds of advanced scientific texts, which use a very high proportion of Sumerian words as logograms, many of them with specialised meanings particular to those genres and not in everyday use. Texts on divination and astronomy can consist of up to 85 per cent Sumerian logograms, meaning that they are not even written in sentences but as a series of symbols. The symbols could be understood as sentences only by those who knew what they meant in the context – the ancient equivalent of academic jargon.

In cuneiform there are nearly a thousand different signs in total, though no one person at any one time would have needed to know all of them. For the purposes of basic communication it was only necessary to know between sixty-eight and 112 cuneiform signs depending on the period, which is a manageable amount. Thus merchants were able to write letters home to their wives and the wives would write back; contracts and receipts were relatively uncomplicated; and Mesopotamia boasts the world's first customer services complaint, a lengthy rant about having received the wrong quality of copper (which went viral on the internet in 2016).[9] Despite cuneiform's potential for complexity, plenty of people could use it for everyday purposes. A scholarly tablet, however, was another matter – the flashy use of obscure sign values and technical terms meant that no ordinary person would be able to pick up an omen tablet and understand it. Tablets often end with special instructions not to show the uninitiated the secret knowledge contained within them. Texts from all five branches of Mesopotamian scholarship (astrology, divination, exorcism, medicine, and lamentation) are found with this instruction. Their secrets were probably safe, since the uninitiated were unlikely to be able to read them anyway.

⁂

It is not surprising that Libbali-sharrat, Ashurbanipal's wife, found cuneiform difficult. Even in everyday instances, cuneiform could be confusing. A Babylonian writing to the king in the fourteenth century BC complains, 'Why did you send me pots when I asked for straw?'[10] The source of the confusion is the fact that the signs for pots and straw look very similar and someone mistook one for the other. The Akkadian word for scribe salutes those who managed to master cuneiform, since it translates as 'tablet king'.

What is striking is the fact that Ashurbanipal's wife was expected, as a royal woman, to be literate and well educated in ancient traditions. Other women in the Assyrian palace could clearly read and write too. Female scribes are known from lists of people working there, as are female administrators (alongside female singers and hairdressers, blacksmiths, and stone borers).[11] The manageress of the women's quarters bought slaves for which we have the receipts,[12] and it seems unlikely that someone in such a position of responsibility would not be able to check these documents for herself. Most tellingly of all, we have tablets where a question was presented to the sun god with an apology asking him to 'overlook it if a woman has written it and put it before you'.[13] Women were not supposed to write in this ritual context, but evidently they could and sometimes did. It has even been proposed that the woman in question was Libbali-sharrat – if so, she had clearly improved her skills.

In all periods of Mesopotamian history women were active in business, able to be witnesses in court, and could own, buy, and sell property. It was much rarer, however, for them to reach the higher levels of education. There is no evidence for any female scholars in Ashurbanipal's time who could have used his library, for instance. Yet some women did attain the heights of erudition – Enheduanna, the first named author in Mesopotamia, and by extension of all time, was a priestess of the moon god in the city of Ur in the twenty-third century BC. Daughter of the Akkadian king Sargon, Enheduanna wrote a number of fiendishly difficult Sumerian poems that make full use of the complexities of cuneiform, revelling in puns and multiple meanings, making her poetry among the most difficult in all Mesopotamian literature to translate.[14]

It is also likely that there were more female authors in Mesopotamia than we currently know of – only in 2020 was it recognised that the author of a famous hymn to the healing goddess Gula was a woman. Normally it is easy to tell whether a name belongs to a man or a woman, because all names are preceded by a cuneiform sign indicating the gender of the person. However, in this case, the ancient Mesopotamians themselves had forgotten that the poet Bullussa-rabi had been female and had been writing her name with the masculine determinative. The mistake was noticed by researchers in Munich who also looked at administrative documents and realised that only women were ever called Bullussa-rabi. The scribal art was strongly associated with men in Mesopotamia, but there were remarkable women who defied the trend.

⁂

Beginners like Libbali-sharrat wanting to improve their cuneiform had three stages of education available to them. First there was the primary training that taught the essentials, which was enough for those who wanted to read and write for simple business and accounting purposes. Those who wanted to take up one of the scholarly professions such as exorcist or astrologer would progress to the second stage that covered more advanced literature. In the third stage they specialised in one of these branches, much like in our tertiary education system.

Most of our evidence of the early phases comes from the Old Babylonian period in the second millennium BC rather than Ashurbanipal's time. The great advantage of clay is that we can see the different stages preserved and can track the progress of beginner scribes. The very first thing they learn is simply how to make wedges, and just as today's young schoolchildren have large and irregular handwriting, so too are there many practice tablets showing comically long and inept wedges as the pupils get to grips with holding the stylus. Next, they practise writing whole signs, then move on to simple words and names. When we learn foreign alphabets one of the first things we do is to write our own name, and the ancient Mesopotamians were similar, writing out a huge number of people's names in great long standardised lists.

Apprentice scribes would learn how to write basic vocabulary by copying lists of nouns, which are grouped thematically. One of my favourites for the sheer strangeness of its content is a list of 'the trees and wooden objects in their totality'.[15] It starts with trees and then proceeds to wooden objects including tools, chairs, boats, ploughs, dead tree branches, battering rams, and musical instruments. The list has 705 entries and is just the first chapter of the series as a whole. The next five tablets set out the names of animals and meat cuts, natural materials such as stones, plants, vegetables, fish and birds, fibres and clothing, geographical names, and types of food, covering three thousand basic nouns, the equivalent of 'My First 3,000 Words in Sumerian'. It is likely that pupils were expected to memorise them all.

Since cuneiform signs can be read in many different ways, the scribes had to become familiar with the multiple potential meanings. They had to copy out other lists that gave the various Sumerian readings of logograms, to set out the signs according to similarity of shape, and to explain how to read compound signs, where two simple signs put together mean something different from the sum of their parts. Learning was by rote, as we can see directly on the tablets. The teacher copied out an extract to be memorised on one side, and the pupil turned the tablet over and wrote the lines on the other side. Signs of boredom are also preserved on the tablets, as pupils dug their fingernails into the clay and played with it. One tablet even has bite marks in it – which allowed a dentist to identify the child in question as being twelve to thirteen years old.

Finally, the learners started writing in full sentences, starting with example contracts and moving on to proverbs, hymns, and complex poems such as the story of Gilgamesh's battle against the monster Huwawa. This education was cultural as well as functional – all scribes in the Old Babylonian period would have been familiar with numerous difficult works of Sumerian literature regardless of what professions they were training for, much as schoolchildren in the UK all have to read Shakespeare. Although Sumerian had already died out as a spoken language it still made up the entire school curriculum – Sumerian truly was the language of education.

In Ashurbanipal's time education was similar. There was more emphasis on Akkadian literature than Sumerian, though the latter was still studied. By the first millennium the vocabulary lists had got even longer – hundreds of entries were added, with individual lists now running to thousands of entries, because the lists with their multitude of alternative readings and meanings had become important tools for interpreting other texts. One scholar ends a letter to the king recommending that he send for one of the dictionaries, since they now had lists giving synonyms for obscure Akkadian words as well.[16]

Remarkably, some of Ashurbanipal's own schoolwork survives. One tiny tablet in the British Museum, just 3 cm wide and 6 cm tall, preserves the beginning of a letter from Ashurbanipal to his father when he must have been young: he uses the easiest possible spellings and the signs are wobbly. It reads simply: 'To the king, my lord, your servant Ashurbanipal. Good health to the king, my lord! May Nabu and Marduk bless the king, my lord!'[17] We do not know what message followed, since the rest of the tablet is broken. Standard greeting formulas like these were taught in school – in the Old Babylonian period pupils learned to write formal letters by copying fictional ones from famous kings.

After learning the basics of writing as a boy, in his late teens Ashurbanipal studied with the court astrologer Balasi for two years before ascending to the throne. As we've seen, he studied medical ingredients and instructions for making glass,[18] which support his claims to have mastered cuneiform knowledge. Other advanced texts he was instructed in include ritual prayers. One of these survives on a tablet which his tutor would have made as a model for him to copy – this is written in a particularly large script, almost twice as big as the writing on the library tablets, and there is a bit of space between the lines so that he can see the signs more clearly.[19]

The standardised prayer has also been personalised for him – his name and personal gods filled out where the other library copies have 'so-and-so' – since the prayer is meant to be adapted for the person reciting it: 'I am your servant, Ashurbanipal, the son of his god, whose god is Ashur and whose goddess is Ashuritu. O great gods, speak my favour!' Another prayer to a personal god is written in script three times the size of professionally written cuneiform, with the wedges unusually spaced out, making it the equivalent of non-joined-up handwriting.[20] Even when starting the advanced second level, the young Ashurbanipal needed some extra help.

That he needed this help is not surprising. Cuneiform signs are tiny – just 3 mm high – and are closely crammed together with no spaces between words. The fact that the script is three-dimensional makes it even harder, since effectively we are reading the shadows. Tablets had to be read outside in strong sunlight, where the scribe could turn the tablet in his hand and manipulate the direction of the light so that it cast shadows into the impressions made by the wedges. Assyriologists today work with lamps and magnifying glasses to reproduce the effect (though my favourite trick is to take a photograph and blow it up to 300 per cent on the computer). Nor is this a modern deficiency – many older Mesopotamian scholars tasked their apprentices with writing out tablets for them since their eyesight was not up to it any more, though I can't help but wonder if this is not the ancient equivalent of getting the intern to do the photocopying.

Connected as it was with divine knowledge, ascending to the next level of the scribal art could become an act of devotion to the gods. Scribes often dedicated tablets to Nabu, the patron god of writing, depositing them in his temple as a gift.[21] Ashurbanipal himself did this, showing himself to be a serious student, and included prayers at the end of more than one tablet reading:

> For my life, the protection of my vitality, prevention of illness, the confirmation of the foundation of my royal throne, I placed it in the library of the temple of Nabu in Nineveh of the great lord, my lord,

for all time. In future, O Nabu, look on this work with joy, and constantly bless my kingship. Whenever I call out to you, take my hand! As I repeatedly go into your temple, constantly protect my step. As this work is placed in your temple and stands firm before you, look constantly with favour and ever consider my wellbeing![22]

As many other such prayers show, mastery of writing was pleasing to the god of scribes, a way of acquiring his favour.

Since advanced level cuneiform was so difficult it gave authority to the scholars who had mastered it, who claimed to be the guardians of tradition bequeathed to them by the gods themselves. A catalogue found in the library tells us that the god of magic and wisdom, Ea, was thought to be the author of the entire corpus of exorcistic texts and of all lamentations needed in rituals, as well as the various series of astrological omens, physiognomic texts, and medical texts, and two Sumerian epic poems about the god Ninurta[23] – in other words, the foundations of all scholarly learning.

This knowledge was believed to have been given to human beings by mythical sages long ago, before the great flood. The Mesopotamians placed this flood thousands of years in the past, and saw it as a pivotal event that separated myth from history. The Sumerian King List, written at the end of the third millennium BC, calculates that the flood occurred at least 28,876 years before the time of its writing and also lists eight kings who ruled before the great flood, reigning 241,200 years between them.[24] It was during this antediluvian time that the sages bestowed all the arts of civilisation upon mankind. They came in the guise of fish-men; much later, the Babylonian priest Berossus, writing a history of his country's traditions for the new Greek rulers, describes the first of them: 'it had the whole body of a fish, but underneath and attached to the head of the fish there was another head, human, and joined to the tail of the fish, feet, like those of a man, and it had a human voice.'[25] This sage was called Oannes, and according to Berossus he taught the Mesopotamians writing and mathematics, but also how to build cities, found temples, make laws, and farm the land. Here, then, is a very different tradition from that preserved in the Sumerian story of Enmerkar, envisaging writing as not invented by any human, but as a gift of the gods. Oannes is listed second only to Ea in the Assyrian catalogue of texts and authors, as the one who passed on some of these compositions to humankind.[26]

Perhaps the strangest element of the story is the fish–man hybrid form taken by the sage. Berossus says that at the end of the day he would go back to the sea and spend the night there. Other texts describe the sages as 'pure carp',[27] and depictions of fish-men can be found carved in temple reliefs in Ashurbanipal's Nineveh – these are the fish-gods that the Victorian excavator Layard described as guarding the chamber of records. But why would fish be the bringers of knowledge? The answer may lie in the association of water with wisdom in Mesopotamia. Ea dwelled in the Apsu, a watery abode beneath the earth that was the source of all the rivers. His domain was associated with him, and the fish may well have been his messengers, though this is never spelled out in the texts.

As cuneiform developed it was first adapted to Akkadian, and later it also came to be used for Hittite in the west, an Indo-European language spoken in Anatolia, and in the east it was adopted to write the Elamite language in Iran. But although it would take a couple of thousand years, the signs of cuneiform eventually had competition from a newer invention – the alphabet.

The alphabet was inspired by another extremely complex writing system – Egyptian hieroglyphs. The earliest alphabetic script is found in Egypt in the early second millennium BC, scratched into rocks by the sides of roads in the Western Desert, and on the walls of turquoise mines and temples in the Sinai Peninsula. These were written by foreign workers and troops in the Egyptian army who spoke a West Semitic language from the Levant related to Phoenician. Though they probably did not know hieroglyphs themselves, they took the general idea of using pictures to write, and for the first time abstracted them so that one symbol stood for a single letter. This formed the basis for the Phoenician alphabet, which appears for the first time in the twelfth century BC. The Phoenician heartland is in modern-day Lebanon, but the Phoenicians were a maritime power who traded extensively and founded colonies all over the Mediterranean, settling even as far as Spain. It was the Phoenicians who brought the alphabet to Greece and Italy in the eighth century, and their system was adapted to write the Greek letters that we know today, as well as Etruscan, from which the Latin script developed. Like the scripts of many other early languages in the region, including Hebrew and Egyptian, Phoenician does not write any of its vowels, so the sign that we label as 'A' actually represents the consonant aleph. The Greeks, however, do not have this consonant, or quite a few others, so they redeployed the unused signs for vowels: aleph became alpha.

This alphabet was not an isolated development. By the thirteenth century BC, a cuneiform alphabet had already developed in the Syrian city of Ugarit. Ugarit was a multicultural hub where at least eight different languages were spoken from all over the Near East. The scribes of this city created their own signs inspired by Mesopotamian cuneiform – thirty symbols, each standing for one consonant. Amazing mythological tablets have been discovered in Ugaritic relating adventures of the gods that have striking parallels with the Bible, giving us a window into the development of Israelite religion and that of their neighbours.

Cuneiform alphabets were not only used to write Ugaritic – examples have been found all over the eastern Mediterranean, from southern Israel to Cyprus and even Tiryns in Greece. However, these examples are few, and in the Near East they did not really catch on. Instead, alphabets were used in parallel with traditional cuneiform, each for a different language and for different purposes. By the first millennium BC the dominant language in the Near East was Aramaic, a West Semitic language with its own alphabetic script. This is what most people spoke in everyday settings, and increasingly record-keeping and administration was carried out in Aramaic as the millennium went on. Even the Neo-Assyrian kings used it:

reliefs from Ashurbanipal's palace show two scribes counting a pile of enemy heads, one inscribing cuneiform on a writing board, the other writing on a parchment scroll, in what must have been Aramaic. The medium was important for the message. Cuneiform is ideal for writing on clay, but alphabets with simpler characters are much easier to draw with ink on parchment. Clay was much cheaper than parchment, since it could be found everywhere for free and did not require the same amount of processing, another point in cuneiform's favour.

Alphabets have considerable advantages, but they did not displace cuneiform completely for many hundreds of years after their invention. While they are quick to master, they did not have the prestige that cuneiform did. This is exemplified by the fact that the Persian king Darius ordered his scholars to create a type of cuneiform script to write his country's traditional language in the late sixth century, a time when Aramaic had already surpassed cuneiform in use. Darius wanted a cuneiform script because of the weight of tradition behind it, seeking to prove himself equal, if not superior, to the other powerful kings of the Near East. After the Persians conquered Babylon, they also appropriated the Babylonian writing system, adapting it to their own purposes. Old Persian is based on cuneiform but has actually a much simpler syllabary, with thirty-six phonetic signs and just seven logograms. It is a compromise between modernisation and tradition – the signs are made up of the same types of wedges as Babylonian cuneiform, and thus look suitably impressive, but it is much easier to read.

It is thanks to Darius that cuneiform was ultimately deciphered and rediscovered in the nineteenth century AD. Darius commissioned monumental inscriptions narrating his deeds and listing the peoples he had conquered. The most famous of these is the Behistun inscription in western Iran, carved into the cliffside a hundred metres above the ground alongside a royal road, visible to travellers from far away, and accompanied by a relief showing rulers of all the rebel lands submitting to the Persian king. Many other inscriptions were found in his capital city of Persepolis and the surrounding area. Like the Rosetta Stone which enabled the decipherment of Egyptian hieroglyphics, these inscriptions displayed the same text written in three different languages. The Rosetta Stone had ancient Greek as one of its three, a language that was already well known and so could unlock the others. In contrast, all three of the languages in the Persian inscriptions were a complete mystery: Old Persian, Elamite, and Akkadian. With no head start and without the benefit of knowing what the inscription said, the decipherers were in for a considerable challenge.

The Behistun inscription was not the only Rosetta Stone of cuneiform, but it is the most photogenic of all the trilingual inscriptions, showing Darius with his foot on the neck of the usurper Gaumata, the leaders of seven other provinces in distinctive local dress with their hands tied behind their backs, and the Persian god Ahura Mazda looking on approvingly from above. The inscription and relief are so high up the cliff that the images would have been the only part of the monument actually visible to passers-by, and make a powerful statement by themselves. The dramatic story the text narrates tallies with the account given in Greek sources describing Darius's rise to power, which was helpful for deciphering the Old Persian portion of the text, the first of the three languages to give up its secrets.

The decipherment of all three cuneiform scripts took more than fifty years, and was the achievement of many talented scholars. The British diplomat Henry Rawlinson, an aristocratic adventurer and major general stationed in Baghdad, usually gets all the credit, but much like the Behistun inscription itself, this is largely because he was the most glamorous. Rawlinson deserves recognition for his role in the decipherment of Old Persian, but many scholars contributed, and others had greater input when it came to Akkadian.

As had been the case with the decipherment of hieroglyphics, the first element to yield was the name of the king. It was a German schoolteacher, Georg Grotefend, who made this first step in 1802 in Göttingen, after making a bet with his drinking buddies that he could decipher cuneiform. Working with inscriptions from

Persepolis, Grotefend guessed that the royal inscriptions would start with a list of the king's titles, and so was able to identify the name of Darius. In 1835 Rawlinson came across the Behistun inscription while he was out with the British Army in Iran and made 3D copies of the text using a sort of papier-mâché, an immensely difficult undertaking given that the inscription was engraved on a cliff. One of the languages (Old Persian) turned out to be related to modern Persian, a language in which Rawlinson was fluent, and in 1846 he published an edition and translation of the inscription. Meanwhile, a learned Irish cleric called Edward Hincks had already determined how the signs in the writing system worked, building on the efforts of others, meaning that scholars in Europe could confidently read the Persian portion of the inscription. Rawlinson's work enabled Hincks to refine his understanding of the script, and with Old Persian deciphered, he could focus his efforts on the other two languages.

In 1846 Hincks worked out that Akkadian was a Semitic language related to Hebrew, another language that was well understood and could be used for comparison. By this time many more sources had been discovered and Hincks did not have to rely solely on studying Persian inscriptions. He could also consult inscriptions of Nebuchadnezzar from Babylon, a growing number of cuneiform tablets, and more inscriptions from Lake Van in Turkey, which used the same script to write another language in the independent state of Urartu. Hincks worked out the peculiar way that these languages spell out their syllables, with the sound *bab* being spelled *ba-ab*, as well as the fact that one sign could have many different meanings and that one sound could be represented by many different signs: in short, the main features of the cuneiform system. Perhaps most significantly of all, he proposed that some of the signs might represent sounds from another language, which of course turned out to be Sumerian. This crucial observation was made in a mere footnote but turned out to be one of the most important keys to cracking the script.

By 1852, tablets from the chamber of records had reached the British Museum. Among them Hincks recognised lexical texts that listed the different sounds and words represented by various cuneiform signs. Those same texts which the ancient scribes had copied out while they were learning cuneiform now helped Victorian scholars to learn it, three thousand years later. Many bilingual texts – Sumerian compositions with Akkadian translations underneath each line – were also brought back to the museum, ultimately enabling the study of Sumerian as a language in its own right.

Rawlinson continued to work on Akkadian, as did others. Much like today, results were published in scholarly journals, and so each scholar was able to benefit from the discoveries of others, though they also had fierce rivalries and competing theories about how the languages worked. Rawlinson was initially convinced that cuneiform represented letters rather than syllables, and that its origin was in Egypt. When he changed his mind and started reading the signs as syllables, he claimed to not remember how he had come to these conclusions, but seems to have plagiarised Hincks, since he also ended up copying some of his mistakes. In any case, by 1857 enough progress had been made to propose a test – four different scholars would each make a translation of a new inscription none of them had seen before and send the results in a sealed envelope to the Royal Asiatic Society in London. Rawlinson, Hincks, and two others, William Fox Talbot and Jules Oppert, took part – their translations more or less agreed, and cuneiform was declared deciphered.

This was only the very beginning. Understanding Akkadian and Sumerian in all their subtleties would take far longer. The Akkadian perfect tense was only discovered as recently as the 1930s, and experts continue to debate the nuances of Sumerian grammar today. Nor are all Mesopotamian scripts fully cracked – proto-Elamite, a type of cuneiform found in Iran that is contemporary with early Sumerian, is still only partially understood, and a handful of scholars are working on its decipherment as I write. There are still many mysteries to unravel in the cuneiform system, many secrets for us yet to discover.

Throughout history and across cultures, writing has often represented power and authority, even bordering on the magical. In Mesopotamia amulets have been found inscribed with cuneiform-like characters that do not actually spell any words – the mere presence of writing was thought to have magical power, regardless of what it said. The mystery of undeciphered scripts has always had a strong allure, due to the phenomenal challenge of breaking their codes but also because of the fascination exerted by writing itself. As we have seen, many myths have grown up around the origins of writing – from Enmerkar's stroke of brilliance to the fish-man delivering it complete from the sea. What these myths have in common is attributing something that took place over a long period and was the work of many different people to a single time, place, and person. Exactly the same thing happened in our own time with the decipherment of cuneiform, a long and complex process involving more people than I can mention here, which most accounts attribute solely to Rawlinson. Compressing a long story into the genius insight of a single figure makes the story much easier to grasp and easier to tell, but loses much in the process. If anything, the mythical accounts from Mesopotamia should serve as a reminder to us that we are just as capable of mythologising and oversimplifying our own history.

The lasting value of cuneiform over thousands of years shows that there is strength in complexity, which can be both practical and mystical at the same time. It is a system that privileges diversity over standardisation, and communicates more than just words. What began as a utilitarian accounting system evolved into a script that was thought to represent the keys to the universe. An object of wonder to the scholars of the library, cuneiform served as an inexhaustible source of inspiration revealing the minds of the gods, the laws of nature, and the fabric of reality itself. To read cuneiform, both now and then, is to go on a journey through time and space. We will undertake these journeys with the ancient scholars as they explored the limits of human knowledge and enshrined their efforts in the ever-enduring clay.

2.

The Power of the Gods

Ashurbanipal's grandfather Sennacherib is feeling triumphant. Standing on the roof of the palace in the city of Ashur, he watches the New Year celebrations taking place. It is March and the Assyrian spring is beginning to bloom. A procession of gods is making its way through the streets – sumptuous statues sitting on thrones are being carried from the temple to the city gate, passing through streets thronged with people eager to catch a rare glimpse of the gods. At the centre of the procession is the state god of Assyria, Ashur. He is on his way to the New Year festival house, a special building outside the walls of the city where he will symbolically battle the forces of chaos and re-establish order in the universe, guaranteeing stability for another year, before being returned to the temple.[1]

Sennacherib is pleased to see the celebrations underway, for he built the New Year festival house and remodelled the temple specially for this purpose. The New Year festival has not been celebrated in this way in Assyria since the eighteenth century BC, 1,100 years ago. Subsequently it had become more of a Babylonian ritual, a twelve-day event celebrating the supremacy of the Babylonian god Marduk and his control over the cosmos. But the Babylonians have not been able to celebrate the festival since being conquered by Assyria; this interruption to a long-standing custom has been a great blow to the city's pride, making them feel their change in status all the more. They have never really accepted their loss of independence and have continuously fought to regain it.

Sennacherib's reign has been plagued by uprisings in Babylon, a constant thorn in his side, but now it is all over. He finally defeated Babylon in 689 BC, putting an end to those years of rebellion and subduing those troublemakers who cannot accept that the world has changed. To mark his triumph, he has rebuilt the Babylonian temples and shrines that he destroyed, sites where key parts of the old festival took place – only not in Babylon, but in Assyria. By relocating the New Year festival from Babylon to Assyria, and now glorifying Assyria and its god Ashur, Sennacherib is sending a clear message about who really wields power in the Near East.

Sennacherib had very personal reasons for his aggressive attitude towards Babylon and its gods. After years of struggling to keep the region under control, he had installed his son as king of Babylon, which resulted in peace for six years. However, as we saw in the Introduction, a group of Babylonians betrayed their king to the Elamites in Iran, who kidnapped him and took him back to their country. Sennacherib's son was never seen again.

Sennacherib's grief unleashed his rage. It was the last straw. After so many years of frustration and conflict with Babylon, the murder of his son drove Sennacherib to destroy the city completely. Not only did he raze it to the ground, he even dug canals to flood the city, and sowed the fields with salt so nothing could grow there again.[2] He captured the statue of Marduk, the god of Babylon, and held it hostage in Assyria. Yet he rebuilt the shrines in the city of Ashur in the image of Babylon. It was a remarkable thing to do – clearly Sennacherib could never truly destroy or forget Babylon, despite all the problems it caused him; but he was absolutely determined to subsume it into Assyria symbolically as well as politically, and to celebrate this fact every year.

The New Year festival was the culmination of a whole host of reforms that saw Sennacherib transfer Babylon's ancient rituals of power to Assyria. Many texts describing these reforms are preserved in the library.[3] Most strikingly of all, Sennacherib had his scholars rewrite the Babylonian *Epic of Creation*, changing its hero from Marduk to Ashur.[4] All Marduk's great deeds were now ascribed to Ashur, including the creation of the world, the vanquishing of chaos, and kingship of the universe, giving a mandate to Assyria for its political ambitions. Not content with making Ashur king and foremost warrior of the gods, Sennacherib went even further. He changed the spelling of Ashur's name to a Sumerian one, writing it as a logogram, AN.SHAR$_2$. This could still be pronounced 'Ashur', but in writing it looked the same as the name of the king of the gods before Marduk. As this character was one of the first to be mentioned in the poem, the change effectively implied that Ashur existed before all the other gods. In this rewriting of mythological history, Ashur is first, foremost, and always the mightiest, just like Assyria. The new rendering of Ashur's name stuck, and two generations later was still used in the writing of Ashurbanipal's name.

Assyria was indebted to Babylon for much of its culture – many of its customs, literature, and knowledge originated there. Nowhere is this clearer than in the realm of religion. While the Assyrians had their own national gods, their basic pantheon was that which had been worshipped all over Mesopotamia for more than a thousand years, developed in the lands of Babylonia and by their predecessors in Sumer. As politics shifted, so did religion: the rise of one city catapulted its patron god to the top of the hierarchy, and this is reflected in mythology as the gods battle for supremacy.

But religion was not only about the state, and the gods were complex beings. They were portrayed both as like humans in their personalities and weaknesses, and simultaneously as utterly mysterious and incomprehensible. From the squabbles and power struggles depicted in mythology to the earnest hymns and prayers uttered by individuals, the library holds a wealth of texts that give us insight into not only Assyrian religion but older traditions also. We cannot understand Assyrian society without understanding its religion, and we cannot understand Assyrian religion without exploring what came before. We will have to look further back in time to piece together a picture of their gods.

Though Sennacherib's actions in overwriting Babylonian religion were extreme, what he did was nothing new. Ashur's replacement of Marduk was merely the latest in a string of battles among the gods that had been going on since the beginning of Mesopotamian history. Over this long time span, many different gods would rise and fall along with the fortunes of those who worshipped them. The history of religion in Mesopotamia is one of competition between deities, with new gods arriving on the scene, merging with older ones and absorbing their identities. There are so many deities, cities, and complexities over such a long time span that there is much work still to be done to piece it together. We will sketch the outlines and introduce some of the main characters, though we will not be able to meet them all.

Each city had a patron god which it worshipped alongside the rest of the pantheon. These gods were worshipped elsewhere also. Nabu, the god of scribes, was the patron of Borsippa, a city in northern Babylonia, but as we have seen, was worshipped by Ashurbanipal in Assyria too. The gods were thought to dwell in their statues, so that when the statue of the god left the city, it meant that the god had actually left, and was tantamount to the god abandoning their people. In this way, Sennacherib's capture of Marduk's statue was effectively him kidnapping the god himself, which the Babylonians would have interpreted as Marduk forsaking them. This 'godnapping' was a common practice, and Sennacherib was not the first to do it. The statue of Marduk had been looted from Babylon several times, so much so that one Babylonian text describes this history as Marduk travelling around the world.[5] Without the god being present in his temple, the Babylonians could not perform the rites showing their devotion to him; and, most crucially of all, they could not perform the New Year festival, which reaffirmed his power and support for his city.

By Sennacherib's time in the early seventh century BC Marduk was one of the most powerful gods in Mesopotamia, but it had not always been this way. The Mesopotamian pantheon begins with the gods of Sumer. Similarly to how Greek and Roman deities have different names in each language but came to be considered the same, the same gods were worshipped by the Sumerians, Babylonians, and Assyrians under different names. These gods had originally been distinct deities, belonging to the Akkadian speakers who are first evidenced in southern Mesopotamia around 2500 BC, but soon merged with the older Sumerian gods. Inanna, patron goddess of Uruk in Sumer, is called Ishtar in Akkadian; the god of fresh water and wisdom Enki becomes Ea; the sun god Utu is later called Shamash. But newer deities could rise to power also – Ashur was not originally Sumerian, and Marduk was little known before the second millennium BC.

The rise of Marduk is very much connected with the political and military power of Babylon: as the city grew in importance from an obscure backwater to the dominant power in the south, so Marduk grew in influence, being exalted as king of all of the gods just as Babylon ruled over all other cities in the region. The Babylonian *Epic of Creation* that Sennacherib later tampered with was in itself a rewriting of mythological history to reflect Babylonian domination over southern Iraq. Both the Assyrians and the Babylonians were presenting the divine world as a mirror of realities on earth, which justified their actions. They probably would have seen it the other way round, of course – that in order for them to have achieved what they did they must have had the backing of the gods, and so were only explaining how things had to be.

Although the heyday of Sumerian culture was in the third millennium BC, the texts that tell us about the adventures of its gods usually date to the second millennium, many centuries later. In Sumerian sources the three most powerful gods were An, Enlil, and Enki (Anu, Ellil, and Ea in Akkadian, respectively), joined at the top by the mother goddess Ninhursag (sometimes called by other names, and known as Belet-ili in Akkadian). These four determined the destinies of humanity. Ninhursag was the creator of human beings, while An, Enlil, and Enki created the universe and divided it between them. The Babylonian poem of the flood describes how they cast lots for their different realms of power.[6] An received the sky, Enlil the earth, and Enki the Apsu, the source of the rivers running under the earth. As ruler of the heavens and father of the gods, An was an ultimate authority who bestowed kingship upon human rulers, but did not intervene in life on earth as much as other gods. Enlil and Enki were very different. Enlil was the de facto king of the gods, and as the one with responsibility for the earth, he was the god that many ordinary human beings considered a supreme authority. Enki, meanwhile, was a creator god who organised the natural world.

All three of these gods sired many others, in often dubious circumstances. An's most notable offspring was the goddess Inanna, but he also copulated with the earth to produce many demons. Enlil caught sight of the pretty maiden goddess Ninlil walking by the riverbank and repeatedly raped her, which resulted in her giving birth to the moon god among others.[7] Ninlil became Enlil's consort – her name is simply the feminine version of her husband's name, En meaning lord and Nin meaning lady. The gods did not condone the rape, however, for they arrested Enlil and forced him to leave the city as a punishment. Enki behaves similarly atrociously and fathers his children by impregnating his daughter, the daughter of his daughter, her daughter, and so on.[8] Unlike the Greek gods, at least the Sumerian gods only harass other deities and leave mortals alone. The exception to this is the goddess Inanna, who subverts so many norms, and takes a human husband, the shepherd Dumuzi.

The Babylonian *Epic of Creation*, written in the second half of the second millennium BC, some hundreds of years after the Sumerian texts, has a very different story about how the gods came into being.[9] In this beginning, there was water – Apsu, the freshwater domain personified, and Tiamat, whose name means sea. From the mingling of these waters the first generation of gods is born. The sky god Anu is third in sequence, and in turn begets Ea, who later becomes father to Marduk. Struggles among the gods erupt almost immediately – the younger generation make an awful lot of noise, which stops their father Apsu from sleeping and in a rage he threatens to kill his children. Ea intervenes and murders Apsu before turning his body into the cosmic location of the Apsu, which explains how the god of wisdom came to live there. Spurred on by her children, Tiamat spawns an army to avenge the killing of her husband, giving birth to demons, scorpion men, dragons, and other monstrous beings, and marches upon the gods. None of the gods want to face Tiamat; all are too afraid. But then Marduk volunteers to fight. This young warrior, hitherto with no place among the great gods, demands that if he succeeds the others must acknowledge him as king. They agree to his terms, and Marduk duly proves himself worthy, easily defeating Tiamat and her horde. After the battle, Marduk creates the earth out of Tiamat's corpse and sets up a whole new world order, assigning the gods their places in the sky, establishing the regular movements of the heavens, and creating human beings. The story culminates with the gods volunteering to build Babylon and Marduk's temple within it as the greatest creation of all.

The Babylonian *Epic of Creation*, then, was not universally believed in Mesopotamia but was a distinctly Babylonian version of events geared towards proving the superiority of Marduk and his city. It depicts a universe built on struggle and conflict from the very earliest days, ultimately ruled by a supreme warrior god. It is aggressive towards earlier traditions also. Other stories existed telling of the creation of the world and of human beings, but this epic incorporates them into its own version of events and rewrites them for its own ends. For example, the gods that created human beings were originally Enki and the birth goddess Belet-ili, but in the Babylonian version Marduk is the one who comes up with this brilliant idea; Enki is portrayed as just a follower of Marduk's orders, with no mention of a birth goddess at all.

The Babylonian *Epic of Creation* is ruthlessly comprehensive in rewriting earlier traditions to depict Marduk as supreme, and does so with dazzling virtuosity, weaving together different strands of theology, mythology, and literary history. More than any other, this poem is a portrait of absolute power in all domains, 'a text that tolerates no rivals', so overpowering is its hero. The story unfolds over seven tablets, and ends with a list of Marduk's fifty names, many of which formerly belonged to other deities whom Marduk has now superseded. The poem culminates with the instruction to study these names – the father should teach them to his son, and the scholars should discuss them together.[10]

Marduk did not just take over the names of earlier gods, he took their whole identities. Not only was he king of the gods, but he was also the storm god, the warrior god, the god of wisdom and magic, and a creator god who made the world. The *Epic of Creation* shows him accomplishing feats traditionally ascribed to these other gods, rendering them almost superfluous. All these other gods now become just aspects of Marduk, whose statue is even venerated in their temples. As one list of gods puts it:

Urash	Marduk of planting
Lugalidda	Marduk of the abyss
Ninurta	Marduk of the pickaxe
Nergal	Marduk of battle
Zababa	Marduk of warfare
Enlil	Marduk of lordship and consultations
Nabu	Marduk of accounting
Sin	Marduk who lights up the night
Shamash	Marduk of justice
Adad	Marduk of rain
Tishpak	Marduk of troops
Shuqamuna	Marduk of the container
[name lost]	Marduk of everything[11]

To many this sounds like the beginnings of a kind of monotheism, as one god is now fulfilling the functions of all of the gods. Yet it does not fit the definition of monotheism as we know it, the belief in one and only one God. There is no demand to only worship Marduk above all others, and contrary to what these kinds of lists imply, Marduk does not displace other gods altogether. People continued to worship other gods, and we may well ask how far Marduk's takeovers really went. Even after the ascent of Marduk to kingship over all the gods, the original triad of Anu, Enlil, and Ea was still honoured in the temples. When the *Epic of Creation* was recited before the statue of Marduk during the Babylonian New Year festival, the priest threw a veil over Enlil's cultic pedestal, perhaps to shield the god from the story of someone else taking his place, or, alternatively, as a symbol of his subordination. Either way, the old king of the gods was still relevant in Marduk's new era, despite what the poems would have us think.

It is difficult to reconcile these different traditions about the gods, and the apparent contradictions between mythology, abstract theology, and real-life worship. Yet this is the very nature of polytheism, which is a flexible system where different ideas can exist side by side. The closest parallel may be in modern-day Hinduism, where thousands of deities are worshipped as individuals, but understood on a higher level to be different manifestations of one supreme power. One god list in Ashurbanipal's library has about two thousand entries giving the names of the gods, with Marduk having 172 to himself.[12] Yet many of them are only known from the lists, abstract entities who may not have been worshipped in real life but who were part of the scribes' attempts to order the universe. The gods have many names and many faces, each one telling us something different about life in Mesopotamia.

Given the heights to which Marduk had climbed, Sennacherib's triumph over him in the seventh century BC was a major feat. The capture of his statue showed that Ashur was the king of the gods now. Yet Ashur is a very different kind of god from Marduk, indeed from any of the other Mesopotamian gods. He has no personality, and no myths tell us about his deeds or his character other than Sennacherib's alterations to the *Epic of Creation*. Instead, he is the idea of the city god taken to the extreme, a pure personification of its might. Ashur the god is so much identified with Ashur the city that it is impossible to know which came first. As the territory controlled by the city of Ashur grew it came to be called 'the land of Ashur', which is the Akkadian name for what we call Assyria. Whereas other gods chose particular cities as their home, Ashur *is* the city, or at least the spirit that dwells in it. After taking over from Marduk he was celebrated as a supreme creator and omniscient ruler as well as patron of the Assyrian state. But while Marduk's power was tied to Babylon, Marduk was also worshipped outside that city and those controlled by it, as a god of wisdom, magic, and healing. Ashur, by contrast, was synonymous with Assyria and its political power, and may have had reason to be jealous of Marduk's popularity.

The second most important deity in Assyria was Ishtar, a goddess distantly related to Aphrodite, but whose personality changed substantially on the way from Mesopotamia to Greece. Ishtar is not a goddess of romantic love and fuzzy feelings, but a goddess of sex and war, of deep drives and strong emotions. If Ashur lacks personality, Ishtar more than makes up for it: she is power hungry and threatening, a goddess who wages war against the mountains and attempts to overthrow her sister as queen of the dead. She is contradictory and ambiguous: a woman with male ambitions who possesses the traits of both sexes; who personifies violence and disorder, yet is nurturing and supportive; patron of all members of society, from kings to prostitutes.

Ishtar had a special relationship with the Assyrian kings. In one hymn to the goddess, Ashurbanipal called her his mother and creator, speaking of how she gave him confidence and blessed his weapons: 'I knew no father or mother, I grew up in the lap of my goddesses.'[13] Actually, this hymn addresses two Ishtars – Ishtar of Nineveh, and Ishtar of another city called Arbela. These had originally been different goddesses who were subsumed into the single identity of Ishtar when the cities came under Assyrian dominion, just as Marduk took over from other gods as Babylonian territory expanded. By Ashurbanipal's time, these two Ishtars were considered different aspects of the same goddess, with the lady of Nineveh in the role of divine mother and the lady of Arbela as the one who bestows kingship. However, 'Ishtar', without any specific city attached, is also frequently invoked, transcending and incorporating both. There is also great overlap between their roles. Ishtar of Arbela had an oracle in that city which frequently sent messages of encouragement to Esarhaddon and Ashurbanipal, in which she too speaks like a mother:

> I will carry you on my hip like a nurse, I will put you between my breasts like a pomegranate. At night I will stay awake and guard you; in the daytime I will give you milk.[14]

At other times she promises: 'I will flay your enemies and give them to you', 'your enemies will roll before your feet like ripe apples', and 'I will abolish the frontiers of the lands and give them to you',[15] perhaps the extreme manifestation of her protective instincts.

The name Ishtar came to be synonymous with 'goddess' in Akkadian, as if she were the only one, or the very definition of the word, which is itself a paradox given that she is so different from other goddesses. Two notable figures among these others are the birth goddess Belet-ili and the goddess of healing Gula, both women in traditional nurturing roles who do not share Ishtar's vengeful streak. Yet overall there are not that many prominent roles given to female deities in Mesopotamia, which may explain why Ishtar comes to dominate. Any important goddess in a city conquered by the Babylonians or Assyrians was labelled as simply 'the goddess', and the traits of the most powerful personality became the default. Hymns describe Ishtar as gathering all the divine powers to herself, a reflection of how the cults of so many other goddesses became her own.

The fact that disorder personified was the highest-ranking goddess in Mesopotamia says a lot about the Mesopotamian conception of the universe: it is a contradictory place, where disorder is not only natural but worshipped, perhaps as a way of keeping it under control. That Ishtar was especially venerated by the Assyrian kings may seem somewhat strange given their obsession with order: in their view of the world, it was the king's duty to impose order on the chaotic periphery surrounding Assyria and bring it into the cosmic harmony of Assyrian rule. Ishtar, goddess of unbridled violence and passions, accompanies kings into battle and ensures their victory over the very chaos that she in some ways represents.

Perhaps it is better to have disorder on your side when your aim is to tame it.

The elevation of Ishtar is also unusual given that overall there was a trend to demote the status of goddesses after the third millennium. Many female deities who had important roles in early Sumerian religious texts were later displaced by male deities. For example, the goddess of scribes was originally Nisaba, but by Ashurbanipal's time this role was filled by Nabu. The underworld was originally ruled by Ereshkigal, but a first-millennium myth tells of how she fell in love with Nergal and he became king of her domain instead. Unlike what we see with Marduk, these minor goddesses do not all become aspects of Ishtar, who retains a very distinct personality, but their attributes are rebranded as male. The Babylonian *Epic of Creation* particularly sidelines female deities – except for the monstrous sea, Tiamat, but even her name is not written with the cuneiform sign that indicates divinity. The reason for this shift may be that the third-millennium pantheon was based on the household, where women had important roles, whereas in the second and first millennia the pantheon was based on the state, where they did not.

⁂

The gods that Sennacherib watched parading through the streets would have looked human in form. None of the statues have survived, since they would have been made of precious materials that were looted and recycled long ago. But we know what they looked like from depictions in art. A relief commissioned by Sennacherib's father Sargon II, carved into the rock above a great canal, shows a procession of Assyrian gods each standing or sitting on their totem animal – Ashur is riding on a dragon (borrowed from Marduk), Ishtar stands atop a lion, the thunder god Adad is on a bull.[16] Images on the walls of the palace at Nimrud show a procession of gods taken captive from an enemy city being carried back to Assyria, seated on thrones. We also have many depictions of them on cylinder seals – a cylinder seal being a small object that people would use to sign their name, by rolling it across the clay, usually decorated with motifs as well as inscribed with cuneiform. The gods in these images are distinguished from humans by their horned crowns, a special signal of divinity, and are usually sitting down while the humans worshipping them stand.

The gods also show human emotions such as grief, desire, fear, joy, and anger. The mythological poems held in the library tell of their deeds and misadventures. They gather in assemblies, have discussions and arguments, trick and betray each other, go on journeys, and fight battles. They have viziers to keep them company and give advice. They have families and relationships, which in the Babylonian and Assyrian traditions are usually less dysfunctional than they are in the Sumerian. Most of Mesopotamian literature is about the adventures of gods rather than humans. Occasionally the gods interact with certain special humans, but often as part of their own squabbles.

One of my favourite examples of the humanlike nature of the gods is the way that Enlil behaves in the story of the flood.[17] The Mesopotamians had a flood story very similar to the one in the Bible – a god decides to destroy the human race by sending a universal flood, but one man gets away by building a boat. He is instructed to take on board two of every kind of animal and discovers that the flood is over by sending out three birds to find dry land. The story is so similar to the biblical version that it seems likely that the biblical authors encountered it during their long years of exile in Babylon and composed their own version which deliberately reacts against the Babylonian one, for the alterations speak volumes about the differences between their religious perspectives. Enlil, the god in charge of the earth, sends the flood not as part of a grand plan, but out of a fit of sleep-deprived rage. Human beings, far from being wicked, are simply making too much noise, which prevents him from sleeping and provokes him to destroy them all. After he sends the flood the other gods rebuke him for this rash decision, rhetorically asking why he didn't think this through. If human beings are wiped off the face of the earth, then there will be no one to make offerings to the gods and they will starve. It is a rash and stupid decision, and the other gods have no problem telling him so. Not only do the gods need sleep as much as humans, then, but they need humans as much as humans need them.

The biblical version has the Israelite God punishing humankind for their wickedness. This portrays the God of the Hebrew Bible as a higher moral authority, in stark contrast to the highest authority among the Mesopotamian gods. Enlil is much more fickle and couldn't care less whether human beings are good or bad, he just wants them to shut up. It is a very different concept of divinity, a polemical alternative arguing against the dominant narratives of the time. Yet from a Mesopotamian point of view, their version simply says something different about divine justice: the universe is unpredictable, and catastrophes can happen for no good reason. That is the nature of natural disasters, which even today many find difficult to reconcile with belief in a just God. The Mesopotamian gods are not perfect and make mistakes, just like human beings, which is one way of explaining why bad things happen to good people.

The noise generated by the people was a result of the normal activities and hustle and bustle of everyday life, and of overpopulation, which amplified this to an unbearable level. That is no one's fault, yet at the same time it was displeasing to the gods. Like the biblical story, then, the Mesopotamian version is also a cautionary tale that stresses the need to be on the right side of the gods. Humans were still to blame for the flood, in a way, but their transgression was an accident. This is a common theme in prayers from Mesopotamia, where people utter lengthy apologies to the gods for having offended them without knowing exactly what it is that they have done.

That the gods were imperfect is clear from another story about Enki, the god of trickery, who was once tricked himself.[18] The goddess Inanna got Enki drunk and talked him into giving her all the essences of civilisation, which she packed on her boat and took back to her city of Uruk. When Enki woke up, very hungover, and realised what she had done he was furious and chased after her, but it was too late. These essences included everything needed for human life, including various crafts and types of knowledge such as reed-working and copper-smithing, sacred offices and priesthoods, but also abstract qualities like heroism and kindness and their opposites, wickedness and deceit. Kissing, sex, and the tavern are also prime essentials, as are prostitution and plundering cities. This is yet another story about the origins of civilisation, which explains why Uruk became the first great city, but it recognises the bad that comes with the good, a realistic view of the complexities of people and of society.

The gods were vulnerable like humans and could not take their power for granted. In the Akkadian poem *Anzu*, Enlil loses control of the universe when the demon Anzu steals the tablet of destinies while Enlil is in the bath.[19] Without this magic object, Enlil no longer wields supreme power, which belongs to whoever possesses the tablet. And the flood is nearly the end of the gods as well as the humans, which shows that the gods can even die, the most human trait of all. Marduk killed his adversaries in the *Epic of Creation*, and several other 'dead gods' lurk in the background of Mesopotamian mythology. This is the ultimate result of the battles of the gods. Yet death is also a fundamental ingredient in life: as both the flood story and the Babylonian *Epic of Creation* tell us, the creation of human beings requires the blood of a god to be mixed with clay, which imparts a divine spirit to mortals.

Despite all this it would be a mistake to see the gods as overly like humans, for that would be to underestimate them. The Mesopotamians were truly in awe of the gods, filled with reverence, fear, and wonder towards them. Prayers typically begin by enumerating their many awesome qualities, reminding the suppliant of just what the gods were capable of, and the power they held over life, death, and destiny. Reciting these lists could have strengthened the person's confidence in the gods' ability to fulfil their request and humbled them before the divine, though they also were a way to flatter the gods and make them more likely to accept their pleas. Either way, tales of the gods behaving badly do not seem to have detracted from the very real respect people had for them. This can be seen in the ending of the flood story. Though it is a narrative that condemns Enlil for being thoughtless and rash, it ends by addressing him and declaring 'this song is for your praise. May the gods hear, let them extol your great deed to each other.'[20]

All these foibles and misadventures raise the question of how far the Mesopotamians really believed in their gods. Why worship powers that were ultimately so flawed? Yet we ask these questions because the dominant religions of our own time have conditioned what we expect from religious devotion. Monotheistic religions such as Judaism, Christianity, and Islam demand allegiance to one supreme deity, forsaking all others. They sprang up in a climate where this was not the normal practice. In a world of multiple gods, naturally people had multiple allegiances of differing strengths and bonds. If you asked Sennacherib whether he believed in the gods, he would be baffled by the question. Belief was not a choice; the gods were just a part of the world that everyone took for granted. It would be like asking whether we believed in the sun.

For the Mesopotamians, the sun and the sun god were one and the same. As well as manifesting in their statues, the gods manifested in the sky as the heavenly bodies. This explains why many prayers and rituals took place outside, so that people could address the gods directly, facing them as they spoke. The moon was a deity called Sin (nothing to do with sin in the sense of transgression, just a linguistic coincidence), the planet Venus was the love goddess Ishtar, Mars was the war god Nergal, Mercury was the god of scribes Nabu, Jupiter was Marduk, king of the gods. That these identifications are similar to the ones that we still use today is no coincidence – the Greeks got the names of the planets from the Mesopotamians and changed them to those of their own gods, and those we use are the Roman equivalents.[21] But for the Mesopotamians the planets really were the gods and were not just named after them. The gods lived both in the sky and on earth – they could manifest in different places and in different forms, all at the same time.

Why the gods behaved as they did was not always clear. Time and time again hymns and prayers emphasise that the gods are ultimately unknowable. Enlil is described as of 'unfathomable mind', as are his successors Marduk and Ashur.[22] It is the ultimate rulers who attract this description more than any others. As one hymn to Marduk puts it:

> The lord divines the gods' inmost thoughts,
> but no god understands his behaviour.
> Marduk divines the gods' inmost thoughts,
> no god understands his mind.[23]

This extract is taken from a poem dubbed in modern times *The Poem of the Righteous Sufferer*, which has parallels with the biblical book of Job. The sufferer is afflicted with a whole host of misfortunes – from every kind of ill-health imaginable to being ostracised by his friends and family, yet he has no idea what he has done to offend the gods, for he has revered them all his life. In the end he is visited by an exorcist in a dream sent by Marduk, and when he wakes, he is restored to health. No explanation for this change in affairs is given. The lesson seems to be that all fortune depends ultimately on Marduk's will, which we can never understand since it does not follow the same expectations as ours:

> what seems good to oneself could be an offence to a god,
> what in one's own heart seems abominable could be good to one's goddess!
> Who could learn the reasoning of the god? It is like the centre of heaven.
> Who could grasp her counsel? It is like the abyss.[24]

People may not have doubted that the gods existed, but they did doubt whether they heard their prayers, and whether there was any point in worshipping them. Perhaps this comes as no surprise given the inscrutability of the gods, the randomness with which they seemed to bestow their favour, and the quick turns of human fortunes. A poem we call the *Babylonian Theodicy* portrays a man in crisis, bitterly lamenting how a lifetime of serving the gods has brought him nothing but suffering, and arguing that it makes no difference:

> Indeed in my youth I tried to find out the will of my god,
> with prayer and supplication I besought my goddess.
> I bore a yoke of profitless servitude:
> my god decreed for me poverty instead of wealth.[25]

Over thirteen stanzas he gives examples of how the gods do not reward piety or care for justice. His parents died when he was only a child, his life is a misery and his finances are ruined, while idiots, the wicked, and tyrants flourish. The injustice is even evident in nature: the wild ass who eats grass to its heart's content has made no attempt to follow the will of the gods, and the savage lion makes no sacrifices and still has its fill of choicest meat. Yet this is not the only point of view put forward in the poem – it takes the form of a dialogue between the sufferer and his friend, and for every bitter remonstration there is a counterargument. Death is part of life, but those who look to the gods are protected. Evildoers will get their comeuppance eventually, and even the wild ass and the lion will meet with the arrow and the pit. Better not to earn the same fate – the rewards of the gods will be longer in coming, but longer lasting. The poem seems to end with each character sympathising with the other's point of view – the friend speaks of how lies and falsehood are endemic among humankind, since they were given to us by the gods, and acknowledges the suffering that this causes the downtrodden, while the complainant makes one last plea to his god and goddess for help, giving them another chance to save him. The ending is thus inconclusive, and we do not know if he is really persuaded.

While each god had their own domain of responsibility, in practice any of the gods could be asked for any of the big things that people wanted – long life, good health, a favourable destiny. People often cultivated special relationships with individual gods. Ashurbanipal with all his learning makes many dedications to the god of scribes Nabu. As we have seen, Mesopotamian names are miniature sentences which are in themselves prayers to the gods or affirmations about them. Sennacherib's name in Akkadian is Sin-ahhe-eriba, which translates as 'the god Sin has replaced the brothers', likely a prayer of thanksgiving for a living child after the death of older siblings. The names of other characters we will meet are similarly meaningful – the chief physician Urad-Nanaya's name means 'servant of the goddess Nanaya', while the name of the exorcist Adad-shumu-utsur exhorts 'Adad protect the name!' In addition to these favourites, everyone had a personal god who would intercede for them with the great gods. Bad luck and suffering were not only consequences of angering the great gods, but of angering your personal god, who would then abandon you and no longer make your case. People seem to have had closer relationships with their personal gods than those of the higher pantheon, since prayers to personal gods dispense with lengthy formalities and get straight to the point.

The flood may not have been sent as a punishment for human wickedness, but the Mesopotamian gods were not indifferent to how humans behaved. The sun god Shamash was also the god of justice, as he could see everything happening on earth and had an objective perspective. Prayers to Shamash exalt how he will punish dishonest merchants, those who call in loans before the agreed time, corrupt judges, and men who covet their neighbours' wives, cursing them with no heirs and desertion by their own families. Conversely, he will rescue the falsely accused, and give extra life, wealth, and offspring to the honest merchant and doer of virtuous deeds.

Nor is Shamash the only Mesopotamian god to be concerned with human morality. Misfortune of all kinds was thought to be the result of angering the gods through sin and wrongdoing. One of the rituals to cleanse a person of their sin gives a very long list of 123 things that they might have done to anger the gods.[26] It includes stealing, adultery, murder, lying, spreading gossip, estranging family members from one another, and disrespecting the gods. Failing to do certain good deeds also counted: he who did not free a prisoner or clothe the naked man was also unwittingly committing a crime against his god. In a phrase reminiscent of Jesus's words teaching moral integrity in the Sermon on the Mount, 'let your yes be yes and your no be no' (Matthew 5:37), the Mesopotamian ritual text states that the man who said 'no' for 'yes' and 'yes' for 'no' has done wrong.[27]

The gods would also punish transgressions that do not seem obviously immoral to us. Some of the stranger crimes listed by this ritual tablet include obscurities such as the 'curse of bellows and stove' – what this refers to is anyone's guess.[28] There were many ways to offend the gods, and in addition to the first 123 offences the tablet lists punishments for another 173 very specific actions.[29] For instance, urinating or vomiting in a river was a major sin – since rivers were divine, presumably the river god would not have been well pleased. Then again, anyone who has walked through a British town centre on a Saturday night may wish that public urinating and vomiting were similarly taboo today. People could also pick up guilt like a stain without even knowing about it and through no fault of their own – sleeping in the bed of a cursed man or drinking from his cup was another way people could accidentally acquire sin and need to be cleansed. This required elaborate rituals which were the domain of the exorcist; these will be explored more in the next chapter.

Each individual had to take care to maintain a good relationship with the gods for their own sake, but on the level of the state it was the responsibility of the king, as the gods' representative on earth, to maintain divine favour for his land as a whole. Thus, there were several royal rituals that the king had to take part in to reconcile himself and the country at large with the gods.

One of the most important of these rituals was the New Year festival with which we opened this chapter. The texts that describe the key components of this Babylonian ritual come from the Hellenistic period, and so can only tell us about how it was celebrated long after Sennacherib, though the Babylonians were performing it in some form as early as the second millennium BC. The festival was a twelve-day programme of events which saw all the gods assemble in Marduk's temple, meaning that their statues were brought from neighbouring cities in lavish processions. Central to the festival was the re-enactment of Marduk's battle against Tiamat, the story told in the *Epic of Creation*; the re-enactment confirmed Marduk's power among the gods every year and renewed his favour for his city. But one of the most remarkable things about the ritual was the role of the king, who was ritually humiliated in the ceremony. He was stripped of his regalia, his ears were pulled, and then while he knelt before the statue of Marduk a priest would slap him – hard.[30] If he shed tears, it was considered a good omen, that all would be well for the coming year, whereas a lack of tears was a bad sign, which certainly gave the priests an incentive to do their worst. The king then had to swear that he had not committed any sins against Marduk, his temple, his city or its inhabitants, thus promising that he would continue to take care of them in the coming year. The Babylonians may have developed this part of the ritual in response to the aggression of Assyrian rulers like Sennacherib, since it was the Assyrians who had done wrong against Marduk rather than any native Babylonian ruler. Or it may have been an even later response to the declining interest of Persian and Greek kings, who often ignored Marduk altogether.

⁂

Most of the festival activities would have gone on behind closed doors rather than in front of a public audience – only the priests would have seen the king being slapped. Temples were not places of individual worship, but houses for the gods, and accordingly were private spaces for deities and their servants. Unlike in today's monotheistic religions, priests did not have the job of ministering to people, but were engaged in keeping the gods' households running. The Sumerian word for temple is simply 'house', and households they really were – everything was geared towards the feeding and care of the divine statue, which was treated as having the same needs as a person. The statue was washed and clothed, provided with food four times a day, and put to bed at night. The Assyrian king took an interest in the temples' interior design – priests often wrote to him about refurbishment plans, and in one case he asked to see the sketch of the designs for the new bed.[31] When the statue was taken out on procession during festivals it was carefully watched, and the king wanted to know when the god arrived safely.[32] Caring for the statues of the gods was of utmost importance, for if they were neglected they would abandon the city and disasters would follow. This may seem strange from a Judaeo-Christian or Islamic perspective, but this way of treating the gods is alive and well in India, where Hindu temples follow many of the same practices.

The gods were kept apart from ordinary mortals in their temples and would not have been seen except when they were taken out on processions. Only a very special class of priest was allowed to enter the innermost sanctum where the statues resided and present the gods with their meals. These priests were called 'temple enterers' and had to be of the utmost purity in order to come before the gods. Priesthoods were often passed down in families, but background checks were still carried out on potential initiates.[33] Candidates had to be of good character, have lived a morally good life, and be in good health, as it was offensive to present the gods with anything less than perfect. One text tells us that the bodies of certain kinds of priests had to be 'pure as a golden statue'.[34] New priests underwent an initiation ceremony in the bathhouse before they approached the god for the first time, where their bodies were checked and their heads shaved as a mark of their new status. Temples employed barbers to make sure they stayed that way.

Being a priest was a big job. The obligations were numerous since there were many expensive and time-consuming rites to perform in the temple. Priests were paid, but it was not a large amount; holding a priesthood was more a mark of status than something wanted for financial gain. In fact, it was common to sell off priestly offices or subcontract someone else to perform your duties for you.

Many priests came from well-off families and had other sources of income, but this was not the case for all. Status and wealth were not necessarily connected, and even though these were prestigious titles to hold, it was not only the rich who possessed them. Remuneration was usually paid in kind, and priests were given the grain they would need to turn into bread or beer for the gods, with some left over for themselves. They could also eat the 'leftovers' from the meals served to the gods, who enjoyed the aroma more than the taste.

What did the gods eat? We know more about the standard daily menu in Babylonia than Assyria, the temple records being better preserved there. There the diet of the gods consisted of beef, mutton, poultry, vegetables, dates, cakes, bread, and beer, which was served in vast quantities. Some kings made a special effort to upgrade the offerings – in 598/7 BC the Babylonian king Nebuchadnezzar II said that he made sure Nabu was served one fattened bull; sixteen sheep; fowl, fish, mice, eggs, vegetables, fruits, special dates from Dilmun, figs and raisins, honey, butter, cakes, milk, oil, three types of beer, and wine – every day. Sacrifice was a key part of the temple's activities, since as we have seen in the flood story the gods need offerings to survive, but these offerings are also proof of human devotion and a form of gift-giving. The Ishtar temple in Uruk sacrificed 4,300 lambs every year as part of its daily operations, and some special occasions required ninety lambs in a single day. One hundred and twenty herdsmen were needed to steward such a large flock, which gives a sense of the scale of the institution.

In light of this, temples needed a whole host of personnel. The temple of Nabu in Borsippa, a city just south-west of Babylon whose records are especially plentiful, employed people working in twenty-eight different professions in the Neo-Babylonian period (which overlapped with and followed the time of the Assyrians). These included persons responsible for producing the statues' meals, such as ox herders, butchers, fishermen, bakers, oil pressers, and brewers, while the temple enterers were the waiters. They also needed craftsmen to maintain the temple and its luxurious goods: builders, carpenters, potters, reed-workers, stonecutters, goldsmiths, and jewellers, as well as those concerned with the clothes of the gods and the priests – tailors and washer men. The gods demanded entertainment, so acrobats and singers were employed too, performing for the gods on a regular basis. Inevitably, scribes were needed to keep track of the enormous bureaucracy involved in running such a large household, as well as measurers and gatekeepers. Temples even hired their own boatmen to take care of transport, both of the statues of the gods when they had to go to Babylon for the New Year festival, and of commodities such as bricks for new buildings.

The households of the gods were powerful economic institutions. They owned huge estates and produced commodities which they sold, like the wool from their sheep. Other temples made money from selling their agricultural goods, and even functioned as early banks, offering loans to business ventures and to poor people in need. The riches of the temples made them prime targets for theft, which is dealt with in several letters in the royal archives. In one case, thieves stole sheets of gold from the temple of Ashur, though these were thankfully recovered.[35] The city mayor wrote to the king to report it, noting that this was the second time it had happened. Thieves did not necessarily have to break in as insiders were also tempted to go rogue – in the city of Arbela a priest of Ea peeled off gold from the offering table,[36] while in Kalhu a temple guard conspired with a lamentation priest to cut off 'beams of gold from the head of Ninurta' and bands of silver from the walls.[37] Worst of all, a cook stole a golden statue of the god Erra – when he was found out and apprehended he was beaten to death.[38] Stealing from the gods was a serious matter. This explains why it was so important to perform background checks on new priests – those with access to the inner sanctum were in a uniquely privileged position that could be easily abused.

The whole system revolved around the belief that the statue really was to be treated as if it were the god itself. But at the heart of this is another paradox – how can a statue made of earthly materials and by human hands be divine? How could mere wood be the flesh of the gods? First, the most rare and precious materials were chosen – pure gold that came straight from the mountains and gemstones that had not been used before for any other purpose, along with wood from a special type of tree. But the transformative factor was that, when the statue was completed, it underwent a special ceremony called the mouth-washing ritual, a ritual that brought the statue to life and changed it from an inanimate object to a manifestation of the god.[39] The statue was taken down to the river at sunset and lavished with offerings, libations, sacrifices, and incantations. During this ritual all associations with human craftsmen were symbolically broken, with the work now being attributed to the gods rather than to mortals. The tools which were used to make the statue were bound up inside the body of a sacrificed sheep, along with figurines of a tortoise and turtle made of gold and silver, and thrown into the river. In the morning the craftsmen were summoned before the gods of each of their crafts, and their hands were bound and symbolically 'cut off' with a wooden knife. The goldsmith swore, 'I did not make you: Kusibanda, god of the goldsmith, made you'; the carpenter swore, 'I did not make you: Ninildu, god of the carpenter, made you', and so on, each substituting their respective profession and its patron god.[40] The human craftsmen finally threw their tools in the river, to send them back to the divine craftsmen they were borrowed from, to the Apsu where those gods dwelled.

Although I have mixed examples from both Assyria and Babylonia in painting a picture of their shared religion (necessary simply because of where the evidence falls), there were differences between the two. One of these is that in Babylonia objects belonging to a god were also considered divinities in their own right. Chariots, thrones, sceptres, drums, and even branding irons were not only labelled as gods with a special cuneiform sign indicating divinity, but also received sacrifices and food offerings just as the statues of the gods did. This was not the case in Assyria, where they were treated as more ordinary objects. Yet the Assyrians knew that these items were revered in Babylonia, and sometimes showed a certain cultural sensitivity towards them. On one occasion during the reign of Sennacherib's father Sargon, a bed belonging to a god was moved from Babylonia to Ashur, which posed an existential problem – should it still be treated as divine in its new location?[41] The official in charge of the operation arranged for the bed to be transported by boat, and for practical reasons it had to stay on board overnight before being moved to the temple. The official, Ṭab-shar-Ashur, made sure that as long as the bed was on board it received sacrifices of sheep just as it would have done in its original temple, and informed the king of what he was doing. The Assyrians did not believe that beds were divine, but in this case Ṭab-shar-Ashur thought it best to treat it as if it were until it was securely on Assyrian soil. He must have felt uncomfortable treating the bed in a manner different from that to which it was accustomed simply because it had moved upstream.

Not all Assyrians then shared Sennacherib's contempt for Babylon. In fact, his destruction of the city and theft of its god deeply shocked Assyria. Sennacherib's son Esarhaddon made it his mission to undo his father's damage, rebuilding the city and sending the statue of Marduk back so that he could be cared for in his own temple, and take part in the New Year festival again. No matter how mighty Assyria's god Ashur was, it did not feel right to treat Marduk as a second-class citizen. The battles between Assyria and Babylonia would continue for generations – Ashurbanipal sacked the city yet again after it broke away from his control, repeating his grandfather's mistakes and storing up more trouble for the future. Marduk had the last laugh in the end, for the Babylonians led a coalition of all Assyria's traditional enemies in an attack against Nineveh in 612 BC, setting the city on fire and putting an end to Assyrian rule, just two decades after Ashurbanipal died. Ultimately, then, it was the anger of Marduk that destroyed Ashurbanipal's palace and his library.

From the rise and fall of cities and empires to the changing of the seasons, the weather, and people's fluctuating emotions, the gods were the forces that shaped existence. Ultimately, all personal fortune and misfortune could be attributed to their influence or anger. They were embedded in the very fabric of the world and could not be separated from it for better or for worse, with violence and disorder honoured as much as justice and might. It is a view of the workings of the universe that has profound respect for the unknown and the uncertain, where humans must be humble in the face of nature. This is by no means the last time we will hear from the gods, since they are to be found in every aspect of Assyrian life.

While very different from the dominant monotheistic religions that shape much of the world today, Mesopotamian religion significantly influenced the Judaeo-Christian tradition. Israel and Judah were part of the Near East, small kingdoms at the mercy of the political giants of Assyria and Babylon. Assyrian and Babylonian kings therefore appear in the Hebrew Bible because of their impact on its peoples. The Bible is full of polemics against the old gods, too, and full of stories that show just how different the Hebrew God is from them. In order to make a claim of superiority, deities have to be mightier than their competitors, and religious competition was a feature of Mesopotamian religion throughout its history too, even culminating in something approaching monotheism as all gods ultimately became seen as merely aspects of Marduk.

Yet ancient Judaism not only defined itself against Mesopotamia, but also shared much with it, since both sprang from the broader cultural sphere of the ancient Near East. Both practised animal sacrifice, uttered similar types of prayer and worshipped gods who were at once vengeful and merciful. Both had ecstatic prophets; both composed lamentations over the destructions of cities, and poems of righteous sufferers. Indeed, the similarities between the two traditions were what so excited the Victorians when the original Mesopotamian sources were first discovered – and what caused so much controversy, since those sources were used as arguments for and against the reliability of the Bible.

Although Mesopotamian religion seems a world away from religion in the Western world, when we trace back the connections, the ties are much closer than they might at first appear. Given the substantial influence of Mesopotamian religion on the Hebrew Bible, and considering how significantly this in turn influenced Western culture, we arrive at the surprising truth that the power of the Mesopotamian gods can still be felt today.

3.

Magic and Witchcraft

Adad-shumu-utsur is sweeping the ground by the riverbank in the dead of night. He has come down from the citadel and chosen a secluded spot, next to the walls but away from the town, for this is no gardening chore but an important part of creating a ritual space. The sweeping is mostly symbolic, as much about clearing away invisible impurities as any visible dirt. As he sweeps, he runs through the arrangements in his mind. The figurines are ready, the special robes have been prepared, and his attendants have brought the holy water. He picks up the vessel and sprinkles water around the area to finish the ritual cleansing. He sets up his portable altar to the sun god, ready to receive the sacrifices. The queen mother will arrive just before dawn, and then they will begin. Adad-shumu-utsur has chosen the most favourable day possible for the ritual to take place – it is the latest in a long string of rituals he has performed, but none has yet worked, and he needs everything on his side to prevail.

It is June 670 BC and the king's mother Naqia has fallen gravely ill. This incredibly powerful woman is a trusted adviser to the king and wields enormous influence at court, so rumours begin to circulate that this is the work of witchcraft. As the highest-ranking exorcist in Assyria, Adad-shumu-utsur is on the case, trying to release her from the malicious energies and direct them back upon the witch who sent them.

It has been a stressful time for the king's exorcist. In this period, Esarhaddon is king, and Ashurbanipal his studious younger son. For two months Esarhaddon had been extremely sick, the most intense phase in an illness that had waxed and waned for years.

Never before had the king been so ill, and his physicians and exorcists alike had become increasingly desperate in their attempts to restore his health. Earlier in the year a huge conspiracy had broken out and the king had retaliated by executing much of the top level of the administration, which was bound to leave the survivors feeling jumpy. As soon as the king himself had recovered his mother fell ill, and curing her became Adad-shumu-utsur's charge. He is under a lot of pressure to succeed.

Although we do not know what Naqia's symptoms were at the time of this illness, others typically ascribed to witchcraft include depression, headaches, vertigo, ringing in the ears, loss of appetite, pallor, weakness, paralysis, impotence, and terrifying dreams. This is quite a specific set of ailments, which were often found clustered together, making witchcraft a diagnosable cause of disease like any other. The first response would usually be to attempt to reconcile the patient with the gods with prayers, rituals, and offerings. If this failed, there had to be an underlying reason for the gods' disfavour, and it was thought that witches could turn the gods away. Ultimately magic could kill: a witch using 'cutting of the throat magic' would get astral deities and evil omens to terrorise the target, with symptoms including bleeding from the mouth and derangement. When this type of magic was diagnosed as the cause, the prognosis was usually death.

It was unclear what type of witchcraft had been performed on Naqia, and so Adad-shumu-utsur had to try many different remedies to cover the potential bases. The witch may have cursed her, performed a spell to alienate her from the gods, or Naqia could have ingested a bewitched substance in her food. Adad-shumu-utsur informed the king that his team were performing rituals against something that might have been 'loss of flesh', a term for extreme weight loss.[1] As well as these, the team were performing numerous spells for undoing witchcraft, and all this was just the start.[2] The situation must have been serious – a second letter reported that they had performed ten more tablets' worth of incantations and rituals.[3] They were trying everything they could think of to keep her alive.

Magic in Mesopotamia was both ordinary and extraordinary. It was ordinary in the sense that it was an accepted part of the world – there was no such thing as the supernatural, since the word implies a division between reason and unreason, explicable and inexplicable. Magic was perfectly rational – you appealed to the gods and if they decided to help you, they would lend their strength to your actions. As with the gods, there was no question of believing in it or not, it just was. At the same time, a magical ritual was a special event that created a sense of awe and wonder for the people involved. Exorcists – the specialists in charge of such rituals – would go to great lengths to create an atmosphere that was highly charged and set apart from normal life, a space where extraordinary things could happen. It was a matter of degree – there were simple rituals that in principle could have been performed by anyone, even the untrained, such as those performed to banish the effect of a bad dream, and then there were highly elaborate rituals that would have taken many hours and costly resources for specialists to carry out. It is the latter that we know the most about, since folk magic by definition was not written down and preserved in the libraries. What we have is the knowledge of the professionals, where magic is taken to its highest and most complex form.

The professionals that we know of are all men. This did not mean that women could not perform magic, only that they were excluded from the scholarly elite that received professional training as exorcists. Ordinary people who could not afford to call an exorcist may well have improvised. Incantations for babies hint at this: in a society where all the childcare was done by women it seems unlikely that spells to stop babies crying would have been invented by male academics. Anti-witchcraft rituals show that women were considered capable of magic, since the incantations mostly target female witches. Males are mostly mentioned in the pair 'my witch and my warlock' when trying to cover all bases, implying that women were far more often thought to be the cause. The only time that the word for exorcist appears in a feminine form is in an anti-witchcraft ritual, as a synonym for witch. Only in literature do female magical practitioners appear in a good light – in the Sumerian poem *Enmerkar and Ensuhgirana*, a Sumerian witch does battle with a non-Sumerian one from Aratta, and the Sumerian spells always win.[4] It is a tale with a similar agenda to the poem we encountered in Chapter 1, where a battle of wits between two rulers culminated in the invention of writing by the Sumerians, proving their superiority. Here too, the Sumerians are the best at everything, magic included.

Since it is the gods who ultimately decide whether magic succeeds or fails, exorcists were made rather than born. Like most elite professions in Mesopotamia the art of the exorcist was kept in the family and handed down from father to son, but no innate gift was needed as his accomplishments were all the result of training. Exorcists studied a set body of knowledge comprising traditional incantations and rituals. The list survives today as the so-called *Excorcist's Manual* and includes temple rituals, medical incantations, anti-witchcraft rituals, purification rituals, incantations for driving out demons, and formal prayers, as well as venturing into other specialist domains such as divination and medical prescriptions.[5] These overlaps show just how widely applicable the exorcist's skills were, and that he did far more than drive away demons. The Akkadian word for the profession is *ashipu*, derived from the verb 'to cast a spell'. The Assyrian exorcist was a professional magic worker, who used those incantations and rituals as tools to effect change.

Adad-shumu-utsur's family had served the king for generations. He traced his ancestry back 150 years to Gabbu-ilani-eresh, who had been master scholar to two kings in the ninth century BC. His father had been chief scribe to both Ashurbanipal's great-grandfather Sargon II and his grandfather Sennacherib. Now Adad-shumu-utsur was the personal exorcist of Ashurbanipal's father Esarhaddon, and his two brothers were the king's chief scribe and a court astrologer, respectively. This was an extremely powerful family, holding between them three of the highest offices in the land at the same time. Their father had prepared them and secured positions for them, as was normal for all professions in Mesopotamia. Adad-shumu-utsur would in turn obtain a position for his own son Urad-Gula as an exorcist at the royal court, and would also find employment for his nephews and cousins.[6] Yet although family ties certainly opened doors of opportunity, they were no guarantee of success. Advisers could fall from favour just as easily as they had risen if they failed to deliver results. Adad-shumu-utsur would have to be careful, then, and hold himself to the highest professional standards.

Letters preserved in the archive reveal an intense correspondence between the king and his scholars. More letters survive from Adad-shumu-utsur than from any other adviser – forty-eight written just by him, and six co-authored with other scholars. Although Adad-shumu-utsur lived in the time of Esarhaddon, the collection that would become Ashurbanipal's library was already taking shape. Adad-shumu-utsur would have had his own tablets to consult at home, but Ashurbanipal's library contains an abundance of magical texts, some of which the royal exorcists may already have had access to. In any case, the library collection gives us an excellent idea of the arts of the exorcist needed at the royal court, and Adad-shumu-utsur's letters give real-life examples of when they were used, spanning both everyday matters and serious emergencies. It is to one of these emergencies that we now return.

The last incantation Adad-shumu-utsur tried in the prolonged battle against the queen mother's illness was 'You are the river who creates everything.' This incantation was an ingredient in many different rituals for undoing evil, but it turns up in one particular anti-witchcraft ritual found in the library, which could well have been the one that Adad-shumu-utsur used. The tablet states that the ritual is for a person who has ingested bewitched substances, slipped into their food or drink. As a result, the patient is unable to tolerate their food any more: 'when he eats bread and drinks beer his face is sallow and he vomits.'[7] This kind of witchcraft would certainly be a convincing explanation for extreme weight loss, so our reconstruction assumes it is the one that Naqia performed.

Adad-shumu-utsur helps the queen mother to recite 'You are the river who creates everything' as part of a bigger ritual. She does not perform it alone but is accompanied by the exorcists who prescribed it to make sure everything is carried out correctly. These are highly elaborate procedures that require Adad-shumu-utsur's expertise.

To perform the ritual, the queen mother starts on the riverbank with a prayer to the sun god Shamash. As the god of justice, Shamash is often asked to correct any misfortune that is undeserved, with witchcraft being a prime example. The ritual takes place early in the morning when the sun has just risen, the ideal time to make a petition to the sun god, before he becomes busy with anything else. Adad-shumu-utsur has been at work since long before sunrise, setting up the portable altar where he has placed the sacrifice, a libation vessel, and two clay figurines, one male and one female. These are the images of the unknown witches who are suspected of having caused the illness, who will soon get their comeuppance for what they have done.

Adad-shumu-utsur instructs Naqia to stand on the riverbank facing the sun, and to repeat after him, explaining to Shamash that 'the evil of the witchcraft, magic, sorcery and machinations' have left her 'frightened, scared and constantly terrified every day'. She finishes with a plea:

> May that evil not come near me and my house, not approach me, not reach me,
> May that evil cross the river and pass over the mountain!
> May that witchcraft distance itself 3,600 miles from my body,
> may it steadily rise into the sky like smoke,
> like an uprooted tamarisk tree may it not return to its place!
> May the river receive this witchcraft from me, may the river spare me![8]

As the first rays of the sun reflect on the water, the exorcist and his patient hope that Shamash will accept their appeal and approve the cleansing that will now take place in the river. Immersing herself in the river three times, Naqia faces upstream and addresses the river directly, asking it to remove these evil influences:

> You are the river who creates everything.
> When the great gods dug you, they placed good fortune on your banks,
> Ea, the king of the subterranean ocean, built his dwelling in your midst.
> You are just, your waters put things in order.
> Receive from me the evil of the witchcraft affecting me, let your banks receive all my illnesses!
> Carry away the evil, river, bring it down to your depths, river!
> Let that evil not come near me in my house, not approach me, not reach me!
> Let me live and become healthy, then I will praise your glory![9]

After bathing in the river clothed in a special robe, Naqia strips off her garments and washes herself with holy water in front of the figurines, the water dripping over them as she recites another incantation: 'I have stripped off, I have stripped off.' This means that any last remaining traces would be transferred from her to the witches who had cursed her, sending the evil back where it came from. As far as anti-witchcraft rituals go, this is a rather mild punishment. Others involve tying them up to symbolise their imprisonment, smearing them with disgusting-smelling fish oil in order to humiliate them, beating them with date thorns or iron spikes and/or stamping on the figurines to crush and vanquish them completely. Sometimes the figurines are made with their arms already tied behind their backs. In this way the patient acts out their victory over the witches, but also inflicts hurt on them in return.

Next Adad-shumu-utsur purifies Naqia by waving incense and a torch over her, and giving her a final wash with pure water to remove any last traces of evil. In leaving, they have to take care not to use the same route they had used to get to the river, lest they should pick up any evil that had been shed on the way. Like sin, witchcraft is understood to be contagious. At the same time, this transferability is what makes it possible to cure the patient, since the rituals ultimately direct the evil back to the witch.

It is also important to cleanse any trace of witchcraft from the house so that it cannot reattach itself to the patient. This particular ritual, however, instructs the exorcist to take the patient to the brewer's house first for a drink. Alcohol is recognised for its great powers of release – just as it releases people from their inhibitions, so too does it release people from any evil that is bound to them. A drink on the way home is a good way to shake off any lingering witchcraft in pursuit and put it off the scent.

When the queen mother and her exorcist return home they purify the house with a scapegoat ritual: a goat is tied up in the house while the exorcist rings a mighty copper bell and beats an ox-hide drum, scatters seeds, burns aromatic substances, and sprinkles pure water. Adad-shumu-utsur must now decide what to do with the goat. In other rituals the animal is killed and its remains buried, so that the witchcraft transferred from the patient to the goat is safely deposited in the ground. This ritual does not specify the goat's fate, but given all the trouble he had been to, the exorcist wants to be sure.

It was a key principle of Mesopotamian magic that evil could not be destroyed, only deflected. Like the principle of conservation of energy in modern physics whereby energy cannot be created or destroyed, merely changed from one form to another, the Mesopotamians believed that witchcraft, sin, guilt, and disease could not be completely eradicated but merely transferred. Substitutes of all kinds are frequently involved in magical rituals, and it was not always necessary to kill a goat when a clay model would do. However, the scapegoats were brought out for the really serious cases, when the stakes were life or death, as was the case here. Similar rites are found all over the Near East, including in the biblical book of Leviticus, which describes how all the sins of the community would be put upon a goat, which was then released into the wilderness, taking the people's transgressions with it.[10] Adad-shumu-utsur would have completed the ritual by smearing the gates of the house with gypsum and bitumen – magically charged chalky and sticky substances – which would repel evil energies and prevent witchcraft approaching it again.

Strange noises heard near the house could alert the owner to the presence of witchcraft, perhaps the ancient equivalent of installing a burglar alarm. Indeed, Naqia's incantation mentions evil signs witnessed in her house, one of which was a creaking gate. This was thought to be a message from the gods indicating that the house's occupant was at risk of attack. Another tablet in the library's collection advises what should be done: smear the gateposts with silt, then smear them with a mixture of gypsum, sulphur, red paste, and a mash used to make beer, while reciting an incantation.[11] Further attacks could be prevented by burying magical plant mixtures underneath the gate and putting them in the door sockets.[12] Another copy of the same ritual that Naqia might have performed states that if these rites are performed on the seventh, fourteenth, twenty-first, twenty-seventh, twenty-eighth and twenty-ninth days of the month then 'as long as he lives witchcraft will not come near him'.[13] Adad-shumu-utsur probably did all of these things on Naqia's behalf to keep her safe from being bewitched again.

Naqia recovered from her illness, to everyone's relief. After the crisis had finally passed, Adad-shumu-utsur returned to dealing with the day-to-day concerns that were the exorcist's normal responsibilities. Some of the more mundane tasks of the exorcist included purifying garments for a ritual,[14] burying protective figurines in the palace bedrooms,[15] and helping out in the temple. Priests had to be purified before they could enter the inner sanctum, and even the soil used to make the bricks of temples had to be purified before it could be used. The exorcist would also preside over all kinds of rituals in the temple, such as bringing the statues of the gods to life, making new kettle drums, performing sacred marriage ceremonies and holding annual festivals. In short, he was a busy man with many demands on his time, as another letter from the end of June shows. Already exhausted from the trials of the previous months and the fight to save Naqia's life, Adad-shumu-utsur was feeling harried by the many different requests made of him. Recently there had been an earthquake that greatly worried the king, who was now badgering his exorcist to advise him how to deal with it. Adad-shumu-utsur talked to the other scholars and they were not concerned – it had taken place in a city far away and did not count as an evil omen, for the king at least. In the meantime, Adad-shumu-utsur had other duties to attend to. The king wrote to him again about the earthquake, but he was out and couldn't consult his library. He returned home only to find another letter from the king asking why he had not replied to his previous message. He dashed off a response:

> Concerning what the king my lord wrote to me 'why have you not sent an answer to my letter?' – I had to drive to the palace those rams which the chief cook had brought for me, and the writing board was in my house. Now then, I can look at the board and extract the relevant interpretation.[16]

As this relatable excuse for a late reply shows, Adad-shumu-utsur was often rushed off his feet. Magic was so pervasive in Assyria that he would have been involved with almost every aspect of the personal life of the king and his family. From spells to stop babies crying and curing diseases to fending off demons and pleading with the gods to avert the evil portended by omens, the exorcist was an all-round problem solver who was called in to put right a whole range of issues. In this instance, in his eventual response to the king's letter he juggles both ritual and medical responsibilities – he advises that a ritual be performed against the earthquake and then tells the king that he has examined a sick child and found him to be normal ('is there a child who does not behave in this way sometimes?').[17] Sounding rather harassed, he complains that no one had told him about the child the first time he went to the house and had to go back, and promises to return again to check on him tomorrow. No wonder he had forgotten the writing board in his house.

Adad-shumu-utsur didn't shoulder this work alone: he worked with a team of exorcists to carry out all of these activities and collaborated with the other scholars too. For instance, he worked with astrologers to perform prayers to retrograding Mars, and to ward off the evil portended by an eclipse, as well as with physicians on medical matters. When the king assigned another exorcist, Marduk-shakin-shumi, to assist him, he was effusively grateful for the favour,[18] though Marduk-shakin-shumi also struggled to keep up with the workload; he wrote to the king complaining that he could not possibly make the deadline for an eclipse ritual: 'the tablets are too numerous, god only knows when they will be written. Even the preparation of the figurines which the king saw yesterday took us 5 to 6 days.'[19] Such elaborate preparations were common – for example, the performance of one anti-witchcraft ritual required 48 different figurines made of many different materials: tallow, clay, bitumen, tamarisk, cedar, wax, sesame pomace, and gypsum. The figurines all had to be carefully constructed, only to then be burned during the ceremony.[20]

While the exorcist spent a lot of time dealing with the supernatural causes of illness, illness was not the only affliction to be caused by witchcraft. 'Hate magic' could make its victim a social outcast, spurned by former friends and colleagues alike. 'Distortion of justice magic' and 'seizing of the mouth magic' could cause people to become speechless and inarticulate in court or at other critical times when they needed to defend themselves. In fact, one of the terms for 'witch' translates as 'adversary in court', which might imply this was thought to be a common occurrence, as well as conceptualising the witch and the patient as legal opponents. Usually, though, the identity of the witch was not known – the texts tend not to accuse anyone by name, but speak in general terms of 'my witch and my warlock', or sometimes prescribe the making of figurines of various groups of people who might have malicious intentions, such as 'my enemies', 'my litigants', 'my accusers', 'my slanderers', 'my evildoers'.[21] This was another way of covering all bases, to catch the witch whomever they might be.

Although belief in witchcraft was widespread in Mesopotamia, there were never any witch crazes like those seen in medieval Europe, where accusations spiralled out of control. The reason for this is twofold. Firstly, as we have seen, the effects of witchcraft were limited to a small number of scenarios, and its physical effects were medically diagnosed – witches were not held responsible indiscriminately for anything that could go wrong in a person's life. Secondly, accusations of witchcraft were discouraged in Mesopotamian law. Witchcraft was a serious offence that merited the death penalty, but precisely because of its serious punishment anyone bringing a charge had to be very certain that the accused was guilty. This is true of any capital crime – the beginning of Hammurabi's law code states that if a man accuses another man of murder but cannot prove it, the accuser will be killed. In the case of witchcraft in Hammurabi's time, if there was no proof the accused would have to undergo the river ordeal. Like in the European witch trials, this involved throwing the suspected witch into the river and seeing whether they sank or not. Sometimes the suspect also had to swim a certain distance. Unlike in the European witch trials, the Mesopotamians concluded that if the person sank they were guilty and if they floated they were innocent – the god of the river was the one who decided whether to spare the accused or put them to death there and then. If they were innocent, the accuser was put to death instead and the wrongly accused took possession of all of his property. Making specific accusations of witchcraft was very risky and only a few examples are known. One suspicion is preserved in the library: a report to Esarhaddon complains that the women of a certain family in the city of Guzana 'bring down the moon from the sky'.[22] This probably refers to astral magic, in which the witch addresses the gods in the night sky, and which was part of the most serious form of black magic, the 'cutting of the throat'. We do not know, however, if the accusation was followed up. The Middle Assyrian laws from a few hundred years earlier leave us in no doubt as to what would happen if the witch were found guilty: whether a man or woman, they would be put to death.[23]

Between black and white magic there was an ambiguous area of 'grey magic', neither illegal nor strictly about correcting injustices or reconciling with the gods, but a kind of aggressive magic concerned with increasing one's own personal power. This includes incantations to seduce women, bring back runaway slaves, and silence enemies at court. Ashurbanipal's library does not seem to contain many tablets of this type – the king did not need to resort to magic for these purposes.[24] However, they can be found in the private libraries of exorcists, and Adad-shumu-utsur may well have had some in his house for his own personal use. Although these kinds of texts never refer to themselves as witchcraft, the intentions behind them are certainly manipulative and the people targeted by them would most likely have considered it sorcery. Witchcraft in these cases was a matter of perspective.

Since anti-witchcraft rituals were a mirror of the rites of witchcraft, we can see how witches were imagined to have carried out their evil deeds. The exorcists used the same principles of magic as the witches did, turning it against them. As well as reciting spells and appealing to nefarious gods as in astral magic, they made figurines of their target and destroyed them by piercing, burning, or dissolving them in water. Collecting the victim's fingernail clippings, hair, thread of clothing, or another substance that had been in contact with them and embedding it in the figurine would ensure a link between the model and the person. Instead of destroying the figurine the witch could also bury it between the walls of the victim's house, or in the ground, symbolic of the grave. As we have seen, witches could also slip a bewitched substance into a person's food or drink, or write curses to afflict them. Esarhaddon was concerned about this latter possibility – a letter from his chief scribe reassures him that 'I have checked and there is none. The curse has not been written there.'[25]

Curses are among the list of suspected causes of Naqia's illness. But why would anyone want to curse the king's mother? Royal women could be extremely powerful in Assyria – queens were highly visible figures and even had their own armies. Ashurbanipal's mother Esharra-hamat was said to have wielded influence beyond the grave – a letter tells us that her ghost appeared to the young Ashurbanipal, who reports that the gods have ordained him to be crown prince of Assyria 'because of her righteousness'.[26] As we will see in Chapter 7 the ghosts of dead family members had to be treated well, otherwise they could come back to haunt their descendants, and other ghosts were often blamed for bringing disease, which would also fall under the exorcist's remit. It is Adad-shumu-utsur who reports Esharra-hamat's ghostly appearance to the king, saying she has blessed Ashurbanipal because he revered her ghost. Filial devotion paid off, and doubtless they would have all been glad that her intentions were benevolent.

Naqia was one of the most influential of all Assyrian women. Assyrian kings could have multiple wives, but usually only one queen. Here again Naqia is exceptional, for she had not been the first wife of Sennacherib, yet it was her son who inherited the throne, which put her in a position of immense power even after her husband's death.

Unusually for a woman, Naqia was actively involved in helping her son to govern his empire, down to the small details of policy and decision-making. The king's officials wrote directly to her about political matters, including asking for military reinforcements after the enemy destroyed a bridge.[27] Modern scholars have sometimes used this fact to bolster the portrayal of Esarhaddon as a weak king, controlled by his overbearing mother. But it is just as likely that Esarhaddon made use of her because, in a reign plagued by rebellions, she was somebody competent that he could trust. Another exorcist writes to Esarhaddon praising her wisdom: 'the mother of the king is as wise as the sage Adapa!',[28] while astrologers address her with the words 'the verdict of the mother of the king my lord is as final as that of the gods. What you bless is blessed, what you curse is cursed.'[29] She even received letters from the gods – the oracle of Ishtar of Arbela wrote to her regularly with prophecies about how her son would prevail over all his enemies. And letters are not the only witnesses to Naqia's influence. She built a palace for Esarhaddon and dedicated a temple to the gods, actions which were previously only undertaken by kings, putting her on a level equal with that of her son.

Women in such high positions of power were unusual in Assyria, and it would not be surprising if others at court envied and resented her. The conspiracy that threatened to unseat Esarhaddon towards the end of his reign may well have targeted his mother as well, and she kept a close eye on unfolding events. The oracle of Ishtar of Arbela often wrote to them both about the political situation, conveying the goddess's promises to 'cut those conspiring shrews and weasels to pieces before his [Esarhaddon's] feet'.[30] In 672 BC Esarhaddon made all of his subjects swear an oath that if they heard any rumours of rebellion or treason they had to report them, or else suffer a litany of curses inflicted by each and all of the major gods, ranging from 'just as honey is sweet, so may the blood of your women, your sons and your daughters be sweet in your mouth' to 'instead of dew may burning coals rain down on your land' to 'just as this bug stinks so may your breath stink'.[31] The strategy was effective, for Esarhaddon unmasked and defeated the conspiracy and stayed on the throne. Indeed, the exorcist Adad-shumu-utsur once wrote to the king about an informer whose mother had information that she should have reported to the palace, but did not. Instead she told her friends, none of whom said anything, and all of whom later died.[32] To the Assyrians it would have seemed as though the oath and its curses were effective.

Naqia survived the witchcraft attack and carried on in her powerful role. Remarkably, she instigated another loyalty oath for Ashurbanipal, much like the one Esarhaddon had drawn up, compelling 'the whole nation' to swear allegiance to her 'favourite grandson' and report any rumours of insurrection not to the king but directly to her.[33] It is a notable example of her autonomy and the reach of her power.

Whether the queen mother lived or died would have consequences for the whole empire, making her a prime target. But however powerful she was, the king was of course more powerful still, and more vulnerable. He was most at risk of attack by witchcraft and had the most power to lose.

Once every year the king's exorcist performed a special ritual to cleanse the king of any witchcraft. So likely was it that the king would be a target of bewitchment that this ritual was performed whether or not he was showing any signs of it. The ritual, called *Maqlu*, took place in late summer in the month of Abu, a month associated with Gilgamesh, judge of the netherworld. The focal point of the ceremony is specified in the name, which means 'burning' – a great crucible was set up and figurines of witches were continually cast into the fire. The ritual took place in the darkest period of the month as the moon was disappearing, a darkness which would have made the glow of the fire seem even brighter. Abu is the hottest month of the year in Iraq, with temperatures today averaging 35°C and sometimes reaching as high as 51°C. It was certainly a time for burning.

The king would address the gods as if he were a prosecutor in a lawsuit, stating his case and making his accusations against the witches. Since they acted in secret and could not be identified, he was unable to bring the witches to justice in the normal way or exercise his kingly authority against them directly. He thus appealed to the gods, who alone would know the identity of the sorcerers and be able to act against them. These are the words that began the ritual:

I call upon you, gods of the night,
with you I call upon night, the veiled bride,
I call upon twilight, midnight, and dawn.
Because a witch has bewitched me,
a deceitful woman has accused me;
because she has thereby caused my god and goddess to be
 estranged from me
and I have become sickening in the sight of anyone who
 beholds me
and consequently I am unable to rest day or night:
because a gag that is continually filling my mouth
has kept food distant from my mouth
and has diminished the water which passes through my
 drinking organ;
because my song of joy has become wailing and my rejoicing
 mourning –
. . .
Because she has performed evil against me and has constantly
 conjured up baseless charges against me,
may she die, but I live.[34]

The object of the ritual was to destroy these witches. Burning was the most effective method, as it attacked the witch's body and also her ghost, denying her existence beyond death. For this reason, cremation was not usually practised in Mesopotamia, since destroying the soul was a fate that only witches deserved.

The ritual lasted all night, with the continual chanting of incantations through the dark hours and concluding at dawn with the rising of the sun. After all the figurines were burned, the focus turned from fire to water, dousing the witches' ashes to extinguish their power and symbolically drown them. As in the ritual with Naqia, the king would finally be washed to purify him. Other special measures were taken to protect the king from any future attack. He was fumigated with sulphur, salt, turmeric, and asafoetida, and anointed with healing oil which would expel any illness or other traces of the witchcraft from his body. Strands of multicoloured wool would later be woven around his bed, forming a protective barrier so that witches could not attack while he slept. As the longest anti-witchcraft ritual known in Mesopotamia, *Maqlu* is a compilation of many other rituals, bringing together every known type of anti-witchcraft measure for full and comprehensive effect.

Not every day of Adad-shumu-utsur's working life would have been quite so dramatic; plenty of rituals warded off more every-day evils as well. Known as *namburbi* rituals – the word is Sumerian for 'its undoing' – the aim of these was to undo the effects of bad omens. The series of tablets collecting the most important namburbi rituals is the longest of any series in the library, spanning a staggering 135 tablets. There are namburbis against sensational omens like eclipses and earthquakes, but also more ordinary threats: the evil portended by seeing a snake in the house, lizards, ants, howling dogs, ominous flashes of light, and fungus growing on the outer north wall, to name just a few.[35] These portents were messages from the gods announcing misfortune was on the way, and can be compared to folk beliefs such as a black cat crossing your path being bad luck. Once the message had been received, the next step was to perform a ritual to make sure that the evil never arrived.

Namburbi rituals range from the simple to the complex. If a man saw a snake on the first day of the year it was taken as a sign he would die within that year, but all he had to do to avoid this fate was gash his head and shave his cheeks. As the text itself tells us, unsurprisingly he would be miserable for three months, but he would live.[36] The ritual prescribed for seeing ants in the house was more practical, and involved magical substances which were probably effective in their own right at driving the ants away even without the incantations – sweet-smelling oil, gypsum, and horned alkali, as well as the more symbolic mixture of dust from a ship, clay from a river meadow, and dust from an outer gate. All these were scattered on the nest, which was then fumigated in a manner reminiscent of modern pest-control techniques.[37] But many namburbi rituals required elaborate sacrifices and petitions to the gods, which is where the exorcist came into his own.

In its basic form this type of ritual is set up as a legal appeal to the gods. This is a formula we see again and again in the exorcist's activities, as he pleads with the gods to change their mind. Whether the injustice is an attack by witches or an unknown evil announced by a frog in the house or an earthquake, the exorcism sets up a ritual court where he can ask the gods to change their verdict. We have already seen this in action with Naqia addressing the sun god, asking for his permission for the river to remove evil. That the gods can change their minds is fundamental to the workings of magic, since it means they can be called upon to intervene. Bad omens were the gods' way of telling people they had done something wrong or that someone else wished them ill – the exorcist then had a chance to put things right.

As we have seen, Adad-shumu-utsur spent much of his time rushing from one problem to the next; driving away demons was only one part of his busy workload. But the exorcist of our popular imagination does have its roots in the Mesopotamian profession. In Mesopotamia not only witchcraft but also demonic attack was thought to cause all manner of diseases, both physical and mental. When the demons struck, Adad-shumu-utsur would have performed rituals to cast them out, calling on the great gods for help. The fact that so many diseases are ascribed to demons implies that exorcism was not uncommon, though it tended to be serious cases that received this diagnosis. Demons were a fact of life in Mesopotamia, not an extraordinary phenomenon, though this did not make them any less terrifying.

When we think of exorcists, we generally think of priests battling evil spirits and people possessed and tormented, taken over by invading demons. The 1973 film *The Exorcist* is the best-known illustration of this idea. But that film also has a Mesopotamian connection.

It opens in northern Iraq at a site near Nineveh, with an archaeologist discovering a statue of a monstrous being. While the face grins out at him dogs start to fight and an evil wind blows, foreshadowing the showdown that will be their final battle when the exorcist is called to cast the demon out of a twelve-year-old American girl. This is none other than Pazuzu, one of the most ubiquitous of all Mesopotamian demons, and one of the most evil-looking. But appearances can be deceptive, for the real Pazuzu would never possess anyone, and was in fact the exorcist's ally. Contrary to our expectations, not all demons are malevolent.

Pazuzu is certainly terrifying to behold, and Hollywood can be forgiven for assuming he was malicious. With goat's horns, dog's jaws, tongue hanging out over his bared teeth, bulging eyes, beard and human ears, he is a grotesque hybrid of human and animal. His body is wasted with starvation, his predator's talons outstretched, his wings spread about to beat in flight. To top it off, his penis takes the form of a literal snake. But despite this Pazuzu was helpful to the exorcist, a force of evil that could be harnessed for good. He was king of all the wind demons and so had the power to keep them in check. One incantation relates how he broke the wings of other demons who were on their way to plague mankind, stopping them in their tracks.[38] Pazuzu's alarming appearance scared away other evil spirits, and so his image was used as a protective amulet. It was common for ordinary people to wear small Pazuzu heads as beads on necklaces or threaded through a garment pin, or they might have small statues of him in their house to ward off evil. This demon is a prime example of the fact that it was possible for supernatural beings to switch sides. In Mesopotamian myths it was also common for defeated monsters to serve the gods who had vanquished them, a victory of order over chaos where evil forces were realigned for the common good.

Adad-shumu-utsur would have known how to contend with a huge range of demons. More than a hundred demons are known by name, but there may have been even more – one of the great incantation series against them states, 'in the census of heaven and earth they are not counted.'[39] Most of them are shapeless, ethereal beings that slither under doors or manifest as winds. Perhaps this was what made them so frightening, for it is hard to counter an enemy you can't see. When anything is shadowy and ill-defined, our imagination rushes in to fill in the blanks with our worst fears. Some demons are in fact diseases personified, and we will meet more of them in the next chapter on medicine. Others are named after what they do – 'the lurker', 'the snatcher', 'the watcher'. Others are visualised as monstrous hybrids: a lion's head with the talons of an eagle, or a snake's head with human hands.[40]

One of these demons stalked the corridors of the palace at Nineveh, causing particular problems for the royal family – the *alu* demon. Ashurbanipal's grandfather Sennacherib had been afflicted by this demon, which seems to be some kind of wind, though it has the same name as the constellation Taurus and may originally have been identified with it. The *alu* is an indeterminate spirit – it has no mouth, no limbs, no face; it does not listen, and cannot be seen.[41] Incantations describe it as 'like a wall that caves in and collapses upon the man'.[42] It 'muzzles the mouth and binds the hand and foot'.[43] The *alu* is a dark cloud, a bringer of psychological troubles and depression. A medical manual from the library tells us that one afflicted by the *alu* demon does not know who he is, has constricted pupils, something like a stupor afflicts him, his limbs are tense, his ears roar, and he cannot talk.[44]

We only know of Sennacherib's struggles with the demon from an oblique reference in one letter. Sennacherib's advisers had made a pact not to tell him if an unfavourable sign occurred, but to report it as an 'obscure' sign instead.[45] Presumably this is because the king did not take well to bad news and his advisers felt they had to tiptoe around him. He must have found out about it, because the letter recounts that when the *alu* demon had come, an angry Sennacherib warned his advisers: 'if a sign that is untoward to me occurs and you do not report it to me . . .'[46] Here the tablet is broken but for us the ellipsis is just as menacing as anything that could have ended the sentence. Sennacherib's problems clearly preceded the attack of the demon, but its arrival may have coincided with a crisis point. Sennacherib may have been suffering from a kind of post-traumatic stress following the death of his father in battle – he never speaks of him in his official inscriptions, which is highly unusual, and might reflect a repression of his memory and unwillingness to speak about him more generally. Given that demons were often blamed for what we would consider mental illness, the *alu* demon may have been a way to externalise and talk about this trauma.

We do not know anything else about Sennacherib's battle with the *alu*, or whether he overcame it, mainly because we do not have any letters preserved in the archives from Sennacherib's scholarly advisers or doctors. But the demon did return in the next generation. Although it's not clear whom the *alu* was after this time, a letter from the chief exorcist to Esarhaddon mentions the demon again – it was back. Esarhaddon had asked what a certain incantation was for and was told it aimed to drive out the *alu* demon and epilepsy. The exorcist explains to the king what normally happens in the ritual. The exorcist 'hangs a mouse and a shoot of a thorn bush on the vault of the patient's door'. He then 'dresses in a red garment and puts on a red cloak', with a raven on his right arm and a falcon on his left. Somehow also holding a torch and a whip at the same time, he strikes the whip and recites the incantation 'verily you are evil'. Another exorcist goes around the bed of the patient with a torch and an incense burner, reciting 'be gone, evil demon'. He repeats this morning and evening until the demon is driven out.[47]

We don't know why Esarhaddon was asking after this incantation. The letter associates the *alu* with epilepsy, and another letter tells us that a child was attacked by this illness.[48] But there were many royal children, and this second letter cannot be dated. If one of Esarhaddon's children was beset by the *alu* I suspect we would have heard more about it. It's possible – though this is only speculation – that it was being considered as a treatment for Esarhaddon himself, who suffered from a mysterious illness and had great difficulty figuring out what was wrong with him, as we will see in the next chapter.

The library holds a classic collection of incantations called *Evil*

Demons that describes the same ritual discussed above.[49] Here we get a fuller picture of what the exorcist would have said to the *alu* demon, as well as what he did. First of all he describes its nefarious activities, which gives us a wonderful illustration of what this demon was thought to be like. It seems to have attacked particularly at night, snaring the victim as if with a net, disturbing a man's sleep with sexual attacks, flitting about like a bat or a bird in the dark, and prowling around like a fox.[50] To name something is to bring it under control, and in this way the exorcist would have defined this being that escapes definition, and pinned it down.

Before addressing the demon, the exorcist would have protected himself with a whole roster of incantations, like putting on his battle armour. He calls upon Marduk and Ea, and declares himself to be their messenger, sent by those gods and speaking their words: 'he placed his pure incantation over mine, he placed his pure mouth over mine'.[51] He praises the power of Ea and Marduk and asks for their protection as he approaches the patient. Then he addresses the demon and commands it to depart from the man's body, his house, and the shrine of the family god, sending it off into the wilderness.

There are many elements here that we can recognise in the exorcists of our own popular imagination. Many other incantations specify the use of holy water and a special holy wooden staff that the exorcist held as he approached the patient. Others involve casting magic circles with flour to create a protected space. Using the power of the gods, the exorcist commands the evil spirits to leave. They are sent back to the liminal regions whence they came, whether that is the wastelands of the steppe, the wild mountains, or the netherworld. In these respects, Mesopotamian exorcism is not so different from what we see in Hollywood. As is so often the case, the Mesopotamian exorcists are the originals.

In this complex spiritual realm, where spirits could switch sides and gods could hurt as well as help, it was vital to have experts like the exorcists at hand for guidance. This led to a closeness between the exorcists and the royal family. Adad-shumu-utsur was particularly close to Esarhaddon and was put in charge of the very serious task of curing his mother and attending to his children when they fell sick. When a royal child died, Adad-shumu-utsur comforted the king with words that still move us more than two and a half thousand years later: 'had the illness been curable, you would have given away half of your kingdom to have it cured! But what can we do? O king my lord it is something that cannot be done.'[52] On other occasions he wrote with encouragement, reassuring the king that he did not need to worry and everything was being taken care of.

Yet this closeness would not last. Adad-shumu-utsur and his family were extremely successful during the reign of Esarhaddon, but when Ashurbanipal came to the throne something changed. Adad-shumu-utsur's son Urad-Gula fell out with the king and was dismissed, leaving behind a trail of desperate letters as he and his father pleaded for him to be reinstated. It was a dramatic fall from grace – Urad-Gula had been close to Ashurbanipal while he was crown prince, and may even have been one of his tutors. When he reminds the king of his former devotion, touchingly he relates how in those days he stood at the windows keeping watch and appeasing Ashurbanipal's god. The letters he wrote to the king are confident in tone, showing he felt secure in what he could say. No one mentions the reason for the rift, so we don't know what exactly Urad-Gula did to anger the king. But he seems to have been involved in a childbirth that went wrong – perhaps he was blamed for the loss of a child.[53]

Adad-shumu-utsur remained in post as the king's exorcist and begged him to restore his son to his former position. In a routine letter concerning an eclipse that did not take place, Adad-shumu-utsur remarks at the end, 'nobody has reminded the king about Urad-Gula, the servant of the king, my lord. He is dying of a broken heart and is shattered from falling out of the hands of the king, my lord. The king, my lord, has revived many people.'[54] Ashurbanipal did not take the hint to reinstate him. Six months later Adad-shumu-utsur wrote again, this time a long letter specifically dedicated to making his son's case. He opens the letter by praising the king for his good reign: 'the old men dance, the young men sing, the women and girls are merry and rejoice; women are married and provided with earrings; boys and girls are brought forth, the births thrive'[55] – this last point would have been particularly pertinent if Urad-Gula had been blamed for a stillbirth in the past. The letter continues, describing how the king has released the imprisoned and pardoned the condemned, how the sick have recovered, the hungry have been fed, the naked have been clothed: 'why then must I and Urad-Gula amidst them be restless and depressed?'[56] It is a touching picture of a reversal of fortunes. Adad-shumu-utsur seems to have suffered too, saying that he has no friends left in the palace who will accept any gifts and speak on his behalf. He begs the king to have mercy on his servant so that he will not die of shame.

This time Ashurbanipal does seem to have had mercy – but only some. The next time we hear from Adad-shumu-utsur he is much happier, profusely thanking the king for his kindness, for treating his servants as a father treats his sons, describing how his heart became happy and grew strong as a bull's. It seems Adad-shumu-utsur has been forgiven. But we need to read between the lines – what the king wrote to him was 'I have gathered you, your nephews and your cousins, you belong now to my entourage' – there is no mention of his son.[57]

It was Adad-shumu-utsur's job to intercede with the gods on behalf of the king, pleading with them to change their minds or to reconcile them after any wrongdoing. Yet despite being a professional mediator who had saved the king and his family many times from the wrath of the gods, it seems he was not able to make peace between the king and his own son. Urad-Gula was not restored to his position and writes again to the king describing the lamentable situation he finds himself in. He has no transport since his animals died two years ago, which means he has to walk between cities on foot, and has to endure the shame of people asking him why he is walking such long distances. By now he is around fifty years old and has to watch assistants pass his house in carts, and even people of junior rank go by on mules, reminding him of his indignity.

Furthermore, his wife has abandoned him and he has no son. With no farm to sustain him, he cannot even afford a pair of sandals, and is in serious debt. He reminds the king that he has known him since he was a child but does not now ask to be reinstated: he only asks for some simple beasts of burden and a spare change of clothes, his desires pitifully downgraded to match his new circumstances. He seems to have lost all hope of ever regaining his former position, and is now more concerned about how he will support himself in old age. His misconduct must have been severe indeed for him to have reached such a position after once being so close to the king. We do not know if his petition was ever answered.

Urad-Gula's story is a pertinent reminder that no one could take their power for granted at the Assyrian court. He was born into the right family and had risen to a high position thanks to the influence of his powerful father, but could only keep it if he stayed on the right side of the king. It should remind us, too, that the arts of the exorcist were taken extremely seriously and that it was quite possible for exorcists to fail in their duty. Getting it wrong could have serious consequences – these are the people who guard the king's life against supernatural enmity, and just as a physical bodyguard could fall short, so could a spiritual one. Court exorcists were extremely important positions because the stakes were so high.

Magic is a nebulous word that can be used to describe many different practices. It can cover defensive magic, such as using amulets to ward off evil or staging elaborate rituals to cast out demons, or it can refer to aggressive magic whereby witches incapacitate their victims, inflict curses, or influence the behaviour of others whether by rendering them speechless, calming them down, or making them fall in love. Ultimately, magic was a way to use supernatural means to effect change, an additional resource to rely on in order to make things happen.

Crucial to the belief in magic is the idea that fate is not fixed but that people can have influence over it. While we tend to see magic as a way of harnessing esoteric forces to bend the cosmos to the magician's will, in Mesopotamia it was much more about getting the gods onside. Without them, the whole enterprise was hopeless and no spell would work, no matter how sophisticated. Magic and ritual are essentially forms of persuasion, of appealing to the gods and asking them to intervene. Going through an elaborate ritual shows that people took the petition seriously, that this was not just a half-hearted prayer but something they were prepared to spend time, money, and effort on, all of which would please the gods and make them much more likely to support the request. The more serious the problem, the more elaborate the ritual would be, reflecting the greater desire for the gods to pay heed.

The gods could turn against you at any time without you knowing why; demons could attack, and witches could curse. But despite the capriciousness of the divine world, the Assyrians did not feel helpless, because they always had a chance to influence these powers and change the minds of those responsible. The exorcist could not guarantee that the gods would bestow their favour, but he could at least guarantee his client that they had done all they could to ask. The elaborate rituals would have been psychologically powerful, which is reassuring in itself. In the case of purification from sin, the rituals would have brought about a state of genuine contrition that may have changed something in the client's psyche, while a simple amulet hung on the wall would remind its owner every time they looked at it that they had the gods' protection. Magic, then, gave the Assyrians a sense of control, a way to cope with their difficulties, even when those difficulties were so great that they didn't know what else to do, when they were ill or grieving or in deep depression. Every society needs its own way of addressing these human concerns, of boosting confidence and restoring hope, and magic was the Assyrians' way of being proactive in the face of hardship, giving them a sense that they had a hand in their own destiny.

4.
The Treatment of Disease

Urad-Nanaya reaches out and puts his hand on the king's forehead. Esarhaddon's skin is hot to the touch, fevered, but the chief physician cannot tell what has caused it and cannot say how long it will last. When the fever abates the king suffers chills, his temperature constantly changing. Debilitated and depressed, the king has shut himself away for days now, lying in bed in the dark and shunning all human contact. Urad-Nanaya is one of the few at court who is allowed to see him in this condition, one of the few who may be able to help. Yet he is running out of options.

Urad-Nanaya gives the king a thorough examination but fails to make sense of his symptoms. They do not match any known disease in the tablets he has studied, and he has never seen anything like it before. The king has been unwell for many years with all kinds of afflictions that have waxed and waned – stiff joints, weak limbs, mysterious sores and blisters, a horrible skin rash, inflamed eyes, and ringing ears. But now, with this fever, the illness has reached crisis point. The king is becoming increasingly desperate, asking, 'Why do you not diagnose the nature of this illness of mine and bring about its cure?', but all Urad-Nanaya can say is that he doesn't understand the symptoms, and suggests that he ask the diviners to sacrifice a sheep and ask the gods.[1] The gods are now the only ones who can fathom the king's condition.

Nevertheless, the chief physician is determined to keep on trying, and will go on to recommend another four remedies on this occasion alone. Assyrian medicine is a sophisticated discipline that has diagnoses and treatments for all manner of ills, and a vast literature he can consult. Like most Assyrian scholarship it is based on a long-standing tradition going back many hundreds of years, with several elements inherited from the Babylonians, lending it authority.

Urad-Nanaya is not entirely alone in his hunt for a cure. One of the chief exorcist's main responsibilities is healing, and incantations are as important as drugs to the treatment of disease. The exorcist and physician work together, addressing the physical, spiritual, and psychological causes of the issue, although the spirit of collaboration can also descend into personal rivalry and mistrust. Whether or not the Assyrians are aware of it, this double-pronged approach harnesses a mind–body connection that later practitioners of modern medicine would long overlook.

Mesopotamian medicine was fundamentally holistic. Much of it was pharmaceutical in nature, using herbal medicines that have been shown to be effective and are still in use today, though magical components were equally important. The performance of rituals reassured the patient that they had been reconciled with the gods, helping them to believe that they would get better. Putting their mind at rest in this way made it more likely that they would actually improve. We usually treat this placebo effect rather dismissively, but the medicinal benefit of belief is very real.

Ritual sets the stage for medicine to work regardless of what that medicine is, in our own culture as well as in ancient Mesopotamia. When we go to a doctor we also go through rituals where belief and expectation have a huge influence: we go to a professional invested with great authority whom we trust and respect, and collect a prescription from the pharmacist who is appropriately dressed in a white coat, another symbol of their expertise. The pronouncements of these professionals can have a great impact on the course of the illness. Even in modern times there have been cases where patients were misdiagnosed, incorrectly receiving a fatal prognosis, and then gone on to die simply because they believed they would; but more often the opposite is true, that the reassurance of a doctor gives people confidence and peace of mind, which helps the body to heal. The Mesopotamians would have had the same trust in their physicians, but the addition of magic and ritual took it one step further and added a specifically psychological dimension, although they would not have thought of it in those terms. Often the two sides worked together. For instance, tying magical stones on to someone's forehead to treat a headache may seem pure ritual to us, but may have activated pressure points that do relieve the pain. Understanding both of these aspects, and their interplay, is critical to understanding how Mesopotamian medicine worked. This is especially true in a case as complex as Esarhaddon's, where the longer he suffered the more depressed he became.

The king's exorcist Adad-shumu-utsur was extremely worried about Esarhaddon's state of mind. Not only had the king shut himself away in a dark room but he had also stopped eating. Then as now, it was not a good sign. Although the king would not see him in person, Adad-shumu-utsur wrote to him telling him to end his isolation:

> Why today for the second day now is the table not brought to the king my lord? You stay in the dark much longer than Shamash, king of the gods, staying in the dark a whole day and night and again two days! The king, the lord of the world, is the very image of the sun god Shamash. You should keep in the dark for half a day only![2]

This letter is a touching example of Adad-shumu-utsur's concern for Esarhaddon. He begs the king to eat something: 'good advice is to be heeded: restlessness, not eating and not drinking disturbs the mind and adds to illness. In this matter the king must listen to his servant.'[3]

The personal tone is poignant. The advisers rarely tell the king what to do outright, preferring to lay out the facts and their opinions and let the king decide for himself. But here the exorcist crosses this boundary and urges the king to follow his advice. Nor is he the only one to do so – when the fasting extends to the third day, two of his senior astrologers write: 'the king, our lord, will pardon us. Is one day not enough for the king to mope and eat nothing? For how long still?'[4]

As well as being a personal nightmare, the king's illness was a national crisis, for the Assyrians took it as a sign of the displeasure of the gods. Just as only a physically perfect man was fit to enter the presence of the gods in their temples, only a physically perfect man was fit to be the representative of the gods on earth, and a chronically sick king most definitely did not meet this criterion. Esarhaddon faced many uprisings during his reign and an outbreak of conspiracies in 671/70. If his condition had become known it could have been the perfect excuse for these rebellions – a justification for overthrowing his regime and setting up another contender as the legitimate king. All the more reason, then, for Esarhaddon to hide away.

Esarhaddon's depression worsened even after he spectacularly crushed the conspiracies in March 670. As seen earlier, he successfully rounded up and executed the leaders, many of whom were members of his own court. But the fact that he was betrayed by those in his inner circle caused him to take extreme measures to root out all possible conspirators, and he executed a significant proportion of the Assyrian elite, leaving the empire in disarray without its most experienced administrators.[5] In the wake of this chaos the king trusted no one and became deeply cynical, even of those who were trying to help him. His chief physician Urad-Nanaya gently pointed out that he was seeing enemies where there were none, saying that the conspirators have made everyone hateful in his eyes, 'smearing them like a tanner with the oil of fish'.[6] The atmosphere at court became extremely tense and Esarhaddon terrified his servants with his rhetoric. On one occasion the king made a speech to them about how the attendants of former kings had been much more dedicated than his were – in the past when kings fell ill, their servants sat up with them all night and carried them on litters, he said, implying that his own servants were not showing the same devotion. Urad-Nanaya told the king what effect this rebuke had on them, saying, 'all the attentive servants who have remembered their orders were scared to death at the speech of the king.'[7] Esarhaddon's outlook had become so bleak that he could only see danger, and discounted the efforts of those loyal to him.

In fact, Esarhaddon's medical team worked around the clock, just like doctors today. During a particularly difficult time when they were faced with multiple emergencies, the king's exorcist assured him they were 'working sleeplessly and unremittingly' to get everything done.[8] Aside from the king's health – he had now added aching teeth to his long list of ailments – the exorcists were preparing for a major eclipse ritual that would hopefully stave off further disaster. There was much to do, and the stakes were high. The physicians were equally busy: the royal children had all been unwell, one of them coming down with a fever several times, which the king found especially alarming. Urad-Nanaya was working so hard that he started to worry about his own health suffering. News of this reached the king, who wrote and asked him how he was. Urad-Nanaya's reply was candid:

> When am I ever free? I take care of the prince and as soon as I saw him healthy again, I came for the health of the king. Now, O king my lord, I should be released for a full month! I must do something otherwise I shall die.[9]

We do not know whether his request was granted, but the fact that the king asked after him and received such a blunt answer attests to a close relationship between this doctor and his patient, or at least a frank and honest one. While many of the king's other advisers tiptoed around him, Urad-Nanaya was not afraid of delivering home truths.

It may well have been the stress caused by the conspiracy that sparked a flare-up in Esarhaddon's symptoms. The king's advisers went to great lengths to reassure him and put his mind at rest, aware of the difference this would make. Urad-Nanaya declares that the gods will not abandon the king, while sending herbs and explaining their effects. Meanwhile, the king's exorcist Adad-shumu-utsur dispenses self-care advice exhorting Esarhaddon to eat properly and get out of bed in order to lift his depression. The arts of these two practitioners overlapped and intertwined to the extent that it is difficult for us to tell where one ends and the other begins. But how did they see themselves? Let us take a closer look at the tablets they studied and the knowledge they had to acquire.

On the face of it Urad-Nanaya and Adad-shumu-utsur had quite different domains of responsibility. As chief physician, Urad-Nanaya primarily dealt with the aspects of medicine that we would recognise most easily – dressing wounds and administering drugs, concentrating on the physical causes. The king's exorcist Adad-shumu-utsur on the other hand addressed the metaphysical causes of disease – cleansing the patient from sin, spiritual impurities, demons, and witchcraft, and bringing him back into a state of harmony with the gods. Each specialist had their preferred treatments – the physician prescribed pharmaceutical drugs while the exorcist mainly used incantations. However, in practice these responsibilities were not quite so neatly divided, as both exorcists and physicians were interested in the other's tactics – exorcists kept tablet texts dealing with physical healthcare in their libraries, while Esarhaddon's doctors were as likely to prescribe amulets and magical substances as medications and salves. A prime example of this can be seen in Urad-Nanaya's instructions on how to cure a nosebleed, which involves soaking red wool in a mixture of martakal-seed, cedar resin, and dust from a crossroads, and reciting an incantation over it before inserting it into the nostril, a perfect combination of magic and medicine.[10]

Urad-Nanaya and Adad-shumu-utsur both attended to the king when he was unwell and, despite their differences, gave him similar advice. When Esarhaddon had diarrhoea and vomited bile, they both had enough knowledge of what his physical symptoms meant to reassure him that he would be fine.[11] Their different perspectives can be glimpsed in how they chose their words. The chief physician bases his opinion on prognoses given by the lists of prescriptions, while the exorcist uses the language of favourable and unfavourable omens – 'he vomited a lump with the bile settling downward; this sort does not portend good.'[12] Each was coming at the problem from a different theoretical background. The physician dealt with practical remedies, while the exorcist was concerned with the gods, who communicated with humans through divination and signs.

The exorcists and physicians did not always agree, and Urad-Nanaya was not afraid to criticise his rival. When Adad-shumu-utsur advised that the princes should not go outside before a certain date Urad-Nanaya challenged him and demanded to know why: 'Has he seen some portent?'[13] Urad-Nanaya apparently felt so strongly about this that he tracked down Adad-shumu-utsur in another city by writing to his colleagues there, who made the exorcist explain his decision and swear to it by the gods. It turned out that Adad-shumu-utsur had a perfectly good reason – a ritual was underway that was designed to protect the king from imminent death, and for one hundred days the king had to go into hiding. Adad-shumu-utsur did not want the royal children to go out during this dangerous period and was only acting to keep them safe. What seems like common sense to a physician – that there was nothing wrong with being out and about – has wider consequences from the perspective of the exorcist, concerned as he is with otherworldly phenomena.

The royal library collection is rich in material relating to both branches of the healing arts, and Ashurbanipal seems to have been particularly interested in medical knowledge. He specifically commissioned an encyclopaedia of therapeutic medical texts, bringing together both traditional teachings and more experimental ideas. This *Nineveh Medical Compendium* – an up-to-date and state-of-the-art collection of treatments – has only recently become available, published online by a dedicated team at the British Museum.[14] The tablets are organised from head to toe, starting with diseases of the cranium such as headaches then proceeding to eyes, ears, neck, nose, and teeth, all the way down the body to the anus and hamstrings. A separate catalogue of medical texts from Ashur further adds to our knowledge of the physician's expertise.[15] It replicates this list but also adds tablets addressing divine anger, mental illness, sex, pregnancy, and childbirth. There is some debate as to whether Esarhaddon's doctors would have used the treatments in these texts, since they do not quote them in their letters and use different terminology for their recommendations. However, given the extremely technical nature of the medical texts (which are difficult to understand even for Assyriologists who are not specialists in the genre) it makes sense that the physicians would write to the king in plainer language, just as doctors today use Latin terms among themselves and have simpler explanations for patients.

Judging from these tablets, the range of conditions that Urad-Nanaya would have been able to treat was considerable. From minor ailments like headaches and digestive problems to serious disorders such as mental illness and epilepsy (known as AN.TA.ŠUB.BA in Sumerian, which literally means 'fallen from the sky'), the *Nineveh Medical Compendium* has something for everything. The Assyrian physician could treat injuries from lion maulings and bites of scorpions and snakes; coughs and fevers; strokes and paralysis; heartbreak and depression; impotence and difficult births. He was a dentist as well as a doctor,[16] and even a vet, since the last few tablets of the compendium are dedicated to horses and cattle.

The other main medical text in the library is a series of forty tablets describing the likely causes and outcomes of disease, a collection that has been called the *Diagnostic Handbook* (a modern misnomer – forty clay tablets is not exactly a pocket-sized handbook).[17] This is one of the few texts in the library and in Mesopotamia as a whole that is not anonymous or attributed to the gods but is the work of a named individual. Esagil-kin-apli was the chief scholar of a king of Babylon in the eleventh century BC, and came from a long line of eminent advisers, tracing his lineage back to the chief scholar of the famous Babylonian king Hammurabi, who lived in the eighteenth century BC. In an editorial note, Esagil-kin-apli tells us that the *Diagnostic Handbook* had become a bit of a mess as it was copied through the ages, with different versions being used in different places, and describes the texts as being 'like twisted threads'.[18] Esagil-kin-apli sorted out this mess and organised the texts in a sensible way so that they would be easier to study and learn from, producing an authoritative edition. His version of the handbook became standard, and earned him fame – hundreds of years later Babylonian scholars working under Greek rule still remembered him as a great sage.[19]

Like the *Nineveh Medical Compendium*, the *Diagnostic Handbook* is organised from head to toe and describes various symptoms that could affect a person in different parts of the body. Based on each of these it offers a diagnosis, specifying the name of the disease, its cause, and the likely prognosis. Mostly it tells us whether the patient will live or die, which would have helped the doctors to know whether to treat them or not. But it gives more subtle prognoses too: sometimes it tells us how many days it will take for the patient to get well, or describes the progression of the illness as the symptoms change. These descriptions show that the Mesopotamian healers observed their patients very closely, since they took into account variations in the patient's condition at different times of day, and the exact number of days when new symptoms appeared after the first onset of the illness. They measured five different grades of temperature variation, noted how the patient felt mentally as well as physically, and considered the age of the patient. The history of medicine usually credits Hippocrates with inventing the concept of diagnosis based on observation but, as so often is the case, the Mesopotamians had got there a thousand years earlier.

Although we would assume that diagnosis is a matter for the physician, the *Diagnostic Handbook* clearly belongs to the exorcist. The very first words of the series are 'when an exorcist goes to a patient's house' and it begins by describing what he might see on the way there, providing valuable information before he even meets the patient. For instance, 'if he sees a potsherd standing up in the street: that patient is dangerously ill, he must not go near him.'[20] If a donkey passes the exorcist on his left the patient will die, but if he sees a red ox the patient will live.[21] If the exorcist was attentive to his surroundings he could sometimes diagnose the disease before even reaching the patient's house. Things that happened to the exorcist himself on the journey also mattered – if his right eye started twitching he would not achieve his goal, and if he stubbed his right toe the patient would die within seven days. He also had to consider omens at the patient's house – for instance, if the door creaked on his way in, the patient would die.[22]

Modern scholars usually treat these opening tablets as separate from the rest of the series, which deals more recognisably with medical prognoses such as 'if his face is full of black lesions he will die'[23] or 'if the muscles of his abdomen continually hurt him, his left temple continually hurts him intensely, he is continually rigid, inability to eat afflicts him, his body is feverish and he has wasting away of the flesh, that person is sick with a venereal disease.'[24] But what the exorcist saw on the way to the patient's house was just as relevant as what he found when he got there, and to the Mesopotamians these were all simply different kinds of ominous signs. Even for us today, predicting the course of an illness is an attempt to predict the future, although we base our forecasts on empirical evidence. The Mesopotamians used both real-life experience and the logic of divination – they knew how diseases progressed from observing patients closely, but they also treated symptoms as omens, and understood them using the same codes of omen interpretation that we will see in the reading of entrails, and astrology.

Divination not only was a way of predicting the future but could also be used to obtain knowledge about the present. This meant that reading the secret language of the gods was one way to find out what was wrong with the patient. The sage Esagil-kin-apli clearly thought that medicine and divination were closely related. When he edited the *Diagnostic Handbook*, he edited an omen series along with it and grouped them together – this text, called *Alamdimmu*, was a physiognomic treatise that diagnosed a person's character from the way that they looked. But the principles of divination can be seen throughout the *Diagnostic Handbook* itself. The symbolic codes of left and right, of different colours, and wordplay are common, and exerted a strong influence on the verdict of whether the patient would survive. The codes do not work in exactly the same way as in other types of divination, however, since medicine has a more obviously empirical dimension to it. It is all very well if green is a favourable colour to find on the fungus in your house, but it is not such a good colour for human skin.[25] Here the divination codes are combined with real experience of the progression of disease to create something that is a mixture of empirically based science with the other schools of Mesopotamian scholarship.

The *Diagnostic Handbook* reflects the thinking of the exorcist, who dealt with supernatural entities. The exorcist often blamed gods, ghosts, or demons for causing disease, as the handbook gives diagnoses such as 'hand of Ishtar', 'hand of a ghost', or 'the lurker-demon afflicts him'. This does not mean that the Mesopotamians thought that disease was only caused by such beings, rather that these were the causes that the exorcist could do something about. Physicians, on the other hand, might have had different ideas about how much influence these ethereal beings had – they do refer to them in therapeutic texts, but write the words as if they are fossilised and ancient rather than current and up-to-date, implying they are not so relevant. A close reading of these texts can also detect other hints of professional rivalry as both exorcists and physicians find subtle ways of mocking each other. For instance, exorcists often use incantations containing very serious dialogues between the gods of magic about what is to be done about the illness. A therapeutic text dealing with stomach ailments parodies this dialogue style by having a patient talk to his own belly about passing gas – a scatological way of bringing the gods back down to earth. The exorcists get their own back and also make fun of the physicians – one of the incantations against eye disease includes a deliberately garbled Sumerian spell recited by an incompetent physician, who then unsurprisingly fails to cure the patient. These jibes show that although the physicians use bits and pieces of magic in their work, they ultimately view the elaborate formulations of high ritual as something of a distraction. The exorcists meanwhile see themselves as superior thanks to their higher learning, and make fun of the physicians' lack of education.

Nonetheless, both agreed that any of the gods could strike a person with disease. The same god could specialise in a number of afflictions: Ishtar was responsible for venereal disease, thematically in keeping with her domain of sex, but also for particular types of black sores that could be anywhere on the body.[26] Certain gods seem to have favourite colours – 'hand of Ishtar' is associated with parts of the body turning black; the sun god Shamash is associated with white, and the moon god Sin with red. A particular type of jaundice was caused by the hand of the warrior god Ninurta, while diarrhoea was sent by Gula, the goddess of healing. These deities were thought to strike when the patient had committed some kind of offence against them rather than attacking randomly. Sometimes they sent deputies on their behalf, which would result in yet another variation in how the illness presented.

Demons and ghosts seem to be more commonly blamed for neurological and psychological disorders. Tablets 26 to 30 of the *Diagnostic Handbook* describe differing symptoms of epilepsy and name a rich selection of demons and spirits among the possible causes. Spittle flowing from the mouth was attributed to the Lilu demon, loss of bowel control was attributed to the ghost of someone who had been murdered, while inability to talk was more specifically caused by the ghost of someone who had burned to death.[27] Angry ghosts came back to vent their rage upon the living, especially if their descendants were not taking care of them by making offerings (see Chapter 7 on literature). Some had more specific grievances. The Lilu and Lilitu demons were the spirits of young people who had died before marriage and had never had sex (the female version Lilitu is the equivalent of Lilith in the Hebrew tradition). They sought out unsuspecting humans to be their partners instead, causing all manner of nasty symptoms, especially at night, like the incubus and succubus of Western folklore. Symptoms occurring in the daytime could be attributed to them as well, such as confusional states accompanied by rolling eyes and nosebleeds.[28] Babies were also targets for their spite, being born from marriages that these demons had never enjoyed themselves.

The real terror of infants was the demoness Lamashtu, daughter of the sky god Anu, who was thrown out of heaven because she developed a taste for eating babies. Forced to wander the earth, she particularly attacked pregnant women and children, apparently out of jealousy that she did not have her own. Incantations tell us how she pretended to be a midwife and then poisoned the children with her milk or strangled them, an explanation of infant death that would have made sense to a society with extremely high child mortality. In fact, one of the classics of Babylonian literature explains that a similar type of demon was created by the gods as part of a population-control programme.[29] But babies were not Lamashtu's only targets: she grasped at men and women alike, of all ages. She inflicted fever, fluctuations of body temperature, chills, trembling, dizziness, depression, and weakening eyesight – a list that sounds similar to Esarhaddon's cluster of symptoms. Ashurbanipal's library housed a whole series of incantations against Lamashtu. When the exorcist suspected she was the cause of a child's fever, the texts tell him to try a complex ritual. It required him to make a figurine of Lamashtu as a prisoner, and place twelve bread rolls 'made from unsifted flour' before her. He then had to libate well water, make the Lamashtu figurine hold a black dog, and place her at the head of the sick baby's bed for three days. The figurine was then given a piglet's heart and some hot soup, along with a flask of oil, travel provisions, and bread. The exorcist would then recite an incantation to her three times a day, and on the afternoon of the third day bury her in the corner of the wall.[30]

In this ritual the dog is for Lamashtu to suckle instead of the human baby and the soup is provided as more appropriate food than human flesh. The bread rolls are to sustain her on the journey she is about to undertake, for the incantations send her back to the mountains where she lives. This rather touching gesture is to make sure she doesn't get hungry before she's reached her destination and turn around and come back. But the ritual did not end here – the exorcist would also have anointed the child with a mixture of pitch from the rudder and oar of a boat, dirt from the embankment, lard, fish oil, ghee, hot bitumen, and a couple of plants: 'Anoint him thoroughly and he will recover.'[31] These unpleasant substances may have served to repel Lamashtu and make the baby seem like a less appealing snack. The exorcist could also give his patient an amulet to keep Lamashtu away, a great many of which have survived for us today. These amulets show us what the Mesopotamians thought Lamashtu looked like – she has a lion's head, donkey's teeth, talons for feet, and an otherwise human body with pendulous breasts. It was especially common for pregnant women to wear these amulets, as a visible sign of protection, since they were among those most vulnerable to Lamashtu's attack.

The idea that disease is caused by invisible spiritual entities shares some similarities with our understanding of disease being caused by invisible bacteria and viruses. The Mesopotamians knew that some diseases were contagious. The *Diagnostic Handbook* warns the exorcist to keep well away from some patients, presumably because it was known that he risked catching the disease himself. But more explicit references to contagion can be found. In the Old Babylonian city of Mari in the second millennium BC, one of the women in the palace became ill and the king ordered:

> nobody is to drink from the cup from which she drinks, nobody is to sit on the seat on which she sits, and nobody is to lie on the bed on which she lies and many women are not to mingle with her. That illness is contagious.[32]

Sometimes physicians give instructions to isolate the patient:

> you move him to a place next to the house, cover him with a sack and fumigate him with any fumigant at hand. See to it that he sees no bright daylight, that nobody talks to him, and that nobody goes in where he is lying.[33]

Omens predicting epidemics also indicated that people would not enter each other's houses, and that someone who had grasped the hand of a patient who later died would go on to contract the disease themselves.[34]

Consequently, the Mesopotamians were aware of the need for good hygiene. Larger private houses at Ur and Larsa in the early second millennium had indoor toilets connected to a drain, and hand washing with soap was frequent. There was even a particular demon who was believed to frequent the lavatory, Shulak, whose name is interpreted as meaning 'hand not clean' in one fifth-century commentary from the city of Uruk.[35] Doctors knew it was important to change dressings for wounds often, and the fact that medicine was often boiled may suggest that they understood the importance of sterilisation as well.

However, it was not only illness that the Mesopotamians kept at bay with cleanliness – they believed that washing was a form of purification, and that physical dirt and metaphysical impurity were closely connected. Ultimately, they thought that it was spiritual pollution that was contagious, and which was the cause of disease spreading from person to person. As we have already seen in the chapter on magic, sin itself was thought to be catching, and people could pick up all kinds of misfortune from coming into contact with afflicted individuals. Coming too close to a person who had transgressed against the gods would bring their anger down on you, even if you yourself were a model of piety.[36] Just as microorganisms take no heed of how blameless is their victim, so it was with spiritual impurity, which could attach itself to anyone who came into contact with it.

Urad-Nanaya will have had a rather different understanding of disease causation. Physicians understood that diseases could be caused by the body and its organs without any supernatural beings necessarily being involved. Medical texts speak of various body parts as simply 'sick' without reference to a spiritual entity. They describe the body using metaphors involving gardening and technology, with incantations describing how the system must be corrected. The intestines are seen as a kind of irrigation system, and the incantations exhort:

Whom should I send to the canal inspector of your innards?
May they carry silver spades and golden shovels!
May they open the canals, may they open the ditches!
May his excrement escape and come out!
May the storm in his belly come out![37]

The texts describe other bodily functions in terms of cooking, brewing, and pottery. For instance, the womb was equated with an oven that produced a fully formed human being in the same way that a kiln fired a pot. This picks up the theme running through mythological texts where the first human beings were created out of clay. Interestingly the birth goddesses are also associated with other crafts, including carpentry, again underscoring the relation between pregnancy and active making. Among the physical causes of disease, Mesopotamian physicians also recognised the influence of the environment on health, such as wind invading the body, which has parallels in Greek, Tibetan, and Chinese medicine.

Although Adad-shumu-utsur and Urad-Nanaya came from different standpoints their approaches were nevertheless complementary. The physician could treat the disease in the physical body, but why had the patient been afflicted by it in the first place? This was the domain of the exorcist, who could fix the underlying cause in the spiritual realm. It is easy to see how this could lead to feelings of superiority in the practitioners steeped in higher learning, while the physicians were down-to-earth and may have seen themselves as more practically and immediately useful. But regardless of what they thought of each other, they would have had to put their differences aside to get to the bottom of the king's illness.

Although they did not know whether Esarhaddon's problems were spiritual or physical – a punishment from the gods or simply a malfunctioning body – the king's healthcare team still had to come up with solutions. If we take a closer look at the library's texts, we can see what they might have tried, as they struggled to pin down his odd set of symptoms.

Beginning with the head, as the medical texts do, we know that Urad-Nanaya treated the king's ear problems with smoke therapy – burning aromatic substances and wafting the aroma into the ears.[38] This was a treatment for tinnitus caused by the hands of gods or ghosts, who caused the strange noises by whispering into the patient's ears.

Although ghosts are usually the exorcist's problem, the physician would have found many different prescriptions for ghost-induced ear ringing among his tablets.[39] After gathering the medicinal substances, he would have recited incantations asking the gods to keep the ghosts away, and then inserted the substances into the ears. The most common ingredients were myrrh, cedar resin, and magical stones. The first two are powerful pharmaceutical substances – myrrh is a potent antibacterial and anti-inflammatory agent that speeds the healing of wounds, while cedar resin is an antiseptic. Since tinnitus can be caused by ear infections, this would be a perfectly sensible treatment that may well have worked. We also know that the physician could treat more ordinary earaches by inserting wool sprinkled with juniper oil, another antiseptic substance that helps wounds to heal.[40] In this case no incantations are necessary, since there is no suggestion that ghosts are involved.

Esarhaddon had also suffered from eye inflammation since early in his life, at least from the time when he was crown prince.[41] Luckily for him, ophthalmology had a long history in Mesopotamia, with eye surgery even mentioned in the law code of Hammurabi in the mid-eighteenth century BC.[42] The *Nineveh Medical Compendium* has four tablets devoted to eye prescriptions, over more than five hundred lines.[43] Here we find treatments for dimmed or blurred vision, ingrown eyelashes, conjunctivitis, jaundice, bleeding, and all kinds of visual distortions. The text informs us that inflamed eyes can be treated by crushing a type of resin (probably mastic) and flour made from roasted grain and infusing them in beer. Bandages could then be soaked in the mixture and applied to the affected area.[44]

Moving down the body, the king also complained of both fever and chills, which can alternate in the same illness. The most common treatments for fever were salves and herbs bandaged to the patient. These tended to use different substances ground into flour and then mixed together into a dough. Some of these substances are aromatics of the kind we have already seen – cedar, juniper, and cypress – while others are humbler, such as chickpea, lentil, date rind, and cress. The doctor would shave the patient's head and bandage the dough around it. The reason for using foodstuffs might partly be explained by the Babylonian idea of disease as a hungry ghost, an entity with an appetite that feeds on human beings.[45] The fever is described in one incantation as an all-consuming fire that eats up everything in its path – the forest, the canebrake, cattle and sheep, a young man and a young woman. In the medical texts when something hurts it is described as 'eating' the patient. The solution, then, is to give the attacker something else to eat instead, and to tell the disease to go off to the mountains where it can eat all the almonds and pistachios it wants. The dough used to bind the ingredients to the patient would also have been effective in a practical way, as the Nineveh medical texts tell us it cools the head.[46]

Urad-Nanaya sent a salve for Esarhaddon to rub on his body. But he was not going to stop there: he threw everything he had at the fever, recommending four different treatments in the same letter.[47] Along with salve, he sent poultices in little bags designed to be hung around the neck – a combination of drugs and magic. He instructs the king to take an enema, which apparently he had done several times before, so he was familiar with the procedure. The doctor assures him 'it will remove the illness'.[48] Finally, he prescribes a special medication to be administered under his personal direction, though he warns it might make the king sweat.

This warning seems to have been warranted, and yet not strong enough, as the king later complained that he felt very hot. However, he doesn't complain to Urad-Nanaya, but to one of the exorcists, perhaps hoping for a second opinion. The exorcist backs up his physician colleague, saying that the medication was supposed to be hot as sweating was the whole point of the treatment. He does however offer his own perspective, and comments how strange it is that the king also has chills in summer: 'This does not make any sense. It is the work of the gods.'[49] Typically for an exorcist, he sees the ultimate cause in the divine sphere, and uses magical means to combat it: in this case, amulets. The king has queried whether he should use one particular string of stones that he had picked up somewhere abroad, to which the exorcist replies, 'Did I not tell the king my lord already in the enemy country that they are unsuited to Assyria? Now we shall stick to the methods transmitted to the king my lord by the gods.'[50] Newfangled foreign fads were not to be trusted.

Some of the methods of administering drugs that seem strange to us would have been very efficient from a pharmaceutical point of view. The enemas that Mesopotamian physicians were fond of prescribing deliver medicinal substances much faster through the wall of the bowel than through the stomach.[51] Similarly, Mesopotamian doctors often prescribed fumigation with aromatic herbs, and while this might sound ritualistic, it is basically a type of aromatherapy. Inhaling volatile oils is one of the fastest ways for medicinal compounds to get into the bloodstream, much faster than taking them by mouth.

Another of Esarhaddon's many woes was his skin rash, which we cannot identify precisely. The *Diagnostic Handbook* lists twenty-nine names for different skin problems, but none of them match the terms used to describe the king's malady. The exorcist would not have had much luck in treating it. As we learn from the handbook, the exorcist could deal with sores that are hot like a burn, hard as a rock, full of pus, or which cover the patient with dark spots or itchy skin. The closest entry to Esarhaddon's condition reads: 'if the nature of the sore is that it is red and the person continually gets feverish and continually vomits, it is called *Samanu*.'[52] *Samanu* is a disease caused by the hand of Gula, the goddess of healing, and so perhaps the exorcist could try to reconcile his patient with her.[53] Although this description sounds similar to Esarhaddon's symptoms, unfortunately it is not so easy for us to diagnose him as his doctors have not left us detailed enough records of his condition. We know that Esarhaddon was feverish, but we don't know the colour of his rash or how frequently he vomited.

In this case Esarhaddon had to rely on Urad-Nanaya. Perhaps tellingly, in two of these places describing a skin problem, the *Diagnostic Handbook* specifically recommends getting a physician to look at it.[54] But if the patient does not get well after the swelling goes down, the handbook states that a goddess has put it there.[55] The treatment Urad-Nanaya recommends for Esarhaddon's rash is in the end rather simple – he suggests the king rub himself with bird fat, which will protect the king from draughts. He also advises the king not to wash himself with hot water, and assures him that then the rash will soon be gone.[56] This is sensible advice by modern standards as well, since standard care for eczema involves keeping the skin moisturised and ensuring it is not aggravated.

Animal substances like bird fat were often used as medicinal ingredients. To cure eyes that feel 'under pressure', the physician could prescribe sheep bone marrow, the gallbladder of a turtle, the dried head of a lizard, or a lamb chop. Some of these treatments may have been more rational than they sound – for instance, in the case of night blindness the patient was instructed to eat liver, a rich source of vitamin A, which we now know to be an important nutrient for good eyesight. In other cases, their power was derived from their symbolism. For instance, turtles are known for their longevity and can be found in remedies for strength, youth, and endurance, such as eating turtle head for preventing grey hair and turtle penis for ending nocturnal emissions.[57] Parallels can be seen here with traditional Chinese medicine, which considers turtles a tonic for the kidneys, which supply vital energy that diminishes with age. Symbolic connections like these are not necessarily pure inventions, but can also be real.

Physicians also used minerals and stones as ingredients in their medicines. One prescription for 'rotten' eyes includes lead,[58] while a combination of lapis lazuli, two other stones, kohl, and two types of clay boiled in milk was considered 'a tested daub for dimness'.[59] Urad-Nanaya once tells the king that he has been busy cooking the gemstone beryl for use in a remedy, though we don't know what it was for. Here the closest modern analogue is practitioners of traditional Tibetan medicine, who will sometimes give patients small bundles of ground-up precious stones and metals to soak in water overnight; the water is then drunk the next morning. As far as traditional medicine goes, then, from a global perspective Mesopotamian medicine is not so unusual.

However, some of the ingredients do sound rather more alarming: human fat, human skull, dragon's blood, dog's tongue, and excrement of ox, lizard, sheep, gazelle, and dog are not substances we would want to ingest. Thankfully, we need not envisage Urad-Nanaya digging around in the graveyard or collecting animal faeces – these are actually secret names for much more palatable ingredients. For example, 'human fat' actually refers to the oil of the *irru* plant (which is probably the plant we call colocynth), while 'lion fat' is another name for the plant itself.[60] This may have been an attempt by physicians to keep their knowledge to themselves by using codes that outsiders would not understand – in fact, one text in the library makes fun of physicians prescribing seemingly disgusting substances, such as 'onager dung in bitter garlic and emmer chaff in sour milk'.[61] It may or may not have been a private joke among the doctors that ingredients they referred to as 'ox and gazelle dung' were only used in texts relating to rectal diseases and were to be inserted into the anus. But cryptic names of plants are used in other cultures too, and are not necessarily attempts to disguise them. We only have to think of Macbeth's witches chanting 'eye of newt and toe of frog, wool of bat and tongue of dog'.[62] At least one of these is in fact a name for a common plant – dog's tongue is an English folk name for both borage and plantain, weeds that grow on many lawns and meadows and do in fact have medicinal properties. In Mesopotamian texts too, dog's tongue refers to a common medicinal plant.

Assyriologists try to link ancient plants with modern ones through etymology – if two names of plants sound extremely similar in, say, both Arabic and Akkadian, or any other related Middle Eastern language, we can guess they might be the same. Mesopotamian descriptions of the plants help corroborate this, as do comparisons of their traditional use in Middle Eastern herbal medicine with mentions in other historical texts, while plant remains found in excavations can provide further evidence.

For example, sesame is called *shamashshammu* in Akkadian, *simsim* in Arabic, *shumshum* in Hebrew and *shumsha* in Aramaic. Its name gives a further clue: the Akkadian means 'oil of a plant', while its Sumerian name means 'oil-containing grain'. Additionally, we know that sesame does grow in Iraq, its seeds have been found in the archaeological record, and its medicinal uses in the cuneiform texts match those known today.

This does not always work out so neatly, however. Although we can be reasonably confident that *ninu* is a type of mint, the mint family is so large that we cannot be sure exactly which type it is. Then as now, the same plant could have many different names, which could lead to a great deal of confusion for non-specialists. To use a modern English example, the plant that Macbeth's witches refer to as dog's tongue is known by many other folk names: waybread, snakeweed, soldiers, kemps, fireleaves, white man's foot (or footsteps), waybroad, ripple grass, Englishman's foot, broadleaf, cuckoo's bread, and rat-tail. But it also has a Latin name, *Plantago lanceolata*, which is assigned to it precisely to cut through the profusion of alternatives, and to place it within a scientific taxonomy. Anyone using this herb medicinally would check the Latin name to make sure they had the right one – after all, there are many other plants that look like a rat tail and might casually be described that way.

The Mesopotamians faced the same issue and compiled herbal encyclopaedias to deal with it. Remarkably, Ashurbanipal himself took a personal interest in this problem, and commissioned a new edition of the plant list *Uruanna = mashtakal*, an authoritative text that grouped different names for the same plant together and made it easy to find drugs with similar properties. For instance, a plant that people would have known as *mashtakal* in Akkadian could also be called 'plant whose place is in heaven', 'plant from the mountain', 'pure plant', and 'plant for purification'.[63] Mashtakal is the plant most frequently used in purification rituals, which explains the last two names, but it is not the only one used for that purpose. 'Plant from the mountain' tells us where it grows, but again this would not narrow it down if we had to go and look for it. The name 'plant whose place is in heaven' is the Sumerian term, the equivalent of a Latin name today, which would only have made sense to specialists. Ashurbanipal's encyclopaedia of drugs is organised with these academic names first and more common ones grouped after them, just as herbal handbooks are today. What's more, it gives equivalent plants that have similar effects to mashtakal so that the physician could substitute them if he didn't have any mashtakal to hand.

We know that reorganising the plant lists was Ashurbanipal's own personal project because of this comment written at the very end:

> It contains drugs, which since times of old have not been systematically redacted in commentaries and explanatory texts. Ashurbanipal, king of the universe and king of Assyria, checked all those drugs and their equivalents which had been indiscriminately lumped together without applying any criterion as far as sequences are concerned and for the first time he methodically arranged these drugs and their equivalents. He removed those entries that appeared two or three times. In doing so he did not change the old handbooks but rather followed the old order of entries, then checked and collated them.[64]

For hundreds of years Mesopotamian scholars had copied and recopied the knowledge of their day, adding new information whenever they found it, preserving older traditions alongside newer ones and incorporating ideas from other cities when they came across them. But over time all this accumulation of knowledge had become quite chaotic. Now Ashurbanipal saw a chance to make a difference – just like Esagil-kin-apli had straightened out the twisted threads of medical tradition to produce the *Diagnostic Handbook* four hundred years before him, so Ashurbanipal could do the same for the lists of plants and make a name for himself as a pioneering scholar. With this editorial comment Ashurbanipal is deliberately putting himself on the same level as the great sages of old, laying claim to an intellectual achievement.

Ashurbanipal claims to have done all this work himself, but do we believe him? Given how much labour would have been involved, it seems more likely that he ordered his scholars to take care of it. As a parallel, the annals describing Ashurbanipal's military conquests are written in the first person even when he was nowhere near the battlefield. Statements like 'I cut off his head and beat it against the face of the ally who could not save him' most likely refer to the work of Ashurbanipal's soldiers acting on his behalf, rather than the king executing people himself.[65] The same is probably true for his library's large-scale projects, like this one. In general, the texts of the library are written in an extremely neat and professional hand that looks almost the same on every tablet, meaning we cannot distinguish different kinds of handwriting. It is almost like an official font, and indeed some Assyriologists refer to it as 'typewriter cuneiform'. But we should not judge Ashurbanipal too harshly for delegating the labour; he did after all have an empire to rule. To his credit, we see in his words a special concern for orderly arrangement shared by the modern librarian and scientist, as well as respect for the academic tradition. The Assyrian king shared the values and attitudes of his scholars whether or not he did all the checking himself, and focused one of his library's most important projects on medicine. Perhaps seeing his father's reign cut short by illness inspired Ashurbanipal to make medical research a priority.

We have explored some of the treatments Urad-Nanaya might have tried on Esarhaddon, but what about his diagnosis? What was this mystery illness he was suffering from? We already know that Urad-Nanaya was at a loss. Unfortunately, the exorcists have left us no suggestions either and we know little about how they attempted to treat him. None of their letters name the particular rites they performed for the king's health, speaking only generally of purification rituals and rituals 'against loss of flesh'.[66] In one of these rituals the king had to sit in a reed hut for seven days reciting prayers to his personal god and goddess, trying to appease their anger and persuade them to return to his side.[67] But whether their abandonment left him vulnerable to the hand of a god or a ghost is unknown to us.

In writing this I have come to sympathise deeply with Esarhaddon's doctors. It is no wonder that they could not diagnose his illness – the descriptions they have left us do not match any ancient medical texts. Nevertheless, scholars have been tempted in modern times to find a match for his disease. It has been suggested Esarhaddon had lupus, a chronic autoimmune condition whose primary symptoms are joint and muscle pain, skin rash, and extreme tiredness. Fever and eye inflammation are also common. Lupus causes inflammation more generally, which can strike anywhere in the body, meaning that no two cases are exactly alike, and it can wax and wane in severity just as Esarhaddon's illness did. It is the closest modern diagnosis that we have come up with, and there is no known cure for it even today. Given that modern medicine has difficulty understanding and treating this disease, it would be unsurprising if the ancient Mesopotamians also struggled.

Although this sounds like a convincing diagnosis, in reality it is not so simple. We don't know if Esarhaddon suffered all these symptoms at the same time or whether they were in fact produced by different diseases. People weakened by chronic illnesses are often susceptible to all kinds of secondary infections and problems, so the cluster of symptoms that made up Esarhaddon's illness may have had multiple different causes. We simply do not have enough information to be precise enough to reach any real conclusions.

But the problems go deeper than a lack of records. In fact, it is difficult for us to correlate any description of an ancient disease with a modern one. The Mesopotamians understood disease in a completely different way from us, and grouped symptoms together differently than we do. Anyone who has ever tried to google their symptoms will know how the same combinations of symptoms can be signs of many different diseases (none of which we probably have) – if we cannot even identify diseases precisely through modern descriptions of them, how on earth are we to identify them from the far more laconic ancient texts? The opposite is also true, in that one cause of disease can rear its head in many ways. The *Diagnostic Handbook* is full of pronouncements that the patient is afflicted by 'hand of Lamashtu', 'hand of Ishtar', or 'hand of a ghost', but each of these agents could be responsible for a number of problems. As I was reading the *Diagnostic Handbook* in preparation for writing this chapter, I diagnosed myself with 'hand of Lamashtu', but since Lamashtu can strike in different ways that alone is not enough to tell you what I was suffering from.

Even the way in which the ancient texts describe parts of the human anatomy shows that they understood the body's workings in a way that does not correspond to ours. While we have a detailed interest in physiology – the intricate workings of the body – Mesopotamian terms are often vague, and use one word to refer to a general area that could include several different parts. This is in striking contrast to their extremely detailed knowledge of the anatomy of sheep that they sacrificed in divination. There are eight terms describing different parts of the sheep's heart, while the Babylonian word for a human heart really just means 'middle' or 'inside' and can be used for any part of the chest or general abdominal area as well as the heart itself. The same is true of the word for liver, which can also designate the stomach. Though this seems baffling to us, it is true that abdominal pain is often referred pain, meaning that a problem in one part of the abdomen is felt as if it is in another part, and that from the patient's perspective a vague description might be more accurate than a precise one. Nevertheless, it illustrates how difficult it is to put modern labels on ancient ailments.

With all these caveats, I still cannot help but speculate. Esarhaddon's doctors were unable to give a diagnosis, but they must have had theories. And though there is no clear match in the *Diagnostic*

Handbook, some entries do come close. These can illustrate some possibilities they might have considered.

Several of Esarhaddon's symptoms point to one supernatural entity: the moon god Sin. 'Hand of Sin' was a diagnosis for various skin conditions and also for constantly fluctuating body temperature. The handbook pronounces:

> If the patient's body gets hot and then cold and his affliction keeps changing: it is the 'hand' of Sin.[68]

Other factors may support the diagnosis of hand of Sin, at least for Esarhaddon's skin condition. On the way to Egypt, he stopped to pay a visit to the sanctuary of the moon god in the city of Harran. It has been suggested he did so precisely because of his skin troubles, and that it may have been an attempt to pacify the god who had inflicted this disease.

But other spiritual causes could also have been to blame. Another entry in the *Diagnostic Handbook* is reminiscent of Esarhaddon's situation:

> If the patient vomits bile and he burns with fever, it is the 'hand' of his father's god.[69]

We know Esarhaddon suffered both ailments, though not necessarily at the same time. Another caveat is that there are many types of fever. This particular one is a kind of 'sun heat', whereas Esarhaddon's doctors only speak of fever in general terms. Given Esarhaddon's family history, the exorcists might have thought it plausible that he could have been haunted by his father, since Esarhaddon seems to have made it his life's mission to reverse his father's policies. Sennacherib had destroyed Babylon; Esarhaddon rebuilt it and went to considerable effort to support the city. The library preserves a story about Sennacherib enquiring piously what his father had done to offend the gods in a manner that seems much closer to how Esarhaddon would have liked his father to have acted than how he actually behaved.[70] Of course, being haunted by his 'father's god' and being haunted by his father are not exactly the same thing, but it could have been one possible explanation for Esarhaddon's distress.

There is one more contender. A rare letter from the king himself to one of the exorcists queries a ritual against 'fall of the heavens'.[71] In bemusement he asks, 'What is this? The heavens do not fall but exist for ever.'[72] The reason for his confusion is the arcane language: 'fall of the heavens' is a technical term for epilepsy. A fragmentary letter tells the king that an exorcist has given amulets against epilepsy to a couple of children in the royal household, though since we cannot date the letter accurately we cannot be sure if the king in question was Esarhaddon or Ashurbanipal. As we have already seen in the chapter on magic, Sennacherib was tormented by the *alu* demon, which could also cause epilepsy – the condition may have run in the family.

In summary, our list of possible ancient causes includes the hand of Ishtar, the moon god Sin, a ghost, Lamashtu, being haunted by his father's god, and epilepsy. It is not surprising that the exorcists found it difficult to narrow down.

The cures for kings can tell us how medicine was practised at the royal court, the very highest level of society, but what was available to those who lived outside the palace? Both physicians and exorcists practised privately and could be hired by anyone who could afford their services. The law code of Hammurabi from the eighteenth century BC stipulates that in Babylon physicians had to charge different amounts depending on the social class of the patient: ten shekels of silver for performing eye surgery upon a man of the upper class versus five shekels for a commoner and two for a slave.[73] The surgeon had to be extremely careful that the operation was a success, as the same law code states that if he blinds the man in the process or the patient dies after the operation, the physician's hand will be cut off.[74] If a slave died during an operation, the surgeon would have to replace them with a slave of comparable value, since he had essentially deprived the owner of their property with his mistake.[75] We do not know if the same regulations applied to Assyrian physicians a thousand years later, but Hammurabi's laws were kept in the library and studied by the king's scholars, so it would have been familiar history, at least.

The house of a family of exorcists has been discovered in the Assyrian city of Ashur, which gives us a fascinating window into the practice of medicine away from the court. Exorcists would normally visit their patients in their own homes, taking whatever ritual equipment they needed with them, but this house in Ashur also has a room, covered with red plaster that may have been specially dedicated to rituals. We can imagine what a powerful atmosphere this must have created: the burning braziers casting the room aglow like a furnace, and the exorcist blending into the room, also dressed in red. But the tablets in this family's library show that exorcists were just as involved with treating physical ailments as spiritual ones, that they knew complex plant remedies, and had practical experience with testing drugs. Apprentice exorcists would practise on animals in the early phases of their training, applying similar remedies to animals as they would to humans. Although the Mesopotamians did not practise human dissection, they probably also learned about anatomy by analogy with animals, which they did regularly sacrifice and butcher for food.

The exorcists in this family were all male, but women could practise medicine as well. Women as professional magical practitioners would have been deeply suspicious. But there were female physicians, at least in the earlier periods of Mesopotamian history, and the most important healing deities were goddesses, which suggests that healing was not necessarily considered a masculine activity. Women were also involved in the preparation of medicines, as female herbalists mixed up medicinal oils and plants.[76] Midwives in particular were female, but since childbirth was one of the most dangerous events in a woman's life a male exorcist would provide spells and magical strategies to help ensure the mother survived. Women's health was not the preserve of women alone, then, as can also be seen in other scenarios. Ashurbanipal's library contains complex medical recipes for gynaecological issues such as the abnormal flow of menstrual blood, which would have been copied and studied by male scholars.[77] The *Diagnostic Handbook* also contains prognoses for the exorcist to determine the health of an unborn baby, its sex, and whether a woman who fell ill during pregnancy would live or die.[78] It is in matters of childbirth and pregnancy that we find texts dealing specifically with gynaecology, but as in medicine today women were otherwise treated in the same way as men. Similarly, there is no need to assume that female physicians only treated women. We do not have the records that prove who their patients were, but so far there is nothing to indicate that their practice was limited to their own sex. Ashurbanipal's library may reflect a male-dominated world, but outside in the community women may have been more powerful than the texts let on.

All in all, by the standards of ancient medicine, Mesopotamian doctors were probably fairly successful. Admittedly, an ophthalmologist friend of mine was horrified to hear that Mesopotamian physicians were fond of putting lead and copper in people's eyes. But more generally the remedies seem to have been less dangerous than the medicine of some other eras, and some of their plant remedies had real pharmaceutical effects. Bloodletting was not often practised, for instance, and toxic ingredients like heavy metals were not used in very many instances. The *Diagnostic Handbook* describes problems of septuagenarians and octogenarians, suggesting that many did live to such an advanced age.

Esarhaddon was not so lucky. He eventually died of his illness after only eleven years of rule, while he was on the way to campaign in Egypt. He must have recovered sufficiently to feel well enough to travel and even to wage war, but the illness came back when he was not expecting it. Thankfully his doctors had more success with the crown princes Ashurbanipal and Shamash-shum-ukin, both of whom had been seriously ill as children but were brought back from the brink.

Like the other branches of Mesopotamian knowledge, Mesopotamian medicine spread across the ancient world. In early Greece there was a school of thought that took a very similar approach to medicine. The Methodists, as they were known, followed different teachings to those of Hippocrates, who would go on to become the leading medical authority of the day. Although Hippocrates would emerge triumphant, it is thanks to him that we know about the existence of the Methodists, since his writings are highly critical of them. For instance, the Hippocratic treatises on epilepsy attack those who blame gods for causing diseases and make fun of those who use purification rituals to treat them. Both the explanations and the treatments critiqued there have very close parallels in the Mesopotamian texts.

On the other hand, the way that the Hippocratic texts describe symptoms and give prognoses is very similar to the structure of the *Diagnostic Handbook*. Although Hippocratic doctors may have disagreed with their predecessors on the causes of disease, they still owed much to them in terms of method, and some individual treatments. Ancient Greek doctors used the same ingredients for treating eye problems as the Mesopotamians did: recipes in the Hippocratic treatises on sight bear a remarkable resemblance to those found in Ashurbanipal's library. Roman medical treatises on eye disease have even more similarities with Mesopotamian ones, and quote other Greek physicians as their source. The details of how Mesopotamian medical knowledge influenced the classical world are still being worked out, but our understanding of the history of Mesopotamian medicine is rapidly developing and it may well turn out that there are far more connections than we currently recognise. Closer to Mesopotamia itself, we can see the influence of Mesopotamian handbooks in medical texts from medieval Syria, attesting to the former's influence on later Arabic medicine. Perhaps it is the technical knowledge of Mesopotamia that has had the most impact beyond its borders – practical, useful, and applicable to human beings wherever they are, regardless of the language they speak or their culture. In theory, medical recipes could be picked up and reused by others, either in conversation, via translated texts, or using ingredients directly given, if doctors were willing to share their secrets with international colleagues.

Modern clinical medicine has made huge advances in the last few thousand years, but we also live in an age where traditional medicine is booming. The popularity and success of alternative medicine are in part due to the extra time and personalised attention that these practitioners give to the patient, treating them as a whole person, listening to them and taking all their concerns seriously. While we should not project our modern ideas of empathetic counsellors on to the ancient Mesopotamian exorcists, it is nonetheless true that the time and attention they spent on what we would see as psychological aspects of illness would have helped the patient feel better. This was truly holistic healthcare that considered the patient's emotional state and their relationship with the gods as well as their physical symptoms. Here the interdisciplinarity of Mesopotamian scholarship is very much on show, with omens, magic, religion, physical examination, and botany all coming together to play their part in the healing arts. In matters of life and death it was more important than ever to draw knowledge from wherever it could be found.

5.
Reading the Signs

The first streaks of red hit the sky as the sun begins to rise. Dannaya has been waiting all night for the sun god's arrival, presenting offerings and prayers in an elaborate ritual that began at sundown. The cold air under the open sky has kept him awake, but in any case, he was not in danger of drifting off to sleep in front of the seven gods present in their statues – there was much to do during the lengthy vigil. He has already set up and cleared away altars piled high with honey-sweetened loaves, poured libations of the finest beer throughout the night, and sacrificed two rams to Ashur, the personal god of the king of Assyria. Sunrise is the signal for the main part of the ritual to begin. As the glow begins to spread beyond the horizon, Dannaya's attendants set up three more altars and bring out another ram. Next, three basketfuls of loaves stuffed with honey and butter, twelve for each altar, are placed before the gods. Dannaya sprinkles the loaves with salt, bowing as he approaches each deity. When his apprentice has set four more jugs of beer on the main altar, he motions for the ram to be led forward, and scatters the incense in front of the sun god as the sky brightens. His colleague Dari-sharru ties the feet of the ram together and they hoist it on to the table. Dari-sharru holds it down while Dannaya raises the knife and asks the question they have been waiting all night to ask:

'O Shamash, great lord, give me a firm, positive answer to what I am asking you! Ashurbanipal, king of Assyria, a king created by you, has heard: "Shamash-shum-ukin, unfaithful brother, who stirred up the country and caused a major uprising, is fleeing to Elam." Is the rumour true? Is he indeed fleeing to Elam?[1] Does your great divinity know it?'[2]

The year was 651 BC and Ashurbanipal was fighting a bitter civil war against his brother. When their father Esarhaddon had died, he had split the empire between his two sons, giving the title of king of Assyria to Ashurbanipal, and making his elder son Shamash-shum-ukin king of Babylon. It was a strategy designed to prevent the bloody disputes over succession that had plagued the dynasty for generations, and an attempt to mollify the rebellious Babylonians. It was thought that if both brothers were given their own sphere of royal authority, perhaps they could live in peace. But it was not to be.

Although Ashurbanipal was given the lion's share of the empire, he seems not to have been satisfied, for he acted as if he were king of Babylon too. He rebuilt and dedicated temples in Babylonia, which should have been his brother's privilege, and sent spies to the capital. Some local Babylonian governors wrote directly to him instead of to their own king – the interference was so great that it is difficult to tell whether Babylonia was even intended to be an independent state or whether it was always supposed to be just another vassal of the mighty Assyrian empire. From the outset there were signs that Ashurbanipal was stringing his brother along, showing him who really held power. Ashurbanipal succeeded to the Assyrian throne immediately after the death of their father, but the installation of Shamash-shum-ukin as king of Babylon did not take place until the following year. When Babylonia was invaded by the Elamites, long-standing enemies based in Iran, Ashurbanipal was slow to send the soldiers needed to expel them. Resentment brewed in the elder brother, who was being pushed around by his younger sibling.

Despite this, the arrangement held for seventeen years, until Shamash-shum-ukin lost patience and declared Babylonian independence in 652 BC, making a pact with the Elamites to invade Assyria. A papyrus preserving a popular story from many centuries after the revolt records Shamash-shum-ukin declaring that he was king of Babylon while Ashurbanipal was merely a governor of Nineveh, and ought to be his subject.[3] All the remaining surviving sources come from the Assyrian side, with Ashurbanipal bitterly raging about how Shamash-shum-ukin had forgotten all the favours he had done him and had treacherously betrayed his brother. An inscription on a clay prism recounting Ashurbanipal's military campaigns laments:

> [Shamash-shum-ukin] whom I had installed as king of Babylon – everything that kingship calls for I gave to him. I assembled soldiers, horses, and chariots and placed them in his hands. I gave him more cities, fields, orchards, and people to live inside them than the father who engendered me had commanded. However, he forgot these acts of kindness I had done him and constantly sought out evil deeds. Aloud with his lips he was speaking friendship, but deep down his heart was scheming murder.[4]

In these accounts of the war, written from Ashurbanipal's point of view, Shamash-shum-ukin's name is scarcely mentioned without the epithet 'faithless brother', implying that treachery was part of his very being. This is a marked contrast with the inscriptions from the early part of Ashurbanipal's reign, in which he calls him 'my favourite brother' and wishes, 'may his days be long and may he experience the fullness of old age!'[5] A once-happy relationship had turned sour, and led to a vicious war.

A year in, it was still not clear which side had the upper hand, which is why Ashurbanipal's diviners were consulting the ram's entrails. The Babylonians had recently taken the city of Cutha from the Assyrians, and yet a rumour had just reached Ashurbanipal that his brother was fleeing to Elam, and so could not have been doing so well after all. Was the rumour true? Had his brother given up hope and fled abroad for refuge? Perhaps, finally, Babylon would fall into his hands and be under his control. Ashurbanipal wanted to know whether his military intelligence was trustworthy. In the chaos of war, when loyalties are divided and misinformation is rife, how is it possible to know the truth? The Assyrians had an answer: ask Shamash, the sun god.

Entrail divination, or 'extispicy', was considered a fail-safe method of obtaining information from the supernatural realm. Any question could be posed – will the chief eunuch recover the fortresses taken by the Manneans? Should Esarhaddon marry his daughter to the king of the Scythians? Will Ashurbanipal survive this insurrection? – and Shamash would give his verdict. As both the god of justice and the celestial body who could see all happenings everywhere on earth, Shamash was uniquely placed to reveal the answers to all questions. To ask him, one had to enlist the help of a specialist diviner. At the moment of asking the question, the sun god would write the answer on the entrails inside a sheep. The sheep would then be slaughtered, and the diviner could read the answer by inspecting its organs, primarily the liver and gallbladder, but also the intestines, heart, and lungs.

Nearly 350 of these queries are preserved in the royal archives that were part of Ashurbanipal's library, showing just how important extispicy was to decision-making at the Assyrian court.[6] Questions of military strategy were frequently put to the sun god, as were rumours needing verification, religious matters such as the selection of priests and deciding whether statues should be allowed to travel, and proposed dynastic marriages. But more personal questions were also asked: Will the queen mother Naqia recover from her illness? Was Ashurbanipal's dream anything to be concerned about? Letters were placed before the sun god and he was asked whether their contents were reliable. Peace offers from foreign envoys were subjected to the same test, to question their sincerity. Shamash could deliver a verdict on any matter: past, present, or future.

Whether or not we believe in the will of the gods, extispicy offered many other practical advantages. The wording of the question was crucial, and the discussions that went into formulating it would have helped to clarify opinions. The answer to any extispicy was always yes or no, which helped to distil nebulous discussions down to the essentials and enabled clear decision-making. And since the decision came sanctioned by the gods, it was held to be objective; no individual was responsible if the result did not turn out as expected.

Extispicy was held to almost scientific standards of exactitude. The entrails were always checked by more than one diviner, and in some cases they were inspected by as many as eleven.[7] Even the chief diviner Marduk-shumu-utsur was not left uncorrected: on one occasion the more junior Dannaya pointed out that he had missed two unfavourable omens, and added them to the record.[8] It was common to check the result of the first extispicy against a second or even a third, to ensure that it was accurate, and if the answer was not declared by a clear majority of signs it was always advised to perform the extispicy again.

This exactitude is one reason why extispicy was considered such a prestigious branch of knowledge in Mesopotamia. Its precise nature meant it was considered more reliable than divine signs that came in through other channels. Astrological omens, for example, could be verified through extispicy when it was unclear whether their evil took aim at the king. In these cases it could be put to the gods to confirm whether or not the omens were of any concern. Sacrificial divination, then, could act as a check not only on human advice and intelligence, but also on human interpretations of the divine. For most of Mesopotamian history extispicy was considered more prestigious than many scholarly disciplines that we now consider more authoritative, surpassing medicine, mathematics, and astronomy (although in later Mesopotamian history these last two would eventually overtake it).

It may seem strange to use the word 'scientific' when discussing divination, but from the Mesopotamian perspective it was perfectly rational. Any scientific system is based on certain premises – assumptions about the world that we hold to be true – whether proven or hypothetical. In Mesopotamia, the fundamental premise was the belief that the gods were always sending signs to humanity. For a society that believed in all-powerful gods, it made sense to believe that they could and would communicate with human beings, and the fact that divination has been practised by cultures the world over, from Greek oracles to Siberian shamans and Mayan priests, shows this is not an uncommon belief. Those who believed that the gods could communicate with human beings were quite logically on the lookout for divine signs in the world around them. The Mesopotamians used these signs to understand the intentions of the gods, organising and explaining them according to certain codes, and devised theories of interpretation that were inscribed in vast and technical series of clay tablets that could only be understood by highly trained specialists.

This science was the product of long and serious scholarly thought. The Mesopotamian omen compendia, the standard reference works that collected lists of omens, constitute the earliest evidence available for the history of science itself, since they show how people reasoned in the ways they made connections between certain signs and their outcomes as early as 2000 BC, centuries before other cultures began to record this kind of information. The omens are a product of rigorous logic and systematic thinking, extended into different areas of enquiry. This was a more sophisticated way of making associations than simply assuming that one event caused another. The signs were not thought to *cause* the events that they portended, but rather to announce them: they were messages from the gods rather than entities with power in their own right. The diviners did not think that unusual signs in the sheep's liver could bring about victory in battle or cure an illness, only that they were indications sent by the gods of what would happen if things continued the way they were. Divination, then, was both an abstract system to help make sense of the world, and a practical tool for navigating it.

This intricate, codified system made it impossible for individual diviners to falsify their results in order to influence the king: this was not a shadowy cabal of advisers using 'the will of the gods' to manipulate royal policy to their own ends, but was more akin to a group of scientists performing an experiment and dispassionately presenting the results. As diviners worked in pairs or groups we can even consider them to be engaging in peer review, since they checked each other's work. The reports from the diviners sent to the king never recommended courses of action, only describing the findings of the extispicy and stating whether the result was favourable or unfavourable. Nor would it have been easy for groups of diviners to conspire to control the king; on some occasions the question was asked multiple times by different diviners who were kept separate so that they could not confer. Sennacherib was said to have instructed three or four different groups of diviners to perform the same extispicy so that they could not fix the result, and passed on the recommendation to his descendants.[9] While scholars at the Assyrian court were often well versed in several different branches of divination, the entrail specialists never collaborated with scholars of other disciplines, and were kept apart from them so that they could act as a check on other debates. The king could be certain that an answer from the sun god was reliable, untainted by human manipulation, and that it could bring clarity into any discussion.

Dannaya would have taken comfort in this as he performed the ritual. His task was a supremely important one, but he did not bear the responsibility for it alone, and whatever the outcome, he knew he was just doing his job. At least Ashurbanipal was not literally looking over his shoulder – when extispicies were performed for private clients they often participated, staying up all night with the diviner and taking part in the prayers, sometimes presenting the ram to Shamash themselves, wanting to experience this sacred ritual first-hand. Although a special occasion for an ordinary person, who may have needed to save up to afford it, an extispicy was a routine affair in the Assyrian court, and Ashurbanipal would not have put up with so many sleepless nights. Instead, Dannaya held the hem of Ashurbanipal's garment to represent his royal patron, allowing the king to be present in symbolic form as he offered the ram on his behalf. However, Ashurbanipal's scholarly training did mean that he was able to dispute Dannaya's interpretation of the omens if he so chose: in a famous tablet, the king claims to be 'capable of arguing with expert diviners about the series called "If the liver is a mirror of the heavens," '[10] the name of a learned commentary on extispicy omens which unfortunately has not survived.

⁂

Extispicy was one of the quintessential Babylonian sciences that was adopted all over Mesopotamia. Although a few references to consulting the liver appear in Sumerian texts, it was the Babylonians who developed extispicy into a fully fledged system in the first half of the second millennium BC, organising omen lists into vast compendia. Over time the compendia underwent some changes, narrowing in focus to concentrate more on the liver and less on the other organs, and the language became increasingly technical. By the Neo-Assyrian period they had been standardised into a canonical version, and our best source of knowledge for the discipline is Ashurbanipal's library, where extispicy was an essential part of the king's collection.

The system for decoding the signs was vast and complex. The series of omens explaining how to interpret the entrails was at least ninety-nine tablets long, and each tablet contained around a hundred entries, meaning that there were nearly ten thousand omens to choose from. Learning how to interpret these signs was no easy task. The texts are written in highly specialised language, and even basic grammar often must be inferred. Omens are phrased in two halves, with a conditional formulation: 'if *x* happens, then *y* will happen'. This was the sentence structure for all Mesopotamian scholarly texts, from medicine to astronomy and law, firmly anchoring extispicy in this academic context.

The omens are full of highly esoteric language, and although they might seem mysterious and even poetic, they are in fact highly specific and technical. For example:

> If a design is drawn from the centre of the Palace Gate to the right door jamb of the Palace Gate to the Finger: auxiliary troops will approach.

If a design is drawn from the centre of the Palace Gate and it goes out: a famous person will arrive riding on a donkey.

If a design is drawn from the centre of the Palace Gate to the Increment and its centre is speckled white: the accountants will plunder the palace.[11]

The 'design' probably refers to track marks left by parasites, for a sheep's liver makes an ideal home for them and is often scarred by their movements. The 'Palace Gate' was the umbilical fissure between the two lobes of the liver, and its 'door jambs' were mounds that could appear beneath it, while the 'Finger' was a protruding part (modern vets call the latter by its Latin name *processus caudatus*, meaning 'tail coming forth', showing how both ancient and modern anatomists simply named it after its shape). The 'View' and the 'Station' were different names for a crease in the left lobe, and the 'Increment' is another fleshy protrusion, near the lower edge.

The names of the zones often related to the omens that occurred in these locations, just like in palmistry where the 'life line' relates to length of life and the 'Mount of Venus' to romance. For instance, the 'Path' often concerns military campaigns, and the 'Palace Gate' to comings and goings in the palace. In the first omen listed above, the design connecting the Palace Gate with other parts of the liver symbolises the movement of troops in and out of the city. In the second, the arrival of a famous person on a donkey will remind many of Jesus' entry into Jerusalem on Palm Sunday approximately seven hundred years later, an act loaded with symbolism in the Near East. The link between the Palace Gate and the Increment in the third omen signifies prosperity, but white speckles are a negative mark that often symbolises death, turning this connection on its head – instead of increasing the palace's coffers, the accountants will plunder it.

In addition to the zones, there were other symbolic marks that might appear on the liver – pustules symbolised rain, 'foot marks' stood for journeys, and 'weapon marks' were negative towards whatever they pointed at. There were also holes, fissures, crosses, filaments, and membranes, all of which affected whichever area they were found in and were mostly negative given their origins in disease. This is why a healthy sheep was required, as this gave the best chance of producing favourable omens. The phrasing of the questions usually betrayed this expectation: 'Is Shamash-shum-ukin indeed fleeing to Elam?' clearly expects the answer 'yes', and they would have hoped this would be a more likely outcome from a healthy sheep.

'Reading the signs' is a common metaphor in many cultures around the world, but in Mesopotamia it had a special significance. A fresh liver from a sheep, before it has oxidised, is not the dark reddish-brown colour we are used to seeing at the butcher's or on our plates, but a much lighter brown, the same colour as the wet clay tablets that Mesopotamians wrote on. Furthermore, some of the small wedge-like marks that appear on it look exactly like cuneiform signs. We can only imagine how extraordinary it must have been for a Mesopotamian to have slaughtered a sheep and find inside it something resembling a clay tablet with signs impressed upon it. Who could have written them there if not the gods themselves?

Dannaya would most likely have learned his craft from his father, as it tended to be passed down through families. When it came to learning the anatomy of the liver, he would have been helped by clay models labelled with the different parts. Such models survive even today: one famous Old Babylonian example, in the collection of the British Museum, is inscribed all over with holes appearing in every part.

However, some teaching also took place in the library itself. A letter from the chief diviner and two others to Esarhaddon tells the king that the curriculum needed to be updated:

> two 'long' tablets containing explanations of antiquated words should be removed, and two tablets of the extispicy corpus should be put instead.[12]

Presumably they thought that trainee diviners no longer needed to know quite so much archaic vocabulary, and that it would be more useful to replace them with two new tablets of extispicy omens. The library's collection was in constant use, not just for the preservation of knowledge for posterity or for Ashurbanipal to consult, but as part of the training and daily work of scholars. It had to be kept up to date, much like any university library today.

The strange thing is that despite there being such a wealth of information to consult in the library, it appears that the diviners did not often look things up. Dannaya would have studied the series of tablets explaining the omens during his training, but he did not refer to it during the extispicy itself. Of the omens quoted in extispicy reports to the king, only about 3 per cent of them can be found in the compendia. Ten thousand omens is a large number, but it does not cover every possibility. The series, then, is more like a set of examples that illustrate the theories, or principles, that Dannaya could apply to anything he encountered in the sheep. Even stranger, the details of the 'predictions' that appear in each omen – the plundering accountants, or the famous person on a donkey – seem to have been irrelevant for working out the answer. At the extispicy, it was only noted whether the omen was favourable or unfavourable, with the number of each added up at the end to give an answer of yes or no.

What, then, was the purpose of such elaborate and numerous omens if their content was reduced to a simple yes or no answer? Like many academic books today, the fact that they had no 'practical' use did not mean they had no value. Far from it, they were repositories of a kind of Babylonian philosophy, demonstrating the infinite variety of connections in the universe. By theorising about what different signs meant, the writers of these texts were trying to understand how and why various happenings in the world were interlinked. The same phenomenon can be seen in omen texts of all disciplines – astrological texts show the same pattern, with only a very small proportion of the thousands of omens listed in the tablets ever actually cited by scholars, the majority existing for the purpose of scholarly speculation. All kinds of possibilities – and even impossibilities – are explored in these texts. For instance, one Old Babylonian omen reads: 'If the sheep has no heart: downfall of the prince.'[13] The diviners could never have sacrificed a sheep and discovered that it had no heart, but it shows that they thought it was worth asking the question: what would it mean if the gods really did place a sheep with no heart in front of them? The same is true of astral events such as the omen 'If the sun comes out in the night and lasts until morning' – the Mesopotamians did not think that such an impossible thing could happen, but they stretched their hypotheses as part of the quest to understand the underlying workings of the world.

The more practical side of extispicy was a finely honed craft that required perfect execution of the ritual, with much care taken to prepare the ritual space and create a sacred atmosphere. Dannaya would have bathed beforehand and dressed in clean clothes so that his body was pure, and observed dietary restrictions in the days leading up to the ritual by avoiding strong-smelling foods such as garlic, leeks, cress, and fish. This was part of ensuring purity and may have been an act of courtesy so as not to offend the gods with bad breath. However, the Mesopotamian love of wordplay may also be behind some of these restrictions: the word for 'leek' is almost identical to the word for 'disaster', and so avoiding one may have helped avoid the other.

There was no set venue for the ritual to be conducted, since the diviners travelled with the king wherever he went. There were only two requirements. First, that it take place under the open sky, so that the diviners could address the gods in their celestial forms. For this reason an extispicy never took place when it was raining or cloudy unless in an emergency, in which case the diviners had to add apologies to their prayers. Secondly, the extispicy had to be performed in an 'inaccessible place', set apart from the hustle and bustle of everyday activity so that it would not be disturbed. It could be performed by the riverbank or on the roof of a temple, or in a secluded part of the palace grounds, so long as the site had been purified. When the first star of night lit up, the attendants would sweep the floor and sprinkle it with water, to purify the place both symbolically and literally – the sprinkling kept the dust from being stirred up and dirtying the clothes of the diviners or the fleece of the ram. Incense of juniper and cedar would be burned, filling the air with a sweet and spicy fragrance, particularly necessary to mask the smell of the butchering that was to come.

The incense may not have been there only to cleanse the air. Juniper has hallucinogenic properties and is used in shamanic rituals in Central Asia and the Himalayas to induce altered states of consciousness. Cedar is also known for its psychoactive effects, and there are hints in Mesopotamian texts that it may have been used for this purpose. One Old Babylonian prayer describes the diviner coming into close contact with the incense and declaring that it will invoke the gods:

> O Shamash, I place incense to my mouth,
> . . . sacred cedar, let the incense linger!
> Let it summon to me the great gods.[14]

The incense may have helped Dannaya feel he was coming into contact with the gods by inducing a subtle shift in his state of mind. Furthermore, he had to hold cedar chips in his mouth for the entire ritual, supposedly to purify any words he uttered, but cedar oil taken internally is also reputed to be psychoactive, with reports that it sharpens the senses, giving heightened hearing and vision. Such an effect would be useful in an extispicy ritual when he was examining the flesh at the first light of day.

The ram he was inspecting had to be pristine, since it was an offering to the gods and had to be of the highest quality in order to be worthy of their favour. This requirement of perfect health applied also to the diviner himself – like anyone who served the gods, as we saw with priests, the diviner has to be physically faultless. One text tells us that 'one with squinting eyes, chipped tooth, or cut-off finger cannot approach the place of extispicy', and stipulates that his limbs must be perfect too.[15]

Somehow, Dannaya was an exception to this rule: he was a eunuch. The Assyrian court was full of eunuchs, frequently depicted in reliefs on the palace walls and easily identifiable by their slightly chubby and beardless faces. They could be mistaken for women, but a quick look at their muscular arms shows them to be male. Nor was their defined role in any way feminine: the head of the army, perhaps the most masculine position possible in Assyrian society, was often a eunuch. Eunuchs were castrated at a young age, the removal of their testicles meaning they would not undergo puberty, and were willingly volunteered for the role by their families. Becoming a eunuch was in fact an attractive career prospect since it guaranteed a secure livelihood in the royal administration. As loyal servants of the king, eunuchs could reach the upper echelons of power, and were also granted their own tracts of land, a labour force to work it, and tax exemptions to boot.

Despite this, it was rare to find eunuchs as diviners, probably because of the requirements of physical perfection. Only one other eunuch is known in this role – Shamash-sabatanni, who also worked for Ashurbanipal and Esarhaddon. It is unclear what made these two able to bypass the regulations: perhaps while other diviners had had to work their way up to obtain royal patronage, these two had been in a favourable and secure position at court from the very beginning.

⁂

We left Dannaya with his knife raised above the ram. After asking the question, 'Is Shamash-shum-ukin indeed fleeing to Elam?', he slits the ram's throat, and an attendant collects the blood in a bucket. They bleed the animal dry before beginning the inspection. This means that the actual examination of the entrails is nowhere near as bloody a business as we might expect. He can cleanly cut into its abdomen, and the surfaces of the organs are nicely visible.

Dannaya takes out the entrails and puts them aside – guts first, followed by the liver, heart, lungs, stomach, and all the rest. Finally, the answer to Ashurbanipal's question can be read.[16]

He begins by examining the liver, the 'tablet of the gods'.[17] The surface glistens in the morning light, reflecting the brightening sky, with all its ridges and colourings jumping out at him under Shamash's illuminating gaze. Most important is the crease in the left lobe, the 'Station', which shows whether the gods were present in the sacrifice. Thankfully the Station is there, but its base is protruding and pointed, which he knows from experience is not a good sign. Dannaya continues reading the liver in an anticlockwise direction. The Path, another crease along the edge of the left lobe, is present and looks normal – he tells his reporter Dari-sharru to note this down. He prods the gallbladder and is pleased to find that it is securely attached on the left. Neither of these two findings adds to the tally of signs, but it is important to note them down for completeness, to show that nothing has been overlooked.

There is nothing more unusual to note as he works his way round, until he reaches the Finger, which does not look healthy – parasites have burrowed a large hole in its left side. As if this were not bad enough, at the top left there is a 'weapon mark', an extra arrow-shaped piece of flesh that has grown outwards, and it faces the top of the Finger. Dannaya remembers the entry corresponding to this in the omen series: 'the enemy's onslaught will be successful' – not good news in wartime. Another weapon mark rises above the Increment, pointing from left to right, but he is relieved to find this, as it is a positive omen: 'my army will take the enemy's booty.' At this point, however, Dari-sharru points to the gallbladder – there is something sticking out on the left side, hidden away towards the back. The other diviner quotes from memory: 'If the "mass" rides upon the left of the gallbladder: the mass of the enemy's army will march against my country.' Another negative to add to the list.

Dannaya moves on to the lungs. They are mostly healthy, but he spots a 'foot mark' on the left side – a bad omen. He also checks the skeleton – the top of the breastbone is split, also not a good sign. By now the intestines have cooled enough for them to be visible amid the mass of fatty tissue and he counts the number of coils of the spiral colon – fourteen. Thankfully this is normal. Finally, he checks the heart, which also shows no signs of abnormality.

Dari-sharru has been keeping track of the signs, noting down their findings on a tablet that will be sent to the king, like in modern minute-keeping. Dannaya waits for him to go through them and make a quick summary at the end, but he already knows what the outcome will be – he can only remember one favourable sign occurring in this extispicy, and many more that are unfavourable. By now the sun is up and it is easy to read the tiny sharp wedges on the clay. The whole process has taken about twenty minutes. Dari-sharru looks up and gives the result: 'There are five unfavourable features in the extispicy.' The answer, then, is no – Shamash-shum-ukin has not given up all hope and fled to Elam. Ashurbanipal would not be pleased.

It was not the first time Ashurbanipal had asked the sun god about the war with his brother, nor would it be the last. He had been particularly concerned that others would join the revolt and go to his brother's aid. In March 651 he asked whether the governor of the 'Sealand' would switch to his brother's side, and four months later he asked, 'Will the Elamites join the war?', both of which received the answer 'no'.[18] The concern was justified, for the Elamites had been a thorn in Assyria's side for generations, and did ultimately make common cause with the Babylonians against Ashurbanipal. When it had looked like the Assyrian army might have a chance of taking Babylon, Ashurbanipal had asked whether Shamash-shum-ukin would fall into their hands.[19] The answer was 'no', and indeed the city had not fallen. 'Will the army of Shamash-shum-ukin leave Babylon and flee?'; 'Should the men, horses and army of Ashurbanipal cross the marshes and wage war against the men and army of Shamash-shum-ukin?'; 'Will the weapons of the Assyrian army prevail?'; 'Will Shamash-shum-ukin flee Babylon if the Assyrians take Sippar?' – the questions kept coming.[20] Thirteen different queries about this war survive in total, and Dannaya was present at almost half of them.[21]

Assurances of Assyrian victories would have boosted the king's confidence in his strategy. But some of the answers turned out to be wrong. Just a few weeks after asking whether the rumour of his brother's flight was true, Ashurbanipal again tasked Dannaya with finding out whether Shamash-shum-ukin would fall into his hands if he attacked.[22] This time the answer was 'yes', but it did not happen – the war lasted another two years. Nor had the entrails been correct about the treacherous governor of the Sealand, Nabu-bel-shumati. As Dannaya had recorded at the time, there had been no favourable features in the extispicy at all, a decisive outcome. Yet Nabu-bel-shumati did indeed join the war and became one of Shamash-shum-ukin's closest allies. What would Dannaya have made of this – how could the gods have been so mistaken?

There were several factors that could explain an inaccurate divination. First of all, the answer to a question was only valid for a certain time period. The Babylonians used a mathematical formula to work out how long the answer would apply for, which depended on the length of the Finger in each liver. The Assyrian diviners did not usually record this, and instead their queries specify the length of time that they are asking about, ranging anywhere between seven and one hundred days, with one month as the usual standard. During that time circumstances could change – a week is a long time in politics, a month or three even more so. Perhaps Nabu-bel-shumati was not going to join the war this month, but a few months later it would be a different story. The answer to the question was not seen as a definitive, 'This will happen', but rather, 'This will happen *if things carry on the way they are.*' It is possible that the answer to an extispicy was considered a comment on a policy being proposed, and that if the sun god delivered a verdict that was not what the king had hoped for he would consider alternative strategies. Perhaps the Assyrian army would not prevail if they used that particular battle plan, or perhaps they would capture Babylon only under very specific circumstances, which cannot always be controlled in the chaos of the battlefield.

The exact nature of extispicy, which gave it its authority and prestige, may also have served to protect it from criticism when it failed. Had the question been too precise, or simply been the wrong question? 'Will Shamash-shum-ukin flee Babylon if the Assyrians take Sippar' is in fact two questions in one – a verdict of 'yes' might mean that he would flee, but not necessarily that Sippar would actually fall. And there is also the possibility that the diviner may have made a mistake and not conducted a flawless ritual – in the prayers that preceded each enquiry we find a whole list of pleas for the gods to overlook it if the diviner stumbled over his words or if a ritually unclean person had accidentally come near the place of extispicy. The gods, of course, did not necessarily have to accept the apology.

There is no doubt that the Assyrians sincerely believed in the reliability of divination, and took its answers very seriously. They would not have taken so much care over the ritual and gone to so much effort to check and recheck the results if they were not going to make use of the sun god's verdict. Among the cases that we can trace from proposition to action are Esarhaddon's question of whether he should invade Egypt and if his armies would prevail – this was asked four times, and we know that the campaign did take place and was successful.[23] Ashurbanipal appointed Nabu-sharru-utsur as chief eunuch, an immensely powerful post that put him at the head of the army, only after the gods had approved.[24] It is hard to believe that if an extispicy had given the opposite answer he would have been installed. Though an extispicy could be performed up to three times as a check, the king was not allowed to go on asking for ever until he got the answer he wanted to hear: there are omens that predict death and disaster for any diviner who asks the same question too many times.

Entrail divination, for all its peculiarities, was not merely a Babylonian eccentricity. It became an extremely popular practice that spread from Babylon all over the ancient world. Mesopotamian extispicy was adopted by the Hittites in Turkey and adapted by the Greeks and the Etruscans, and from there it spread to Rome, where it formed a major part of the state ritual. Remarkably, extispicy survived into modern times. It was used by Catherine de' Medici in sixteenth-century France, and in pre-Buddhist Tibet. Even today, consulting the entrails of goats is common among some tribes in East Africa; in Cuba it is done with chickens, and in Peru with guinea pigs. It must, then, genuinely be useful in some way. But how?

In modern times it is often said that the purpose of divination is to help people cope with anxiety about the unknown by giving them more certainty about what is to come, but this is too simplistic. After all, the gods can give answers that we don't want to hear. More accurately, it is a tool for navigating possibilities, focusing and narrowing options to arrive at a decision. Even if extispicy cannot guarantee that something will definitely happen, it can provide reassurance that a course of action is heading in the right direction, and allow for it to be changed if it is not. The process of asking draws on human counsel as much as the divine, since discussion was required both to formulate the question and to decide what to do in response. Nothing is ever certain, as the Mesopotamians knew, but the opinion of the gods could be a helpful guide.

In matters of statecraft there are seldom easy answers: the modern world has its own methods of divination, which are not necessarily any more successful than asking the entrails. We try just as hard to forecast politics as the Mesopotamians did, trying to predict the outcomes of elections by conducting opinion polls, for example. These vast and expensive undertakings require a lot of investment, of both time and money, employing specialists who have trained for years in their art and who use complicated systems and formulas to try to ensure a correct result. Yet despite the fact that these surveys are based on real-world data, the results are still often wrong. People are not always entirely truthful, as the Mesopotamians recognised when they asked the sun god to verify rumours, and they can change their minds, just as the Mesopotamians knew their gods could. From the Mesopotamian point of view, then, extispicy could be seen as a kind of opinion poll that bypassed the fallible human realm and went directly to the gods, who were the only ones with a complete picture of human hearts and minds and world events.

Our methods of divination are directly linked to whatever they are trying to predict – tomorrow's weather forecast is based on today's climatic conditions and the direction they seem to be headed in, while advertising algorithms try to predict what we will buy based on what we have already bought. This may seem like an obvious advantage, and works much of the time, but it is also a weakness. Because most forecasting depends on data about what has already happened, it cannot take account of the unknown. Algorithms that are only fed data from the past cannot necessarily predict how things will change and cannot incorporate unknown unknowns. Thus, YouTube endlessly feeds us the same songs we already know rather than helping us to discover new genres we might prefer, and economists rarely see a crash coming. Change can be sudden and unexpected, and often cannot be foreseen.

Extispicy provided a way out of this feedback loop. Its answer was independent of the patterns of history and incomplete human knowledge. It did not care what experts thought was likely, or what vested interests may have wanted to happen. Because it was not reliant on these things, it was not contaminated by their biases and could provide a check on them, a reminder of the influence of the unknown. It was a single method of divination that was universally applicable to any question; going directly to the gods bypassed human expectations, and forced the enquirer to rethink matters from other perspectives, sometimes when they least wanted to. Our models may be more accurate than predictions produced by chance, but throwing randomness into the equation can have unexpected benefits. We may not choose to sacrifice a sheep, but we need to find ways to account for the unexpected if we are to become truly skilled at divining the future.

6.
Messages in the Stars

On top of the temple roof Balasi is scrutinising the sky. From this vantage point he has a good view of the black surface that the gods write on, seeing over the palace's crenelations, clear of any other buildings. Looking out towards Virgo he can see Saturn, the king's star. On the other side of the sky is a tiny, faint point of light hovering above the horizon. This planet is the reason he has come up here tonight, for its sighting has caused a furore at the court.

It is 27 March 669 BC, the twelfth – and what will be the final – year of Esarhaddon's reign. The previous year had been tumultuous: conspiracies were crushed and the top officials executed; the queen mother almost died, and the whole royal family was exorcised twice (the last occasion just a few months ago). The king's advisers were on edge, having seen all too recently what happened to those who were disloyal to their master. In this charged atmosphere it was more important than ever to be truthful with the king, but all the advisers had to tread carefully, since Esarhaddon was often depressed and easily unsettled.

As the king's chief scholar and astrologer, Balasi has the job of watching for messages from the gods and advising the king on their meanings. But Esarhaddon has many other astrologers advising him, and some clearly ought to be sacked. Balasi has just received a letter from the king saying he has been told that Venus has become visible, which is obviously wrong. Anyone who has studied the cycles of the planets would know this is not the time for Venus to appear – it is a basic error that should not be made by any student of astrology, let alone an adviser to the king.

Balasi has come up to the roof to verify this and is furious. Venus is nowhere to be seen and the planet in question is in fact Mercury. The mistaken report has sparked a huge row and Balasi is the one who has to sort it out. Having confirmed it for himself he will now write to the king to inform him:

> The man who wrote this to the king my lord is in complete ignorance. He does not know . . . the cycle . . . Or the revolutions of Venus! . . . The ignoramus, who is he? . . . Who is the man who writes to the king my lord? I repeat, he does not know the difference between Venus and Mercury![1]

Tensions at the royal court could run high, especially where astrology was involved. Balasi's anger at the mistake above shows just how high the stakes were when it came to interpreting the stars. The Assyrians believed that the gods communicated with the king through celestial portents, providing a kind of commentary on his reign. Mixing up the planets not only gave the king incorrect information when he needed to make decisions, but also twisted the words of the gods, a translation error of the most serious kind. If that were not bad enough, the king had been worried unnecessarily, which would create all kinds of other problems for his scholars, who now had to reassure him.

Astrologers come at the top of a list of experts working at the Assyrian court,[2] a mark of the prestige of this branch of scholarship and its importance to politics. They wrote reports on all manner of celestial events, from eclipses to conjunctions of planets and the rising and setting of stars, all of which had to be analysed. The stars could portend the death of the king, enemy invasion, famine, or economic disaster, but the task of interpreting them was not always straightforward. The tablets in Ashurbanipal's library set out a vast array of potential configurations of stars and planets, with principles, yet their principles are so complex that astrology is the most mysterious and least understood branch of Mesopotamian scholarship today.

Astrology as we know it is very different from that practised in

Assyria. Mesopotamian astrology was originally geared towards the state rather than the individual. Balasi would not have cast a horoscope for the king, or sought his own destiny in the stars, but saw himself more as a translator of a divine code, reading the messages that the gods were sending in the sky and conveying them to their intended recipient. The grand scale of the medium corresponded to the lofty concerns of the gods: the king was the gods' representative on earth, and these cosmic messages related to events of national and international importance rather than the everyday lives of ordinary people. The shift to focusing on the individual would be a later development, an innovation of the Babylonians in the fifth century BC, as we will see.

The Assyrian royal archives contain letters from more than fifty-two named individuals on astrological matters, and their correspondence makes up one-third of all surviving scholarly letters and reports. Yet astrology was ultimately a Babylonian science, and it was the Babylonians who invented the zodiac, horoscopes, and mathematical astronomy, all of which are still with us today. The Babylonians could predict eclipses and the movements of any star or planet to a remarkably accurate degree, using formulae based on hundreds of years of observations. Their work was borrowed by the Greeks after the conquest of Alexander the Great and formed the basis of Greek astronomy and mathematics, a huge influence on subsequent cultures whose Mesopotamian debts are all too often forgotten. With their mathematical work the Babylonians even developed one of the pillars of the modern scientific method. And all this is rooted in the observations of people like Balasi seeking the gods in the stars.

Every night the king's astrologers kept watch over the sky, monitoring the ever-changing heavenly landscape. The Mesopotamians believed the gods were always sending them signs, not only in the sky but also in unusual happenings on earth – from date palms growing out of season to creaking gates and pigs dancing in the city squares.

The world is full of signs, and it was up to the king's scholars to be vigilant enough to observe them, and decode their meanings.

The stars had a special place in this scheme, and are explicitly referred to as 'the heavenly writing'. The sky was a surface for the gods to write on, and the Sumerian word for 'star' can also refer to a cuneiform sign, the very basis of the writing system. The sun god was said to look down upon earth and read everything he sees as if it were cuneiform signs. Heaven and earth were interconnected, a principle that underpins the whole system.

This principle is stated in a text in the library dubbed the *Babylonian Diviner's Manual*,[3] which lists the names of key collections of both celestial and terrestrial omens. Most of these texts are lost, which is a shame because they have fantastic titles such as 'If a wildcat opens its mouth and talks like a man' and 'If a rainbow that is curved like the intestines is seen in the sky' (if I could have back any text lost from antiquity it would be 'If bundles of reeds walk about in the countryside').[4] After listing these important compositions, the manual states:

> The signs on earth just as those in the sky give us signals. Sky and earth both produce portents, though appearing separately they are not separate because sky and earth are related. A sign that portends evil in the sky is also evil on earth, one that portends evil on earth is evil in the sky.[5]

Strange happenings on earth were thought to be reflected in the heavens, and signs produced in the heavens were reflected on earth. Therefore it was the job of the diviner to observe both realms and check whether the signs confirmed each other. For this reason, astrologers not only write to the king about what they see in the stars but report on other unusual omens too. One series that was particularly important for the state dealt with anomalous births – miscarried foetuses or live young of both animals and humans with abnormal features – which, like astrology, portended events of great political significance.[6] One Babylonian astrologer reports that an archer's sow has given birth to a piglet with eight feet and two tails. He pickled it in salt to preserve it, knowing that it would be of national importance. According to the astrologer, it means 'the ruler will seize the kingship of the world'.[7] Other anomalies were not so fortuitous, nor did they have to be so weird to be significant. As the king was also informed, a cow giving birth to twins indicated destruction of the land, while triplets could mean an enemy attack, or an exceptionally cold year and failure of the harvest, depending on the sex of the offspring.[8]

In the Assyrian conception of fate, destiny is not fixed, but ever-changing. That something is written in the stars does not mean it is a certainty, only a message. As with extispicy, the sign announced what would happen if things stayed on their current trajectory. This is reflected in the very nature of the sky: planets move across it, appearing and disappearing, and the constellations move with the passage of the seasons. The sky is never still, and neither are the minds of the gods.

The flexibility of fate is key to understanding astrology in Assyria. If the evil sign was spotted in time the disaster could be averted, since the scholars could perform a ritual to ask the gods to change their minds. Far from being fatalistic, then, reading the messages in the stars gave the Assyrians a way to respond to what the gods were telling them, change course accordingly, or ask the gods to reconsider.

In the Assyrian calendar the day began at nightfall, and while most of the population were on their way to bed, for the astrologers work was just beginning. It was their job to regulate the calendar – the month began with the sighting of the moon's first crescent, an event which they then reported to the king. The lunar cycle is twenty-nine-and-a-half days, that last pesky fraction meaning that it will always be out of step with the solar calendar. Because of this discrepancy, a month might have twenty-nine or thirty days depending on which evening the crescent first appeared, and it wasn't always obvious which it would be, so the scholars had to keep watch. To stop the lunar calendar getting out of sync with the seasons, a leap month was added periodically by royal decree, on the advice of the astrologers. Observing the sky therefore had some very practical functions, as well as ominous ones.

Though the celestial skyscape changed every night, not everything that took place was deemed significant. The scholars had to take care to only report omens of real importance, so as not to overwhelm the king with unnecessary information. Keeping watch on the skies was like triaging the king's email inbox: deleting junk, ignoring inconsequential mailing-list updates, and only forwarding the most urgent items. In a way it is a very modern problem – how to make sense of the deluge of information and distinguish what is important from what is not. From all this noisy data, the scholars had to pick out what mattered most, and they did not always agree.

A network of scholars observed the heavens not only in Nineveh but in cities all over Assyria, and in Babylonia too, so the king received information from many different sources, and could check them against each other. Having scouts in a variety of locations was especially important in astrology because the weather made such a difference to whether they could work or not. If the sky was cloudy in Nineveh nothing could be observed, but perhaps further south in Babylon the stars would be visible. However, the further away the scholars were from the king, the more distant their relationship.

As astrologer-in-chief and tutor to the crown prince, Balasi was close to the king, and more able to speak his mind than some of the others. In his letter about the Venus/Mercury mix-up, he gets directly to the point rather than opening with elaborate greeting formulas and good wishes for the king's health, as some of his colleagues do. His candour in this letter is extraordinary, as he voices his anger not once but three times. What is especially interesting, though, is what the mistake would have meant. The rising of Venus is usually a good sign. Other reports of the planet's appearance predict abundant rain, good harvests, and the reconciliation of kings.[9] On one occasion the chief scribe is so happy about an early appearance of Venus that he exclaims: 'what is this love by which

Ishtar loves the king my lord and has sent the very best to the king my lord!',[10] and reports that an early rising indicates a long life for the king.

Balasi probably assumed that the astrologer who mistook Mercury for Venus had written to the king with similar promises. Now Balasi has to deliver the unwelcome news that no such good omen has been observed. It is easy for us to assume that the court was full of flatterers who were just telling the king what he wanted to hear, but the fact the Balasi gets so angry about accidental good news shows us that if this did ever happen, there were others who would speak up. After all, it would be far worse to reassure the king that all was well and find disaster around the corner than to warn him of problems that thankfully never came to pass. Not all the advisers would have felt able to do so, though. Astrologers working at the royal court reported negative omens more often than those who were further away, who were perhaps afraid of the consequences of being the bearer of bad news when they did not know how the king would react that day.

Balasi was not the only one who was annoyed by the erroneous report. Another senior astrologer is even more heated in his condemnation, calling the sender 'a vile man, an ignoramus, a cheat!'. Accusing him of being deceitful, he demands to be allowed to scrutinise all reports made by this unknown person, continuing, 'Why does someone tell lies and boast about it? If he does not know he should keep his mouth shut.' He concludes with a biting piece of sarcasm: 'the king my lord should not hesitate but promote him at once!'[11]

On the one hand we might take pity on the poor ignoramus who confused Venus and Mercury. At the time the two planets were extremely close together, and as one of the quickest-moving planets, Mercury is one of the more difficult ones to spot – its name in Akkadian translates as 'the jumping one', which reflects its elusiveness.[12] Nonetheless, this would be no excuse for a man who was supposed to be one of the foremost experts in the land.

Knowledge of the cycles of Venus was fundamental to the

astrologer's art. What seems like an arcane piece of knowledge to us was in fact quite simple to find out for those with access to the right tools. The movement of the planets follows a predictable schedule, known as the synodic period. In the case of Venus, it takes eight years to complete a full cycle of five synodic periods and return to the same point in the sky as it started in. The Mesopotamians had been keeping records of the precise positions of Venus since the second millennium BC, so all an astrologer had to do to find out where the planet would be on any given day was look up where it had been on the same day eight years ago. The same is essentially true for other planets, though the patterns and timings are different. However, Assyrian scholars would not rely on either observation or data tables alone but had to be adept with both. When they were expecting a planet to rise above the horizon after being invisible for long periods, they would confirm it by making sure they observed it themselves. Conversely, they would check what they had seen against their knowledge of the cycles to make sure they matched up – or at least they should have done, as Balasi would have grumbled.

Throughout Venus's cycle of eight years the planet appears and disappears many times and even switches sides in the sky, moving between east and west. Venus's pattern of disappearing in the east and reappearing in the west, only to vanish again and reappear on the other side of the horizon, means that many cultures have historically thought it was two different planets, the 'morning star' and the 'evening star', but the Mesopotamians knew these were one and the same. They tracked the dates of these appearances and disappearances, allowing the scholars to follow the cycle and, of course, to interpret its significance. As one tablet puts it:

> In the month of Shabatu on the 15th day Venus disappeared in the west. It stayed away in the sky for three days, and on the 18th day Venus became visible in the east: it means springs will open, Adad will bring his rains, Ea his floods, king will send messages of reconciliation to king.[13]

What is especially remarkable about this tablet is that these observations are dated to the reign of Ammisaduqa, a Babylonian king who ruled in the mid-seventeenth century BC – a thousand years before the assembling of the library. This is not stated outright, but one of the entries gives the year when it was observed, 'the year of the golden throne', which was the name that Ammisaduqa gave to the eighth year of his reign.[14] Because we now have the ability to calculate where Venus would have been in the sky on any date in the past, these dated observations allow us to synchronise the Babylonian calendar with our modern dates and confirm when this king was on his golden throne. The tablet is thus hugely significant, as it is one of the key pieces of evidence in establishing Babylonian chronology. It also shows that the Assyrian scholars already had information stretching back a thousand years available to them. No wonder Balasi considered knowledge of Venus's cycles so obvious – by his time it was hardly cutting-edge.[15]

In the end the squabble over Venus and Mercury may all have been a misunderstanding. Two days earlier another adviser had written to the king mistakenly predicting that Mercury would rise in the next month, when in fact it was already visible. Frustrated by the idiocy of this error, the chief scribe ranted to the king about his colleague's incompetence, but forgot to explain what exactly he had got wrong. In the same letter, the chief scribe then replied to a different question the king had asked about Venus, and the king thought he was predicting the rising of that planet instead, and so he wrote to Balasi to check. All these miscommunications led to a big argument between the chief scribe and senior astrologer, who settled it by going out to look at the sky together. Mercury was indeed visible – 'they saw it and were satisfied.'[16]

Understanding the communications between the gods and the king was difficult enough; miscommunications between the king and his scholars made it all the harder. If the chief scribe had explained his reasoning rather than laying into his colleague, perhaps this never would have escalated. But Venus is a beneficent planet that brings peace and harmony, and as we have seen, its appearance is a sign of reconciliation. According to the omen series a sighting of Venus in the month when these letters were written also meant 'king will send messages of reconciliation to king'[17] – fittingly it seems that everyone made up.

The scholars drew their interpretations from the celestial omen series known as *Enuma Anu Enlil*. This is an abbreviation of the text's first line, which translates as 'When Anu, Enlil, and Ea, the great gods, by their firm counsel established the designs of heaven and earth . . .'[18] This mythological introduction explains how the gods ordained the movements of the heavenly bodies. The series is well represented in the library, where it consists of seventy tablets in all, setting out which events in the sky were important and what they meant.

The series begins with twenty-two tablets devoted to the moon. That the moon comes first in the series implies it was the most important, perhaps because of its role in regulating the calendar, and indeed about half of the astrological reports to the king are concerned with the moon. The tablets take into account many different aspects of the moon's appearance: the dates when it could be seen, the length of the horns of the crescent, and the brightness of the halo that could surround it during a full moon, as well as its position relative to the sun, stars, and planets. The moon was thought to be the heavenly manifestation of the god Sin, and many of the descriptions of the moon's appearance reflect the god's actions. A lunar eclipse is described as Sin in mourning, while a halo was the god riding around in his chariot.

The sun, or the god Shamash, comes next. As well as looking out for obvious dramas such as solar eclipses, it was important to observe the appearance of the sun as it rose, including the colour of the clouds that surrounded it, along with the timing of it and the accompanying weather conditions. One scholar observed a halo around the sun as it rose, and wrote to the king that 'if in the month of Adar the sun is surrounded by a halo in the morning: in this month the flood will come, or it will rain'[19] (an ancient equivalent to our 'red sky in the morning: shepherd's warning'). The sun god could play many other tricks: the tablets also describe parhelia, the two bright lights that can appear either side of the sun when its light refracts through ice crystals in high cirrus clouds. When these appear it looks like there are three suns in the sky, which must have seemed terrifying to the ancient Mesopotamians who did not have the scientific explanation for how this could take place. This alarming event could have different implications: *Enuma Anu Enlil* predicts 'destruction of the cities and their pasture lands', but some versions add another possibility, that 'the king will proclaim a remission of debts'.[20] While one seems negative and the other positive, the two are not mutually exclusive – it was precisely in hard times that such debt forgiveness schemes were necessary.

The next fourteen tablets concern the storm god Adad and all the weather that he could cause: lightning, thunder, complex cloud formations, rainbows, earthquakes, and winds. Here again the god is very much portrayed as the active agent. Where we would say 'it thundered', *Enuma Anu Enlil* says 'Adad shouts'. The storm god had many ways to communicate with mortals. The more Adad rumbled, the more he commanded attention; and the number of thunderclaps made a difference to what he was trying to say. Shouting one, two, or three times was bad news for commerce, business, and the harvest, but if he shouted four or five times abundance and wealth were on the way.[21] At six he reverts to warning of famine.[22] By the time he has reached eighteen shouts, Adad is fed up and says that the palace of the prince will be plundered, but at nineteen he changes his mind and declares that the harvest will prosper. His change of mood is brief, as by twenty shouts there will be a violent flood storm, and the list goes all the way up to thirty, piling up catastrophes.[23] The tone of his voice also mattered, as the sound of his thunder is compared to a whole range of different birds and animals. Adad could vary his messages by sending rain on different days of the month, as the interpretation was different depending on this. Contrary to what we might expect, rainbows were not always good news but could portend murder, violence, and rebellion.[24] However, it very much depended on which direction the rainbow stretched, as it could also indicate that the gods would have mercy on the land. As ever, a small change could indicate a completely different answer.

Only in the last twenty tablets does *Enuma Anu Enlil* reach the planets and stars, which get surprisingly little space considering how many of them there are. Not much of the other planetary sections have survived apart from the Venus omens, so we have to rely on astrologers' reports for a sense of what these tablets contained. Balasi writes to the king about the movements of all five planets that could be seen with the naked eye: Mercury, Venus, Mars, Jupiter, and Saturn. Their relationship with the moon seems to have been especially important – the presence of Mars in the lunar halo indicated destruction of cattle, while Jupiter and Saturn approaching the moon strengthened the king.[25]

As well as giving omens, this part of *Enuma Anu Enlil* sets out some general principles that would have been useful to the diviners keeping watch over the heavens. It outlines brief explanations of some of the basic meanings of the stars and planets; for instance, we are told that 'the fox star is for breaking into houses',[26] meaning that the appearance of Mars could be a warning of break-ins. But rarely are such principles stated outright in the omen series itself. The scholars would have learned mostly by oral instruction, and from commentaries that were compiled to explain the deeper meanings of certain omens in a kind of meta-analysis. The library contains an abundance of these commentaries, which the scholars used to help them understand *Enuma Anu Enlil* itself.

The meanings of planets were related to the gods they represented. As we have seen, Venus is often associated with peace, rain, and agricultural fertility, because this planet was the celestial manifestation of the goddess Ishtar, goddess of sex. But Ishtar had many faces, and which one she was showing depended on where her planet was. As goddess of war, Ishtar could also turn vicious: if 'on the eighth day of Addaru Venus rises in the west: king will send messages of hostility to king'.[27] As an extension of this, Venus could also stand for the enemy country of Elam, and its conjunctions with other planets could forecast war, a clash of heavenly bodies. Similarly, Mars represented the war god Nergal, and his movements often announced war, plague, and death to men and cattle.

But the planets could also represent political actors on earth: as the brightest planet, Jupiter was thought to be the king of the gods Marduk, so his presence also represented the human king by analogy. Mercury was identified with Marduk's son, Nabu, and thus the human crown prince. These kinds of analogies were also at work in the ways that the planets interacted with each other. If Mercury moved in front of the star Regulus, another star of the king, it meant that the crown prince would revolt against his father, taking his place on earth just as he had usurped him in the sky.

Mesopotamian astrology used binary codes of opposition where the right side is good, and the left is bad, a principle that operated throughout the other types of omen series as well. For instance, if the right horn of the crescent moon pierces the sky it is a good omen, since the good side is higher than the bad. Wordplay is also paramount, my favourite example being the backwards reading of a star's name. Tablet 50 of *Enuma Anu Enlil*, which deals with the meanings of particular stars and constellations, mentions an obscure star called LUL.LA (meaning 'false'). It then reads the name backwards to produce AL.LUL, the name of the constellation Cancer, telling us that 'the false star is Cancer'.[28] In this way a difficult name is explained with a simpler one, revealing something about the star's nature in the process. All these principles – analogies and substitutions, binary codes, and linguistic codes – were part of the interpretation of all the omen series, not just stars and entrails but also dreams, abnormal births, and other unusual occurrences in nature, and can thus be seen as the pillars of Mesopotamian scholarly thinking. However, compared with other areas of scholarship there are far more instances in astrology where we cannot understand the connection between the omen and its meaning – whenever we find what seems to be a rule, we also find many exceptions that seem to confound it.

Celestial divination was so complex because there were so many different variables in the system. Each planet, star, or constellation could stand for several different concepts, multiplying the possible readings. Then there were all the other factors to consider: which day of the month the omen was sighted, at what time, how bright the planet was, which constellation it was in, and so on, each of which would add yet further possibilities. Take for example this letter from the astrologer Akkullanu, who gives Ashurbanipal a list of potential meanings for the current activities of Mars, the astral manifestation of the war god Nergal:

> The planet Mars has gone on into the constellation Capricorn, halted there, and is shining very brightly. The relevant interpretation is as follows: 'If Mars rides Capricorn: devastation of Eridu; its people will be annihilated.' And the interpretation of the great brightness is as follows: 'If Mars shines brightly: the king will gain in strength and prosperity.' 'If the effulgence of Mars is seen in the sky: there will be an epidemic, variant: an epidemic among the cattle of the country.'[29]

Here we have three different options – two negative, which are in keeping with the nature of Nergal as a god of war and plague, and the other an unexpected assertion that a bright Mars means strength and prosperity for the king. Although the negative omens outnumber the positive – and this letter reported a whole host of other negative omens – Akkullanu concludes by saying that 'the king my lord can be happy'.[30] How can this be the case?

It all depends on who is affected by the negative omens. The letter was written on 10 June 650 BC, in the middle of Ashurbanipal's war against his brother, who was king of Babylonia – it is he who should be worried rather than the king of Assyria, and indeed around this time the Assyrians were gaining the upper hand. The first omen states that the devastation will afflict Eridu, a city in southern Babylonia that had defected to the rebels. Even so, the bright Mars still seems unfavourable at first sight. When Mars is bright it usually means that the god of war is angry, which only portends well for the king's enemies. But the Babylonians who originally wrote the omens – that the Assyrians had since adopted – had associated the planet with their own enemies in Subartu in the north. Since the Assyrians were also in the north, they were now equating Subartu with themselves. Hence a bright Mars that was good for Subartu in the original omen series was now interpreted to be good for Assyria. This complex chain of logic illustrates how the scholars could turn a negative into a positive. While the omens themselves are overwhelmingly negative in the series, the astrologers tend to find ways to look on the bright side, often finding a reason why the evil will afflict another country rather than their own.

At other times, however, a danger was portended which the astrologers could not interpret their way out of. When such an omen was observed, the exorcists would be called in and a *namburbi* ritual performed to avert the evil it portended. As we saw in the chapter on magic, the ritual was set up like a kind of court where the exorcist appealed the verdict and asked the gods to reconsider. With enough prayers and offerings, perhaps the gods would change their minds.

The type of ritual performed depended on the omen. Two different exorcists report to the king on a retrograding Mars, which announces an invasion of locusts and bad news for Assyria generally. The king is told, 'we are constantly performing rituals and prayers against the evil . . . There is nothing to worry about, the king . . . can be at ease.'[31] One ritual was not enough, it seems; several were needed. Special prayers were performed for the crown prince as well.[32] Other rituals required the participation of the king himself. During an eclipse in the first month, the king was supposed to prostrate himself towards the south while the exorcist smeared his bed with swallows' blood and cypress oil in order to keep the evil away.[33] Others still were highly elaborate affairs performed in the temple. But the beauty of these rituals is that they could be performed even if the scholars were unsure if the omen was a problem, just to reassure the king. Balasi had noted a conjunction of Mars that would normally be a source of anxiety, but he was not too worried since he had measured the distance between the two planets and considered them to still be far away. However, his response to the king was: 'What does it matter? Let the pertinent namburbi ritual be performed.'[34] It was always better to err on the side of caution and appease the gods, rather than ignore their wrath until it was too late.

The most dangerous signs to be observed in the sky were lunar eclipses, since these could predict the death of the king. The king would certainly be worried on such an occasion, as it was a time of great uncertainty, but he himself was not necessarily the target of the moon god's displeasure. As we saw in the letter from Akkullanu, he could comfort himself that *a* king was to die, but which one? The question of which king became the subject of fierce debate after one particular lunar eclipse during Esarhaddon's reign in the year 678 BC. One scholar helpfully explains to Esarhaddon that the evil of the eclipse could affect several different people depending on the month, the day, the time, and where the eclipse starts and ends.[35] Two of the astrologers writing to the king claim that the fourteenth day means Elam[36] – but this did not mean Esarhaddon was off the hook, as there were other variables to take into account.

The moon was divided into quadrants, each of which correlated with a geographical region. The direction in which the eclipse shadow travelled as it moved over the moon influenced which land was affected. In this case, the eclipse started on the upper east side and cleared on the lower west. The two astrologers notify the king of what it means:

> The king of Ur will experience famine; deaths will become many; as for the king of Ur, his son will wrong him, but Shamash will catch the son who wronged his father, and he will die in the mourning-place of his father; a son of the king who has not been named for kingship will seize the throne.[37]

The verdict was unanimous – trouble for the king of Ur. But since the Assyrians ruled Babylonia as well as Assyria, this city in the south was now within Esarhaddon's territory. Technically Esarhaddon was now king of Ur – would he be the one to experience famine, deaths, and betrayal? Fortunately, the planet Jupiter was present during the eclipse, which meant 'well-being for the king, a famous important person will die in his stead'.[38] The king of Assyria did not have to worry after all. The same adviser who pointed this out suggested how to ensure that this more favourable prediction came true. He recommended that the king 'remove one prince from among the nobles of the Chaldeans or Arameans', so that they can bear the ill of the omen, 'and the king my lord can be happy'.[39] The prediction could be fulfilled, and this way the king could even choose which unlucky noble would absorb the evil for him.

There is no doubt that the Assyrians sincerely believed in these omens. One of the scholars reminds the king of a previous occasion when Jupiter was present in an eclipse, and quotes the same prediction, 'well being for the king, a famous noble will die in his place'.[40] Sure enough, in this case, 'A full month had not yet passed before his chief judge lay dead!'[41] As the gods had said, so it came to pass. In other cases, the scholars tried to fulfil the predictions themselves so that they would still come true without causing too much damage, a kind of controlled explosion to prevent a larger disaster. When a lunar eclipse indicated that a flood would come and break the dikes, one astrologer suggested, 'let someone cut through the dikes in Babylonia at night . . . No one will hear about it!'[42] Making this small breach in a specially chosen location would ensure that the gods had their way without ruining the crops as might happen if the dikes failed on a larger scale. Negative predictions could not be dismissed, something had to be done to mitigate them, and the scholars took their responsibilities very seriously.

We consider astronomy and astrology to be very different subjects: the scientific study of the sky versus a more esoteric theory of the planets' influence on human lives. But in Mesopotamia they were one and the same. Those who observed the stars and planets did so in order to interpret their meaning. Scholars who could predict astronomical events had a head start on reading the minds of the gods, and sought ever more accurate understandings of the heavens to help them interpret their messages better. Mathematical astronomy is one of Mesopotamia's greatest achievements, one that forms the very basis of modern science. Yet without astrology there would be no astronomy – the history of the two are intertwined, and developments in one drove developments in the other.

Although it may seem strange to us that hard sciences are so linked with mystical pursuits in Mesopotamia, separating them is a very modern concept. For most of human history and in many different cultures, astronomy and astrology have been studied by the same people, with astrology considered the apex of technical and scientific knowledge. Similarly, as late as the eighteenth century AD the great scientist Isaac Newton, who is famous today for his advances in physics and mathematics, spent most of his time working on alchemy, which he considered his most important area of enquiry. The economist John Maynard Keynes wrote that Newton was 'not the first of the age of reason' but 'the last of the magicians, the last of the Babylonians and Sumerians, the last great mind which looked out on the visible intellectual world with the same eyes as those who began to build our intellectual inheritance'.[43] The Babylonians and Sumerians are closer to us than we might think, both because we have only recently started to think differently from them, and because we owe so much of the intellectual foundations of our culture to them, though it has long been forgotten.

The extreme longevity of cuneiform culture and transmission of knowledge through the ages gave Mesopotamian scholars an extraordinary bank of data to work with, and an extraordinary opportunity to refine it. As we have seen, the Assyrians knew when to expect the appearances and disappearances of the five major planets that were visible to the naked eye, as well as their synodic periods, that is, the time it took for them to return to exactly the same place in the sky. These are set out in an important text in the library called MUL.APIN,[44] a sort of astronomical handbook that was probably compiled by the Babylonians in the late second or early first millennium BC. This model of the heavens was the culmination of early Babylonian astronomy, and formed the basis for further developments. It begins by naming the stars and constellations and setting out in which part of the sky they could be seen, alongside key dates such as their first appearances and last disappearances. It also contains important information relating to calendars – the length of the night at different times of year, the times of the rising and setting of the moon, and the rules for calculating when extra months had to be introduced to keep the solar and lunar calendars in sync. It ends with a list of omens such as 'if a star flares up from the west and enters the Lisi-star: there will be revolution',[45] crowning this astronomical compilation with astrological information.

Stars and planets follow a fairly regular schedule, but the Assyrians struggled a little more with forecasting eclipses. Although they could not yet predict these precisely, they had some good rules of thumb that allowed them to make educated guesses. For example, they knew that lunar eclipses could occur every sixth lunar month and were only possible at full moon, while solar eclipses were only possible at new moon. Ashurbanipal's scholars were also beginning to understand that eclipses recurred in regular patterns, such as the cycle of forty-seven lunar months that we call the octon. The astrologers often wrote to the king informing him that they were expecting an eclipse to take place, and then watched to see whether it would happen.[46] They were not always right, so it was critical that they kept watch to verify their predictions. However, the Babylonians would soon create a system that rendered this superfluous.

In the fifth century BC, two centuries after Ashurbanipal's reign, the Babylonians made one of the greatest breakthroughs in the history of science: they developed mathematical astronomy. This is no exaggeration: in doing so, Babylonian scholars came up with the very concept of creating mathematical models, and the idea that it is possible to extrapolate trends from data, which remain essential tools in science today. Their careful record-keeping enabled them not only to spot patterns but even to develop mathematical formulae that would enable them to calculate the positions of the stars and planets to a remarkable degree of accuracy. No longer did they have to consult tables of the planets' past positions to know where they would be in the future. Now they could plot the major positions of the planets for the coming year using calculations alone and predict eclipses within an accuracy of four minutes.

It began with the invention of the zodiac. The Mesopotamians had long paid attention to which constellations the moon passed through in its journey across the sky, as we can see when Assyrian astrologers refer to them in their letters. But constellations are of different sizes, and the moon spends more time in some than in others. The zodiac system divided the sky into twelve equal chunks and named each one after a constellation, rather than strictly adhering to exactly how much space that constellation took up. This would make their calculations far easier. This system was picked up by the Greeks, along with many other astronomical theories and methods, and consequently the names of most of these constellations are still familiar to us now:

^{mul}LU$_2$.ḪUN.GA$_2$	The Hired Man	Aries
^{mul}GU$_4$.AN.NA	The Bull of Heaven	Taurus
^{mul}MAŠ.TAB.BA.GAL.GAL	The Great Twins	Gemini
^{mul}AL.LUL	The Crab	Cancer
^{mul}UR.GU.LA	The Lion	Leo
^{mul}AB.SIN$_2$	The Furrow	Virgo
^{mul}*zi-ba-ni-tum*	The Balance	Libra
^{mul}GIR$_2$.TAB	The Scorpion	Scorpio
^{mul}PA.BIL.SAG	Pabilsag	Sagittarius
^{mul}SUḪUR.MAŠ$_2$.KU$_6$	The Goat-fish	Capricorn
^{mul}GU.LA	The Great One	Aquarius
^{mul}KUN.MEŠ	The Tails	Pisces

Even those connections that are not obvious at first sight can be explained. 'The hired man' referred to the deified shepherd Dumuzi. In its translation to the Greek system, the symbol morphed into the ram in his flock rather than the man himself, giving us 'Aries', which means ram in Latin. Similarly, Virgo was known as 'the furrow' in Babylonian, but this was depicted by a woman holding an ear of wheat, and Virgo the virgin took over as the more important element in this image. Pabilsag is an archer god, just as Sagittarius is. 'The great one' was identified with the god Ea, who is commonly depicted with streams of water flowing from his shoulders, much like the water carrier Aquarius. As for 'the tails': before the zodiac, the Babylonians thought of Pisces as two separate constellations, which later coalesced into one. Sometimes they are described as two fish tied together with string, or as a bird and a fish bound by a cord, or as two rivers, while 'the fish' is sometimes used as an alternative name for the whole constellation. In these respects, the Babylonian map of the sky is closely connected to ours.

Mapping the sky in these mathematically equal divisions meant that the astrologers could record their observations more precisely, observations which they then set down in astronomical diaries. The earliest such diary surviving today dates from 652 BC, but the diaries most likely began much earlier. The Greek astronomer Ptolemy tells us that he used Babylonian records and that the earliest available to him were eclipse reports from 747 BC.[47] The last diary that we know of dates to the year 22 BC. This means at least six hundred years' worth of data going by primary evidence alone, seven hundred if we take Ptolemy at his word, making this the longest running scientific project in history. In contrast, our current Met Office weather data only extends back one hundred years. By the fifth century BC the Babylonians would have had around two hundred years' worth of extremely precise data to work with in this format, in addition to the rules they and the Assyrians had already assembled. Such a depth of detail meant that they could refine their knowledge of planetary cycles increasingly over time until they were so secure that they could extrapolate mathematical formulae from the data.

The diaries show that Assyrian and Babylonian astrologers had common concerns, as they record all the same phenomena that the Neo-Assyrian astrologers considered important in their reports to the king: the first sighting of the moon each month; the appearances and disappearances of the planets, now with their exact zodiacal positions; eclipses; halos around the sun and moon, and any stars that could be seen there; and weather such as strong winds, rain, and rainbows. They also note rarer occurrences such as meteors and comets, including sightings of Halley's comet in 164 and 87 BC. The diaries keep track of everything considered ominous in *Enuma Anu Enlil*, all the messages the gods were writing in the sky. But the diaries are not only astronomical, despite their name. We also find recorded events on earth that were significant in other omen series too, such as a wolf entering a city and killing two dogs, and a ewe giving birth to a lamb with three heads, three necks, and three buttocks.[48] As the *Babylonian Diviner's Manual* asserts, sky and earth are related, and the diaries are a systematic attempt to understand these correlations better.

The astrologers went further still in this attempt, for the diaries also track the price fluctuations of barley, dates, mustard, cress, sesame, and wool. These six commodities were the most frequently traded staples in the Mesopotamian economy, making this the Babylonian equivalent of tracking the FTSE 100 or the price of oil. The economy was linked with the stars, and astrologers produced forecasts of business conditions for the year ahead. Several tablets even state rules for predicting market rates. For example, in the Hellenistic period one astrologer wrote out a tablet explaining how to predict the price of grain, and whether prices would increase or decrease depending on the positions of the planets.[49]

The astronomical diaries trade in political predictions, too. When Ashurbanipal went to war against his brother, the king of Babylon, and defeated him in battle in 652 BC, Babylonian scholars duly noted it in the diaries. But most strikingly, the diaries record Alexander the Great's entry into Babylon in 331 BC, the moment that Mesopotamia was absorbed into the Greek world.[50] This diary is a particularly fascinating example, as we can see dramatic celestial portents correlating with dramatic political events on earth. Early in the month there was a total lunar eclipse, which usually indicates the death of the king. The king of Babylon at this time was the Persian king Darius, and although the Persians were not very interested in messages from the Mesopotamian gods, the Babylonian astrologers certainly were, and kept a close eye on what happened next. Deaths and plague occurred during the eclipse, which was already a bad start. On the fifteenth of the month a meteor fell. The omen series tells us that this signifies enemy invasion ('if a star flashes and goes down in the east: an enemy host will attack the country, and the enemy will ravage the country').[51] This is exactly what came to pass, of course, with the approach of Alexander and his army. At the same time there were two flashes of lightning (the term used by the Babylonians translates as 'fall of fire'), one of which struck a dog, which seems unlikely to be a good omen. The next month, the king of Babylon was in trouble: panic spread within his camp, his troops were defeated, and he fled to the land of Guti. Soon afterwards, Alexander, 'king of the world', entered Babylon. To the Babylonians none of this would have been coincidence. Perhaps Darius should have paid more attention and been on his guard – after all, the signs were blatantly obvious to anyone familiar with the language of the gods.

The Persians had ruled Babylon since 539 BC, seventy years after the fall of Assyria. The Persian empire is famous for its religious tolerance, particularly because the Judaeans who had been resettled in Babylon were now allowed to go home, and the Babylonians were able to continue with their traditional worship, caring for the gods in their temples and cultivating their scholarship. Even so, temples and scholars started to become less relevant to those in power. Astrology had always been practised on behalf of the king, but now the kings were no longer interested. This may have been the driving force behind another major shift in thinking about the stars: the invention of the horoscope.

The lack of royal patronage spurred astrologers to seek out new clients and other uses for their skills. Babylonians had long believed that a person's date of birth had meaning for the individual, a belief which had spread across the Near East. Hittite translations of Babylonian texts contain omens such as 'if a child is born in the 12th month, this child will grow old and have many sons.'[52] But it is only from the fifth century BC that astrological principles were applied to individuals other than the king and crown prince. The Babylonians began to compile nativity omens more systematically in the Persian period, with one tablet predicting that 'if a child is born in Taurus . . . that man will be distinguished, his sons and daughters will return and he will see gain.'[53] These rather general predictions are the forerunners of horoscopes, which would be much more detailed in terms of what was deemed to be significant.

The earliest horoscope known to us dates from 410 BC.[54] By this time mathematical astronomy had taken off, and so the astrologers could calculate the relevant planetary positions rather than look out for them in the sky. This development was extremely useful since it enabled them to plot horoscopes for any individual no matter what time they were born and regardless of the weather. It would be impossible to observe exactly where the planets were during the day, and it is rare for all the planets to be above the horizon on the same day. Even at night when the planets were out it was often cloudy and difficult to see the sky – 'it was overcast' is an extremely common phrase in the astronomical diaries explaining why there is no record for the night. But now the astrologers could work out exactly which constellations the planets were in at any time, day or night, cloudy or clear.

Our modern horoscopes are the direct descendants of the Babylonian ones, although they use many concepts that were added and developed by the Greeks. Like the birth chart used by astrologers today, Babylonian horoscopes give the positions of the sun, moon, and each of the planets in the zodiac, specified to the precise degree. However, they also include information that ours do not. Babylonian horoscopes are not limited to the date of birth alone but include celestial events taking place several days or even months on either side. They tell us when the moon was last visible in that month, the date of the winter solstice that year, and the nearest eclipses – the same kind of information recorded in the astronomical diaries.

Unfortunately for us the Babylonian horoscopes are mostly pure data, and the interpretations are not usually written down. This is again similar to the birth chart used by astrologers today, which looks all but incomprehensible to the untrained eye – grids of strange symbols and numbers and geometrical diagrams with lines crossing a circle. It is likely that the Babylonian astrologers would have explained the meaning of the data to their clients in person rather than sending a written report, and the horoscopes we have are likely for their own professional use. A very small group of texts from Uruk contain a few short predictions, but they are vague. For example, the horoscope of an individual called Anu-belshunu reads:

> Year 63, (month) Tebetu, evening of day 2 Anu-belshunu was born. That day, the sun was in 9;30° Capricorn, moon was in 12° Aquarius: his days will be long. Jupiter was in the beginning of Scorpius: someone will help the prince. The child was born in Aquarius with/or in the region of Venus: he will have sons. Mercury was in Capricorn; Saturn in Capricorn; Mars in Cancer.[55]

All that the horoscope predicts is a long life, children, and the rather mysterious comment that someone will help the prince – it is unclear whether this will be Anu-belshunu himself. Yet perhaps these were the most significant things from a Babylonian point of view – living to old age was not a given in a society with high infant mortality, and having sons to continue the family line was of utmost importance. As for someone helping the prince, this sounds like the kind of prediction found in the old series *Enuma Anu Enlil* that concentrated on the fortunes of the king. But perhaps this could still be significant to an individual: if the fortunes of the royal family intersected with those of a private person it could have a huge impact on their life.

Anu-belshunu was born in the Hellenistic period, a time when Babylon was ruled by Greeks. Year 63 refers to the sixty-third year of the Seleucid dynasty, named after Alexander the Great's general who ruled in Mesopotamia after his death. Anu-belshunu's day of birth therefore corresponds to 26 December 249 BC in our calendar. This is not all we know about him – Anu-belshunu was a lamentation priest and astrologer with a great collection of tablets, including one that illustrates the constellations.[56] The dates on his tablets show that he was active as a scholar until the age of eighty-three, so his horoscope was right: his days did turn out to be long. He went on to have sons, too: his son Anu-ab-uter copied tablets for him, and his grandson was a lamentation priest in the Anu temple in Uruk, as he himself had been, continuing the family tradition.

Anu-belshunu came from a family of lamentation priests who were responsible for singing to the gods in their temples. Anu-belshunu's family claimed their descent from Sin-leqi-uninni, the composer of the Babylonian *Epic of Gilgamesh*. This family was part of a tight-knit community in Uruk, the old nobility who clung to the old ways as the world around them came more and more under Greek influence. Keeping cuneiform alive was the job of a privileged few, and just as it had always been a small circle of intellectuals who studied the stars, it is likely that the use of personal astrology was also limited to the elite.

It was these elites in the cities of Babylon and Uruk who pursued mathematical astronomy, and by Anu-belshunu's time this had become very advanced indeed. By the second half of the fourth century BC Babylonian scholars had developed two main types of algorithm to predict celestial events, which we call System A and System B. System A enabled them to calculate the positions of planets using step functions, a technique familiar to mathematicians today. The accuracy that could be achieved is astonishing. When planetary positions are calculated according to both Babylonian and modern methods, we see that the Babylonians are only out at the extremes; otherwise they are remarkably close to what we can do with modern computing power.

System B was the linear zigzag function. Astrologers were using this technique as early as the second millennium BC, since we can already find examples of it in *Enuma Anu Enlil*. However, it was astrologers in Uruk who developed this technique to its most sophisticated level in the 260s BC, making it a speciality of Anu-belshunu's home city.

The astronomers used linear zigzag functions to predict astronomical phenomena. Their most sophisticated achievement was in modelling the behaviour of the moon. The length of time during which the moon is visible each night varies over the month and year, and the astronomers came up with a way to predict this in advance. Their models were based on an idealised lunar month of thirty days where the moon's visible hours increase by the same amount each day in the first fifteen days to reach a maximum, and then decrease by equal amounts in the second fifteen days back to the minimum. The same principle was applied over the whole year, so that the moon's visibility was assumed to vary from a minimum at the summer solstice to a maximum at the winter solstice, and then back to the minimum again in summer. When plotted, this looks like a zigzag – hence the name of the function. In reality, the curve of the graph is closer to a sine wave, but this model captures the major factors affecting the moon's visibility and is the earliest example of its kind that we possess in the way that it separates such a complex phenomenon into different components and describes each of them with a simple mathematical function.

The concept can be expressed both as an algebraic formula and on a graph, although these are later inventions, and the Babylonians mainly entered the data in tables. Again, what is striking is the sophistication of the calculations. More than 2,000 years ago the priests of Uruk and Babylon were using advanced mathematics of a type well known to today's scientists. The Babylonian lunar theory of System B underpins the calculations of Greek astronomers such as Ptolemy and Hipparchus, and must have been explained to those scholars by Babylonian astronomers directly, since only those well versed in the technical details would have been able to describe it accurately. Many other Babylonian mathematical concepts have reached us via the Greeks, especially in the realm of astronomy, while others were forgotten and had to be invented for a second time. Babylonian schoolchildren were calculating the lengths of the sides of triangles in the second millennium BC with a version of the theorem that Pythagoras formulated independently 1,400 years later in the sixth century BC. Our knowledge of the extraordinary achievements of Babylonian mathematics is increasing all the time. For instance, in 2016 a newly translated tablet showed that Babylonian astronomers were using a concept essential to modern calculus, calculating the distance travelled by Jupiter by finding the area of a trapezoid.[57] Using a graph to understand motion or speed over time is usually credited to scholars in Oxford and Paris around AD 1350, but the Babylonians were doing it 1,500 years earlier.

In the last years of cuneiform culture, astronomy was the main preoccupation of Mesopotamian scholars. Tablets from Seleucid Uruk, where Anu-belshunu and his colleagues worked, show just how much their priorities had changed: almost half contain mathematical astronomy, vastly outnumbering any other genre of text. It would be easy from a modern standpoint to see this as a decline in the belief that the gods speak through the stars; science and rationalism replacing religion. Yet the messages of the gods must still have had meaning, for if the scholars had truly ceased to think that the omens had any validity they would not have copied them any more. The scholars still kept *Enuma Anu Enlil* in the temple library, as well as the omens about sheep giving birth to lions,[58] foxes crossing a man's path,[59] and markings on the entrails of sacrificial sheep.[60] The astronomical tablets were written by lamentation priests who sang to the gods on a daily basis and used their increasingly accurate data to ensure the correct timing of rituals and festivals. Astronomy was central to the correct running of the temple, and mathematical calculations were carried out in service of the gods. But now that Mesopotamia was ruled by foreign kings who were not interested in what the native gods had to say about their reign, it made more sense for the scholars to keep their heads down and focus on keeping the gods happy rather than relaying messages that would never be heeded. If anything, mathematical astronomy might show a greater interest in understanding the divine, the scholars turning inwards to study what interested them most rather than what their patrons demanded.

Other aspects of cuneiform culture fade away during the long periods of foreign rule, but astronomy holds out to the very end. It is fitting that Uruk is one of the cities where cuneiform lasts the longest, given that it was the first Mesopotamian metropolis, and the birthplace of cuneiform culture. But Babylon also held on, as the city that throughout Mesopotamian history was regarded as the cultural centre. The last cuneiform texts we know of were written in Babylon and Uruk and are sets of astronomical predictions for the coming year. One of these predictions, written in Babylon in AD 74/75, opens with the standard invocation, used for hundreds of years, 'By the command of the deities Bel and Belti may it go well', showing that the gods were still front and centre.[61]

Eventually astrology surpassed extispicy to be considered the most authoritative branch of Mesopotamian science. Its gift was its predictability: you can never know in advance what the gods are going to write inside a sheep, but when they send stars and planets across the sky in recurring patterns their will starts to become more fathomable, and subject to human investigation. Yet the same principles of interpretation are used in astrology as in extispicy and all the other types of omens, from snakes taking up residence in the temple to the shape of the curls in a man's hair. In all of these, certain codes applied: the division of left and right and subdivisions into other zones, the meanings of colours, and, foremost among these codes, the linguistic features that bound the universe together – puns on both Akkadian and Sumerian words, and associations with similar-shaped signs. This framework binds all the Mesopotamian omens together and shows that they belong to a common conception of science, the same methodology applied to different areas, a unified system for understanding the world. While our science uses the experimental method and testing of hypotheses as its fundamental system, theirs is based on the concept of reading messages, both in the belief that the gods are writing messages all around us, and in the idea that esoteric principles of language can help to read them.

The Assyrian king's astrologers, then, were the equivalent of modern scientific advisers, their remit science rather than policy. They did not push the king towards specific courses of action, merely informed him of what was happening in the sky and what it meant. Only occasionally did they use the stars to justify political recommendations, though it may well be that such discussions took place in person after they sent the data in advance. Science is neutral, though can be used in different ways.

Drawing conclusions from this data was not an easy enterprise. The scholars had room to apply their own creativity and judgement in interpreting the omens. Just as happens today, two scholars could disagree about what the data means, and could come to different conclusions. There were also variations in the texts they used, as *Enuma Anu Enlil* seems to have existed in different versions in different cities, and even the same text could give contradictory predictions for the same celestial event, pointing to differences of opinion within the same tradition.

Once again, the mirror can be turned back on us. The way that modern governments use data to inform high-level decisions is not so different from how Mesopotamian diviners selected and presented theirs. What is economics if not a branch of divination, constructing complex models to try to foresee the future rises and falls of markets and the societies that are tied to them? We may consider the sources of that data to be more reliable than the messages of the gods, though predicting the future is a difficult business, no matter how sophisticated our methods. At every point in history, including our own, our understanding of how the world works has been imperfect. This should give us pause for thought when we look back at the Mesopotamian astrologers, whose warnings of the anger of the gods bequeathed to us the foundations of our own scientific methods.

7.
Literature

Thirty-six years before Ashurbanipal's reign, on a hot summer day at the end of the eighth century BC, bad news reaches the city of Kalhu: King Sargon is dead. The chief scribe Nabu-zuqup-kenu can hardly believe what he is hearing. The messenger sent ahead of the returning army is saying that not only has the king been killed in battle – a rare and unexpected thing in itself – but even worse: the enemy has seized the body, and the Assyrians have not been able to wrest it back again. The implications of this are huge. In a state of shock, Nabu-zuqup-kenu retreats to his study and takes down from the shelf Tablet XII of the *Epic of Gilgamesh*.

This tablet contains a dialogue between the legendary King Gilgamesh and his friend Enkidu, who has journeyed to the netherworld and returned. There, Enkidu encountered the souls of various people, rich and poor, and learned of their fate after death. Gilgamesh asks what became of them, and Enkidu answers:

> 'Did you see the one who was killed in battle?' 'I did.
> His mother and father honour him and his wife weeps
> over him.'
> 'Did you see the one whose corpse lies in the steppe?' 'I did.
> His ghost does not rest in the netherworld.'
> 'Did you see the one whose ghost has no one to provide
> for him?' 'I did.
> He eats dregs from the pot and crumbs of bread discarded
> in the street.'[1]

These lines are of such profound significance that Nabu-zuqup-kenu copies the tablet and dates it – the twenty-seventh of Du'uzu 705 BC.

The lines from *Gilgamesh* explain why the failure to recover the body of Ashurbanipal's great-grandfather was such a disaster, since there could not be a proper burial. While this is considered a tragedy in many cultures, leaving bereaved relatives unable to say goodbye, in Mesopotamia it had even more troubling consequences. It was the duty of descendants to provide offerings to the ghosts of their ancestors, which they did in a strikingly literal way. Normally family members would be buried underneath the floor of the house. Their relatives would insert tubes into the ground and pour libations of water into them so that the dead would be able to drink. These offerings fed the ghost in the netherworld and kept it happy. Without these offerings, the ghost would be driven mad with thirst, and in revenge would come back to haunt the family members who had neglected them. The violent manner of death was also important: one who died a natural death had the best conditions, 'drinking clear water on the bed of the gods',[2] while one who was set on fire was not there at all – as the original Sumerian tells us, 'his smoke went up to the sky'.[3] As we saw in Chapter 3, cremation was not usually practised in Mesopotamia, for it was thought to destroy the soul.

The fate met by Sargon, then, matches exactly what is described in the epic – killed in battle, the corpse abandoned and unable to receive offerings, his ghost doomed never to rest, and to forage for scraps like a beggar. It must have been a sombre moment as Nabu-zuqup-kenu wrote out these lines, in the full knowledge that his former master would now be reduced to these circumstances. It had implications for all those who knew him, too, as Sargon's angry ghost would likely soon return.

Then as now, the literary classics were not only great stories but had tangible meaning for people's lives. Nabu-zuqup-kenu turned to a poem at a highly charged time, but he certainly would not have found consolation in these lines. If anything, they would have confirmed his worst fears. He was consulting the poem as a source of philosophical knowledge, a reflection on what happened to the souls of the dead. Its warnings were taken seriously: soon afterwards, the new capital city that the king had founded was abandoned in case Sargon's ghost came back to haunt it. The seat of governance was moved to Nineveh, where Nabu-zuqup-kenu's tablets eventually ended up in the royal collection that formed the beginnings of Ashurbanipal's library. His signed and dated version of *Gilgamesh* Tablet XII was found among the library tablets when the hill was excavated in the nineteenth century AD.

The library's great works of literature have much to tell us about Mesopotamian culture more broadly. Many of these poems are still read today because of their universal themes and resonance with our common humanity, but at the same time, they preserve a very Mesopotamian mindset, showing us what the Mesopotamians considered to be the big questions and giving us their answers. These works were treasured by both the Assyrians and Babylonians – to travel deeper into their world we will consider three of their most influential works of literature. The poems encode the values of the society that produced them, from the position of women to the meaning of good rule. They deal with the meaning of life and death, the problem of human suffering, and the nature of the gods, and stand as a testament to the depth of Mesopotamian thought and feeling.

We begin with the *Epic of Gilgamesh* since it is so central to Mesopotamian culture and to our modern understanding of it. *Gilgamesh* now appears as the first item in many 'great books' courses because it is increasingly recognised as the first work of 'Western' literature, even though it comes from the Middle East. *Gilgamesh* is far from the oldest work of Mesopotamian literature – the library contains many stories that are even older – but it is the first to conform to the model of storytelling that has become dominant in our modern culture: a hero goes on a journey, driven by a thirst for meaning; he overcomes many obstacles, and returns home changed. This is the archetypal hero's journey identified in 1949 by Joseph Campbell that has become mainstream among storytelling gurus and Hollywood films. *Gilgamesh* has enough highs and lows for any blockbuster, with its heroic battles and quests, and a protagonist who is deeply flawed yet inspirational. It moves us deeply as Gilgamesh suffers the agony of the death of his best friend and has to come to terms with his own mortality. Love, loss, fame, desire, hubris and comeuppance: *Gilgamesh* has everything, a perfect story.

Gilgamesh was the second most popular poem in Mesopotamia in the first millennium BC. It was beaten only by the Babylonian *Epic of Creation*, which we encountered in Chapter 2. Popularity is inferred here by the number of surviving copies that have been found and the variety of locations they come from. The poem has been pieced together from around seventy-five different clay tablets that were discovered in all the major centres of Assyrian and Babylonian scholarship. It spread abroad both in its original language and in translation, reaching as far afield as Ugarit on the coast of Syria and the Hittite capital Hattusa in Turkey. Gilgamesh was a great traveller, both in the poem and in the real world where his story spread. It is Ashurbanipal's library, of course, that is the best source of our knowledge of the epic, since it has the most copies and the best-preserved manuscripts.

The whole story is subdivided into twelve tablets, each tablet forming a self-contained part of the story much like a chapter in a book today or an episode of a TV series. The library contained five different 'sets' of the poem, meaning that each tablet in the set was written out by the same person and they clearly belong together (like a DVD box set edition). But none of these sets contains every chapter in the series. It is tempting to put this down to an accident of discovery and assume that we simply have not found the missing tablets, but among all the libraries known to us, none of them contained a single complete series, only selected tablets from each of them. Ashurbanipal was the only one who aspired to a complete collection.

This surprising fact strikes at the heart of what these libraries were for. We assume libraries are places to look up information that we do not already know, but in Mesopotamia it may sometimes have been the opposite. Assyrian and Babylonian scholars would have learned many of these texts by heart during their training, and only written them out as proof of what they knew, or copied them as part of the process of memorisation. Of all the collections of tablets that have been found, the one that contains the most works of literature, aside from Ashurbanipal's, is a scribal school in an Assyrian part of Turkey, where trainees were learning to write and studying the Mesopotamian classics for the first time. Many of the personal libraries held by individual scholars are a product of this process, and much of the knowledge that was handed down was oral in nature. No one needed a complete copy of *Gilgamesh* in their library because everybody knew how the story went. But they did keep individual chapters of it, perhaps to help train the next generation of scholars, to preserve the knowledge in written form as a backup, to use it in a ritual, consult their favourite chapters as a means of reflection like Nabu-zuqup-kenu, or perhaps for some other reason still unknown to us. There is still much we do not understand about the interface between the oral and the written in Mesopotamia.

The royal collection contains more copies of *Gilgamesh* than any other work of literature. Given the library's concern with matters of statecraft, this is no surprise. *Gilgamesh* was a source of wisdom and inspiration to the Assyrian kings, who modelled themselves on the deeds of the eponymous king, but who also should have learned from the tragedy of his example.

Gilgamesh himself is extremity personified. He is five and a half metres tall, vastly strong, and indeed is literally superhuman: the epic tells us he is two-thirds divine and only one-third human, but that one-third ensures that he is still one of us. It is built into his nature to push the limits, and not only in his quest to conquer mortality. He takes everything to extremes – on an expedition to the cedar forest he obtains the timber necessary for the construction of splendid buildings back home, but he cuts down too much and reduces the forest to a wasteland. His extreme emotions drive him to rash behaviour as he is quick to anger and assumes everyone he meets is a threat. His automatic reaction is to fight even those who are only too pleased to help him – when he comes to the waters of death he encounters a group of creatures called 'the stone ones' and immediately kills them all, only afterwards realising that they were the ones who would have carried him across safely. Ambitious, headstrong, never satisfied, and always striving, it is easy to see in him the classic tragic pattern of the overreaching hero.

Gilgamesh was a legendary king of the Sumerian city of Uruk. Historical facts about his life have all been lost to myth, and he became the archetype of a strong, successful ruler. This is despite the fact that the epic often shows him behaving foolishly. Tablet I depicts him as a harsh king, oppressing his people, wearing out his young men by forcing them to take part in games to the point of exhaustion, and insisting on having the right of the first night with every new bride in the city. The people cry out to the gods in protest, and the gods answer their prayers, deciding to teach Gilgamesh a lesson. They do so in a rather roundabout way. Instead of intervening directly, they initiate a chain of events that will lead Gilgamesh to realise the value of the human life that he so carelessly abuses.

The gods send him a friend, Enkidu, whom the birth goddess creates from a pinch of clay and throws down into the steppe. Enkidu lives like an animal, drinking at the waterhole with the gazelles and eating game caught in hunters' traps, until a priestess from the temple of Ishtar is sent to bring him to Uruk. The priestess Shamhat seduces Enkidu, and they have sex for seven consecutive days and nights – and, as came to light with the discovery of a new fragment in 2018, then another round of the same again, making the marathon fourteen days in total.[4] After this Enkidu loses some of his superhuman strength and his former friends the gazelles turn away from him. He has lost his animal nature and through this initiatory experience gains understanding and starts to become a civilised human being.

Although Shamhat is not an ordinary woman, the fact that it is a sexual encounter that transforms Enkidu chimes with Babylonian views on sex as positive and celebrated. Other Mesopotamian texts are not shy in their depictions, such as the juicy love songs between the young goddess Inanna and her shepherd husband Dumuzi, with their metaphors of ploughing and growth that express joy and pleasure as well as the creation of life. As these agricultural metaphors attest, far from the view of sexuality being something animal, for the Babylonians it is an elevating force linked with civilisation itself, part of what it means to be truly human, and what separates Enkidu from the herd.

Shamhat gives Enkidu clothes and teaches him how to take food and drink in the civilised way and takes him to Uruk in Tablet II. When Enkidu hears about Gilgamesh mistreating his subjects, he is outraged and takes it upon himself to bring an end to it. He rushes to the house of the bride whom Gilgamesh is visiting and wrestles him in the doorway. The two are a match for each other, a first for Gilgamesh, and after the fight they become firm friends. Enkidu becomes Gilgamesh's close companion and accompanies him on every venture. But the adventures they embark on result in Enkidu's demise.

The next phase of the story begins with Gilgamesh departing on his expedition to the cedar forest in Lebanon. In the forest lives the monster Humbaba, whom Gilgamesh wants to kill to win glory and fame, so that his deeds will be remembered for ever. It's a notion that's familiar from war poetry of all ages, from Achilles and the *Iliad* to the poets of the First World War. But there's a problem – Humbaba is sacred to the god Enlil, who has put him there to protect the forest. Enkidu is initially against the plan, but ultimately joins to support his friend. They fight the monster in Tablet V until he begs for mercy, specifically appealing to Enkidu to persuade Gilgamesh to spare his life. But Enkidu is deaf to his pleas and encourages Gilgamesh to finish the monster off, quoting his own words back at him to remind him of his thirst for glory.

In the wake of their victory Gilgamesh and Enkidu cut down the trees of the forest and bring the timber back to Uruk along with the head of Humbaba. Enkidu, surveying the devastation, fears the gods' reaction: 'my friend, we have turned the forest into a wasteland!'[5] Little does he know that the gods have planned this right from the start. The gods are already angry, and the slaying of Humbaba is part of their plan to set Gilgamesh's quest in motion. This is Gilgamesh and Enkidu's first disregard for the will of the gods: the second is soon to follow.

Back in Uruk and aglow with victory, in Tablet VI Gilgamesh catches the eye of the goddess Ishtar. She is filled with desire for him and in an astonishing inversion of norms she proposes marriage. Mesopotamian marriages were arranged by families rather than being love matches, so a woman proposing would have been unusual. Even more astonishing, however, is Gilgamesh's response. Not only does he refuse the goddess – a dangerous gamble – but he hurls a catalogue of insults at her, describing how she condemned all her former lovers to suffering: the husband of her youth now weeps perpetually, the allallu-bird whose wing she broke now cries in the forest, the horse that she loved is now subject to the lash; she turned a shepherd into a wolf, and when she was refused by her father's gardener he too met a grisly end.[6] Gilgamesh's reply is an extreme case of what the Greeks would call hubris, a catastrophically misjudged display of arrogance and defiance, since his diatribe even includes sarcastic mimicry and mocking. Gilgamesh, who in later traditions is somehow remembered for his wisdom, still has a lot to learn about diplomacy.

Enraged, Ishtar runs crying to her father and mother, the sky god and his wife, and asks her father Anu to give her the Bull of Heaven so that she can punish Gilgamesh for his disrespect. Her father rebukes her for provoking Gilgamesh, but agrees. This passage is often compared with one in Homer's *Iliad* – there, the goddess of love Aphrodite is wounded in battle by the mortal Greek warrior Diomedes, and similarly goes weeping to her parents. She pleads with the sky god Zeus for his help in avenging the slight, and he tells her off for meddling in things she has no business being involved with.

The uncanny correspondence of certain details in these passages hints that this could be more than coincidence. Aphrodite is the equivalent of Ishtar in Greek religion, and her father Zeus is a sky god like Anu. Furthermore, here Zeus's wife is not Hera but another character given a name that is just a female equivalent of his own (Dione, derived from 'Dios', a form of 'Zeus'), just as the Babylonian sky god's wife is (Antu, from Anu). This character is suspiciously absent from the rest of Greek epic. Was this scene copied from *Gilgamesh* by Homer? Or was it a type scene that appeared in many different poems across the Near East and Mediterranean, a formula which was changed slightly each time and adapted to each new story? Or is it just coincidence after all?

Either way, this is just one of many parallels between Mesopotamian and early Greek poetry that points to an interconnected ancient world where ideas travelled along with traders, forming a cultural continuum. East and West are not so distant or separate, but are linked by millennia of exchanges. Such parallels also challenge the idea of Western literature beginning with the Greeks – even Homer drew on earlier material and was influenced by others, and some of that influence came from the East, whether directly or indirectly. Little is known about Greek literature before Homer, since he lived in a world of oral poetry and no other contemporary works survive to the same extent. But while pre-Homeric Greece is a great unknown from the point of view of the written record, Mesopotamia is brimming with stories that may have been part of Greek literary heritage, however distantly.

The Bull of Heaven that Ishtar requests is no ordinary bull but the constellation Taurus. This mighty heavenly body stampedes over Gilgamesh's land, destroying the crops. Its snort opens up immense cracks in the earth, into which people fall and die. Gilgamesh and Enkidu go out to fight the monster, duly dispatching it. But once again, they go too far – Enkidu tears a limb from the bull and throws it in Ishtar's face as she watches from the city walls. His civilising education has not yet included respect for the gods, apparently, but then Gilgamesh is hardly a model to learn from.

Punishment is swift: the next thing we hear, in Tablet VII, is that Enkidu has been struck by a mysterious illness sent by the gods.

Enkidu dies and Gilgamesh is overwhelmed with grief. Unable to believe his friend is really gone, he sits by the corpse for days and days until a maggot falls out of Enkidu's nose, and then he wanders the steppe dressed in the rags of a lion skin instead of his kingly regalia. This is his first real loss – but also a moment of horrified realisation that he is mortal and will die. No one can escape death's clutches, not even a king.

So intense is their friendship that readers have often speculated about the exact nature of the relationship between Gilgamesh and Enkidu. The Babylonian epic gives hints that it may be something more, but is never explicit, comparing the strength of their affection to the bond between husband and wife. When Gilgamesh dreams of a meteorite falling to earth, his mother interprets it as predicting the arrival of a companion, adding, 'you will love him like a wife, caressing and embracing him'.[7] And when Enkidu dies, Gilgamesh covers his friend's face as if veiling a bride.[8] Whether or not it is said outright, many have assumed that Enkidu is not only a friend but a lover, with whom Gilgamesh was intimate in both senses of the word. But the fact that the epic leaves this ambiguous is interesting in itself, and implies that it is not the most important facet of their relationship. Rather, the focus is on love between two people, and friendship – the idea that everyone needs a friend and equal, even those who are lonely at the top.

The life-changing nature of Gilgamesh's friendship with Enkidu provides another parallel with the *Iliad*. There, the warrior Achilles is moved to rejoin the fighting at Troy after the death of his beloved companion Patroclus. He knows that going back into battle will lead to his death, but he chooses this because it will win him immortal fame, whereas if he returns home he will die in peaceful old age but obscurity. Gilgamesh wants actual immortality, but in the end will have to settle for an eternal name. Both epics, then, deal with the issue of how far one can go in the name of glory, and at what cost, with both journeys initiated by the death of a close friend.

Enkidu's death may launch Gilgamesh's journey, but it sends him off in the wrong direction. His response to the realisation that he too will die is not to come to terms with his mortality, but to set off on a quest for immortality instead. Gilgamesh knows that there is one man who did become immortal: Uta-napishti, who lives at the other end of the world, across the waters of death. Gilgamesh travels there through Tablets IX and X, meeting fantastical creatures on the way and having to outrun the sun as he uses the tunnel it passes through each night to get to the other side of the world. When he arrives, desperate and exhausted, the sage Uta-napishti tells him the story of how he attained immortality.

The story told by Uta-napishti in Tablet XI is that of the deluge, when the gods sent a flood to wipe out all humanity. The story is certainly not what Gilgamesh had hoped for. Uta-napishti's immortality turns out to be a one-off, a reward for surviving the deluge, but one which he can only enjoy if he remains exiled from society, at the very edges of the earth. One cannot imagine Gilgamesh would be very happy with such an existence, stripped of his royal powers and living in relative solitude. In any case, the flood was such an extraordinary event it was unlikely to be repeated. There's also a note of 'who do you think you are anyway?' in Uta-napishti's tone when he asks, 'who will bring the gods to assembly for you so you can find the life you search for?'[9] Gilgamesh is not as special as he thinks he is.

Yet even after all this, Gilgamesh is still not ready to give up. Uta-napishti challenges him to go without sleep for six days and seven nights to see if he has what it takes to live for ever. Exhausted by his journey, Gilgamesh fails the test and falls asleep immediately, his deep sleep betrayed by a series of increasingly mouldy loaves of bread that Uta-napishti's wife leaves beside him to measure the time. As an alternative, Uta-napishti tells Gilgamesh about a special plant that will give him a different kind of vitality – if he can recover it from the bottom of the seabed, he can eat it and regain his youth. Gilgamesh succeeds in obtaining the plant, inventing deep sea diving in order to do so. But on the way home, he leaves the plant on the shore while bathing in a pool, and a snake gobbles it up. The snake gains the ability to continually regenerate itself by shedding its skin, a mythological explanation for how it acquired this power. Gilgamesh has thrown away the tools that he used to obtain the plant, and cannot get any more. Devastated, he weeps at the futility of his quest and his own carelessness, and has no choice but to return home empty-handed.

At this point the story ends rather abruptly. Gilgamesh returns to Uruk and gazes at the walls of his mighty city. These will be all that is left of him when he dies. They may not be much consolation to him, but the walls were still standing centuries later and were evidence to a contemporary Mesopotamian audience of Gilgamesh's existence and fame. In an earlier version of the poem, the tavern-keeper's wife Siduri counsels Gilgamesh to accept his mortal fate and take what pleasures he can from life while it lasts, filling his belly with fine food, dancing, and making merry, delighting in his wife's embrace, and gazing at his children. The implication is that the only immortality he will have is through his descendants. This speech is omitted in the first millennium version in Ashurbanipal's library, where instead it is Uta-napishti who delivers the sermon on the impermanence of life. The message is similar, but gloomier, focusing on the inevitability of death and the fleeting nature of life:

> No one sees death,
> no one see the face of death,
> no one hears the voice of death:
> yet savage death is the one who hacks man down.
> At some time we build a household,
> at some time we start a family,
> at some time the brothers divide,
> at some time feuds arise in the land.
> At some time the river rose and brought the flood,
> the mayfly floating on the river.
> Its countenance was gazing on the face of the sun,
> then all of a sudden nothing was there![10]

Gilgamesh at the end of the epic is very different from how he was at the start – the arrogant and overbearing king has been reduced to weeping and regret. The prologue tells us that he gained great wisdom through his journey, but the poem does not show how he puts that wisdom into action. We are left to imagine the future Gilgamesh without being told what this wisdom is and how it changes him. Does he become a better man, a more compassionate ruler? Is he broken by his failed quest, or does he recover? This elliptical nature is typical of Babylonian poetry, which is full of suggestions that invite us to imagine for ourselves rather than telling us outright. This appeal to the imagination and the raising of questions rather than answering them is to my mind one of its greatest appeals. The omissions are what makes the imagination spark like static electricity jumping across a gap, or like synapses, the spaces for signals to carry our thoughts.

For this reason, the mirror of Gilgamesh allows us to see whatever we want in it. We can identify with him as a grieving friend, or as a man struggling to find meaning in his life and to deal with difficult emotions. At the same time he is rash, foolish, and arrogant. In modern times he has been interpreted as a queer icon, a superhero, and even an out-of-touch business tycoon. Gilgamesh is a complex character, one of the most complex in all Babylonian literature.

But what would Gilgamesh have meant to the Assyrians and Babylonians? The poem's multiplicity of meanings make this harder to determine. To intellectuals like Nabu-zuqup-kenu it was a source of wisdom in its own right. Although we will never know why exactly he chose to write it out on that fateful day, the circumstances of Sargon's death suggest that he was consulting it for what it said about the afterlife. As a scholar he surely would have known the fate that awaited Sargon, but perhaps copying out the tablet was a way for him to reflect on it. The epic is philosophical in other ways too. Enkidu tells us what happens to us after death, but the rest of the poem has much to teach us about life and how we should live, largely by not following Gilgamesh's example.

One aspect that would have especially appealed to the scribes was its emphasis on the need for a king to take advice. Gilgamesh heedlessly rushes into action without consulting his advisers, and comes to grief because of it. Incapable of restraint, he does not listen to Enkidu when he warns him not to kill the sacred monster Humbaba, nor to the elders of the city, nor to his mother, who also counsels him not to go. After Enkidu's death his wanderings in the wilderness are a complete abdication of his kingly responsibilities – we hear nothing at all about the city he is supposed to be ruling while he is off on his adventures. One moral of the story must be that unrestrained power is destructive, and kings need to be guided by others. This is certainly a view that the king's advisers would have shared. One tablet in Ashurbanipal's library contains a list of warnings of terrible things that will happen to a king who ignores his advisers: 'if he has no regard for the due process of his land, Ea, king of destinies, will alter his destiny and misfortune will hound him', and 'if he has no regard for his scholarly advisers, his land will rebel against him.'[11] Esarhaddon's former exorcist Urad-Gula even alluded to this text when asking the king to restore him to his position, a subtle way of reminding him of his commitment to listen.[12]

The Assyrian kings do not seem to have picked up on this message. For them, Gilgamesh was a superhero adventurer, the embodiment of power and might. The same Sargon who would later be killed in battle portrayed himself as another Gilgamesh wandering over the mountains and journeying to the cedar forest in his account of his military campaigns. Esarhaddon, too, alluded to Gilgamesh when he described how he drove his usurping brothers out and seized the throne as the true king. Schoolchildren mocked these pretensions by writing fictional letters purportedly from Gilgamesh that take the tropes of Assyrian royal inscriptions to absurd extremes, such as demanding a foreign king send him '80,000 jugs of wine, 80,000 bundles of crocuses, 90,000 great tabletops of dark rosewood, and 100,000 donkeys laden with cedar and juniper'.[13] But omen texts, too, prefer Gilgamesh as warrior, as omens invoking Gilgamesh are connected with great military strength. Both of these Gilgameshes exist, the superhero to be emulated and the reckless king who should not be, and could be repurposed as needed. One of the library's many manuscripts of the poem is labelled with a declaration that it was copied and checked by Ashurbanipal himself – which Gilgamesh would he have identified with?[14] As both a mighty king and a trained scholar, perhaps Ashurbanipal would have seen both sides.

Despite his portrayal as a heroic, war-mongering man, women play a key role in supporting Gilgamesh throughout his journey. Many crucial elements in the plot turn upon the actions of women – Shamhat brings Enkidu to Uruk, Gilgamesh's mother prays for them to return safely from the cedar forest and consequently Shamash looks after them; the alewife Siduri gives him directions to Uta-napishti, and it is Uta-napishti's wife who suggests that Gilgamesh look for the plant of life. Women have the power to change the course of Gilgamesh's story, and without their intervention he would not have got far. Mesopotamian women had a moderate amount of freedom by the standards of the ancient world, since they were able to own property, run businesses, and divorce their husbands, although they still lived within a highly patriarchal society. Accordingly, women in *Gilgamesh* are highly influential, and have key roles at every step.

Gilgamesh returns to Uruk at the close of Tablet XI, which finds him gazing up at the walls of his city. But the lines quoted at the beginning of this chapter, which Nabu-zuqup-kenu copied out, are from Tablet XII – an extra tablet that was added on to the end of the story. It translates part of an earlier Sumerian poem about Gilgamesh and Enkidu which cannot belong to the story as it is here told, since Enkidu has already died in Tablet VII, but which provides a reflection on the poem's main theme: death and what follows it.[15] In this tablet, Enkidu and Gilgamesh are playing a game when a hole opens up in the earth and the ball and mallet fall into it, right down into the netherworld. Enkidu decides to go and retrieve the items. He ignores Gilgamesh's instructions not to draw attention to himself, however, and ends up being 'seized' by the netherworld. It is his ghost that comes up to the world of the living to tell Gilgamesh of the conditions endured by the dead. In another scene reminiscent of classical epic, Gilgamesh embraces his friend's shade, but while Homer and Virgil stress the impossibility of this, the ungraspable spirits vanishing to the touch, for Gilgamesh and Enkidu the embraces are real.

Babylonian literature paints the afterlife as a gloomy place. One did not enjoy a happier stay for being a good person or adhering to any particular religious cult, as was the case in Greece and Rome. The best one could hope for was to have one's thirst quenched and a measure of respect, but this is hardly paradise, and in any case was not linked to good deeds but simply the number of children who would be taking care of the person's grave. The netherworld is further described in another poem from the library, the *Descent of Ishtar*, which describes the goddess's journey there:

> To the house that none leaves who enters,
> To the road whose journey has no return,
> To the house whose entrants are deprived of light,
> Where dust is their sustenance and clay their food.
> They see no light but dwell in darkness,
> They are clothed like birds in garments of feathers,
> And dust has settled on the door and bolt.[16]

There is nothing to eat but dust, no sunlight and no water. Not only is it dark, but it is dry, and deathly still – the dust that gathers on the door and bolt testament to its eerie silence. The dead are described as like birds, which may reflect the movement of spirits flitting around. In a similar vein, birds flying into the house unexpectedly were thought to be the souls of dead ancestors. This was not a positive omen, however, and required a ritual to avert its evil. The return of the dead was not a good thing.

With such a miserable afterlife, Siduri's words to Gilgamesh gain a real immediacy: enjoy life while it lasts. To be blessed with many children was not only an advantage in death, but in life also for the family-oriented Babylonians. Ultimately, the Babylonians did not glorify death but celebrated life in the here and now, and life is as present a theme in *Gilgamesh* as death.

Gilgamesh is the culmination of one and a half thousand years of literary tradition. The popular version of the epic as told here is a reworking of Sumerian tales about Gilgamesh, which were originally separate and short. The expedition to the cedar forest and the killing of the Bull of Heaven were two distinct stories, which were then joined together in an Akkadian version of the poem written in the early to mid-second millennium BC, the classic period of Babylonian literature and culture.[17] There was also another poem, about the death of Gilgamesh, which does not feature in the Babylonian epic. The version that we read today, then, the 'Standard Babylonian version', is a reworking of a reworking carried out in the late second millennium BC. The late addition of Tablet XII, plus a prologue framing the king's journey as a quest for wisdom, changes the emphasis from a tale of heroic deeds to a meditation on death. Gilgamesh has been reinvented many times in Mesopotamia already, even before he gets to us.

As we have seen, one of the most important myths in all Mesopotamian culture was that of the great flood. Gilgamesh is not the only poem to tell this story; it had earlier been enshrined in another Babylonian classic, the poem of *Atrahasis*, named after its hero who survived the deluge.[18] The account of the flood that Uta-napishti gives Gilgamesh in Tablet XI is a retelling of what was originally a much longer story. In the poem of *Atrahasis* the flood is also the pinnacle of the narrative, but it is embedded in a different kind of tale, one that explains how and why human life was created as well as how it was nearly destroyed, and shows the power structures that govern the universe being set up for the first time. Uta-napishti and Atrahasis are in fact the same person: having originally been known as Atrahasis ('exceedingly wise'), after the flood he is given the new name Uta-napishti ('he found life') by Enlil.

Like the *Epic of Gilgamesh*, *Atrahasis* has a long history – both the myth of the flood and its hero have Sumerian origins, though they are best preserved in an Akkadian poem from the second millennium BC. This was passed on into the first millennium BC and seems to have been re-edited, though with a light touch. Not very much of the first-millennium version survives, but what does differs from earlier versions only in wording and minor details. Ashurbanipal's library contains copies of *Atrahasis*, though the tablets are broken and only parts of the text can be reconstructed from it. Nevertheless, Ashurbanipal's version is extremely important since it became embroiled in a fierce, decades-long debate between Assyriologists about the meaning of the poem's first line. The Old Babylonian version begins, 'when the gods were men'. This is an extraordinary statement that implies that gods had once been human, and that the boundary between god and man was thinner than had been thought. However, the Assyrian version is 'when the gods were *like* men', explicitly stating another interpretation that had been argued for the earlier version as well. This was one ancient scholar's attempt to explain a grammatical ambiguity in the original that had become obscure in Assyrian times: adding the extra word was supposed to clarify the meaning. But when it was discovered by modern scholars it heaped fuel on the raging argument. Such tiny differences in grammar can have huge ramifications. After forty-seven years of scholarly debate, it was finally agreed that the gods were never human after all, but they were once in the same position as us – toiling upon the earth.

Atrahasis begins by outlining hierarchies among the gods and explaining how these came to be. The three top gods of the pantheon – Anu, Enlil, and Ea – draw lots for the different realms of the cosmos. Anu draws the sky, Enlil the earth, and Ea the Apsu, the watery domain beneath the earth that supplies the rivers and groundwater. Already this tells us that the universe is governed by chance – there is nothing special about Enlil that makes him lord of the earth, for instance: he simply won it in a lottery. These three gods are part of the 'Anunnaki', a group of gods who imposed forced labour upon an underclass of gods called the 'Igigi'. The Igigi gods were forced to work the land, digging canals and watercourses just as the Mesopotamians themselves would have done. Such watercourses were essential for the irrigation systems that made the fertile crescent fertile, and enabled the development of agriculture in southern Iraq. The origins of irrigation, then, are enshrined in mythology. However, since the Igigi are gods their work takes place on a cosmic scale – these are not just any irrigation channels being dug, but the very rivers themselves, the Tigris and Euphrates.

This is extremely hard work, and eventually the Igigi gods rebel. In the first workers' dispute in history, they go on strike, and demand that Enlil relieve them of their hard labour. They set fire to their tools and surround his house in the middle of the night. As a tactic it works – the gods decide to create humans as a substitute to do the work. It is worth noting that they don't face much opposition to their demands – Anu immediately agrees that their work is too hard, and the solution is implemented immediately. If trade unions had existed in Mesopotamia it would have been an ideal founding myth.

The strike's success comes at a cost, however; a sacrifice is needed for the creation of the new army of workers. The first human is created out of a pinch of clay, just like Enkidu is in the *Epic of Gilgamesh*, but there is another crucial ingredient – the leader of the gods' rebellion is slain, and his blood mixed in with it. This divine ingredient is what gives rise to 'the ghost', perhaps what we would call the soul, an animating spirit beyond the flesh. We all have a little bit of divinity within us, as is even reflected by the words used for 'man' and 'god' – the Babylonian word *awilum*, meaning man, contains the word for god, *ilum*. Before we get carried away with this thought, though, we should remember that it is an inferior class of deity that resides within people, rather than the all-powerful ruling gods. Nevertheless, this deity led an uprising against the established order and its injustice, and so this is what gives humanity its rebellious spirit.

According to this poem, the meaning of life is work. Humans were created to do the work of the gods and to serve them. Not only to dig irrigation channels, but to produce food, which they must then give to the gods as offerings. This is made all too clear by what happens next, when humanity is nearly wiped out by the flood.

Creating humans has had unintended consequences. When creating life, the gods forgot to create death, and so the numbers got out of control. After 1,200 years, the sheer number of people on the earth has spiralled and the noise is unbearable. The hustle and bustle of normal life is amplified to such an extent that Enlil cannot sleep. As we saw in Chapter 2, Enlil overreacts by deciding to kill off everyone. First he tries plague and famine, but both of these fail because Ea, god of wisdom, foresees the problems this will cause and intervenes. Twice thwarted, Enlil tries another even more drastic approach by unleashing a flood. Ea tells his servant Atrahasis to build a boat, and take on board two of every species of animal life, as well as craftsmen so that human civilisation can rebuild itself again.

The flood is a terrifying event. The sky goes black, darkness is total, the water roars like a bull and the wind screams like a wild ass. Even the gods are terrified; they flee to the highest reaches of heaven and curl up like dogs. With no one to make offerings to them they become parched and famished, and as soon as the flood is over Atrahasis makes a sacrifice to them and they crowd around the smoke of the burning offering to regain their strength. Here the recriminations begin – Enlil is berated for sending the flood with no thought for the consequences. He defends himself by declaring that he was not the only one involved: 'all the great gods together decided on an oath.'[19] Enlil accuses Ea of not sticking to what was agreed and thus sabotaging the plan. The mother goddess blames herself for going along with it as she laments the destruction of her creatures. It is chaos. The disagreement among the gods as a collective, as well as their impulsive natures as individuals, illustrates that the world is a messy place, governed by whim and accident as much as by design. Another moral of the flood story is that the gods make mistakes. Not only was it a mistake to send the flood, but their creations were not perfect the first time around, and required a process of trial and error. Is it any wonder that the world is such an imperfect place, if the gods are making it up as they go along?

After nearly wiping out themselves as well as humankind, the gods have to come up with another solution to overpopulation. They create death, and also sterility. Some women will not be able to have children – and special religious positions are created for them so that they can still have a useful role in society – but most importantly, everyone will die. According to an older Sumerian tradition, after the deluge human lifespans were also reduced – the tens of thousands of years enjoyed by the antediluvian kings become a thing of the past.

Like *Gilgamesh*, this poem was considered a repository of knowledge and was relevant to real life. When one exorcist writes to an Assyrian king advising him what to do in times of famine, his advice mirrors Ea's advice to Atrahasis: perform prayers and offerings to the rain god Adad. He then quotes the poem in support of his recommendations:

> Seek the gate of Adad, bring *upuntu*-flour
> before him, let *maṣhatu*-flour come to him
> as an offering; so that he will rain down a mist in the morning,
> let the field furtively bring a double harvest.[20]

The exorcist's point is that if this tactic worked thousands of years ago, it would work again now. While praying to the rain god for rain may seem like an obvious strategy, the thinking at work here is more subtle than that, since it links into a much wider set of ideas about how the universe functions. *Atrahasis* sets out a fundamental principle about the nature of the gods and their relationship with humanity: it is a reciprocal one. Human beings may have been created to serve the gods, but the gods need us almost as much as we need them. Had they really destroyed us all, they would also have destroyed themselves. While the gods are often remote, incomprehensible, and angry, with human beings despairing in trying to put the relationship right, they do have some influence to bargain with. It was possible to change their minds, and perhaps avert even greater catastrophes.

Both *Gilgamesh* and *Atrahasis* are Akkadian poems based on ancient Sumerian traditions that evolved over the long span of Mesopotamian history. But there was also plenty of Sumerian literature that remained very much Sumerian – the works faithfully transmitted over the years and treasured as classics in the original language.

Sumerian literature is incredibly rich. It spans myths, hymns in praise of the gods, the adventures of legendary kings, and lamentations over destroyed cities, as well as texts relating directly to everyday life such as proverbs, debate poems and satires poking fun at schoolteachers. Most of these were written down for the first time in the Old Babylonian period (2003–1595 BC), Babylon's first era of prominence. Surprisingly, most of it survives not on carefully stored library tablets but in the form of schoolwork – homework that was thrown away and preserved accidentally. For example, nearly one and a half thousand cuneiform tablet fragments were found in a Babylonian scribal school in the city of Nippur that was active in the 1740s BC. These tablets were not neatly placed on shelves but had been built into the very fabric of the building, used as filler material in the walls, floors, and even furniture, with the tablets serving as bricks for school benches. The poems were memorised and written out for practice, then discarded. The school also had a recycling bin where used tablets could be soaked in water and smoothed out again, ready to be written on by another child.

Consequently many of the works of Sumerian literature that we know are educational, either instilling good Sumerian values in children or telling tales exciting enough to hold their attention during difficult lessons – ideally both. The very earliest literature that we know of in the world is probably *The Instructions of Shuruppak*,[21] a long speech from a father to his son giving him advice for life, including such gems as 'you should not pass judgement when you drink beer', 'you should not serve things but things should serve you' and 'a woman with her own property ruins the house'[22] (although women could have a measure of independence, clearly not all men were happy about it). The pupils copied hymns that extol the importance to society of writing and accounting – the skills that they were learning – and this theme crops up in a number of seemingly unrelated poems as well, from creation myths to the goddess Inanna's descent to the netherworld, continually reinforcing the message. On the more exciting end, the Sumerian stories about Gilgamesh bear the hallmarks of court entertainment, and so may originally have been commissioned by the kings who claimed descent from him. The battle against the forest monster Humbaba was extremely popular in schools because it is a rollicking adventure. Most relatable of all were the compositions about school life itself, such as one where a child tells his father how he got into trouble for being late, having bad handwriting, and speaking Akkadian in class when they were supposed to be learning Sumerian.[23] The story has a happy ending, though: the father invites the teacher over for dinner and bribes him with gifts, putting his son back in the teacher's good books.

While Ashurbanipal's library does an extremely good job of preserving ancient traditions, it does not preserve all of them, and not all of these poems from the second millennium made it into the first. One Sumerian epic that did survive is *Ninurta's Exploits*.[24] This poem was translated into Akkadian, and the copies in the library have both languages side by side for ease of consultation. At 726 lines long, it is one of the longest Sumerian poems, and one of the best. Its language is sublime, full of powerful metaphors and vivid descriptions. It contains high drama and emotion, a powerful antagonist as well as a mighty hero, a battle that terrifies even the gods, and a triumph over chaos that results in the taming of nature.

Ninurta was one of the most important gods in Mesopotamia, and was especially honoured in Assyria. He was a bestower of kingship and a model of power. When taking part in state rituals the king would often act in the role of Ninurta – in the lion hunts depicted on the walls of Ashurbanipal's palace the king was understood to be the mortal equivalent of Ninurta fighting his enemies, as he was when fighting in battle. When Esarhaddon describes his struggle against his brothers he interweaves quotations from *Ninurta's Exploits* as well as from *Gilgamesh*, putting himself in the role of the god fighting against evil demons and elevating his battle to a cosmic level. This may be why the poem was especially valued in Assyria, alongside another Ninurta poem, *Ninurta's Return to Nippur*, which describes him returning from his battles, and which was invoked in military processions.[25] These two Sumerian Ninurta poems were certainly special to the Assyrians. The catalogue of texts and authors from Ashurbanipal's library lists the god Ea as their author: the Assyrians must have thought he had imbued them with his wisdom and his knowledge of the magical arts.

Ninurta's Exploits begins with Ninurta's battle against the demon Asag, the king of an army of animate stones. Asag was born in the mountains and has taken them over as his territory. The people appeal to Ninurta for help and he immediately marches to the mountains, accompanied by his talking mace, and crushes the cities of this demonic kingdom, causing poison to flow over the lands, engulfing his enemies like a river in spate.[26] As he heads into battle with Asag the sun and moon recede and the day turns to pitch. The description of the battle is one of the most vivid and dramatic in Sumerian literature:

> The Asag leapt up at the head of the battle. For a club it uprooted the sky, took it in its hand; like a snake it slid its head along the ground. It was a mad dog attacking to kill the helpless, dripping with sweat on its flanks. Like a wall collapsing, the Asag fell on Ninurta the son of Enlil. Like an accursed storm, it howled in a raucous voice; like a gigantic snake, it roared at the land. It dried up the waters of the mountains, dragged away the tamarisks, tore the flesh of the earth and covered her with painful wounds. It set fire to the reed-beds, bathed the sky in blood, turned it inside out; it dispersed the people there. At that moment, on that day, the fields became black potash, across the whole extent of the horizon, reddish like purple dye – truly it was so![27]

But Ninurta and his opponent are well matched, and the god's attack is just as terrifying, advancing like a storm and flattening Asag like a wave. The monster's terrifying aura begins to fade: the similes keep coming as Ninurta rips up Asag like weeds, pounds the demon like roasted barley, and piles it up like a heap of broken bricks.[28] The enemy has been well and truly crushed, 'slain to the condition of a ship wrecked by a tidal wave'.[29] In the aftermath of the battle, Ninurta goes about re-establishing order from chaos, and repurposing all the debris and destruction for a positive use. First, he turns his attention to the destructive flood waters in the mountains. He heaps up a great pile of stones, creating a dam, thus rediverting the water so that it can be used for agriculture. As well as a deity of war, Ninurta was also the god of farming, this poem neatly uniting two of his functions in one story.

Most of Ninurta's time, however, is taken up in deciding what to do with his defeated enemies. Asag himself is transformed into the netherworld, his body making up that gloomy terrain that the Sumerians referred to as 'the mountain'. He had tried to become king of the mountains on earth and is now ironically given over to the shadow of that domain. As for the stones that fought in his army, Ninurta passes judgement and determines a destiny for each of them in turn, allocating them uses in everyday life. Those who were particularly rebellious are destined for hard labour while those who acknowledged Ninurta's superior strength will be used for beautiful monuments. For example, the emery stone which led the army will be used as a grindstone, while diorite changed sides during the battle and defected to Ninurta, and so from now on will be used for the statues of kings. In this way the poem provides an explanation for why particular stones were used for particular purposes. Basic properties of the natural world are given a mythological grounding, and the battles of the gods explain why the world is the way it is, right down to these seemingly mundane details.

The poem celebrates Ninurta's victories in the mountains, which the Assyrian kings equated with their own military exploits. Mountains represent hostile and distant lands throughout Mesopotamian history – indeed the Sumerian word for 'foreign land' was written with a picture of mountains. But the defeat of Asag is more than a simple monster-slaying story. It shows how a new order can come out of the defeat of chaos, another theme beloved by the Assyrians and continually avowed by their kings. The post-battle cleanup leads to important innovations in agriculture that improve life for the people, and all the defeated enemies are reintegrated into society and given a useful role. The message for the Assyrians is that the outcome of military conquest is a good and just society.

Yet the story of conquest plays out in other realms too, and the scribes would have taken another meaning from it. In the everyday world, the demon Asag was said to cause disease, and the exorcist's attempts to cure it were also pitched as a cosmic battle. Medical texts invoke Ninurta as a slayer of sickness, and just as he successfully overcame Asag in this poem, so could the exorcist overcome the demon when it attacked people once again. Just as we talk of curing disease in military terms – from battles with cancer to fighting off a cold – so did the Mesopotamians, but for them the battle was not metaphorical but very real. The victory that has been enshrined in myth can be won over and over. Ninurta has done it before, so the exorcist, with his help, can do it again.

Exorcists found the poem useful and had copies of it in their personal libraries. The house of an exorcist in the city of Ashur held one interesting tablet that contains four different texts: instructions to prevent witchcraft-induced miscarriage, an incantation to protect a crying baby, a list of stones needed to make an amulet necklace, and an extract from *Ninurta's Exploits*. An extract from a poem may seem like an odd choice for what is otherwise a collection of ways to ward off evil. But in fact all of these texts have something in common: stones. The first three prescribed magic stones to protect the person holding or wearing them – magnetite and agate for the pregnant woman, haematite for the baby, and fourteen different stones for the amulet necklace, which work together to deflect all manner of evils. Many of these stones are specifically named in *Ninurta's Exploits*, with Ninurta's victory over them leading to their rehabilitation for human use. Quoting the poem can lend strength to the exorcist in his own battles against evil, a reminder that these forces can and will be conquered.

Ninurta's judging of the stones, and allocation of their new roles, is one of the strangest parts of the story for a modern audience, but for the Mesopotamians it was clearly important – at 240 lines long, it takes up a significant chunk of the narrative. The connections to medicine and exorcism are a plausible explanation for why their destinies deserve so much space, for the stones continued to be relevant to the people studying these poems in the first millennium, the ritual specialists who were steeped in higher learning. The use of magic stones was an integral part of Mesopotamian magic, with different stones having special properties. Although the connections and uses are different, it is the same principle found in New Age shops selling rose quartz to attract love or tiger eye to instil courage: crystal healing is nothing new. As an important part of their art, the exorcists would be interested in stories explaining how stones came to acquire their uses, and *Ninurta's Exploits* was relevant to them in a very practical way.

At first glance these poems can seem terse and cryptic, but each time we read them they give up more of their secrets. Such is their richness that every time I revisit them I see something new. The style is very condensed, making the act of reading them a kind of decoding, and the more we learn about Mesopotamian life the more meanings they yield. Yet they can be enjoyed on many levels. As we have seen with *Gilgamesh* and *Ninurta's Exploits*, the exciting plots would have entertained all audiences, while scholars would find theological and even scientific principles embedded in them. Scholars who understood the omens would have been able to appreciate the poems on yet another level, since omens in the poems themselves foreshadow events that are later to come. The same is true today – we can appreciate these stories simply as the fantastic tales they are, while also having the option of going deeper and deeper to understand this distant society better.

What can the adventures of mortals and gods long dead and forgotten mean to us now? Although the way that we understand the world is quite different, the stories we tell about it are remarkably similar. A hero's battle against a formidable monster is a story told over and over again, from Perseus and the Gorgon to George and the Dragon to *Jaws* and *Godzilla*. Each time, it reveals something about what that society considers to be heroic and what it values. Ninurta's victories in fact closely resemble the plots of modern-day superhero movies, where exceptional strength and power fight against forces of chaos that threaten to destabilise the world, and ultimately restore order. The hero may have a loyal sidekick who accompanies him into battle; in some versions he is inconspicuous and unknown before rising to the challenge, and his victories bring gains not only for himself but for society as a whole. Our superheroes are not gods or kings, and while the principles are broadly the same they show different things about us and what we value. They tell us about the power of the transformation of the individual, about the secret strengths that can be possessed by ordinary-looking people, and the importance of teamwork. People have always told stories to make sense of the world. While many things in Mesopotamian literature may seem strange and unfamiliar, this is still recognisable. Ninurta's exploits are still with us, just called by different names.

But the Mesopotamians also had a sense of humour, and their literature also includes satires and folk tales that were not quite so serious. These range from *The Poor Man of Nippur*, a comic tale of revenge against a corrupt mayor, to the *Aluzinnu* text which makes fun of all of the ritual specialists whose knowledge was held in the library.[30] The exorcist portrayed here advises that the most auspicious diet for the month of February is 'donkey's anus stuffed with dog turds and fly dirt', and gets rid of ghosts by burning down his client's house. Another story pokes fun at the scholars' supposed expertise in ancient traditions when a doctor asks an old woman for directions in the street and cannot understand her reply because it is in Sumerian, the dead language he is supposed to have mastered but doesn't even recognise.[31] This shows a much lighter side to the

Mesopotamians: they could laugh at themselves and what seems odd to us could also seem odd to them.

Ultimately, the incredible wealth of literature from Mesopotamia preserves a great variety of beliefs and experiences. These stories show us how people questioned why the world is the way it is, from concrete aspects of their everyday lives such as why snakes shed their skin and how stones came to have their uses to the deeper reasons behind suffering and death, and what made life worth living. Literature was a place of exploration where the answers could be worked out: the adventures and tribulations of legendary heroes like Gilgamesh and Atrahasis put humanity in the context of the great cosmic scale, but as well as being exceptional stories they had lessons for ordinary people too. As we have seen, the results are multifaceted: the world is a contradictory place, expressed in tales of both order and disorder, with a multitude of human experiences within it, and many different answers to the questions posed by human existence.

8.
The Waging of War

The Elamite soldiers cascade down the hill, chased by Assyrians who pursue with ruthless efficiency. Archers fall out of their chariots and are trampled by horses, are speared in the back, or throw up their arms in surrender. In the midst of the turbulent battle Teumman, the Elamite king, has tumbled from his chariot, his son Tammaritu on the ground beside him, his horses bolting away. His regal hat has fallen from his head, exposing his balding scalp. As he snatches it up an arrow flies into his back. Tammaritu scrambles to his feet and helps his father up so they can make for the forest, but the ranks of shields are close behind them and another arrow hits Teumman in the thigh. On his knees, the king desperately cries out to his son, ordering him to defiantly raise his bow, somehow believing they can still get away. But it is too late – behind them are soldiers with maces lifted high, one of which comes crashing down on Tammaritu's skull. A common soldier cuts off Teumman's head and begins to parade it triumphantly through the battleground.

Holding the head high, grasping it by the hair, the soldier steps over corpses while vultures pluck out the eyes of the dead. Around him the battle still rages but now its end is certain. One Elamite general cuts his own bowstring in a gesture of surrender. Another cries out to an Assyrian soldier to 'Come, cut off my head too and bring it before the king your lord, make a good name for yourself!' Meanwhile Teumman's head makes its way back to the Assyrian camp, paraded past his many fallen soldiers. The soldier steps into a chariot, proudly holding the head before him, and makes haste back to Ashurbanipal, bringing him the sign of victory, the good news.[1]

This Assyrian victory over the Elamites is one of the scenes that would have greeted visitors to Ashurbanipal's South-West Palace, sending a clear message that such was the fate that befell those who crossed mighty Assyria. The relief was carved in stunning panels of gypsum more than two metres high, complete with captions acting as highlights and speech bubbles to make its meaning clear. The battle of Til-Tuba in 653 BC was just one of the campaigns decorating the palace walls, to be seen by ambassadors from all corners of the Assyrian world. As the ruler of the largest empire the world had ever seen, Ashurbanipal constantly had to deal with rebelling vassals and foreign powers encroaching on his land, and was expected to wage war to add to Assyria's territory. The Assyrians had a formidable reputation in this area, one that they carefully curated and preserved, both on their palace walls and in Ashurbanipal's library.

The Assyrian palace reliefs are among the star exhibits of the British Museum. Visitors are often struck by their brutality and are left with the impression that Assyria was a harsh and cruel place. The reliefs show cities burning to the ground, enemy soldiers being flayed alive, captured prisoners impaled on stakes and women and children led off into exile. They are certainly disturbing scenes, as was the intention: it was all part of the strategy of keeping vassal states in their place and maintaining Assyria's power. The strategy has been an effective one, as it has had exactly the impact on us that the Assyrians would have wanted, giving us the image of a mighty war machine.

It is easy to look at these graphic depictions of torture and bloodshed and think that the Assyrians lived in a much more violent age than us, but appearances can be deceptive. Modern states engage in equally barbaric practices, they are just less visible. Imagine if the US Capitol were decorated with scenes from Hiroshima, or the Houses of Parliament in London with reliefs showing the Opium Wars. This would make a very different first impression on visitors, who might not then think us to be quite so enlightened. Power is now demonstrated in more subtle ways, but although modern methods of warfare and diplomacy have changed, many of the principles behind them have not.

Assyria was not unusual among the empires of the world in using such violence against its enemies. The difference is that for many people today Assyria's violence is all that they know about it. The Roman empire was also ruthlessly expansionist and used brutal methods of execution (crucifixion comes to mind), but we are aware of the Romans' great literary and cultural achievements, which shows us a different side to them. We need to do the same for the Assyrians, to put their wars in context and show that they were interested in far more than battle and bloodshed. A closer look at these reliefs reveals far more subtleties than is apparent at first glance, as other Assyrian values are also contained within their carvings.

Nevertheless, war was one of the Assyrian king's sacred duties and thus a key part of his job. Grand accounts of Ashurbanipal's military campaigns show him systematically subduing large portions of the Near East and depict him as a mighty force to reckon with. To oppose Ashurbanipal was to oppose the very gods of Assyria, for whom battle was play and bloodshed a game. These accounts are like miniature historical novels, with high stakes and intense drama. They describe antagonists confessing their wicked intentions, the terrible punishments Ashurbanipal inflicted on those he defeated, and the lavish celebrations in the aftermath of his victories. But how much was history and how much was fiction? Can we tell the difference between Ashurbanipal's own mythmaking and the reality? His scholars would have assisted in this project, using their knowledge of Mesopotamia's traditions to portray Ashurbanipal's victories as inevitable and his kingship as divine. But how successful were they? The official accounts tell one story, but Greek historians tell another, showing that others remembered Ashurbanipal very differently from how he would have liked.

Ashurbanipal was particularly proud of his wars against Elam, a powerful kingdom situated in present-day Iran that had a long history of meddling in Mesopotamian affairs. Ashurbanipal tried to put an end to their interference with a spectacular campaign that culminated in the complete destruction of their religious capital, Susa, and commemorated it both on his palace walls and in royal histories that he commissioned. Particularly galling to Ashurbanipal was Elamite interference in his conflict with his older brother Shamash-shum-ukin in Babylonia, and so the accounts of the two wars are intertwined. Alongside these works of literature and art we have first-hand letters in the archives between Ashurbanipal and the Elamite kings, which reveal another side to the story. The mechanics of diplomacy were more complex than the royal annals would have us believe, and Ashurbanipal did not always get his way. At the same time, the library with its store of knowledge could be useful in times of war, since divination was crucial to formulating strategy, and mythology, literature, and religion were all deployed to justify violence. Military history is never about tactics alone, but is a rich tapestry of politics, ideas, symbolism, and rhetoric. In Ashurbanipal's library we see all of these at work, giving us a sophisticated picture of Assyrian conflict that had far more than brute force behind it.

Assyria was a state founded on military might and war had always been central to its ideology. Ashurbanipal's reign came at the peak of a series of conquests that had started two hundred years earlier. The empire had steadily grown since the ninth century BC, when Assyria started to expand out from its heartland in northern Iraq and absorb more and more territory. The expansion began with Ashurnasirpal II (883–859 BC), who made it his mission to win back the lands that had once belonged to Assyria, land that had been lost three centuries earlier. Ashurnasirpal conquered the land surrounding Assyria in every direction, going on campaign every year in a different place, and by the end of his reign had accomplished his mission. His successor, Shalmaneser III, went further, marching into northern Syria and down through the Levantine states of Phoenicia, Israel, and Judah. This time the strategy was different – the aim was not to make these lands part of Assyria itself, but to turn them into obedient vassal states that would enrich Assyria by sending a yearly tribute, a status that was referred to as dragging the 'yoke of Ashur'. With each military campaign Assyria cowed its neighbouring territories into submission and forced them to acknowledge the Assyrian king as the ultimate authority. So long as they paid the yearly tribute, these neighbouring states would be left alone, but when they did not there were consequences. Rebellions against these heavy financial demands were inevitably frequent, which gave the Assyrians an excuse to invade and take direct control.

Assyria was not blessed with abundant natural resources. One major motivating factor for Assyria's constant wars, then, was to acquire raw materials to make up for what it lacked. This was especially the case in the Levant, which is rich in the timber needed for building. Tribute was paid mostly in gold and silver, but also other materials such as blocks of precious stones and works of fine craftsmanship. After Sennacherib besieged Jerusalem in 701 BC, the king of Judah had to send ivory beds and armchairs, elephant hides, and 'every kind of valuable treasure' to the Assyrian capital,[2] while traditionally the peoples of the Iranian plateau sent the 'fast horses, fiery mules, and Bactrian camels' for which they were famous[3] – each according to their ability, each according to Assyria's needs.

The other major resource in demand was people. The Assyrians needed manpower to serve in the military and to work on infrastructure, and would deploy defeated populations for these purposes, sending them wherever in the empire they were needed. Deportees were often skilled workers and were usually treated well – they were resettled with their families, a proposition which could have its advantages and which was not always carried out by force. As a result, the Assyrian empire was a cosmopolitan place, with different ethnicities and languages to be found in all its corners. These mass deportations were strategic as well as practical, since breaking up these nations and physically moving them far from their homelands made it more difficult for them to organise and rise up against

Assyria again. The Babylonians later used the same strategy, most notably when Nebuchadnezzar II conquered Judah and its capital Jerusalem and resettled its population in Babylonia. Some of the early stories in the Bible's book of Daniel are set during the time of this Babylonian captivity (c. 598–538), featuring Judaean elites held captive at the Babylonian court.

Every country thinks of itself as the centre of the world and the Assyrians were no exception. In the Assyrian worldview Assyria was the epitome of order and everything outside it was chaos. It was the king's duty, therefore, to tame the wilderness and to bring those foreign lands into the cool shade of Assyria, where they would want for nothing ever again. Ashurbanipal certainly seems to think it is to the advantage of these foreign peoples to be part of his empire and the civilised, ordered world. In his account, war takes on an almost religious purpose – the gods Ashur and Ishtar command Ashurbanipal to conquer these peoples, send him messages of encouragement via oracles and dreams, and stand by him on the battlefield. Foreign lands who fail to do as Assyria pleases are said to have sinned and are predictably overcome by the might of Ashur and Ishtar. According to Ashurbanipal it is the gods who have accomplished these victories, having been with him at every turn. The power of Assyria was equated with the power of the gods themselves, and to defy Ashurbanipal was to rebel against the will of the highest deities.

From the ninth century BC up until Ashurbanipal's time, one after another the Assyrian kings continued their campaigns and extended Assyrian influence ever further across the Near East. Ashurbanipal inherited an empire that stretched from Egypt in the west to parts of western Iran in the east, up into Turkey in the north and down to northern Babylonia in the south. It was up to him to keep everyone in check, but these more distant territories were much harder to control than those on Assyria's doorstep. Ashurbanipal had to contend with large states who were used to being independent and resented his interference. His first mission was to quell the rebellion in Egypt that had broken out just before the death of his father, and he swiftly brought the country back under Assyrian control.

1. Tablet XI of the epic of *Gilgamesh*, telling the story of the flood.

2. An ivory writing board found in the city of Nimrud.

3. Shelves in the Sippar library.

4. A clay model of a sheep liver inscribed with omens (second millennium BC).

5. Head of the demon Pazuzu, to be worn as an amulet.

6. Amulet against the demon Lamashtu.

7. Cylinder seal depicting Gilgamesh and Enkidu's defeat of Humbaba.

8. Clay prism inscribed with accounts of Ashurbanipal's military campaigns.

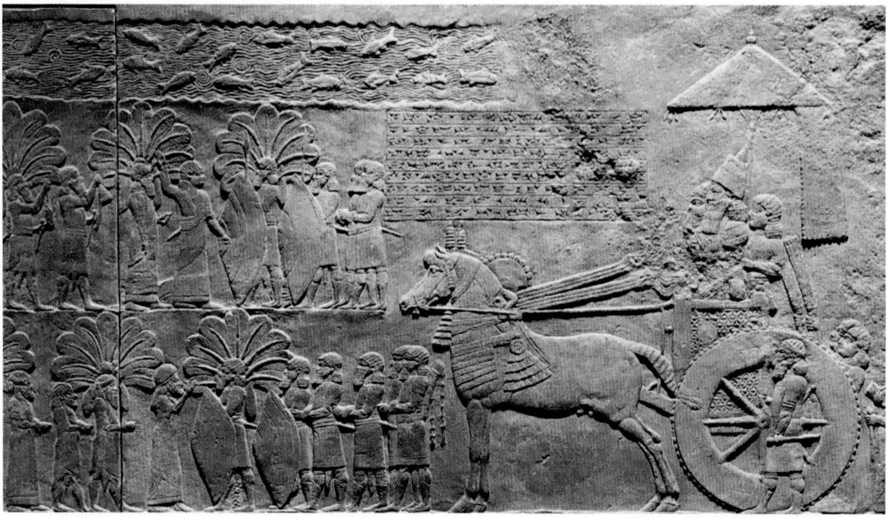

9. Relief from Ashurbanipal's palace showing his defeated brother's royal regalia presented to the king in victory.

10. Relief from the royal lion hunt sequence.

11. Letter from Ashurbanipal's sister to his wife berating her for not being good at cuneiform.

12. Relief showing Ashurbanipal out hunting, with styli in his belt.

13. Relief from the palace of Tiglath-Pileser III showing Assyrian soldiers carrying the statues of gods away from a defeated city.

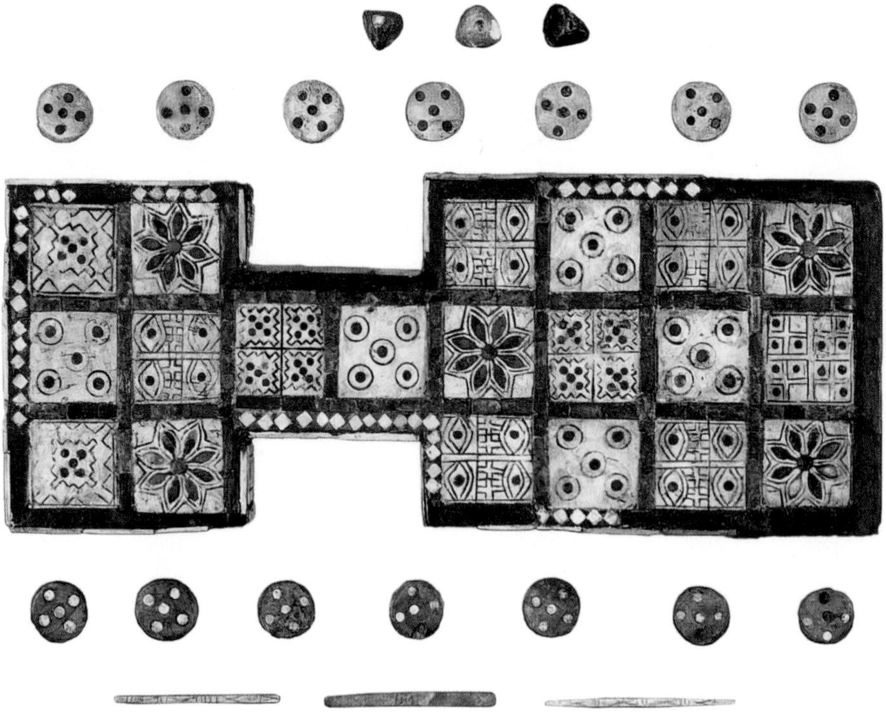

14. The Royal game of Ur, otherwise known as 'Pack of Dogs' (third millennium BC).

We have already seen how Babylon then broke away under the rulership of Ashurbanipal's brother, and was only brought back into the fold after a bitter four-year conflict. Elam had always been a nuisance to the Assyrians, but when they took Babylon's side in this war Ashurbanipal was especially enraged, and he went to extreme lengths to punish them for coming to his brother's aid.

The kingdom of Elam was based in what is now south-western Iran, bordering on Babylonia. This neighbouring state had been in contact with southern Mesopotamians for over two thousand years; they were similar yet distinct cultures that traded goods and ideas. Elam had developed its own type of cuneiform inspired by Sumerian, and built ziggurats as temples for their gods, just as the Mesopotamians did. Yet more often than not the two regions were suspicious of each other, if not outright hostile, their alliances shifting, breaking, and being remade over the centuries. Mesopotamia was not always the stronger of the two. In the early twentieth century AD, the famous law code of Hammurabi was discovered not in its original standing place in Babylonia but in the Elamite religious capital of Susa. It had been there since the twelfth century BC, when the Elamites sacked Babylonia and looted many of its most precious monuments, displaying them on their own citadel as war trophies. At the same time, they kidnapped the statue of the god Marduk, which the Babylonians particularly resented. Thankfully the Babylonians did manage to get the statue back, and wrote the whole embarrassing episode into history as if Marduk had decided to go on a foreign holiday, travelling all over the world before returning home to Babylon.[4]

By Ashurbanipal's time Babylon and Elam had made up but their relationship was still fractious. United by a common enemy, the Elamites had colluded with the Babylonians to revolt against Assyria in the time of Sennacherib, and, as we saw earlier, had kidnapped the Assyrian crown prince, who was bundled off to Elam in 694 BC and presumably put to death. Thirty years later, the Elamites invaded Babylonian territory while Ashurbanipal's older brother Shamash-shum-ukin was in charge. As king of Babylon, Shamash-shum-ukin wrote to Ashurbanipal asking for aid, but his brother was slow to send troops, and then slow to avenge the invasion, which may well have contributed to the tensions between the two that would eventually lead to full-scale war.

Just like in international relations today, events in other countries could have consequences for Assyria, and events in Elam more than most. Elam's internal politics were fraught with frequent power struggles and regime changes, and Ashurbanipal became entangled in them too. In 664 BC the Elamite king who had invaded Babylonia, Urtaku, died shortly after the incursion, and a man named Teumman seized the throne instead of the rightful heir, Crown Prince Ummanigash. Ummanigash fled to Assyria seeking political asylum. Ashurbanipal sheltered the refugees for a decade and refused demands to extradite them, knowing they would be useful to him later. Teumman used this diplomatic spat as an excuse to invade Assyrian-controlled territory in northern Babylonia. This triggered Ashurbanipal's counterattack and march into Elam, culminating in 653 in the Battle of Til-Tuba, commemorated in the reliefs and recorded in numerous inscriptions.

Ashurbanipal commissioned official accounts of his military campaigns, telling the story from his point of view. These were written on clay prisms and deposited inside the walls of his palace, citadel, and temples as a kind of time capsule for later rulers to read. It was standard practice in Mesopotamia to bury objects in the foundations of buildings, stating which king had built them, and recounting his pious deeds. This was especially the case with temples, which were renovated by successive rulers, who would then find the documents written by their predecessors. The Babylonian king Nabonidus who lived in the sixth century BC claimed to have discovered ancient inscriptions of Hammurabi and Naram-Sin, who ruled 1,200 and 1,662 years before him respectively, and wrote about it on his own cylinders, which he then deposited in the foundations of the same temple.[5] Nabonidus has been called the first archaeologist, but he was certainly not the only Mesopotamian king to have dug up dedications from long ago. These accounts were meant to be found – they were written for posterity and speak directly to us. The other intended audience was the gods, who needed to be reminded of their support for Ashurbanipal and what he had done for them in return. Although the prisms were hidden away, the stories they told would probably have been generally known – they might have been read out on public occasions and may well have enjoyed a wider circulation in other forms.

Ashurbanipal also rewrote his history, ordering new versions of the accounts to be written as his perspective on them changed. There are ten different editions of his annals, surviving in around eight hundred copies, making them among the best-preserved pieces of all Mesopotamian literature.[6] The differences between versions are mostly small – some episodes are expanded; details are added or removed as Ashurbanipal chooses to emphasise different parts of the story at different points in his reign. As he got older, the self-revision became more intense, with at least six of these rewritings taking place in the third decade of his rule. The last and most complete version is preserved on an object known today as the Rassam cylinder, a ten-sided clay prism named after the Mosul-born archaeologist who discovered it in Ashurbanipal's North Palace. Interestingly, it is this latest edition that contains the most detail about the war against his brother, which earlier versions had narrated with more restraint. It is as if these episodes gained more importance with time, and hardened in his memory. It is in this last version that Ashurbanipal expresses bitterness and resentment towards his brother, calling him an enemy at every turn, as well as anger at the ingratitude of former allies who defected to him. In the immediate aftermath of the campaign he glossed over these details, as if he did not want to call attention to them, but five or six years later when the Rassam cylinder was written he was brooding again, unable to let the past lie and resurrecting old grievances.

The Assyrian annals truly are works of literature. They are not written in the common Assyrian language but in Standard Babylonian, the artificial dialect that existed only for works of high art. Standard Babylonian would never have been spoken anywhere but is a mixture of dialects from different times and places, embodying the kind of universal heritage that was Mesopotamian culture, shared by Babylonians and Assyrians alike. In this respect it is a bit like Homeric Greek, which also draws on archaic language from many different regions, belonging to all and yet none of them, or modern standard Arabic, a literary language used across the Arab world.

The Assyrian annals are full of allusions to the Babylonian classics, putting their protagonists in the same roles as the great gods and heroes of mythology. They use unusual language and turns of phrase, and similes that compare the king's onslaught to a mighty flood or raging hurricane, with his enemies fleeing like terrified animals before his advance. Ultimately, they raise Ashurbanipal and his wars to a cosmological plane – these are no ordinary battles, but a reordering of the universe itself, depicting an effortless victory of gods against demons, the divinely appointed order against evil and chaos.

The story of Til-Tuba is most fully told in 'Prism B', a treatment of the campaigns written four years after they took place, in 649 BC.[7] In this account Ashurbanipal focuses his rage on the Elamites. He depicts their king Teumman as an evil antagonist from the very start, 'the very image of a demon', plotting to kill the other surviving members of the royal family, who all fled to Ashurbanipal for shelter.[8] Every month, we are told, Teumman sent insults to Ashurbanipal, along with demands of extradition, and constantly sought out evil. Yet the gods punished him for his insolence. In July 653 a lunar eclipse took place and lasted such a long time that even the sun god Shamash saw it when he rose in the morning. Ashurbanipal and his scholars knew this was a message from the gods announcing the end of the reign of the king of Elam. At this very time Teumman had a seizure that left him with facial paralysis, a punishment of the moon god following his eclipse, but Teumman failed to recognise the hand of Sin and shamelessly mustered his troops, preparing to invade Assyria.[9]

News of the invasion reached Ashurbanipal while he was in Arbela, an Assyrian city whose patron goddess was Ishtar. He appealed to the goddess for help, his tears flowing as he spoke of how Teumman had no respect for the gods and was acting without divine approval. Ishtar encouraged him to have no fear. That very night she sent a dream to a dream interpreter, who relayed another message to the king: although he was eager to do battle, he should not set out with his troops, but should instead stay put and 'eat food, drink wine, make music, and revere my divinity while I carry out this work'.[10] Fire flared up in front of her and she departed furiously for Elam. Ashurbanipal sent his troops after her, encouraged by both the eclipse and the words of Ishtar. Rather conveniently for Ashurbanipal, he had a divine mandate to stay at home and celebrate a festival rather than lead the troops himself. Naturally he was only doing what the goddess had told him to do.

Meanwhile Teumman was on the march towards Assyria and had set up camp near the border in the city of Bit-Imbi. Ashurbanipal's troops amassed on the other side of the border at the Babylonian city of Der, ready to cross over into Elam. When Teumman heard the Assyrians were coming he panicked and went back to his capital for reinforcements. Going on the defensive, he took up position at the river Ulai near the city of Til-Tuba, where the Assyrian troops met him in open battle.[11]

Pitched battles like these were not usually Assyria's preferred strategy. Anyone who has played video games featuring the Assyrians will know that they excelled at siege warfare, and it is mostly sieges that are depicted in the reliefs – siege towers approaching battlements; soldiers scaling the walls and defenders tumbling from them; and soldiers chipping away at the stonework, bringing it down from underneath. Til-Tuba is unusual then, both as a piece of art and as a battle. The Assyrian strategy can be inferred from the relief: outflank the Elamites using the cavalry while foot soldiers attack the centre, and drive the enemy into the river.

The official accounts do not describe the battle itself, even though it is depicted so richly on the palace walls. This is most likely because Mesopotamian literature tends to be narrative rather than descriptive – plot-driven and focused on events. Prism B simply narrates the battle like this, from Ashurbanipal's perspective:

> By the command of the gods Ashur and Marduk, the great gods, my lords, who had encouraged me through auspicious omens, dreams, oracles, messages from prophets, I brought about their [Elam's] defeat inside Til-Tuba. I blocked up the river with their corpses and filled the plains of the city of Susa with their bodies like weeds and thorns. By the command of the gods Ashur and Marduk, the great gods my lords, in the midst of his troops I cut off the head of Teumman the king of the land of Elam. The terrifying radiance of Ashur and Ishtar overwhelmed the land of Elam and they bowed down to my yoke.[12]

It is the reliefs that show us just how Teumman came to grief, tumbling from his chariot, making for the forest, but cornered by Assyrian archers and set upon by soldiers who cut off his head. Art and literature work together to give us a picture of the campaign.

The reliefs are carved in a stunning continuous style, leading our eyes through the narrative from one scene to another, rather like a comic strip without the divisions into boxes (as pointed out by the Iraqi-American artist Michael Rakowitz, we can add the graphic novel to the list of Mesopotamia's firsts). We follow Teumman around the wall in a circular route as the Assyrians pursue him, and once Teumman is trapped his head is carried back the way he came, all the way to Assyria. Piles of heads are par for the course in Assyrian art, but Teumman's is instantly identifiable – receding hairline, hooked nose, and squinty eyes, probably a result of his stroke. He clearly stands out from the ranks of anonymous soldiers, who all look the same.

The Elamites can be distinguished from the Assyrians by their different hairstyles and dress, but there is a purpose to the uniformity of the Assyrian troops. They are not individuals, but part of a machine, a body that acts as one to carry out the will of Ashur and Ishtar. Even Assyrian kings cannot easily be told apart from each other – when Ashurbanipal is portrayed it is only the context that would tell us who he is, for he looks identical to any other Assyrian king before him. Rather than being an individual, the king is the perfect man, an embodiment of the very idea of kingship, which is eternal and unchanging. In Assyrian art, to be an individual is to show weakness, for any deviation from the perfect type is considered a fault. While Elamite soldiers might look similar to each other, each of them suffers and dies in his own way. One tugs at his beard in terror as he flees; another looks back over his shoulder at the Assyrians coming for him; another tries to crawl away with an arrow sticking out of his back; others still are trampled by horses, or their eyes are picked out by vultures, or they are speared into the river. There is no such variety among the Assyrians, who simply march, aim, and bring down their weapons one after another.

A modern museum visitor rather sympathises with the Elamites, but this was not at all the Assyrian intention. The same is true of Ashurbanipal's lion hunt reliefs, which seem to depict the dying lions with considerable pathos. Each lion is portrayed as an individual – one widens its startled eyes as Ashurbanipal plunges a spear into its throat; another staggers away vomiting blood; a lioness lies completely still as the king's horses leap over her sprawled body. The king's expression is inscrutable, perfectly calm and in control, above these animal displays of emotion. There are no cracks to be seen in his appearance; he is absolute strength made flesh. Most museum visitors today take the side of the lions, but what provokes sympathy in us would have been derided by Ashurbanipal: these lions represent the wild regions that must be tamed by Assyrian might. We are not supposed to feel sorry for them, for they are only meeting the inevitable fate they deserve as creatures that failed to obey the commands of Ashur and Ishtar. As with the lions, so with the Elamite king and his forces. As the royal annals have told us, he was wicked, insolent, and failed to heed the gods – he only got what he deserved.

⁂

The reliefs may be violent, but like the prisms they are also distinctly literary, full of references to the classics of poetry and divination held in the library. Allusions to these erudite texts pepper the imagery with still more messages that underscore the inevitability of Teumman's defeat and Ashurbanipal's victory. No action is accidental, no depiction without a deeper meaning, mirroring the way that Ashurbanipal's scholars would themselves have seen the world. Those who understood the codes of divination would be able to read the reliefs in the same way that they could read the world around them and decode the gods' intentions. For instance, when Teumman falls out of his chariot it is not a coincidence that he falls to the right side, an event that portends disaster: 'if the prince is riding a chariot and falls to the right of the chariot: hand of the god Shamash, grief.'[13] If that was not bad enough, losing his hat is another bad omen: 'if the prince is riding a chariot and while holding the reins his headdress or his hat comes off: that prince will be slighted.'[14] As the omens warn, so it comes to pass – Teumman's decapitation is a sure humiliation, especially so since the annals make sure to emphasise it is a lowly common soldier who does the deed.

His beheading also has a clear literary resonance. The taking of Teumman's head evokes the famous episode in the *Epic of Gilgamesh* in which Gilgamesh slays the monster Humbaba. Like Teumman, Humbaba is killed in the forest, and the struggle ends with the victorious king cutting off his opponent's head. Just as Teumman's head is paraded at the front of a chariot as it is brought back to Assyria, so does Gilgamesh triumphantly carry the head of Humbaba as he heads home by raft. These parallels compare Ashurbanipal to the legendary king, but others go further and compare his deeds to those of the gods. The *Epic of Creation* is also directly invoked in Ashurbanipal's battle. The reliefs have captions that label key moments, and sometimes even contain dialogue in comic book style. Above the chariot carrying Teumman's head is one such label telling us that the head was sent quickly to Assyria 'as good news'. This is a key phrase from the creation epic which describes the blood of a defeated monster being carried on the wind all the way back to Babylon as a sign of the victory.

Back in Nineveh, Ashurbanipal has heard the good news, and

rides out of the city gates to meet the returning soldiers. Tablets in the library describe how they threw the head in front of Ashurbanipal's chariot and he spat on it. From then on Teumman's head became a ritual object – Ashurbanipal presented it to the gods at the New Year festival in thanks for his victory, and he preserved it so that he could keep it on display.[15] In Mesopotamian mythology, defeated monsters were often used as amulets to ward off evil, their ugliness repurposed to scare away other undesirable forces. Humbaba's head was used in this way, carved at the gates of temples and even worn on necklaces to protect the wearer, just like the demon Pazuzu as we saw in Chapter 3. It seems that the head of Teumman was deemed to have similar powers, as it was carved in a relief depicting a celebratory banquet in Ashurbanipal's garden many years later, dangling upside down from a tree. Ashurbanipal and his wife are drinking in the shade of the vines, fanned by attendants and listening to music as they relax in the wake of the triumph over the Elamites, the gruesome trophy hanging opposite their dining table.[16] Earlier in the conflict, Teumman had boasted that he would not give up until he was dining in the centre of Nineveh – finally, he has his wish.[17] Other captured Elamite kings are forced to serve as waiters, carrying refreshments to the garden, perhaps counting themselves lucky to have escaped Teumman's fate.[18] Meanwhile, back on the Til-Tuba relief, the children of the former governor of Nippur, a city in Babylonia which had sided with Shamash-shum-ukin, are made to grind the bones of their ancestors opposite the citadel gate of Nineveh, before being executed themselves.[19]

Teumman's head was also used to humiliate other rebel kings. Ashurbanipal was determined to punish anyone who had sided with Teumman, and set out again on campaign. Next he went after the Aramean tribe of Gambulu, an area in south-east Babylonia. Ashurbanipal says he covered the whole land like a fog and conquered the city where the leaders were hiding, capturing them alive. He hung the severed head of Teumman around the neck of the Gambulean leader and paraded him through Nineveh to a backdrop of singing and celebration. Further victory parades followed in the city of Arbela, a place sacred to the goddess Ishtar. Spectacular reliefs depict this event as well – the leader of the Gambuleans is led to Ashurbanipal in shackles with Teumman's head hanging around his neck, his captor spitting in his face. Other Gambulean prisoners are tied to stakes and flayed alive, and one man has his tongue ripped out for uttering blasphemies against Ashurbanipal's gods.[20] Ranks of musicians line the bottom panel of the relief, playing harps and singing victory songs. Although the eventual fate of the Gambulean leader is not depicted on the walls the annals tell us what became of him – 'they laid him on a slaughtering block inside Nineveh and slaughtered him like a lamb'.[21]

In this victory parade we finally get to see Ashurbanipal himself – the king is aboard his chariot, shaded by a parasol, looking out over the scene. However, we cannot see his perfect face – it was deliberately gashed out in antiquity. When Nineveh fell in 612 BC all those whom Assyria had oppressed for so many generations finally took their revenge. They burned the palace to the ground, but before they did so, they went around deliberately mutilating images of the king – not only the face of Ashurbanipal, but images of his grandfather Sennacherib too. The Babylonians still remembered him as the one who had destroyed their city seventy-seven years before. They also targeted Ummanigash, the king who had once taken refuge at the Assyrian court. This literal defacing was not an act of spontaneous rage, but most likely a deliberately planned strategy. In Mesopotamia images had power – just as a statue of the god was an embodiment of the god itself, an image of the king was thought to reflect his real presence and power. It is for this reason that the Assyrians erected victory steles – tall monuments – in distant lands as a symbol of their presence: not only was it a visual reminder to distant peoples of who was in charge, but the symbolism took on a reality, for the Assyrian king was held to be truly present there in some sense.

When we take a closer look at the palace reliefs that have been attacked in this way, we notice something rather interesting – it is specifically the eyes, ears, and hands of the king that have been damaged. Erasing these body parts prevented them from seeing, hearing, or acting in the world they had left behind. Even in the lion hunt reliefs, where Ashurbanipal is shown grasping a lion by the tail his wrist has been erased, denying him the satisfaction of winning at his favourite sport. This vandalism was also an act of revenge for deeds that Ashurbanipal had himself committed against Elamite kings, like his desecrating of the statue of King Hallushu-Inshushinak I whereby he 'cut out its tongue that had scoffed, sliced off its lips that had spoken insolent words, and cut off its hands that had seized the bow to fight with Assyria'.[22] These power struggles between kings carried on even beyond the grave.

The battle of Til-Tuba was not the end of the Elamite saga. After the defeat of Teumman Ashurbanipal restored Ummanigash to the throne, assuming he would be grateful to Assyria for its aid. This assumption proved incorrect. When war broke out between Assyria and Babylon in 652 Ummanigash took Babylon's side, along with the kings of the lands of Gutium, Amurru, Ethiopia, and Arabia, some of whom owed their thrones to Ashurbanipal 'by the command of the god Ashur'.[23] The details of this phase of the war are given in the Rassam cylinder, the last account of Ashurbanipal's campaigns. Here Ashurbanipal characteristically blames his faithless brother entirely for the Elamite betrayal, stating that he 'made them become hostile towards me' through bribes of gold, precious stones, and jewellery, bristling with outrage at the ingratitude after all he had done for them.[24]

Although Ashurbanipal rails against his brother's ingratitude in the Rassam cylinder, he presents the war itself as a victory swiftly accomplished. The entire campaign, which lasted four years, is described in a few sentences: 'I confined him together with his fighting men inside Sippar, Babylon, Borsippa, and Cutha, and I cut off their escape routes. I brought about his defeat countless times in city and steppe. As for the rest, they laid down their lives to plague, famine, and starvation.'[25] As we know from other records in the library, it was considerably more complicated than this. However, Ashurbanipal's official accounts are written to demonstrate the awesome power of the Assyrian king and his gods, not to explain the detailed ins and outs.

The reason we hear about the fates of the Elamite kings who take part in this drama is mostly to demonstrate what happens to those who spurn Assyria and dare to follow their own inclinations. Ummanigash is punished for having betrayed Ashurbanipal: he is assassinated and replaced by Tammaritu I (not the son of Teumman, but an earlier king).

The focus now shifts back to the Babylonian war. The people of Babylon 'who had sided with Shamash-shum-ukin and plotted evil' succumb to starvation on account of the siege, resorting to eating the flesh of their sons and daughters and gnawing on leather straps as the only food they can find.[26] All the great gods of Assyria unite to throw Ashurbanipal's brother into a raging fire, and hunt down all those in his court who encouraged him to rebel, ensnaring them in their great net and delivering them into Ashurbanipal's hands.[27] Ashurbanipal must have had mixed feelings about not being able to capture his brother alive. On the one hand, the fact that he glosses over the details of his death implies he was uneasy with the situation. After all, he and his brother had once been close – earlier inscriptions speak of him as his 'favourite brother' and even wish 'may his days be long and experience the fullness of old age!'[28] On the other hand, he was denied the chance to make an example of him – in the victory scene on the palace walls the Babylonian king's mace, ceremonial hat, and cylinder seal are presented to Ashurbanipal as trophies in lieu of the person who would have worn them, which would not have been as satisfying as the real thing.

Ashurbanipal could not let the Elamites go unpunished for helping his brother. Nothing enraged Ashurbanipal so much as the treachery of Nabu-bel-shumati, a governor of an area called the 'Sealand' in southern Babylonia, who had joined forces with Shamash-shum-ukin and been a prominent leader in the rebellion. Ashurbanipal had suspected that he might defect – as we saw in the chapter on extispicy, he specifically asked the gods whether this would happen. This was another person who had once been loyal to Ashurbanipal and had turned against him, a further stinging betrayal. Although the exact chronology of events is unclear, the Elamites later refused demands to extradite Nabu-bel-shumati; it is possible that they had already refused once before, and so Ashurbanipal decided to go and get him himself.

At first this looked like it was going to be easy. Ashurbanipal captured the city of Bit-Imbi, the Elamite stronghold that was the launchpad for their attacks on Assyrian territory, killed the people inside, decapitated them, sliced off their lips, and 'took them to Assyria to be a spectacle for the people of my land'.[29] He also captured some notable Elamite figures and brought them back to Assyria alive. When the new king Ummanaldashu heard the news he fled to the mountains, leaving the way clear for Ashurbanipal to install his puppet Tammaritu.[30]

But Ummanaldashu was not so easy to get rid of after all – he soon deposed Tammaritu and retook control. Characteristically, the Assyrian annals present this as the work of their gods, as if it were a good thing. Amid rumours of rebellion, Ashurbanipal invaded Elam once again, for the second time that year, ravaging the country like never before.

Assyria's favourite military strategy was to terrify the enemy into submission by devastating towns on the way to the main target. This certainly worked in Elam – Ashurbanipal tells us how he conquered, destroyed, demolished, and burned fourteen cities and turned them into ruin mounds on the approach to Susa, the Elamite religious capital. Seeing what would happen once Ashurbanipal arrived, Ummanaldashu again took fright and fled to the mountains for a second time – naked, as Ashurbanipal likes to tell us.[31]

With the king gone, Ashurbanipal was free to annihilate the people, smash the Elamite gods, and plunder the land. It seemed like the country was his to do with as he pleased – at the command of Ashur and Ishtar he marched around triumphantly over an area of sixty leagues. He carried off the statues of the gods, taking them back to Assyria, along with people, young and old, to be resettled in the Assyrian heartland. He delights in telling us the details of the sack of Susa. He opened up the palace treasuries, where no enemy had been before, taking back all the treasures of Babylon that former kings of Elam had stolen over the centuries. He takes particular pleasure in telling us that he reclaimed the gifts that his wicked brother had given Elam as bribes, and stripped the palace of all its furnishings.[32]

This was no mere plundering mission, however – the aim was to systematically destroy Elam's greatest cities so as to prevent them from ever bothering Assyria again. This was both practical and psychological warfare, attacking symbolic targets that would destroy the morale of the people as well as the resources of the city. The ziggurat was the first thing to be destroyed, with all the gods who dwelt within it removed and carried off to Assyria. This was a sure sign to the people that their gods had abandoned them. Ashurbanipal removed statues of protective spirits that guarded the temple and destroyed all sanctuaries in the land. He desecrated sacred places by entering secret groves not usually accessible even to ordinary Elamites, let alone to marauding enemies, and burning them down. Next, he took revenge on the former Elamite kings who had caused problems for Assyrian kings for generations. This was of course couched in religious language – they are the ones 'who had not revered Ashur and Ishtar and who had disturbed the kings my ancestors'.[33] Ashurbanipal destroyed their tombs, exposing them to the sun, that is, to the gaze of Shamash, god of justice, who sees the crimes of all. Destroying their tombs was not enough, for Ashurbanipal actually took their bones back to Assyria, to prevent their ghosts from sleeping and deprive them of funerary offerings, leaving them to torment their descendants.[34]

Finally, Ashurbanipal ruined Elam's agricultural land by scattering salt over the fields to stop anything growing there again. He rounded up people of all ages and classes, from the daughters of kings to officials such as city mayors and workers, including soldiers, engineers, and artisans, and put them to work in Assyria. He forbade the singing of work songs, and allowed wild animals to wander through Elam's cities as if they were meadows. He even took earth from Elam's most important cities and cultural centres and took it back to Assyria, a symbol of his subjugation of the land. It was a thorough and complete conquest that brought Elam to its knees; the kingdom never seriously troubled Assyria again. Supposedly, the Elamite king Ummanaldashu crept back from the mountains and sat down in his destroyed city in mourning.[35]

There was one last matter to take care of – the treacherous governor Nabu-bel-shumati. The way Ashurbanipal presents it, when Nabu-bel-shumati heard the message demanding his extradition he lost all hope: the Assyrian devastation of Elam had been so effective that this long-time traitor's spirit was finally crushed, and he committed suicide. Ashurbanipal's account takes on a novelistic tone, switching to the perspective of Nabu-bel-shumati and telling us his innermost thoughts. Anxious and distressed, 'His life was not precious to him and he wanted to die.'[36] We even get snatches of imagined dialogue when he speaks to his personal attendant, saying, 'strike me down with the sword.'[37] He and his attendant then run each other through with their daggers.[38] At moments of great emotional import the narrative focuses in.

Terrified into obedience, Ummanaldashu packs the corpse of Nabu-bel-shumati in salt and hands it over to Ashurbanipal's messenger, along with the head of the attendant. Even angrier with this traitor than he had been with the Elamite kings, Ashurbanipal refuses to hand over his corpse for burial, and further mutilates the body, cutting off Nabu-bel-shumati's head and making him 'more dead than before'.[39] Ashurbanipal is nothing if not thorough.

Similarly, he did not rest until he had finally captured Ummanaldashu himself, though this took at least two more years. Eventually Ummanaldashu was unseated by a rebellion and he took to the mountains yet again, where Ashurbanipal 'caught him like a falcon and took him alive to Assyria'.[40] The capture of this Elamite king is also depicted in the reliefs – Ashurbanipal must have been pleased to have finally caught him.

This is Ashurbanipal's side of the story, the way he wanted his campaigns to be remembered. The reality was of course rather more complex. The fate that befell Teumman was extremely unusual, as is the attention it receives in the reliefs and the annals. Some of the complications of the story may also be a way of trying to cover up things that had gone wrong. For instance, the fact that Ashurbanipal stayed in Arbela to celebrate a festival instead of going out to fight may look to us like he was shirking battle, but it may in fact have been intended to justify the embarrassing fact that the king of Elam was killed by a common soldier rather than by the king of Assyria himself. Kings should only be killed by other kings, not beheaded on the battlefield in a free-for-all. Ashurbanipal makes a big deal out of the Teumman episode precisely so that he can control the narrative around it, presenting it as divinely ordained rather than unintentional.

Letters from the royal archives give us a glimpse of what else was going on behind the scenes. While the kings are the main characters in the official version, Ashurbanipal also wrote directly to the elders of Elam, and to the city assembly of Babylon, dealing directly with the people, and showing that political power did not reside solely with the rulers. By writing to these other bodies Ashurbanipal could put pressure on the rulers to give in to his demands. For instance, when he calls for the extradition of Nabu-bel-shumati it is the elders he addresses.[41] The elders have been asking themselves why Assyria has been treating them badly, but Ashurbanipal says they know perfectly well why, and it is an insult to even ask the question. He reminds them that when the usurped Elamite crown prince Ummanigash fled to Assyria requesting aid to retake his throne, he sent his army to Elam in support, and did not take any spoils of war but treated the country well – 'did we not pour oil on blood and become friends?'[42] And yet despite this the Elamites are now sheltering Nabu-bel-shumati, a traitor to Assyria. There is no other reason for Ashurbanipal to be hostile towards the country except for their own disgraceful behaviour, as he makes abundantly clear in letters. He demands:

> Why would I persecute your country? If it were a trading post of beautiful stones or anything else, I could think, 'let me see this added to my country', or, 'let me take horses and mules from it and add them to my troops.' I might think, 'it is a source of silver and gold; let me impose tribute upon them', or, 'there are things worthy of kingship there.' But there's nothing of this or that there. Why then would I persecute your country?[43]

Ashurbanipal's contempt for this mountain kingdom is biting. Perhaps it is no wonder that the Elamites in turn disliked Assyria so much. Ashurbanipal closes the letter by giving them a way out: all they have to do to make peace and have their gods returned to them is hand over Nabu-bel-shumati and his accomplices. But if they refuse, 'I swear by Ashur and my gods that under the aegis of the gods I will make the future even more horrible than the past for you.'[44]

The tactic seems to have worked – Ummanaldashu, the king of Elam, did after all deliver Nabu-bel-shumati into Ashurbanipal's hands. In one surviving letter he insists that he had nothing to do with Nabu-bel-shumati coming to Elam, blaming the whole episode on a group called the Martenians who lived near the border. It is they, he says, who have sinned against Ashurbanipal, who brought Nabu-bel-shumati across the river into the country and started the fight between Elam and Assyria in the first place. Ummanaldashu is keen to stress that as soon as Ashurbanipal wrote to him he did as asked, and that these Martenians are rebels whom he will call to account for their sins. In this letter at least, Ummanaldashu takes great pains to cooperate, though whether he is telling the truth is hard to say.[45]

Communications were not entirely hostile, then, even before the very end. After the defeat of Teumman in 653 the elders of Elam appealed to Ashurbanipal for help – the Persians had been raiding the country, and the Elamites asked Ashurbanipal to install a king to preserve the social order. Letters to some of the Elamite kings are quite cordial, with Ashurbanipal addressing them as his 'brother' and wishing them well.[46] In return, Elamite rulers were sometimes quite obsequious towards Ashurbanipal, full of good wishes for his eternal reign: 'May the king, my lord, rule the four quarters of the world! Just as heaven and earth last for ever, may the king live for ever!'[47] There were fleeting moments of peace between the two countries, then, although only when Elam acknowledged Assyria as a superior power, and some kings were more willing to do this than others.

In the war with Babylon there were also other parties involved beyond the two brothers. Letters from the archives show us that Ashurbanipal started out by courting the city assembly, indicating that his dispute was not with them but with their king, and that they could save the city if only they would open the gates.[48] He tells them not to listen to the lies spun by his brother, whom he refers to as his 'no brother', insisting that he has never even thought any of the detestable things that his brother has spoken against him. He assures the people that they are close to his heart, and that they will not suffer for their former hostility, which he blames entirely on the manipulations of Shamash-shum-ukin.[49] The people are not swayed, however, and Ashurbanipal's letters become ever more aggressive. Ashurbanipal declares he will break his brother, threatens to burn the whole land of Akkad, and suggests that perhaps the gods themselves have decreed the Babylonians' destruction since it seems the rebels will persist in their bloody-mindedness.[50]

All this shows that Assyria was not quite as feared and respected as the Assyrians wanted people to think. In fact, there were plenty of people willing to stand up to Ashurbanipal and unafraid of the terrifying radiance of Ashur and Ishtar. The official account, of course, portrays this as an abomination, the rebels rudely forgetting all the kindnesses that Ashurbanipal has done them. But Assyrian kindness came with strings attached, and both Elamites and Babylonians may have felt it wasn't worth it.

Ashurbanipal did not act alone either, but would have sought advice from his scholars. The knowledge held in the library would have come in useful in times of war and would have informed the opinions of king and court alike. As we have already seen, crucial military decisions were put to the gods via extispicy, the sacrificial sheep helping to answer vital strategic questions. The only queries to survive from Ashurbanipal's Elamite wars concern whether or not the Elamites will join forces with the Babylonians, and whether the chief eunuch should be sent to plunder the Elamite allies in Gambulu, both of which did come to pass (even though the extispicy said the Elamites would not march against Assyria).[51] This paucity is likely to be an accident of survival, for many more survive regarding the war with Babylon, and more extensive records from the reign of his father Esarhaddon show that the king consulted the gods about all of his campaigns. Esarhaddon asked about the intentions of the enemy and whether they would attack certain cities,[52] whether it was a good idea to send messengers to foreign kings and whether their replies would anger him, if the messenger would even return home alive,[53] and of course whether battles and sieges would be successful.[54] Extispicy was used to find out these outcomes when there was no word from the battlefield,[55] and to verify whether or not Elamite kings meant it when they proposed making peace. The gods were consulted at every turn and provided valuable intelligence on events happening far away.

Astrology was also a vital strategic tool. We even see one astrologer using celestial omens to recommend very specific military actions. When Esarhaddon was planning to invade the country of Mannea, in what is today north-western Iran, numerous letters from his astrologer Bel-ushezib suggest military strategies based on celestial events. For instance, Bel-ushezib quotes an omen describing the behaviour of a meteor: 'if the flash appears and appears again in the south, makes a circle and again makes a circle, stands then again stands there, flickers and flickers again, and are scattered: the ruler will capture property and possessions in his expedition.'[56] He then tells the king that he should release the army in stages, rather than all at once: the cavalry and foot soldiers should go ahead while the chariots and wagons stay back in the pass. Cavalry and foot soldiers should repeatedly enter the countryside, plunder it, and come back to take a position in the pass, just as the meteor repeatedly flashed and circled in the sky. Only after several rounds of these raids should the whole army throw itself against the cities of Mannea. There is sound political nous behind the recommendation, for there were untrustworthy allies to take account of. The Cimmerians, a nomadic people who control the central Zagros mountains, have promised that they will not interfere and will allow the Assyrians to do as they please to their neighbours, but Bel-ushezib suspects this may be a lie to lure the army into a trap – 'they are barbarians who recognise no oath sworn by a god and no treaty'.[57] Mimicking the movements of the meteor, then, will allow the troops to invade in a controlled way and not commit the whole army before they know whether or not the Cimmerians will keep their bargain.

We don't know whether or not Bel-ushezib's advice was followed, but we do know that the invasion was successful and Esarhaddon captured forts, plundered towns, and pillaged the open country of Mannea.[58] At this point, Bel-ushezib writes again to encourage him that he should return and plunder the rest of the country too, as not to do so would be dangerous.[59] It is reminiscent of Machiavelli's advice that if an enemy is injured the injury should be so severe that you need not fear his retaliation. Bel-ushezib is similarly crafty and strategic in his approaches to the king. He begins his letter with a celestial portent to set the tone and lend credibility to his suggestion – he has seen a lunar crescent that portends evil for the Manneans. He then explains his reasoning: 'wherever an enemy attacks the country, the country will carry this evil portent.'[60] Bel-ushezib then reminds the king that a similar omen had been observed before:

> last year, when the moon was seen with the sun on the 15th day for five consecutive months, did Sidon not carry it? Did the city not fall,

> were its people not chased away? Now in accordance with this, the cities of the Mannean will be plundered, his people taken in captivity, and he himself will be encircled in his palace until he will be delivered into the hands of the king my lord.[61]

Just as the omens were reliable in the past, so they will be now.

There is one caveat – Bel-ushezib's interpretation of these omens is not the standard one that is found in the main series of omens held in the library. The principle he cites, that the evil of the portent will affect whichever country is being attacked at the time, seems to be entirely of his own making. Perhaps it is one he had derived from his own experience and observations, such as when Sidon was invaded, or perhaps he has found other theoretical principles that justify it in his reflections on the omen series. It's not known for certain whether he is the only one to do this or whether these kinds of adaptations were the norm. But what it does show is that Assyrian scholarship was dynamic and evolving rather than beholden to fossilised antiquated texts. It is certainly based on a venerable ancient tradition, but this one scholar at least was willing to interpret those principles in a contemporary way. The temptation from a modern point of view is to see Bel-ushezib as manipulating the king with his scientific-sounding pronouncements. We will never know what his true intentions were, but it seems fair to view him as any other scientific adviser today, using his knowledge, experience, and judgement to build a case that he thought the king would find appealing, and which would be successful.

That the interpretation of omens was so important in times of war throws a different light on Ashurbanipal's bookish tendencies. Knowledge is power, and academic expertise need not be confined to the ivory tower but was extremely useful for fighting a war. Yet Ashurbanipal was the only Assyrian king to embody this and stands out from his predecessors in his approach.

Ashurbanipal as a military man is full of contradictions. His wars are the focus of his annals, yet the gods waged them on his behalf and explicitly tell him to stay at home. His reliefs show him seizing lions by the throat, yet he was often absent from the battlefield, leaving these operations to his generals. As king of Assyria, it was his job to uphold the image of effortless superiority and military might, but he may have valued scholarship more highly and preferred to stay in the library. In the introduction to the annals recording his campaigns he describes how the great gods determined his destiny and gave him gifts of character. The very first thing he lists – before power, virility, and outstanding strength – is a broad mind and grasp of all the scribal arts.[62] This might be explained by his upbringing: Ashurbanipal had not been the first choice for heir to the throne and was trained as a scholar, destined for a very different career before the succession plans changed. Yet even as a prince preparing to become a king, again he tells us that he learned 'the wisdom of the god Nabu, all of the scribal arts . . . the precepts of every type of scholar there is'.[63] This hints at where his priorities lie. He did also learn to shoot a bow and ride a horse and chariot, but in only one version of the many inscriptions does he claim, 'I know how to wage war and battle; I am experienced in forming a battleline and fighting.'[64] One wonders where exactly he obtained this experience. The reliefs depicting the Elamite wars are unique among Assyrian art in their density of literary and scholarly allusions – for all his talk of violence, these were the interests closest to Ashurbanipal's heart.

⁂

The Assyrian war machine was successful against both Babylon and Elam. Despite the constant setbacks, comebacks, and uprisings, Ashurbanipal did finally subdue Elam and capture its kings. But while Elam could be dealt with and forgotten about, the same was not true of Babylon, whose history and culture were so deeply intertwined with those of Assyria. By waging war on Babylon, Ashurbanipal sowed the seeds of Assyria's own destruction, deepening Babylonian resentment and creating the conditions for yet another uprising. Five years after Ashurbanipal's death, an Assyrian general of Babylonian origin called Nabopolassar broke away and established himself as king of Babylon in 626 BC. In 614 BC he teamed up with another rising power in the east, an Iranian people called the Medes, who invaded and took the Assyrian city of Ashur. Various other tribes who had been oppressed by the Assyrians for generations also joined forces with them, and they all converged upon Nineveh in 612 BC, burning Ashurbanipal's palace and library to the ground. The Assyrians held out for another few years, but in 610 they were driven out of their last stronghold in Harran and in 609 failed to take it back. The Neo-Babylonian dynasty inherited Assyria's empire, and the torch passed back south again to the original cultural centre of the Near East.

How was Ashurbanipal remembered? Although he projected an image of himself as both scholar and warrior, the warrior image does not seem to have stuck. The later Mesopotamians remembered Ashurbanipal for his love of learning, perhaps because it was so unusual for Assyrian kings. Ashurbanipal was famous for his tablet-collecting in the ancient world as well as today, so much so that stories concerning the subject were preserved long after him. For instance, when seeking tablets for his library Ashurbanipal wrote to the scholars of Borsippa and ordered them to 'write out all the knowledge in the property of Nabu and send it to me!'[65] The scholars duly complied, working day and night to make copies of every tablet in the temple library. What is extraordinary, though, is the fact that they also copied their reply to him on to special tablets of alabaster, not just on ordinary clay tablets, and circulated it far and wide. It is as if the Borsippans were proud of being asked to provide the king with their knowledge. There may also be a hint of intercity rivalry, as the letter implies that the Babylonians tried to get out of fulfilling the king's request, but that the Borsippans are far more cooperative. The Babylonians certainly learned what the Borsippans had been saying about them, since a copy of this letter turns up in Babylon possibly as late as five hundred years after Ashurbanipal's time. It was written out by an apprentice scribe as part of his studies – Ashurbanipal the scholar had become a textbook figure for the preservation of knowledge in the very last phases of cuneiform culture.

In spite of this, the persona of Ashurbanipal that passed into legend is very different from the one he himself would have approved. A Greek doctor at the Persian court, Ctesias, wrote about the legends of the east circulating there, one of which was the fall of Nineveh.[66] Ctesias' account no longer survives, but fragments are reported by the Greek historian Diodorus Siculus. In this tale, Ashurbanipal is known as Sardanapalus, and is lambasted for his effeminacy, cross-dressing, and indulgence, all things that the Greeks strongly disapproved of. Sardanapalus is the epitome of decadence, more slothful than any ruler before him, and allows his kingdom to fall because he prefers whoring to fighting. Emboldened by a few early victories, he becomes arrogant and overconfident and spends too much time feasting rather than looking after his empire. The enemy besieges Nineveh, and after two years Sardanapalus succumbs. He builds his own funeral pyre and drags his concubines on to it, consigning himself to the flames rather than face his comeuppance.

We should not trust this account for any real portrait of Ashurbanipal and his ways. For one thing, he was already dead when the Medes and Babylonians rounded on Assyria, and many details of the story are much closer to the siege of Babylon than the siege of Nineveh, suggesting that the two had become confused. What it does show, though, is that despite all his conquests not everyone saw Ashurbanipal as the ultimate warrior king. Although this particular story dates from about 150 years after Ashurbanipal's death, one cannot help but think of the goddess Ishtar instructing him to eat, drink, and make merry while she does the real slaughtering on the battlefield. That is a strange detail to include and seems somewhat pre-emptively defensive. Perhaps others at the court were asking questions as to why this self-proclaimed heroic man of outstanding strength was talking the talk but not walking the walk.

The Neo-Assyrian empire dominated the Near East for more than 250 years, systematically expanding and bringing foreign lands into the shade of Ashur. Under Ashurbanipal it really was the largest empire the world had ever seen and set the pattern for later empires to follow. The Persian empire is often credited with being the first ancient empire to have ambitions of world domination, but in reality, they built upon the groundwork that the Assyrians had laid. The Persians inherited the Assyrian system of provinces and governance, along with the incredible network of roads that the Assyrians had built to facilitate fast travel across their territory. They also took inspiration from Assyrian art in creating an image of imperial splendour – the famous palace of Darius at Persepolis has a portrayal of the Persian god Ahura Mazda hovering above ranks of soldiers in a winged disc, depicted in the same way as the Assyrian Ashur flying above the battlefield. These elements borrowed by the Persians in turn went on to influence successive empires in the Near East. Although the Assyrians themselves were no longer a political power, their empire did live on after them.

In some ways the Assyrians were victims of their own success. Their continued expansion was not sustainable, and their methods of frightening people into submission ultimately backfired. Elam could only be controlled by devastating it completely, which did not benefit Assyria as much as if they had turned it into a tributary state. And their tactics and attitudes towards Babylon created deep resentment that directly resulted in their downfall. Ashurbanipal's last wars may in fact have weakened Assyria by exhausting it with prolonged fighting, since the empire collapsed only nineteen years after his death. By destroying Elam, the Assyrians removed a buffer zone, opening the way for the Medes to join forces with the Babylonians and advance all the way to Nineveh. As much as the Assyrians were famous for their prowess in war, perhaps, in the end, they had too much of a good thing. With war comes regret, and Ashurbanipal would have to make amends.

9.
Lamentation

After the war, tears must be shed. Nabu-zeru-iddina stands on the roof of the temple, looking out over war-torn Babylon. The palace is a smoking ruin, and the streets are choked with corpses, scavenger animals growing fat on the flesh of the starved dead. The last time he saw the city it was a thriving metropolis – now it has been devastated by war. Although he has lived in Assyria for many years, Nabu-zeru-iddina comes from a Babylonian family and has a special connection to the city. In fact, his ancestor was once the chief priest of this very same temple where he now finds himself. Ashurbanipal has brought Nabu-zeru-iddina here to perform laments to the gods of the city, but while for Ashurbanipal this is just part of his post-battle routine, for Nabu-zeru-iddina it is deeply personal.[1]

Ashurbanipal's war against his brother has finally come to an end. Babylon was under siege for the last two years of the long war. The city held out for an impressively long time, but the siege took its toll and Babylon fell in the autumn or winter of 648.

Now it is time to clean up. All those who incited Shamash-shum-ukin to rebel against Assyria have come to grief – those who did not die of famine or burn in the fire that ravaged the palace were cut down by Ashurbanipal's soldiers. Ashurbanipal chose a symbolic setting for the final executions: the bull colossus where Sennacherib had been murdered by his sons, since he was the last Assyrian king whom the Babylonians had defied. Now Ashurbanipal was making up for it, killing Babylonians as funerary offerings for his grandfather. He fed their dismembered flesh to creatures of the air, earth, and water, dispersing their remains in all directions.[2]

Such devastation needs more than a physical tidy-up. The city has to be cleansed and purified on a spiritual level if its gods are to be appeased and allow it to become prosperous again. Ashurbanipal has brought in the priests to help, to perform rituals of lamentation, and persuade the angry gods to return to the city. Behind this lies the Mesopotamian belief that all suffering is caused by divine abandonment. Surely the city would not have fallen had its gods been there to protect it. Through outpourings of grief, the priests will make it clear how terribly the people have suffered as a consequence, expressing their contrition, begging the gods to return. When they have proved to the gods how sorry they are, it is hoped that they will come back and all will be well.

As the new ruler of the city, it falls to Ashurbanipal to perform this lament. However, there is an obvious tension here – Ashurbanipal is not sorry at all. From his point of view, the Babylonians absolutely deserved to be abandoned by their gods, since they had committed the cardinal sin of rebelling against Assyria. That is the official line at least, and indeed is how it must seem to Nabu-zeru-iddina, who has been drafted in to orchestrate the performance. Will the gods really be persuaded by something so obviously contrived? But as we will see later, this is not the only occasion where laments are performed as a matter of routine. Perhaps Nabu-zeru-iddina is used to it.

Privately Ashurbanipal may feel rather differently. The laments are, perhaps, an occasion for Ashurbanipal to give vent to his complex feelings about the whole conflict. It was not easy for him to destroy Babylon, especially with all the scholarly wisdom that had originated in that city. Moreover, the capture of Babylon has meant the death of his elder brother, and while Ashurbanipal's inscriptions are full of vitriol against him, the intense sense of betrayal is worsened by the fact they were once close. Behind the outward conqueror's façade, Ashurbanipal's feelings are mixed.

The tensions in the above scene capture the essence of lament in Mesopotamia. Lamentations were performed in response to specific events like those described above, and individuals often poured out their sorrow to the gods in prayers. But at the same time lamentations were sung regularly in the temples, as specialist priests would sing songs of grief in long, formal liturgies, bewailing the destruction of cities and shrines even when no such destruction had yet taken place. Why did they do this? The expression of grief was thought to be extremely important in Mesopotamia, as witnessed by the many surviving prayers that give voice to such feelings. Indeed, it was so important that lament was institutionalised and made a formal part of the temple cult, no longer an individual sorrow but a responsibility of the state to keep the gods onside. It is a very different understanding of the purpose of grief.

The Mesopotamians had many types of laments for different occasions, from personal to formal, all of which survive in Ashurbanipal's library. Laments also find expression in literary forms: the poems that describe the destruction of cities are among the finest in Sumerian and Akkadian. Daily lamentation, however, was a particularly Babylonian practice. Unlike other branches of Babylonian theology and ritual it was not imported into Assyria until relatively late, and was only fully integrated sometime in the early first millennium BC. From the time of Sennacherib onwards, a period that Nabu-zeru-iddina's family lived through, the adoption of lamentation traditions in Assyria intensified. Lamentation illustrates the complex relationship between Babylonian and Assyrian religion and politics, as the Assyrian kings appropriated Babylonian traditions for their own ends. How and why did this come to pass? We will come back to Ashurbanipal's lament over his own destruction of Babylon, but first let us explore how Nabu-zeru-iddina ended up in Assyria.

Nabu-zeru-iddina was a professional lamenter whose job was to perform the daily rituals in the temple. His family had been in the business for a long time – they proudly declared themselves to be descendants of Shumu-libshi, who had been the chief singer in the temple of Marduk in Babylon, the highest rank it was possible to reach in the profession. Nabu-zeru-iddina's grandfather had trained his son in the same skills, teaching him to sing and play music, and to memorise the many formal prayers and liturgies that pleased the gods. His efforts paid off, for his son Urad-Ea became the chief singer in the temple of the moon god Sin in Harran, a city in northern Syria under the control of the Assyrian empire.

Later Urad-Ea was recruited by Esarhaddon to become the chief lamenter of the king. For the first time, a lamentation priest had joined the ranks of the royal entourage and was part of the king's inner circle of advisers. Here he supervised the arrangements for performances during processions of the gods, and even ritual performances in the palace. He probably continued to serve the moon god, or at least stayed loyal to him, since he always sent a blessing from Sin when he wrote to the king. As was the norm in scholarly families, his son Nabu-zeru-iddina followed in his father's footsteps and succeeded him as the king's chief lamenter.

Nabu-zeru-iddina worked with five other lamenters in the palace, who seem to have been of middling rank. In a list of experts working at court during the reign of Ashurbanipal the lamenters are the fifth group, coming after astrologers, exorcists, diviners, and physicians, but before other foreign experts such as augurs and Egyptian scribes.[3] As relative newcomers, the lamenters were not afforded the same status as Assyrian giants of scholarship, but the Babylonian pedigree of their knowledge ranked them higher than the other foreigners. Both Urad-Ea and Nabu-zeru-iddina corresponded directly with the king, while the Egyptian experts did not.

As the children of immigrants, lamenters in Assyria may have felt as though they belonged to two cultures. They had lived in Assyria a long time, but retained a strong connection to Babylonian traditions, which may have given them a dual sense of identity, and an outsider status. There are hints of trouble in letters from temples where other staff accuse lamenters of theft. For example, a priest of Ninurta in Kalhu complains that a lamenter has stripped off bands of silver from the wall and cut away pieces of gold from the beams in front of the god himself.[4] When this kind of thing happened in the king's father's time, he says, such thieves would have been put to death, implying the king should now do the same. The priest is outraged, since he claims the lamenter has stolen from the temple before; nothing was done about it then, and now there the thief is, getting away with it again, with not even a reprimand. Another informant complains of institutional corruption as a larger problem, explaining that a lamentation priest he has accused of theft had previously committed another theft, but the temple authorities had simply retrieved the items and hushed it up.[5]

Other people with similarly important roles in the temple were not usually accused of such misdeeds. Did the Assyrian priests resent these newcomers who were suddenly granted access to the most sacred areas? Another angry letter from Kalhu complains that a lamenter has been changing the way the rites are performed, taking over responsibilities that used to be carried out by others, appointing his own officials, and refurbishing the temples without permission from the king.[6] This priest also points out that all the treasuries are under the control of this particular lamenter and that he doesn't show the god's jewellery to anyone – not exactly a straight accusation but a hint that he thinks this man cannot be trusted. It seems that the Assyrian priests did not like these southerners barging in and taking over. In some cases their suspicions were justified. But prejudice can become a self-fulfilling prophecy, and the fact that two lamenters betrayed the gods in these Assyrian temples may imply they did not really feel at home there. Even Urad-Ea, who worked for the king, did not feel safe – he asks the king for a bodyguard to be sent with him to the New Year festival processions 'because of the traitors'. Who these traitors were and why he was afraid is not known.[7]

Whoever accompanied Ashurbanipal to Babylon would not have needed to worry about a lack of bodyguards. In reality we can't know for certain whether it was Nabu-zeru-iddina who was entrusted with the task, but it would have been someone close to the king. As Ashurbanipal's most senior lamenter it is likely that Nabu-zeru-iddina would have been involved in organising the proceedings, and given that the king had to be guided through the ritual, it seems likely it would have been conducted by somebody he knew. But even if it was not, the scene sketched here would have had the same emotional import for any lamenter. They all practised a profession that originated in the south, and must have grieved the destruction of Babylon, their former home. Despite this, they had to help the Assyrian king reconcile himself with the gods for his terrible crime, a reconciliation which they may or may not have felt he deserved.

⁂

Rituals of lament were originally a response to collective trauma and had been a part of Mesopotamian culture for around sixteen hundred years. The Sumerian poem *The Curse of Agade* describes how the city and empire of Agade were destroyed by none other than the Elamites in the twenty-third century BC, and how the survivors responded to the disaster.[8] For seven days and nights they played harps and drums to the chief god Enlil. The old women and men cried, 'Alas for my city!', the young women tore out their hair and young men sharpened their knives, and the lamentation priests cried out for the destroyed temple.[9] Here we already have professional lamenters leading the whole community in an act of mourning, the people coming together to process their grief.

The destruction of cities in times of war was a common event but was no less traumatic for being so. Certain destructions went down in history and were remembered for many generations afterwards, becoming part of the Mesopotamian tradition that was carefully passed down through the ages. *The Curse of Agade* commemorates the fall of the first Akkadian empire, the dynasty founded by Sargon (r. c. 2334–2279 BC), a king so famous that Ashurbanipal's great-grandfather probably chose his name for that reason. The next event to scar the Mesopotamian collective consciousness was the invasion that brought an end to the Ur III dynasty in 2004 BC, which is the subject of five Sumerian poems.[10] Each of these focuses on a different city, describing the terrible devastation its inhabitants suffered. Here we see a clear attempt to make sense of the misfortune, as the poets attribute it to the anger of the gods, who abandon their cities.

The *Lamentation over the Destruction of Sumer and Ur* is one of these, and is one of the finest examples of the genre, commemorating the fall of the city of Ur and the surrounding land of Sumer, not just the capital city but the whole kingdom.[11] It opens with a long litany of disasters to befall the region, a litany so long that the first sentence describing it stretches over fifty-four lines. The sentence ends by telling us that all these horrors were decreed by the great gods. The gods had decided that the people would be slaughtered, that weeds would grow in the formerly fertile fields, that families would be broken up and the king would be led off to the enemy land in chains – all this is the city's fate. Each of the major gods uses their powers against Sumer: Enki the god of watercourses blocks up the flow of the rivers, the sun god takes away all sense of justice, Inanna the goddess of war hands over the victory to the enemy, and the warrior god Ningirsu throws Sumer away 'like milk poured to the dogs'.[12] The heads of the pantheon An and Enlil strike fear into the people and send an evil storm across the land. The storm uproots huge trees and strips orchards of their fruit, darkens the sky, and stirs up dust. It is a metaphor for the destruction as a whole – Enlil sends down invaders from the mountains: their troops are the storms that gather to strike like a flood.[13]

One by one the gods of the cities of Sumer abandon their destroyed temples. The destruction of the temple is the greatest sacrilege of war in Mesopotamia, for temples were the innermost heart of the city, sacred enclosed places that were normally forbidden to ordinary people, shielded from any impurities. But now their walls are torn down and these quiet sanctuaries are exposed to the light; the statues of the gods are shattered, and enemy soldiers take their pick of the spoils.

The Elamites are key players in this invasion, a testament to the long history of tension between Elam and Mesopotamia. Interestingly, Ashurbanipal boasts of desecrating the land of Elam in the same way that the laments bewail how the Elamites desecrated Sumer all those years before. Ashurbanipal was proud to have destroyed the temple and plundered it, to have ruined Elam's agriculture, and reduced its people to famine. The lamentation over Sumer and Ur says, 'the foreigners in the city even chase away the dead', which brings to mind Ashurbanipal's removal of the bones of Elamite kings from their tombs.[14] Ashurbanipal's claims are general tropes of destruction rather than a response to this specific poem, but he would probably have known of the fall of Sumer at the hands of the Elamites all those years ago, and may have felt their debts were finally being repaid.

Although the destruction of cities was normally taken as a sign that its gods had left, Nanna, the Sumerian moon god and patron god of Ur, does not give up on his people so easily. Nanna approaches his father Enlil directly to plead on behalf of the city, begging him to reconsider his decision. Enlil's response is dispassionate:

> The case, the pronouncement of the assembly cannot be reversed.
> The word spoken by An and Enlil knows no overturning.
> Ur was indeed given kingship, but it was not given an eternal reign.
> . . .
> The reign of this kingship is becoming too long, is exhausted.
> My Nanna, do not exhaust yourself, leave your city.[15]

This is a stark acknowledgement that the rise and fall of empires is simply part of the natural order. Sometimes there may be no fault or blame: things have simply come to their natural end. Usually when a god abandoned their city it was because the people had neglected them or angered them, but this does not seem to be the case here. Nanna does not leave voluntarily but does his best to appeal Enlil's verdict. Yet his intercession is not enough, and Enlil is clear that no city is fortunate enough to rule for ever. There is nothing that can be done. Nanna takes Enlil's advice and leaves. The Elamites are free to do their worst.

The city laments, as these texts are known, sorrowful though they are, are not entirely pessimistic. In fact, they all have happy endings. After the long enumerations of all the catastrophes suffered, the gods change their minds and the cities are restored. After the Elamites have desecrated the temple, the worst sacrilege of war, Nanna tries to persuade Enlil one last time. His words may echo the feelings of the Sumerians as they struggled to make sense of what had happened: 'O father Enlil, the fate that you have decreed cannot be explained!'[16] This time Enlil's response is more favourable. He tells his son that the city will be rebuilt in splendour and its former prosperity will return; all the destruction that it suffered will be turned back and inflicted upon its enemies. The rest of the poem takes the form of a prayer for this better fate and restoration, including a telling refrain: may the gods 'not change it'.[17]

This happy ending is political. The poem was most likely composed during the reign of Ishbi-Erra (c. 2017–c. 1985 BC), the man who took over from the last king of Ur and founded a new dynasty. He needed to present himself as a legitimate successor to this previously mighty empire – the perfect way to do this was to commission poems that acknowledged the very real suffering people had experienced yet also looked forward to the time of renewal that he would bring about. The other Sumerian city laments were probably part of this programme too.

The *Lamentation over the Destruction of Sumer and Ur* was part of the school curriculum in the Old Babylonian period, meaning that children were taught about this key event in Mesopotamian history approximately three hundred years after it happened. The poem does not feature in the tablets that we have recovered from Ashurbanipal's library, but the memory of the event lived on, since many other texts dating to the first millennium associate the last ruler of the Ur III dynasty with catastrophe – his name was for ever entwined with the end of empire. Ashurbanipal's library does contain laments over cities and disasters that are suspiciously similar to the *Lamentation over the Destruction of Sumer and Ur*, implying that this ancient poem was still well known and influential. The tradition of lament remained a strong one, and it was important to commemorate the difficult times, as well as glorify the good.

The city laments are a case of art imitating life, for they were inspired by another genre, formal ritual laments that took place in the temple. The ritual laments would not have been studied in school, but only by those who were training to become lamentation priests (*kalu* as they were known in Akkadian). These specialist performers would have sung to the gods in their innermost shrines, in the silence of the sanctuary away from the hustle and bustle of everyday life. On special occasions when the gods went out in procession the lamenters accompanied them, singing in the courtyard and in the street, and only then would ordinary people have a chance to hear the music of the gods.

Despite its being a very Babylonian practice, our best source of information for ritual lamentation is Ashurbanipal's library. Every ritual lament known to us is preserved there, many of them in multiple copies. The collection contains laments looted from Babylon after the war, some of Nabu-zeru-iddina's own tablets and those of his father, and laments belonging to the temple library of Nabu next door, which have become mixed up in the modern collection.

There were three different types of lament: *balags*, *ershemmas* and *ershahungas*. The first two of these are named after the instrument that would have been played to accompany them. The *balag* was probably originally a harp or a lyre, but the word later came to designate a drum. The *ershemma* is the lament of the *shem* instrument, probably a kind of cymbal or some other small percussion instrument. Nabu-zeru-iddina would have sung these laments and played these instruments too. *Ershemmas* were solo performances by one priest, but *balags* may have been choral pieces, on some occasions including many other temple singers, which would have been dramatic events. The lamentation priest sang the main part to a thunderous beating of drums, answered periodically by the choral refrains that cry out to the gods. Reliefs from the Assyrian palaces show the lamentation priest in his distinctive fishtail-shaped hat standing solemnly next to a drummer, closing his eyes as he waits for his cue. Tablets from the southern city of Ur that date from many centuries after the fall of Assyria contain instructions for performance – vocal ornaments are indicated in tiny script above the lines showing where the singer was to stretch out the vowels or alter his pitch.

Another feature of the laments tied to their performance is their repetitive nature. As well as repeating key words and phrases over and over, the cultic laments contain long passages of nearly identical lines with slight variations, such as 'May you not abandon your city! May each utter a prayer to you!', with the name of the city changed each time.[18] This makes for pretty heavy and monotonous reading, but the laments were not designed to be read, they were designed to be performed, and in performance these repetitions come alive. Together with the beating of the drums they would create a trancelike state – both for the performers, who could have achieved altered states of consciousness, and for the sake of the gods who were listening. These are, after all, laments to pacify the hearts of the gods, and the rhythms created by the repetitions have a soothing quality.

As a professional lamenter, Nabu-zeru-iddina's job was to appease the gods with his singing. Cultic calendars show that laments were sung regularly, probably even every day in the temples in Assyria, accompanying the daily schedule of offerings. The lamenters would sing before the god's statue as if to a person who was really there. In the dead of night before the god arose and was seated in his temple the lamenter would sing a song called 'Come out like the sun!', an expression of hope during the darkest hours that the god would show his favour with the dawning day, which can also be seen as something of an alarm clock. The statue of the god was literally taken out of bed, dressed, and seated in the temple for breakfast, listening to the dulcet tones of the song 'It touches the earth like a storm'. So that the god did not become bored, on the next day a different song was chosen, and he would wake up to the sound of 'The bull in his fold'. There was a standard playlist to pick from, but different temples chose different songs on different days and had their own order. In Ashur there were at least two performances per day.

While it is easy for us to think of this as entertainment, these were serious occasions, no less so for taking place every day. A glance at some of the titles reminds us of their mournful nature: 'Instilling fear like a serpent', 'Flood which drowns the harvest', 'That city which has been pillaged'.[19] The laments enumerate suffering and destruction at length and in crushing detail. For example, in 'Come out like the sun!' the description of the destroyed temple, 'the faithful house', lingers over every part of the building:

> Its crenelated wall has been destroyed. Its dove hovers about.
> Its door frame has been torn down. What was once a place of marvel is no more.
> Its rafters lie exposed to the sun like a man felled by disease.
> Its jutting brickwork is crouching in tears like a mother in mourning.
> Its reed mat is contorted like a person suffering from colic.
> Its reed eaves are lying on the ground like plucked hairs.
> Like a flying bat its . . . has disappeared within the ruin mound.
> In closing the door its door posts have fallen like a man bathing . . .
> The bar and the bolt of the faithful house moan . . .
> The lord Enlil has turned it into a haunted place.[20]

According to the song, the temple has been razed to an absolute ruin. And yet this lament was sung in temples that were very much intact. The terrible desecration of the temple that features in these songs had not actually taken place, and the lamentation priest would be singing it in front of the god in the heart of his house, its crenelated walls and door frames very much still standing. This is not a lament over destruction which had happened, but over destruction which could take place in the future. This pre-emptive strike showed the gods that the people know that they could desert them at any time, and acknowledge how devastated they would be should that happen. The gods would hear these songs and would be pleased that the people recognised their almighty power, and thus would not feel the need to demonstrate it. It is a clever piece of reverse psychology. In this way, a practice that originated in outpourings of grief after a real event was worked into a routine and became a way of ensuring that such horrors would never happen again. It is the very opposite of 'don't worry, it might never happen'. On the contrary, anticipating the worst-case scenario was the very way to avoid it, or to accept it as inevitable.

Nabu-zeru-iddina's songs all had the specific aim of pacifying the angry hearts of the gods, or preventing them from becoming angry in the first place. Because of this they were not only sung as part of the daily liturgy but also on special occasions when there was an extra risk of something going wrong. For instance, during the New Year festival the statues of gods were sent out of their temples to special venues for the performance of the rites, but this made the gods vulnerable and if something happened to the statue it would be very serious indeed. During the processions, then, the lamenters chanted soothing prayers as a kind of insurance policy against any mishaps – the apologies were already in motion. Nabu-zeru-iddina's father wrote at least two letters to the king assuring him these recitations would take place, and that the gods would bless the king in return.[21]

Another particularly risky activity was restoring temples. Like most structures in Mesopotamia these were made of mudbrick, a sturdy composite material, but one that does have to be periodically replaced as the brick eventually crumbles. Unlike in Egypt where temples were made of stone and successive kings added more and more chapels in annexes, Mesopotamian kings were preoccupied with temple repairs, restoring them to their former glory. In order to do this, they had to knock down the existing structures to build them again in new materials, but demolishing the houses of the gods would of course be extremely likely to anger them. All the songs about destroyed temples now come into their own – the lamenters bewail the ruined sanctuaries as they are being deliberately destroyed by way of apology to the gods, and their prayers that the temples will be restored are particularly pertinent. They know that the restoration will happen because the king has organised it, but it is not guaranteed that the gods will return to the temples and happily dwell there. Even though it is necessary to tear down before rebuilding, to destroy before creating, the moment must be marked, grief acknowledged and processed before joy can be felt. Besides, restoration cannot be taken for granted until it has actually happened – even today it is not uncommon for building projects to be abandoned when the money runs out, and the great temple of Marduk himself seems to have suffered this fate when Alexander the Great demolished it and never got around to rebuilding.

The cultic laments are written in Sumerian, though the ones in the library are always accompanied by a line-by-line translation into Akkadian to make them easier for the Assyrians to understand. One of the most important uses of Sumerian in the first millennium BC was in fact for this lamentation poetry, which is one of the largest genres of Sumerian texts in the library. However, laments were uttered and written in Akkadian too, and are among the most exquisite examples of the language.

With their eloquent statements of the horrors of war, laments could be used to criticise the very idea of armed conflict. One of the greatest works of literature to be found in Ashurbanipal's library – the Akkadian poem of *Erra and Ishum* – does exactly this.[22] This poem describes the destruction of the city of Babylon in rich and powerful language, and although we can't pinpoint this event with certainty, the poem was probably composed as a reaction to the city's constant troubles in the early first millennium. It reads as a theological attempt to come to terms with Babylon's fall from splendour, but is clear in its expectation that the city will rise again. Like the earlier Sumerian city laments, *Erra and Ishum* explores the causes of suffering and violence but goes further and deeper into the problem. The city's destruction is not just a decree from the gods that Babylon's time is up; rather, human and divine responsibility are intertwined, and the poem questions the very assumption that the gods are in control. In the chaos and carnage of war it must seem like there is no overarching divine plan: the old gods who were formerly in charge of the universe do nothing to put an end to the slaughter, and new tactics are called for if humanity is to survive.

Erra and Ishum are the two protagonists of the poem. Erra is a god of war and chaos, Ishum is his trusty vizier. Both are middle-ranking gods – they are not on the highest tier like Marduk or Ashur, but the fact that they star in the story is a sign of the changing times. The old gods have been usurped by others. Erra can do as he pleases with no one to keep him in check, and it is Ishum who is exalted as the saviour of the people, not any of the traditional rulers.

The poem opens with Erra feeling restless and eager to start a fight. He feels that the people do not respect him and decides to lay waste to Babylonia to demonstrate what he is capable of and make them sorry. The city god Marduk has grown old and ineffectual – his statue is shabby and in need of refurbishment, neglected by the Babylonians. Erra persuades Marduk to leave his temple to visit craftsmen who can restore him to his former glory, but while Marduk is absent Erra seizes control and goes on the rampage. His wrath manifests as enemy invasion and civil war – civic order collapses and family ties disintegrate, farmlands are devastated, and wild beasts wander the city streets. Marduk looks on the destruction with horror as the governor of Babylon orders his army to plunder its own city and blood flows like ditchwater in the streets. This, at least, is the traditional interpretation of the story's set up, although missing pieces of the tablets have just come to light that may show that Marduk was on board with Erra's plan all along. Perhaps he is all the more horrified when he witnesses the consequences of what he has agreed to.

Erra revels in the carnage, glorying in the havoc he wreaks. Much of the narrative consists of speeches, with Erra describing all the terrible things he is doing in a grim hymn of self-praise:

I obliterate the land and reckon it for ruins,
I lay waste cities and turn them into open spaces,
I wreck mountains and fell their wildlife,
I convulse the sea and destroy its increase,
I bring the stillness of death upon swamp and thicket,
burning like fire,
I fell humankind, I leave no living creatures.[23]

But all is not lost, for Ishum takes pity on the people and steps up to intervene. Ishum stands up to his master Erra and asks him directly, 'why have you plotted evil against god and man?'[24] Erra replies that Marduk has abandoned his temple and that is that – the king of the gods has decided to forsake Babylon, so he is free to do as he pleases. But Ishum knows his master better. He recognises that behind all this is a craving for recognition, and resentment at being overlooked. He points out that Erra is now master of heaven and earth, that all the gods fear and respect him. Yet Erra is so caught up in his anger that he cannot see any of this, and still thinks he is held in contempt. It is a rare instance of speaking truth to power, and an astute observation about the blindness of rage. In the Sumerian city laments it is the destruction of the temple that is the most shocking event, but here it is the death of innocent people that moves Ishum to despair:

He who did not die in battle will die in the epidemic,
He who did not die in the epidemic, the enemy will plunder him,
He whom the enemy has not plundered, the bandit will
murder him,
He whom the bandit did not murder, the king's weapon will
vanquish him,
He whom the king's weapon did not vanquish, the prince will
slay him,
He whom the prince did not slay, a thunderstorm will wash
him away,
He whom the thunderstorm did not wash away, the sun will
parch him,

He who has gone out in the world, the wind will sweep away,
He who has gone into his home, a demon will strike him,
He who has gone up to a high place will perish of thirst,
He who has gone down to a low place will perish in the waters![25]

The slaughter is systematic and brutal; no one survives. Erra has put to death the righteous and unrighteous alike: the high priest who has piously made offerings, old men sitting at home and young girls sleeping in their bedrooms. Ishum's eloquent speech laments the terrible destruction of Babylon and speaks against the senseless destruction of war. It is deeply moving, even today. He quotes the hopes of ordinary people about to be shattered – the man who proudly fathered a son to take care of him in old age, the man who has just built a house and looks forward to growing old there. In a final rhetorical flourish, and one of the most spectacular passages of Akkadian poetry, Ishum quotes Erra's innermost thoughts back to him, as he vows that:

I will make breasts go dry so babies cannot thrive,
I will block up springs so that even little channels can bring no life-sustaining water.
I will make hell shake and heaven tremble,
I will make the planets shed their splendour, I will wrench out the stars from the sky![26]

We might expect such a speech to be confronting, but Erra receives it very differently – he is happy to hear it. After hundreds of lines of this litany of destruction, Erra is appeased. The words have the desired effect. Ishum's speech pleases Erra 'like the finest oil', that is, as a good-quality offering would.[27] This catalogue of disasters is proof that his power has been recognised, and he no longer feels the need to continue his campaign. It is exactly the same principle that is used in the ritual laments – praising the god by acknowledging their power to inflict terrible suffering if they chose to and making it clear that human beings revere and fear them. This was all Erra had ever wanted in the first place, to be honoured and respected. Ishum's lament finally convinces him that he is.

The poem of *Erra and Ishum* has a lot to say about human psychology. After all, Ishum does not attempt to reason with Erra with philosophical arguments, but instead gives him the recognition he craves. Just as Ishum has to acknowledge Erra's influence and power, on a human level anger must be recognised if it is to abate. The difficult emotions embodied by Erra cannot be ignored, for doing so only makes them grow all the more until they spill over in an uncontrolled frenzy. It is important to honour all the gods, no matter what they stand for, not only the gods whom we feel comfortable approaching. And so it is with human emotions – the dark side cannot be repressed altogether, however much we might want to ignore it.

It is rare for Mesopotamian gods to admit they were wrong. Erra comes surprisingly close, acknowledging that Ishum was right to intervene to soothe his rage. If he had not, humanity would be finished, and the gods would have no one left to provide for them. Even so, we get the feeling that Marduk's time is up – just as in the *Lamentation over the Destruction of Sumer and Ur* the message is that no reign lasts for ever, not even that of the gods. The order he had ushered in has crumbled again, and Mesopotamia in the early first millennium felt like a different world, an unstable place repeatedly torn apart by war; many must have lost faith in the gods who were supposed to be regulating the universe. At the end of the poem, it is Erra who enters Babylon in triumph, not Marduk – the implication is that he is the new city god of Babylon, that chaos must be revered to prevent it from being unleashed again.

The poem dramatises the principles of ritual lament and shows that what was going on every day in the temples was extremely necessary. But it was not a strategy only to be used by the priests in the temples – lamentation was integral to all kinds of prayers and rituals, a key part of the exorcist's arsenal, and very likely employed by ordinary people too. Prayers uttered in times of suffering often include heartfelt laments when they ask the gods to turn things around, as well as praise for the deities' mighty power. The same is true in incantations where the exorcist has the patient lament their situation before he takes special measures to do something about it. Lament was a fundamental part of the way that people approached the gods in Mesopotamia – the gods had to be persuaded to take their side, and could be moved with tears as well as with praise. What the poem of *Erra and Ishum* shows is that lament and praise are two sides of the same coin, for weeping acknowledges the gods' terrible power.

The poem of *Erra and Ishum* had a very practical purpose, too. At the end we find a list of the many benefits of praising Erra and of knowing the poem well: the singer who sings it as a lamentation will be spared from the plague, the scribe who masters it will gain fame and honour, the scholars who call on Erra will be granted understanding.[28] But it is not only the specialists who will benefit – displaying a copy of the poem in the house will keep any household safe from the plague, another of Erra's characteristic weapons.[29] This is advice that people followed – the whole poem was written out on tablets shaped like an amulet with special piercings for hanging on the wall, as discovered in the exorcist's house in Ashur, while smaller extracts praising Erra have been found written on amulets as well. As this god of war and pestilence stalked the streets he would be appeased by these displays of respect and leave the houses untouched. These are not just ornamental decorations, but words with real power and potency that people used in their everyday lives.

⁂

Although city laments are usually expressions of collective grief, *Erra and Ishum* is one of the few poems to have an individual author, which suggests it may also have been personal. The poem was supposedly revealed in a dream to one Kabti-ilani-Marduk, who tells us at the end that he wrote it all down when he woke up. The divine source of the poem is clear, for Kabti-ilani-Marduk insists that he left nothing out nor added a single line to what he had heard. Its divine origin may be the source of its power, for Ishum's successful lamenting strategy is passed on to humans by the gods as a model to emulate. It is extremely rare for Akkadian poems to refer to their own authors, who usually preferred to remain anonymous. Yet even this stand-out instance of a claim to authorship ultimately defers to the gods.

The library contains other more personal examples of individuals lamenting in times of suffering too. All kinds of ritual texts contain lamentations as a crucial part, as people name their tribulations before asking the gods to grant relief. One devotee praying to Marduk for deliverance from illness describes their pain:

> You know the illness from which I suffer, I do not.
> It flattens me like a net, shrouds me like a mesh.
> Torment, head pain, fatigue, inflammation, [and anxiety . . .
> have . . .] my limbs,
> foul disease, oath and curse, make my flesh creep.
> They have made my frame feverish, I am clothed in them as if
> with a garment.
> Symbols and images of me are interred.
> They have collected dust from under my feet, they have taken
> my measure, they have taken away my vitality.
> I am infected and beset by people's wicked machinations,
> the fury of my personal god and goddess and humankind
> is against me,
> my dreams are terrifying, awful, evil,
> my signs and omens are confused and have no clear
> interpretation.[30]

So the Mesopotamians poured out their feelings to the gods when they were in difficulty, and did not hold back from expressing sorrow to each other as well. From what we can glean from their letters to the king, the scholars often lamented problems in their private lives when they were looking for help – and not only those scholars who were close to him. One scholar claims to be dying for lack of support and of cold because he has nowhere to live.[31] There are no other letters from him in the archive – we never hear of him again. As we saw, when the exorcist Urad-Gula falls from favour he writes with a litany of miseries describing his pitiful circumstances, and quotes a proverb saying, 'He who has been stabbed in the back has still got a mouth to speak, but he who has been stabbed in the mouth, how can he speak?'[32]

Psychologically there is something very powerful in naming suffering. To give something a name is to acknowledge it, to make it real, but at the same time to lessen its power over us, as we can be soothed by recognising and accepting our feelings. It is not only the gods or the king who might be appeased by laments, but the people uttering them too.

Even mighty kings were not above expressing their sorrow and railing against the unfairness of life. In a highly unusual tablet, Ashurbanipal himself bemoans his situation, bound by unhappiness and ill-health, surrounded by discord and strife despite all the good he has done for the gods. The text begins like a conventional building inscription, recounting the temples he has restored, stating that he has followed the commands of his father in making his brother king of Babylon and installing two of his younger brothers as high-ranking priests of Ashur and Sin. He has done his duty in making offerings to his ancestors, performing good deeds for both the gods and for men, for the dead and the living, but it has made no difference. 'Why are illness, misery, expense, and loss firmly bound to me?'[33] Even though he feels he has done everything right, the gods do not seem to agree, though he cannot see the reason for it:

> I spent days in saying 'woe!' and 'alas!' . . . Death takes hold of me, I am suffering severely. Day and night I wail on account of depression and melancholy. I am exhausted. O god, give these things to someone who does not revere you so that I may see your light! How long, o god, will you treat me this way? Do I myself behave like someone who does not revere god or goddess?[34]

Here the text ends abruptly, leaving this rhetorical question hanging, a direct challenge to the gods. It is a rare admission from a king who elsewhere portrays himself as the perfect embodiment of kingship and strength. Behind the façade Ashurbanipal suffered like everyone else, and questioned the very gods who he boasts elsewhere had chosen him to rule. It is an intensely human moment, where even the most learned of kings struggles to come to terms with his reality. Having carried out his duties as expected all his life, he finds it is not enough. In the words of the *Babylonian Theodicy*, the classic poem on suffering and divine justice we encountered in Chapter 2, 'The will of the gods is as remote as the innermost heaven. Who can understand it?'[35]

As Nabu-zeru-iddina looked out over his war-torn city, he may silently have uttered his own lament. All the laments to the gods that he knew by heart would have echoed within him as he saw the terrible effects of destruction that he had worked every day to avoid. He has sung these laments pre-emptively in other cities, all of which had remained safe. Had the priests in Babylon been doing their duty, he might have wondered? Or had all this come about because of their failure to take care of the god and perform his rites? He would have known of the famous destruction of Babylon described in the poem of *Erra and Ishum* and felt like he was seeing history repeating itself. Ashurbanipal had entered the city as the embodiment of rage and chaos, the god taking his revenge through human actors in another form. And now it was time for the ritual laments to cleanse the city of this pollution, to draw a line under it and start again. If the gods would accept his prayers.

Ashurbanipal tells us in his inscriptions that he performed laments and purification rituals after the sack of Babylon.[36] The purification rituals would have involved many offerings and sacrifices. The exorcist would utter his incantations, invoking the gods to carry out the cleansing. The altars would be piled high with roasted meat, fat, and shoulder joints, libations poured of the finest beer, wine, and milk.[37] Ashurbanipal uttered the type of lament known as an *ershahunga*, which translates as 'heart-soothing tears'. While we do not know which one he chose, many different examples of *ershahungas* to Marduk were held in the library; the text below is taken from the best preserved.

Nabu-zeru-iddina would have prepped Ashurbanipal for this moment, but the king was not a professional lamenter and had to take part in many rites, so was probably not expected to memorise them all. *Ershahungas* are not sung but recited, which would have made the task easier – at least he didn't have to try to stay in tune. Nabu-zeru-iddina probably would have led the king through the ritual, asking him to repeat the words after him, beginning with his penitence:

> Let me speak of my crimes!
> I wail, I cannot hold back my sobs.
> In the bedroom there is weeping.
> In lament and wailing I suffer every day.
> Lord, bitterly I raise a cry to you, hear me!
> Come before my lifted hands, hear my prayer![38]
> I am your servant, I bow down before you
> . . . I constantly seek your shrines.[39]

Lifting his arms up to the sky in supplication, bowing and humbling himself before the god, here the almighty king of Assyria must admit he has done wrong and that he is suffering for it. Whether or not Ashurbanipal actually felt this way, the fact he was made to do it was a powerful symbol. It was a personal lament uttered on behalf of the whole community. The lament is classified as a prayer to Marduk, though it begs many different gods for mercy. As king of all the gods, if Marduk takes pity the others may well follow. The priests can utter all the spells they like, but without the blessing of Marduk it is all for nothing. The lament of the king, his personal apology, is vital.

If Ashurbanipal had not been sorry to begin with, the power of the ritual would certainly make him so. The performance of laments on occasions like this probably lasted hours, for none of them were performed alone but instead were part of a large complex of rituals and prayers. Leading up to the king's personal petition would have been many *balags*, choral set pieces accompanied by clangorous drumming, hypnotic and long litanies of intense and unrelenting grief that could not fail to produce intense feelings in anyone taking part. After so many repeated cries of despair and exhaustion the music would stop, creating a silent backdrop for the king to speak, his recitation made all the more powerful for its stark difference from all that preceded it. Though performed as a prescribed offering to the gods, the ritual was just as valuable for its effects on those who performed it, generating the very sorrow that the gods required. The gods must have their grief, and the king would have to give it to them.

There is no word for 'sorry' in the Babylonian or Assyrian language, just as there is no word for 'please' or 'thank you'. Instead, people expressed their emotions, and showing genuine remorse was good enough to count as an apology (expressing hope or joy was the equivalent of please and thank you). This partly explains why it was so important to express grief – it was proof of contrition, a demonstrable sign of sincerity. We have created a shortcut with the word sorry, but in doing so have bypassed an important part of the reconciliation process. It is one thing to say sorry and not mean it, it is much more difficult to describe in detail the consequences of your actions without feeling apologetic. It is also much more effective in appeasing the wronged party to acknowledge blame so explicitly. While in our language a simple sorry can of course be accompanied by wording that fulfils those other functions, it does not have to be. The difference is that in Mesopotamia it was an inescapable part of making an apology.

It is remarkable that the expression of grief was so highly valued that it was institutionalised, and that scholars like Nabu-zeru-iddina could lament as a full-time job. Lamenting was important not just for the individual, but for the well-being of the whole country.

Disasters were pre-empted by fast-forwarding into the future and lamenting their consequences, and lamentation was one of the most important tools for appeasing the gods, as important as caring for their statues and giving them offerings. Ashurbanipal's laments performed in the wake of his own sacking of Babylon served many functions – to soothe the rage of Marduk and promise he would be better cared for in future; as a ritual of collective mourning for the inhabitants of the city to come to terms with what had happened; and perhaps even as a way for Ashurbanipal to come to terms with his own conflicting feelings in the triumph of his victory and the bitter death of his elder brother. We do not know how Ashurbanipal or Nabu-zeru-iddina really felt, but in one thing at least they were successful: they did indeed coax the gods to return to their home city, for Babylon would soon rise up and engulf Assyria. Marduk would have his revenge, and there would be more tears to come.

Every culture has some form of ritualistic mourning, and our own is no exception, from state funerals that are highly orchestrated by the government to spontaneous mass vigils in the wake of terror attacks. What was special in Mesopotamia was its scheduled regularity, how lamentations were sung even when there was nothing to lament, as insurance against catastrophe. There is no parallel for this in modern Western society, which can make it seem extremely strange. Yet many of us make use of similar strategies without knowing it.

Lamenting a potential disaster when everything is fine is akin to worrying about something before it happens. Sumerian lamentations reflect a society-wide anxiety about the future, about the fragility of good times, about the very real precarity of human existence. The Mesopotamians externalised these anxieties and gave voice to them in a formalised way. When we express our worries, we are doing the same thing, working out our fears by giving shape to them. As we have seen in our study of magic and medicine, ritual of all forms gave the Mesopotamians a way to feel in control of difficult situations, which itself was psychologically helpful.

Less constructively, ritual lamentation could be seen as catastrophising taken to its greatest extreme, taking a fear of a remote possibility and amplifying it by constantly ruminating, endlessly going over the same repetitive scenarios. One could see the daily temple rituals in this light, which devoted several hours every day to mourning and sorrow over events that had never taken place. Yet the Mesopotamian rituals acknowledge this by scheduling set times for the practice, which has also been shown by modern psychologists to stop anxiety from spilling out and constantly dominating one's thoughts (and in the Mesopotamian case, delegating the worry entirely to special professionals so the rest of the population didn't have to think about it). When we think about the psychological functions of lament the Mesopotamians suddenly seem much closer to us than we had previously thought – we too lament in our own way over catastrophes that may never come to pass, and as the Assyrians show, finding formal ways to deal with this can be an effective way forward.

10.

A Day in the Life of Ashurbanipal

Ashurbanipal awakes with a start. He has had a bad dream and the traces cling to him. The details are already slipping away but those he can remember are strange – something about a pot belonging to the goddess Ishtar, and the city of Zikku was somehow involved.[1] He always pays attention to his dreams, since they could be messages from the gods, and he has a bad feeling about this one.[2] He will ask his diviner Dannaya to do an extispicy and ask the sun god about it. In the meantime, though, he has his own remedy. Before he puts his feet on the floor, he says out loud, 'The dream I saw was good, good indeed, by Sin and Shamash!'[3] By making this simple declaration, the evil ought to be averted.

The library at Nineveh was not a place where tablets went to gather dust: this was knowledge that was meant to be used, even before the king got out of bed. As we have seen throughout this book, the library's tablets were a source of practical knowledge that could be called upon in times of illness, grief, concern for the future, war, personal despair, and difficult decisions. So far, we have focused on particularly significant moments or special occasions in the life of the king and his family, but the relevance of Mesopotamian scholarship goes much further than that, into their everyday lives.

To explore this more intimate side to the library, we'll move through one imagined day in the life of Ashurbanipal after the war on Babylon was over. From the dreams he remembered on waking to the food he ate, the games he played, and the sex he had, the library's tablets contain an extraordinary level of detail about the rhythms, pleasures, and challenges of daily life for the Assyrian elite. Bringing together the expertise of the various scholars we've met, we can see the knowledge of Mesopotamia in action, giving structure to life, providing ways of understanding and dealing with its problems, and ultimately giving meaning to daily existence.

Ashurbanipal had not slept well and was not in a good mood. Being king of Assyria was a stressful job and Ashurbanipal had plenty to be testy about. He may have crushed Babylon, but the Elamites were still causing trouble and were refusing to hand over the traitor Nabu-bel-shumati. Ashurbanipal was particularly fixated on this and would not let it go, constantly raging about it in his correspondence. In reply to a letter on a different topic the king of Urartu remarks on Ashurbanipal's irritability, saying, 'Why does the king my lord always write in such a grumbling mood and full of rage?'[4] I can't imagine him as a morning person.

Records regarding Assyrian dream omens give us an indication of some of the bad dreams the Assyrians had: eating human flesh,[5] washing your hands in your own urine, or drinking the urine of an animal.[6] Given the Mesopotamian love of omens, inevitably dreams had meaning, and the library contains a series of tablets that explains them: for instance, eating the meat of a corpse meant somebody will take away what you own, but eating the flesh of a friend meant that prosperity was coming. If a man dreamt of eating his own penis, however, it meant his son would die.

The meanings of dreams were not always straightforward and are often counterintuitive for us. One of the worst things you could do in Assyria was dream of carrying a table down the street: in a cryptic piece of logic, it meant you would die thanks to the wrath caused by your own words.[7] Bad dreams were not necessarily bad omens: for instance, dreaming of eating the faeces of a friend was good luck, while eating the faeces of a wild animal portended riches.[8] Perhaps this was a kind of consolation, similar to how being shat on by a pigeon is said to be good luck in England today. Equally, good dreams were not always good omens – being given wine in a dream was a sign of a short life, while being given honey announced that there would be a death in the family.[9] The dream world can seem like an inversion of the real world, where things that appear to be bad are good and vice versa. But not always – that would be far too simple. Benign dreams included catching a fish in the river ('he will obtain his heart's desire'),[10] being given juniper ('he will have a pleasant year'),[11] and meeting a pig in the street ('he will have sons, his mind will be at peace').[12] Like us, the Assyrians dreamt of flying – and this was always bad luck.[13]

Thankfully, whatever the dream, there were rituals at hand. If Ashurbanipal still felt uneasy after his own declaration he could go to the exorcist for further assistance. The exorcist might suggest that Ashurbanipal pray to Shamash, the sun god who dispersed the night with day, and bring him a clod of earth as an offering, dissolving it in water to represent the evil of the dream disappearing.[14] To avoid the bad dream recurring the next night, the king could instruct his exorcists to perform rituals to ensure good dreams. It seems that one of these rituals was even part of the standard 'rites of the month Elul' (August/September) and was performed to protect the king as a matter of course. The exorcists have left us a letter informing the king of what this involved.[15] They set up a special altar to the moon god made of tamarisk wood, and at the head of the bed put an offering of juniper incense for the god of dreams. Then they washed the king's hands and anointed them with spices and bound lumps of salt, juniper, and cassia to the hem of his garment along with pieces of wood taken from the door. Hopefully this would keep the dream god happy and stop nightmares approaching the bed.

After rising early, the king would go for a hunt. First things first: time to kill lions. Ashurbanipal's inscriptions specify the exact time of day this took place, forty minutes before daybreak, presumably when the animals were drinking at the watering hole.[16] The palace reliefs show him hunting all kinds of creatures, pursuing deer in the mountains, driving them into great nets, and shooting gazelle while crouching in a pit. He hunts onagers on horseback with a pack of hounds, and his attendants bring back hares and small birds from their outing as well as a dead lion, which requires six strong men to carry it. Ashurbanipal never missed an opportunity to vaunt himself over the Elamites and manages to do so here: one image on the palace walls shows Ashurbanipal rescuing an Elamite prince from an attacking lion, shooting over the prince's head while he crouches with arms outstretched, pleading for help. As seen previously, thc Elamitc royal family sought refuge at Ashurbanipal's court to escape from their tumultuous feuding back home where they had been ousted, and he clearly liked to take them on his hunting expeditions to prove his strength. Not only did Ashurbanipal defeat the Elamites in war but he was better at hunting than they were – no wonder they needed his protection.

Hunting was a common pastime for Assyrian kings, as it was for kings in many ancient cultures. But even when hunting Ashurbanipal was not merely relaxing but exercising his duty as a representative of the god Ashur. It was the king's job to bring order to chaos – he mainly did this by conquering foreign lands, but also by taming nature and subduing wild animals. The sport that most epitomised this was the royal lion hunt, a ritual occasion where the king would slay the king of the beasts to demonstrate his control over the natural world as well as the civilised one. By killing the lions, the king was protecting his kingdom, since they were a very real danger and preyed on livestock as well as attacking people (lion attack is an event commonly predicted in omens of all kinds). Turning it into a ceremonial event came to symbolise his protection of his people in a wider sense too.

The royal lion hunt was commemorated on Ashurbanipal's palace walls, and can be seen today in the British Museum. A version of it was staged as a public occasion and drew a large crowd of spectators, as the king demonstrated his power to his adoring people. A makeshift arena was created by two rows of soldiers encircling the space with their shields, plus dogs on standby, and the audience are shown running up the hill to get a better view. The lions have been captured in advance and are released from cages – Ashurbanipal makes for them in his chariot, shoots them down with his bow, and spears them in the throat. He grabs one lion by the neck and stabs it, yanking another by the tail as he raises a mace over its head – acts of ultimate bravery. During the event eighteen lions were killed in all, one for each of the gates of Nineveh, symbolically securing the entrances to the city.

At the end of the hunt Ashurbanipal dedicated his victory to the gods. The reliefs show him pouring a libation of wine over the bodies of the lions before a table heaped with offerings and incense for the gods. Musicians play the harp and eunuchs fan the king, his bow clutched in his left hand, described in a caption as 'the fierce bow of Ishtar, lady of battle'.[17] Having done his duty for the gods, he now gives thanks to them. The lion hunt may have been part of the victory celebrations following triumphs over human enemies too – one text in the library describes an elaborate victory ritual followed by libations poured over a dead lion.[18] Mastery in war and hunting are linked, and a lion hunt would have made a nice addition to the public celebrations. But even when out hunting Ashurbanipal does not forget his identity as a master of scholarly knowledge – one relief shows him seizing a lion by the throat with a stylus tucked into his belt. The king of Assyria never went anywhere without a pen.

What the rest of the day held would depend on whether it was deemed to be auspicious or not. To find out, Ashurbanipal and his advisers could consult what we call hemerologies, which are kinds of calendars prescribing activities that would go well on a certain day and others that should be avoided. There were different types of hemerologies that were relevant to different levels of society, from the ordinary person up to the king. The library holds several copies of the so-called *Babylonian Almanac*, which stipulates whether a day is lucky or unlucky, and lists its suitable and unsuitable activities. There is an entry for every single day of the year, and all of them are preserved, making it one of the best-preserved of all cuneiform texts. The *Babylonian Almanac* is applicable to everyone, setting out which days are best for marriage, going to court, or to achieve a goal. It also points out particularly risky activities for a given day, such as 'he should not cross the river or sickness will seize him'[19] or 'he should not retrace his steps in the street or he will experience loss'.[20] Some days are more likely to see attack by wild animals, confusion, or even insurrection. Others are labelled as favourable or unfavourable with no further explanation. The almanac even dictates when to avoid eating certain foods: pork, beef, fish, leeks, and dates are all singled out as causing disease or bad luck if eaten on the wrong days. No doubt the royal kitchens would have taken note.

Other hemerologies are aimed higher up the social scale and include information such as days when a physician should not see a patient, or when the diviner should avoid consulting the gods. These tend to give more detail about the consequences of doing the wrong thing on the wrong day. One lively example specifies that:

> On the fourth day of the seventh month he should not cross a river, or his sex appeal will fall away. He should not go out to a hamlet or a hostile one will accost him. He should not eat beef, mutton, or pork or he will get a headache.[21]

They even give information about which days of the month the king was likely to be in a better mood, in case any courtier wanted to approach him with a petition. Since Ashurbanipal was perfectly capable of reading these texts himself, I like to think he would have been ahead of the game and would know to expect more obsequiousness on these days. His advisers were also familiar with these calendars and used them to their own advantage – Ashurbanipal's chief scholar Balasi once remarked, 'one should not think on an evil day' as a way of avoiding answering a question.[22]

The Assyrians took these calendars and their prohibitions seriously – documents in the royal archives show that not a single extispicy was carried out on the seventh, fourteenth, or twenty-first days of the month, the days when the hemerology forbids it. Similarly, legal transactions cluster on days that were considered favourable, with people choosing an auspicious day if at all possible. The more important the activity, the more important it was to choose the correct day. The kings tell us explicitly in their inscriptions that they chose favourable days for such important events as setting out on a military expedition or starting construction work on a temple. When he was crown prince, Ashurbanipal was not allowed to visit his father except on a favourable day, something we have numerous letters about between Esarhaddon and his scholars.

Ashurbanipal's diary was organised by his chief scribe. The chief scribe would keep track of what the king needed to do for certain festivals, offerings he had to make, and calendars he had to observe, and find suitable compromises between practicalities and ideals. Sometimes a day that was favoured by the hemerologies did not work for practical reasons, but there were ways to bend the rules. When Ashurbanipal was appointed crown prince, the chief scribe came up with a clever solution to the problem of when all the king's subjects could swear an oath of allegiance to him. It seems it was convenient for the swearing to take place on the fifteenth day of the first month, but that day is specifically prohibited in one hemerology, which says, 'he should not swear on the 15th day or a god will seize him.'[23] The chief scribe gets around this by recommending they start the ceremony in the morning, but only finish it in the evening after the sun has set.[24] Since the Mesopotamian day begins at sunset, delaying the conclusion of the ceremony would mean it had technically taken place on the next day. As it turned out, Ashurbanipal did have an extremely successful reign, so the chief scribe would probably have congratulated himself that his tactic had worked.

Yet another hemerology was aimed specifically at the king and the king alone. This prescribes offerings for him to make every single day of the year. We do not know if the king actually partook in all these ceremonies, or perhaps only observed the most important ones. If he did follow every single instruction in the calendar, making offerings would have taken up a lot of his time. Records from the royal archives tell us that he did make a large number of offerings during major festivals. One of the most important of these was at the end of the year when the king was reconfirmed in his ultimate power over Assyria, as the human equivalent of the divine warrior Ninurta and the agent of the god Ashur himself. Over a period of twenty-five days in the last two months of the year, he visited temples almost every day and performed a complex series of offerings to the gods.[25] He accompanied statues of the gods into temples for the rites and put on the crown of Ashur to symbolise his defeat of the forces of chaos. Then there was a break of two weeks before the New Year festivities began, with another twelve days of ceremonies.

The king's own hemerology also specified days on which he had to abstain from certain activities. On particularly evil days, the king was supposed to refrain from eating grilled meat or baked bread, and from changing his clothes. For example, on the fourteenth day of the first month he should not ride a chariot, should not give orders, certainly should not commission an extispicy or see a doctor, and at night should make offerings to the gods. If he abides by all these instructions, 'income will flow'.[26] To us all these rules might seem like a lot to put up with, but given the promised results, some orders were worth obeying. And at least they occasionally gave him a day off.

Although Ashurbanipal was capable of reading these texts himself, he could save time by having his scholars do the checking. After all, he had plenty of other correspondence to deal with. Letters poured in from all over the empire – from foreign kings and vassals to astrologers and spies in Babylon, to his closest advisers giving daily updates on the stars, the progress of the rituals, and the health of his children. Realistically he probably didn't bother to read the letters himself, but had a messenger read them out to him.

Many of the king's letters were updates from the temples, which frequently got into trouble. Since he represented the god Ashur on earth, it was the Assyrian king's responsibility to make sure that the gods were receiving their proper offerings and that their households were running smoothly. We know from the royal correspondence that this was often not the case. As we have seen already, some priests abused their privileged access to the innermost shrine to make off with precious materials. But the priests were not the only ones who could cause problems. In the city of Ashur there was an ongoing issue with the shepherds who were responsible for rearing the sheep for sacrifice and were refusing to hand them over. After seven years of this, one of the priests reached the end of his tether and wrote to the king several times, pleading for him to do something about it – the situation had become so bad that in order to feed the gods he had to go and buy the sheep from the market himself.[27] He asks the king to send his soldiers to enforce the shepherds' obligations, and to call his servants to account.

Of course, the king had as many people writing to him protesting their innocence as he received accusations of wrongdoing. He received a constant stream of petitions from his advisers complaining about their bad treatment at the hands of others at court, as well as from those who had fallen from royal favour. One Babylonian in prison repeatedly insists that he has no idea why he was arrested as he claims he has done nothing wrong. Strikingly, he even offers to undergo the river ordeal as proof of his innocence – he must have been very confident that the gods were on his side.[28]

Everyone, it seemed, had a request. On at least one occasion Ashurbanipal's little brother writes him a letter, very sweetly referring to himself as 'baby brother'.[29] Unfortunately the middle of the letter with its main content has broken away, as is so often the case with cuneiform tablets, but in the opening and closing formulas he seems very keen to enquire after his older brother's health, which is usually what vassals and advisers do when they need to suck up to the king. Probably Ashurbanipal's baby brother wanted something too.

Letters also poured in from abroad. As well as the disputes with the kings of Elam that we have already seen, the Assyrian king corresponded with his vassals in neighbouring countries. On one occasion Ashurbanipal writes to the king of Urartu insisting he send him blocks of lapis lazuli, presumably as part of the tribute owed. It is in his reply to this letter that the king of Urartu tells Ashurbanipal off for his snappy tone, and further admonishes him for his lack of cultural sensitivity in asking for this precious material – 'Does the king my lord not know that lapis lazuli is our god? If I took the lapis lazuli the country would rebel against me.'[30] Nonetheless, Ashurbanipal still got his way. The Urartian king proposes a solution: the Assyrian army should come and take the lapis lazuli, while he pretends he has no idea what is going on. He won't dine with the Assyrian emissaries, won't be seen marching at their side or talking to his messenger, and certainly won't be seen asking about the well-being of Ashurbanipal. In this way he can concede to Ashurbanipal's demands while saving face at home, pretending he knows nothing about the Assyrians marching into his territory and taking a precious cultural asset 'by force'.[31]

Ashurbanipal did not need to write the replies himself. He had scribes to write the letters for him and would either dictate the response or give them the main points and leave them to compose the letter themselves. They would make a draft to show the king, which he would have to approve before the official version was sent out. However snappy the king might be, the scribes did not water down the king's words for diplomatic reasons – the letters very much preserve the king's character and sentiments. He gives the Elamites hell for refusing to extradite the traitor Nabu-bel-shumati, calls said traitor the whore of one of the Elamite elders, and complains about the Elamite ungratefulness to anyone who will listen.[32] He certainly does not hold back.

Other matters Ashurbanipal had to deal with were more mundane and concerned the management of his palace household. One day the exorcists report they have found an infestation in the eunuchs' wing of the palace but are dealing with it – they plan to perform a ritual against the unwelcome creatures.[33] They don't specify what the creatures are, but the ritual texts prescribe methods for getting rid of scorpions and ants, which may have been the most likely contenders. The exorcists write to the king to ask that they get the right clothes they need for the ceremony. What they wore was an important consideration, although not for physical protection as with the protective clothing worn by modern pest exterminators, or by medical staff in today's hospitals, but rather for magical reasons.[34] For certain rituals the exorcist explicitly dressed in red, taking on the mantle of the gods of exorcism – Marduk and Asalluhi – and acting with their authority. They would get rid of not only the pests, but also of any misfortune that their presence might forewarn of, thus dealing with the practical problem and its existential nature at the same time. If the creatures were in fact scorpions, and anyone trying to catch them had been stung, the exorcists had an incantation to help with that too. Ashurbanipal could call on the exorcists for all kinds of daily nuisances like this, such as fungus growing on the wall or lizards falling on his shoulder.[35] He would also need the exorcists to be present during any building renovations in the palace, such as knocking down walls or digging new wells, as they would need to apply their incantations to make sure everything went smoothly without angering the gods.

After dealing with correspondence, Ashurbanipal sometimes had face-to-face meetings with officials from around the empire. We actually have an agenda of items to be discussed with him written by a Babylonian priest, which gives us an idea of the issues the priest wanted to raise:

- Mounting precious metals on the door of the temple of Marduk.
- Beams of cedarwood to be used in roofing the temples in Babylon, Sippar, and Cutha.
- Suspicious decreases in the offerings of wine given to the gods – 'in the time of your father and grandfather they filled 800 jars . . . now they are only filling 300.'
- One city that used to send 330 sheep every year as offerings to Marduk in Babylon stopped when the crown prince took the throne and now refuses to send any more.
- Following up on the king's promise to tell stonemasons in Cutha to get on with the job.

- Taxes taken for the temple in the form of oxen and sheep, which have been collected by the governors.
- Concerning a palace official that they spoke about last time – the priest recommends that he come to work in Ashur.
- Something enigmatic concerning the king of Babylon, about whom the king said previously 'I shall have enquiries made; as for the report about which you spoke, make it good, explain . . . To me and . . . What you intend to do.'[36]

The tablet shows just how involved the king was in the everyday affairs of the temple, including tax collection, hiring and firing, supplying workmen, and sourcing precious materials for renovations. At the same time, there were many political matters to attend to – either someone was siphoning off the wine for themselves, or they were being stingy with the offerings, both of which are unacceptable. The city refusing to send sheep is surely a bad sign, of either political opposition, personal defiance, or economic problems. And the priest is even involved with a matter to do with the king of Babylon himself. It would have been a busy meeting.

One of the benefits of discussing such matters in person is of course all the non-verbal cues that can reveal so much about a person and their intentions. If Ashurbanipal had studied another text in his library, he would also have been able to draw conclusions about the priest from how he looked.[37] Physiognomy – that is, the belief that a person's character or fate can be glimpsed in their physical features – like so many other branches of mystical knowledge, also has its roots in Mesopotamia. One tablet from the library is devoted to the meaning of different types of hairstyles, my favourite being 'if the hair of his head is totally chewed up like the pelt of a bear, he will have no rival in the palace.'[38] Bad hair days, then, may not always have been such a bad thing, and in the true upending spirit of omen logic, scruffiness was a sign of superiority.

We don't know how much Ashurbanipal knew of this particular text, but he or his scholars may well have scrutinised visitors' appearances for clues as to their trustworthiness. For instance, 'if the hair on the left side of his forehead is chopped off like reeds: he will constantly carry off the possessions of the king.'[39] The king's advisers could stay on the lookout for such people, knowing this was a possibility. The Babylonian priest with the long list of agenda items would have been spared any judging of his hairstyle, since priests had their heads shaved. But that wouldn't necessarily have stopped Ashurbanipal from analysing the shape of his head, the patterns of his wrinkles, or the location of any moles on his face. Most of the time physiognomic omens give clues to the destiny of an individual – for example, 'if a man is covered with moles, he will have food to eat even during a famine.'[40] But sometimes they also reveal something about a man's character: 'if a man's nails are long he will not be talkative; if a man's nails are short he will be noisy.'[41]

Noticing these signs was an integral part of daily life in Mesopotamia. As Ashurbanipal continued with his day, he would have to be alert to any unusual things happening around him. Omens were not only written in the stars or the livers of sheep: the gods could send messages on earth too, as detailed in the series of tablets called *Shumma alu*, meaning 'If a city', which listed all manner of strange things happening in the world at large. Aberrations of nature such as wild animals entering the city,[42] crops growing out of season,[43] or the soil of the land exuding blood[44] all signified something was wrong – that the land would suffer ill fortune, scarcity, or sickness. Yet they can also mean the opposite to what we would expect. For example, date palms are usually symbols of wealth and prosperity in Mesopotamian culture, but they are not always good omens as it depends on where and how they grow. A date palm with two tops indicates hostility in the land, and one that 'repeatedly makes a noise like an ox in a grove' means the man's house will be dispersed.'[45]

Since these kinds of omens were important for the country as a whole, it was important for the king to know about them. One scholar writes to the king specifically to tell him that on the seventh day of the month of Kislimu a fox entered the city of Ashur and fell into a well in a garden. It was hauled up and killed.[46] A consultation of the library quickly reveals that foxes approaching the city gate mean that an enemy will take the city, and a fox running in the city square means the city will become desolate.[47] Presumably this, then, is what the scholar is worried might happen, and they hope the king will call the exorcist to perform a ritual against it.

Animals that gave birth to malformed offspring were also a serious matter for the king. A whole other series of omens specified what it meant when a domestic animal gave birth to young with extra ears,[48] feet growing out of the wrong part of its body,[49] conjoined twins,[50] et cetera. The number of abnormal features stack up as the lists go on and can reach extreme numbers, with one entry listing eight eyes ('If an anomaly has eight eyes, four to the front and four to the back – there will be anarchy in the land').[51] Here the scholars may be getting carried away, but animals with two or three heads do occur in nature, albeit rarely, and their strangeness was thought to be a sign from the gods that something was wrong.

Sometimes these anomalies are described in metaphorical terms, such as a cow giving birth to a lion. Presumably this meant that the calf looked like a lion rather than actually being one, because this really did happen and caused a ruckus. A man called Sin-eresh apparently realised that a cow giving birth to a lion was a serious matter, killed the poor calf, and ate it. Not stopping there, he then killed the farmer who owned the cow to stop news of it getting out. However, he failed to contain the story, since an astrologer tells the king that the man's servants had witnessed what he had done and were ready to testify against him.[52] We don't know who Sin-eresh was or why he was so keen to cover up the prodigy, but it must have portended serious trouble for the king for it to be such an issue. Some of the omens about cows giving birth to lions could actually be positive: 'the prince will have no rival,' or if the calf's front feet were like those of a lion 'the weapons of the king will prevail over the weapons of the enemy'; but if only its back feet were like those of a lion it was the other way round, and the enemy would prevail over the king.[53]

Cows were not the only ones who could give birth to lions – humans could too. Omens describing human births of this nature give a whole range of possibilities. A woman giving birth to a child with a lion's head meant there would be a strong king in the land.[54] A child that looked like a wolf meant carnage; one that looked like a dog meant the land would go mad; and if a baby looked like a monkey it meant that a man with no right to the throne would seize it.[55] If a common child could have such implications for the state, the births of children fathered by the king were especially ominous. If his wife or any of the women in the palace gave birth to a child with a lion's face it meant that the king would have no opponent in the land.[56] Conversely, a child with six fingers on the right hand meant an enemy would plunder the land, in an attitude reminiscent of the Tudor propaganda against Anne Boleyn.[57]

These everyday omens were significant for the individual as well as the state. If a man was going about his business and encountered an animal on the street or in his house it would often be a personal message for him. Here we are in the domain of black cats crossing your path – though for the Assyrians it would have been a white cat that they considered bad luck ('hardship will afflict that land'), or a multicoloured cat ('that land will not prosper').[58] However, the Assyrians were more worried about foxes crossing their path than cats, particularly focusing on which direction the animal came from. If the fox crossed from left to right it was unlucky – 'the man will not attain his wish' – but if it was the other way round it meant the opposite: that he would attain his desires, or would hear joyful news.[59]

Any animal, domestic or wild, could be the bringer of an omen. If a dog jumped on someone it meant the city would be defeated; if it lay down on a man's bed it meant his god was angry with him. Meanwhile, being urinated on by an animal was consistently good luck, seeing one defecate in front of you even better. Domestic animals were supposed to live outside, and so seeing them enter the house was a bad sign, a deviation from how things should be. Ashurbanipal's guards would have done their best to prevent dogs from entering the palace, since that could indicate financial loss and devastation of the city.[60] On the other hand, if one did get through it was not always a disaster since there were some associated situations which could bode well for the palace: if the dog killed something, the palace's assets would increase, and if it lay down on a bed then the palace would acquire something that does not belong to it.[61] A dog entering the temple was also usually positive, indicating wealth and security.[62] Pigs would have been a common sight in the streets, but it was important that they knew their place. If they went into a man's house it meant he would die, and if they danced in the city square it spelled trouble for the city.[63]

We know that these kinds of omens were real issues in Assyria as the king and his scholars discuss them in their correspondence. One day Ashurbanipal's father Esarhaddon was out when a mongoose ran underneath his chariot. The omen series is replete with entries about what it means if an animal passes between the legs of a man, including: 'if a mongoose passes between the legs of a man the hand of the god or the hand of the king will seize him.'[64] The king knew this – he asked his advisers whether the wheels of his chariot would count as the same thing. Clearly Esarhaddon hopes not, since he tries to argue that legs literally means legs, not chariot wheels, but the scholars disagree and insist the same logic applies. The omens are guidelines and, extensive as they are, they cannot cover every possibility – the scholars adhere to the spirit of the law rather than its letter and adapt the omen to the relevant circumstances. Yet they don't change their interpretation just to pacify the king, and are not afraid to stick to their principles.

The omen series dealing with earthly events is the longest one of all and covers many aspects of everyday life. The title we use, *Shumma alu*, is an abbreviation of its first line, 'If a city is set on a height then living in that city will not be good', which sums up the content fairly accurately. All aspects of city life are covered: the settlement's topography and population, the appearance of a house and things that might happen during construction, the conduct of a man's family as well as of animals, the sighting of ghosts and demons, strange lights, infestations of insects, even sex. The omens deal with unusual occurrences and things out of place, but also events that must have been common. More tablets are devoted to lizards and snakes than any other phenomenon, implying that these were a particular nuisance. Indeed, in Mesopotamia there were professional snake catchers on hand to get them out of people's houses. In this way, however esoteric they may seem, the omens give us an insight into daily life in Mesopotamia, showing us people's hopes and concerns, from the king to the ordinary city dweller.

At the end of the day Ashurbanipal would sit down for dinner. Thanks to one amazing text from the archives, we actually know what the protocol would have been for such an occasion.[65] The dinner takes place just before sunset. The king is seated first, on a couch opposite the door. Then, one by one, three of the king's highest officials enter, kiss the ground before the king, and deliver a report (what they reported on is not recorded). After the king has heard from all three of them, the crown prince takes his place, followed by the other sons of the king, and then the king's top officials. The king's chariot driver brings in the incense, setting up the censers to the right and left of the king at the head of the couch. Detailed instructions are given to the servants keeping watch over the brazier. If the incense runs out, they must clean up the burnt residue immediately, and one servant has the specific task of tending the flame and watching to make sure that no coals fall out of the brazier.

There are servants in attendance everywhere: standing between the tables, holding torches and burning aromatics when most of the dinner has been served, collecting dirty napkins and handkerchiefs and giving out clean ones. One servant pours water for the guests to wash their hands, while another picks up any scattered tableware and sweeps the floor. Whereas today the waiter might announce 'dinner is served' before the meal is to begin, in Assyria the chief cook pronounced this afterwards – 'dinner has been served', as a signal for the guests to leave.[66] The crown prince is the first to get up – the magnates stand while the servants clear away the tables.

Complex royal protocol is nothing new, and the order of entering and exiting, standing up and sitting down makes the relative status of the diners clear. That so much attention is paid to the incense, lighting, and sweeping highlights the Mesopotamian concern with ritual purity and cleanliness, in all areas of life.

Along with the highest-ranking officials, palace accounts tell us who else would have been invited to these state banquets. Scholars and priests made the guest list on at least one occasion, as befitting their high status as guardians of knowledge. Bodyguards are also listed among the attendants, understandably for events that brought powerful people so close to the king. Ashurbanipal's sister was also present at state banquets – her name is listed second only to the crown prince on one list of invitees, showing that she had a powerful and prominent position at court.[67]

What would the king have eaten at such a banquet? Sheep, as the most widely reared animals in Mesopotamian agriculture, were the main course, as they were at the meals served to the gods in temples. Nor were the gods forgotten at banquets – sacrifices were offered to them at these meals too, since they were arguably the most important guests of all. At one particular banquet we know that the menu included sixty-five sheep in total, which included those offered to the gods as well as those eaten by the guests.[68] The meat of geese, ducks, and oxen was also part of the feast, while other delicacies included wood pigeon, turtle dove, partridge, and jerboa (a kind of desert rodent which cannot have had much meat on its bones – reminiscent of the Roman penchant for dormice).[69] Wall carvings depicting banquets show servants bringing in trays of food, including plates piled high with grapes and pomegranates. The Assyrians loved fruit – one surviving account is a list of baskets of fruit and bowls of wine given to the queen, and states that the gardener inspected the produce first to make sure it was top-quality.[70]

Accounts from the palace keep track of the animals that needed to be brought into the kitchens for these banquets, but say nothing of how they were prepared. However, a collection of tablets from Babylonia written a thousand years before Ashurbanipal does in fact give cooking instructions for thirty-five different dishes.[71] Here we find a huge variety of different broths for cooking different types of meat, as well as accompaniments of vegetables and grains, often made into a kind of mash or porridge. Just as we today cook recipes from other cultures, so too did the Babylonians – the tablets contain instructions for an 'Assyrian style' recipe and the exotic 'Elamite broth'. Onions, leeks, and garlic were staple ingredients and are found in every recipe – the days when the hemerologies prohibited eating them must have been deprived ones indeed. The meat was stewed in herbs and spices, and sometimes cooked in beer. One recipe for a pie made of unspecified birds involves sprinkling the meat with mint and salt, and making the dough from flour, milk, and a strong fermented fish sauce similar to Roman garum. I once asked the chefs at my Oxford college to try to recreate this recipe (minus the fish sauce), but something must have been lost in translation since it did not go down well with the fellows.

Musicians would have provided the entertainment. One of the palace reliefs shows Ashurbanipal and his queen enjoying a private banquet in a garden, drinking wine from shallow bowls among lush trees and vines. This particular banquet is the victory celebration in the wake of Ashurbanipal's crushing of Elam that we encountered in Chapter 8, with the severed head of the Elamite king Teumman hanging from one of the trees. A female harpist stands nearby providing background music, while other reliefs show male musicians playing horizontal harps and a double flute. The palace kept lists of personnel working in the king's service, and one of them counts sixty-one female musicians at court.[72]

The harps may have been accompanied by singing. Some of the epic poems discussed in Chapter 7 were written as songs and would have been performed. The poem of *Erra and Ishum*, that great lament over the fall of Babylon, explicitly recommends that it should be sung before kings and princes, though Ashurbanipal would probably have wanted something more cheerful most nights.[73] *Anzu* – a poem that celebrates the victory of the warrior god Ninurta over an evil demon – would fit the bill for a festive banquet. The poem has the structure of a song, with repeated sections interweaving much like the verses and choruses of modern popular music. But Ashurbanipal also commissioned epics about his own deeds – the library holds at least three different poems celebrating Ashurbanipal's wars against the Elamites.[74] Perhaps these too would have been sung, which would have been especially fitting under the severed head of Teumman.

Alternatively, for a quiet night in at court the king might have turned to board games. Two different boards survive from the royal palace, for the game that we call 'the game of fifty-eight holes' and one whose ancient name is 'pack of dogs'. Both are race games where the players threw dice (in the form of sheep knuckle bones) to determine how many spaces to move their markers, and the first one to the end of the board won. Esarhaddon himself owned a board for the game of fifty-eight holes, made of marble and labelled as belonging to him. We know much more about pack of dogs because, remarkably, a tablet explaining the rules survives – not from this library, but from Babylon five hundred years later. Each player had five pieces in the shape of dogs, each one with a different starting space on the board. Landing on the same square as another player bumped them off and sent them back to the beginning, while landing on a rosette square earned another throw. Ashurbanipal and his brother must have been fond of this game as children, as Shamash-shum-ukin refers to it in a letter to his younger brother at the height of the war between them. He compares the war to the game and uses it as a metaphor to predict his triumph – Ashurbanipal may be ahead on the board now, but Shamash-shum-ukin will pull ahead with a single move and ultimately win.

Pack of dogs was a popular game throughout the whole span of Mesopotamian history. Several sets were found in the royal cemetery of Ur dating to the mid-third millennium BC, and for this reason the game is more commonly known today as the 'royal game of Ur'. The pieces and dice were found along with the boards, and look more like counters than dogs in this earlier era. These boards are beautiful artefacts, hollow boxes inlaid with white shell and lapis lazuli, truly fit for kings. But the game was played by people at all levels of society. Two soldiers guarding the gates to the Assyrian palace at the city of Dur-Sharrukin scratched the outline of the board into the stone so that they could keep themselves entertained during their long shifts. The game was popular throughout the whole Near East – over a hundred boards have been found from Iran in the east to Crete in the west and every country in between.

But the game was more than simple entertainment – it could also be used for divination. The late Babylonian tablet explaining the rules identifies each of the twelve squares running down the middle of the board with a constellation and gives a corresponding prediction. The square of Gemini means 'you will gain a partner', while Scorpio predicts 'you will draw fine beer'.[75] The tablet comes from an era when scholars had started to map astrology on to all other areas of enquiry, from extispicy to medicine, and even on to board games. Perhaps the game could now be consulted as its own kind of oracle, and throwing the dice could provide an answer to a question for those who knew how to read it. This is the same pattern of communication between gods and human beings that we see throughout Mesopotamian thinking, where ordinary occurrences could be interpreted as omens, messages from the gods to those who knew their language. But this development took place after Ashurbanipal's time, and he is more likely to have enjoyed the game as a way to unwind after a long day.

Come the evening, Ashurbanipal retired to bed. Although his wife lived in a different part of the palace with her own quarters, she would sometimes have joined him. Unusually, we have a fascinating window into Assyrians' sex lives, since even in the bedroom the omens could be consulted. Two tablets of *Shumma alu* are devoted to human sexual behaviour and are revealing about how the Assyrians saw gender relations.[76] Men are supposed to be active, women passive – if women take the initiative, it is considered very bad news for the men. For instance, if a woman 'mounts' a man rather than the other way round, 'that woman will take his vigour; for one month he will not have a personal god'.[77] If the woman pleasures herself while a man is facing her it means the man is 'not pure'.[78] It is hard to know how accurately this reflected people's behaviour, however, and how we interpret the sex omens may well tell us more about ourselves than about the Assyrians.

Knowing which interpretation to choose is made all the more difficult by our incomplete understanding of the omen system. As we have seen, the omens do not only encode the values of Mesopotamian culture but can also reverse them. Cities set on heights are more easily defended than those in valleys, and are far more common since the activity of building and inhabiting a site for generations inevitably raises the ground level – archaeological sites in the Middle East are usually mounds for precisely this reason. Yet the omen series declares that if a city is set on a height, life will not be good there. The reliefs in Ashurbanipal's palace also reflect this view – enemy cities are depicted on hills as they are being besieged and despoiled by the Assyrian army, showing that those set on a height get what is coming to them. But in real life Nineveh was also set on a height, and was held to be the greatest city on earth. We know that the Babylonians and Sumerians at least viewed female sexuality positively from the luscious and explicit language of the love songs of the goddess Inanna to her lover Dumuzi. Perhaps the omens that disapprove of women being active were also one of these reversals, or perhaps they reflect another cultural difference between Assyria and Babylonia, where the Assyrians have a narrower view of what is permissible for women.

The omens are always given from the male point of view, as is the case for most of the scholarly texts in the library. Nothing is said about what it means for the woman if she mounts a man or pleasures herself. Even the female gaze is threatening – if a woman stares at a man's penis, 'whatever he finds will not be secure in his house',[79] whereas a man staring at a woman's vagina signalled good health and that he would obtain what does not belong to him.[80] A man in control of his woman was thought to be in control of his life.

The gods seem to approve of male self-control, since they equate excessive ejaculation with an early death. A group of omens concerning ejaculation make it clear that semen is linked to a man's strength and capital, and spending too much of it is equivalent to draining his finances, although a moderate amount of expenditure foretells financial gain. In this sense, women are a temptation to be resisted. If a man can talk with a woman on a bed – where 'talk' may well be a euphemism – but then gets up and masturbates rather than having sex with her, it is the most auspicious of all of the sex omens: 'that man will have happiness and jubilation bestowed upon him; wherever he goes all will be agreeable; he will always achieve his goal'.[81] Not giving in to a woman's allure shows him to be both fortunate and independent. Whether men knew that getting up and masturbating instead of having sex meant happiness and jubilation, and would consciously do this to obtain these desirable states, we can only guess. Sex with another man also boded well, as the omens declare, 'If a man has anal sex with his equal, that man will become foremost among his brothers and colleagues.'[82] This may not be a simple stamp of approval for homosexuality, but more about power relations: it is the sexually dominant man who will get ahead of his peers by analogy with his role in the sexual act. The omens do not say what it means for the recipient partner, but other texts imply this was not a reputation one wanted to have. A collection of laws written around four hundred years before Ashurbanipal considers it slander for someone to go around saying of another man, 'everyone always penetrates you', and punishes this gossip severely.[83]

Perhaps strangest of all for us is the idea that these human actions can count as omens. If an omen is a message from the gods, how can something we choose to do come from on high? We do not know how the Assyrians made sense of this. It may be that they thought the gods had put the thought in their mind or given them the idea in the first place. Alternatively, the omens could express a moral code, or at least a set of principles about how the world worked, which one could follow to one's own advantage. For instance, the gods have ordained that raping a woman at the crossroads indicates that the rapist will not prosper, and he will be caught either by the hand of a god or the king.[84] Choosing to do this regardless would therefore call down such a fate. Others still follow a common-sense logic where the immediate consequences are extrapolated to the future. For example, if a man masturbates but cannot reach orgasm the omens say he will experience misfortune, which seems like a fairly accurate reflection of how that man would feel at the time.

Yet when trying to read social mores into the omens we must always remember that the primary logic of these texts is governed by language, exploring connections within the cuneiform system and playing with the concept of binaries. The omens say that if two women have sex it will lead to civil war in the land, but this negative outcome does not have to be a condemnation of queerness. Rather, the male scribes are speculating (philosophically, they might say) about the question according to this binary logic – rather than two opposite sexes coming together there is a kind of struggle between people belonging to the same sphere.

Where sexual problems did occur, Mesopotamian medicine had plenty of remedies. One favourite solution for restoring potency was partridge – by either drinking the bird's blood, swallowing its heart, or wearing its penis as a talisman around the waist, wrapped up in the hair from a sheep's perineum.[85] If the king had any trouble in that department, he could also call on the exorcist to supply him with incantations. The incantations do give a more active role to women, who are fully involved in treatments for their partner's impotence. The exorcist would visit the couple at home to facilitate the ritual, giving the woman incantations to recite as well as the man. (Presumably he then left them to it.) These love charms show us what it was like to talk dirty in ancient Assyria. They employ all kinds of metaphors for sexual arousal, frequently comparing the human participants to wild animals. One of them compares the man to a randy he-goat, and goes so far as to recommend tying a goat up at the head of the bed for inspiration, so that the man could magically borrow its qualities.[86] But the imagery could be more refined and poetic too. Arousal is often compared to an oncoming storm – 'wind blow, orchard shake, clouds gather, droplets fall!' – and the man's penis to a taut harp string.[87] Spells for female desire are also known, though these were used by men to make women desire them. And if it was a headache causing her to turn him down, the exorcist had spells for this too.[88] But love magic worked both ways and women also used it to seduce men, exhorting them to 'fawn over me like a puppy' or 'consume me like beer' as they 'lie for ever between my thighs'.[89]

Ashurbanipal may not have done all these activities every day; compressing them into one may make him seem more observant of omens and rituals than he was in practice. However, it certainly illustrates how Mesopotamian scholarship could be called upon in all areas – from choosing dates for the diary and scrutinising the building plans presented to him to interpreting strange things he saw in the house or the street. The library offered numerous ways to deal with situations that cropped up in everyday life, both practical strategies such as incantations and rituals and more philosophical principles such as those embodied in the omens' texts, or the poems that explored the nature of human suffering. Although this was esoteric knowledge, it was also highly practical.

Many of these principles could have been common knowledge among ordinary people. For instance, the servants in the palace may have known it was bad luck for a pigeon to fly through the window because it could have been the soul of a dead ancestor returning, even if they couldn't read the instructions for the ritual against it.[90] The wet nurses employed to look after the king's children most likely knew the incantations to stop children crying without having to consult a professional exorcist. Lists of lucky and unlucky days cover basic agricultural duties that would have been familiar to ordinary farmers rather than academics in the palace. But only the specialist could have explained the complex logic behind the omens, or deciphered the messages written in sheep livers, or appreciated how the gods had structured the universe through language.

Practical knowledge has a larger significance and a higher level of meaning that could be used to study the nature of the gods. Even the dictionaries that helped young scribes learn the dead language of Sumerian were not only straightforward translations but also guides to hidden connections between words and concepts that were only apparent to those who had studied them.

In some cases, we don't know how far the knowledge reached. For instance, the physiognomic texts that describe what it means when a man's hair curls to the right or the left, if his forehead is short or his nose long, are never quoted by the scholars in their letters or anywhere else, meaning that we don't know how they applied them or how many people would have understood them. We can't be sure if the sex omens reflect mainstream views of sexuality or whether they were the speculations of intellectuals playing with language. Yet even if the evidence for the application is lacking it is hard to believe that those who had studied these texts would not have integrated them into their own lives in one way or another. Academic knowledge is never purely academic, but shapes the worldview of those steeped in it, and these were the most powerful people in the land – advisers to the king of Assyria, and even the king of Assyria himself.

What often strikes us today about the Assyrian world is how superstitious it was. We might find it odd for the king to be so concerned about a mongoose running under his chariot, or that a cow giving birth to a calf that looked a bit like a lion would be so politically sensitive that it would lead to intrigue and murder.

But what seems irrational or primitive to us is highly rational within the Assyrian worldview. As we have seen throughout this book, what we would deem superstitious beliefs were the product of extended reflection by highly trained scholars. The meanings of the omens are not random but form a sophisticated system that follows a complex logic. This logic is interdisciplinary, cutting across all the main branches of scholarship, from the interpretation of strange events on earth to the regular movements of the planets, to medical diagnosis and ritual prescriptions. It is found throughout epic poems, the artwork on the palace walls, and in prayers and rites offered to the gods. Few individuals could master all of it, but specialists rarely kept to just one discipline and could use their knowledge to understand texts in many genres.

If you believe in all-powerful gods who intervene in events on earth it is logical enough to think that their intentions can be glimpsed in unusual happenings on earth or in the heavens where they reside. The omen texts collect these happenings in tens of thousands, organise them, and provide explanations of what they mean, which is fundamentally an attempt to make sense of the world. The scholars also explain the meanings of omens which they had not observed themselves and were even impossible, such as the sun coming out at midnight or a sheep without a heart. This shows that they were not simply describing what they saw but must have developed theories and were speculating about what it would mean if these impossible things did happen. This collecting and theorising is a type of scientific activity and is the precursor to modern science. We now start with different assumptions about how the world works and come to different conclusions, based on greater knowledge and testing of those assumptions. But we should not this judge the ancient world by the standards of our own time, for three thousand years from now our own ideas will be seen as primitive. What the ancient scholars achieved was remarkable on its own terms and pushed the boundaries of intellectual enquiry at the time.

Human beings have always been fascinated by freak events in nature like those in *Shumma alu*, or the cow giving birth to a lion, and continue to be today. Stories abound on the internet of animals giving birth to abnormal offspring, provoking a whole range of reactions from shock, disgust, and fear to ridicule. The Mesopotamians probably had the same kinds of reaction as us, but they turned the interpretation of these events into a science. The same is true of many of the other Mesopotamian rituals of daily life, and superstitions. A white cat crossing your path was not merely a sign of bad luck but was worked into a system that made sense of it.

Ashurbanipal's scholars would have been able to tell you exactly why it was bad luck, but also what you could do about it. We may not worry about such things today, but what do we do when we wake up feeling disturbed after a bad dream? Our culture does not have a structured way of dealing with this, whereas the Mesopotamians had many rituals to help shake off the lingering bad feeling and start the day afresh. Ultimately this is the advantage behind all these ideas and practices that we find so strange – they are ways of settling people when they feel unsettled, or when something out of the ordinary happens.

The modern world has plenty of its own superstitions, like Friday the thirteenth, or avoiding stepping on cracks in the pavement or walking under ladders, even if most of us would not actively plan our lives around these concerns. In China it is common for tall buildings to omit the fourth floor since the word for 'four' sounds similar to the word for 'death', a logic the Mesopotamians would instantly understand and approve of. And just as the board game pack of dogs eventually became used for divination, so too did tarot cards in the West grow out of an ordinary card game. We too have read meaning into numbers and wordplay, and repurposed casual pastimes to tell us about the future, even if these beliefs are no longer as mainstream as they were in the ancient world. Mesopotamia's rituals of daily life can be found in similar guises all over the world, then, in the present as well as the past, as people look for special knowledge to help them navigate the everyday.

Epilogue: The Afterlife of Cuneiform Culture

Alexander the Great's last days on earth were haunted by evil omens. In early 323 BC, he decided to return to Babylon – a city he had conquered eight years before – to start planning his next campaign. Even before he got there, the Babylonian diviners sent a message to tell him to keep away. As Alexander approached the walls of Babylon, he was greeted by a murder of crows fighting in the air, some of them falling down dead at his feet. He was then informed that the military commander had carried out an extispicy asking after Alexander's future, and the liver had no lobe, a very bad sign indeed. The king, unsettled, did not enter the city but camped outside the walls.

Other strange things came to pass. A lion was kicked to death by a donkey that had previously been extremely tame, a reversal of roles that showed something was awry. Strangest of all, one day after Alexander had been playing a ball game he came back to find an unknown man sitting on his throne wearing his royal robes and diadem. The men Alexander had been playing with asked the stranger who he was. At first there was a dramatic silence, but he eventually answered that his name was Dionysius from Messene. He had been in prison, but a short while ago a god had released him from his chains and brought him to the palace. The god had told him to take the robes and the crown, sit down, and not say a word. The diviners advised Alexander that this man should be killed, and this time he followed their advice. The stranger's words had got under Alexander's skin – now he saw portents everywhere, and the palace was filled with people performing rituals of purification, divinations, and sacrifices to the gods, which only stoked his fear all the more. Soon afterwards he became ill and died.[1]

This story is told by Plutarch in his *Life of Alexander*, and is recorded also by the historians Arrian and Diodorus Siculus.[2] All of these writers lived centuries after Alexander, giving plenty of time for elements of the fantastic to creep in, but they do preserve echoes of real Babylonian traditions. By Alexander's time Babylon had already been under foreign rule for more than two hundred years – the last native Babylonian king, Nabonidus, had been swept aside by the Persian king Cyrus, who brought Mesopotamia into his empire in 539 BC. The scholars attached to the royal court were forced to seek employment elsewhere, retreating to the temples which had always had the greatest need for their services, and turning to private clients with an interest in astrology and exorcism. In the fourth century BC the temple of Marduk in Babylon was still going strong, employing fourteen astronomers, fifty lamenters, and over a hundred exorcists. When Alexander arrived, the scholars were ready to welcome a new king of Babylon, and as the story from Plutarch shows, offered him the full range of their expertise. Long after Mesopotamia had been conquered by waves of foreign rulers, its knowledge was still alive and kicking.

The most remarkable part of the story is the man who was put to death. This seems to be the Mesopotamian ritual of 'the substitute king', most likely distorted in the retelling. When a lunar eclipse occurred that portended the death of the king, a substitute would be put on the throne for up to a hundred days while the real king went into hiding. At the end of this period the substitute was put to death – in this way the prophecy would come true, but the king would remain safe, as the wrath of the gods had been deflected on to another. The gods were not fooled, but their verdict had to be carried out one way or another, and the exorcists made plenty of apologies to appease them during the accompanying rituals.

The substitute king ritual is one of the most ancient in Mesopotamia, and at the same time one of the last to be recorded. It goes all the way back to the nineteenth century BC, where a chronicle records that it went unexpectedly wrong. While the substitute was on the throne, the real king Erra-imitti died from eating porridge that was too hot, and the substitute simply took over and carried on being king. For the next 1,500 years we hear little about it other than scattered references. Those seeking to ingratiate themselves with the king might make hyperbolic comments wishing they could 'die as a substitute of the king my lord!', though surely not meaning it. But the ritual was resurrected by Esarhaddon and performed three times during his reign, before falling back into obscurity.

While the substitute was on the throne he really did live like a king. Inventories from Ashurbanipal's library show him having an entourage of over three hundred people, including musicians and dancers and courtesans, though one-third of this number were bodyguards to make sure he didn't run away. The substitute was also well provided with wine, as his court was allocated about 10 per cent of the amount consumed by the real court. Meanwhile, the king carried on making decisions and ruling the empire, but his advisers had to address him as 'the farmer' to keep up appearances and not ruin the effect.

The substitute king ritual is a complex one and unites the expertise of several branches of Mesopotamian scholarship. The astrologers had to keep an eye on the eclipse and decide when the ritual was needed. The exorcists would take charge of the ritual itself, subsequently burning the substitute's regalia and the furniture he used before burying the ashes, and purifying the palace afterwards to cleanse any traces of evil. Lamentations were performed during eclipses as a matter of course, where the professional lamenters would play the kettledrum and sing to the gods, both in the temple and in the palace. Substitute king rituals, then, would have been a collaboration of the highest men of learning in the land, all working together to save the king from an evil fate. One of the very oldest Mesopotamian royal rituals was still being used in one of the latest periods of cuneiform culture, under Alexander, spanning a good 1,500 years.

All empires eventually die, and all cultures change and evolve, sometimes beyond recognition. The substitute king ritual encapsulates the attempt to hold on to ancient traditions when they are dying. The ritual may have saved Esarhaddon, but it did not save

Alexander. Yet even though new rulers took over Mesopotamia, and cuneiform gradually fell out of use, the knowledge the library contained was not lost. The knowledge of Assyria lived on far beyond its end.

The library was destroyed in 612 BC, burned to the ground when the Babylonians sacked Nineveh. The opportunity for them to finally throw off the Assyrian yoke came through an alliance with the Medes, joined by other surrounding tribes who had also had enough of Assyrian rule; the combined forces attacked Nineveh. They besieged the city for three months and, when they broke through, set fire to the palace compound. Before they did so they must have rifled through the tablets and taken some with them back to Babylon. Ashurbanipal was not the last king to rule Nineveh, but not much correspondence from either of the kings that followed him has yet been found. The Babylonians may have considered any such recent letters as useful intelligence, and confiscated them so that later they could pore over the inner workings of the court during its last days. As we've seen, they attacked the palace reliefs that depicted the king in his triumph over his enemies. They hacked out the face of Sennacherib looking out over his Judaean captives, and that of Ashurbanipal lording over the defeated Babylonians and Elamites, even chipping away the hand that holds his cup so he can no longer drink a toast to victory. Those the Assyrians had oppressed over many years had their revenge.

After three hundred years of domination, the Assyrian empire was finally defeated. Babylon once again became the centre of power in the Near East, as well as the centre of scholarly activity. For the library of Nineveh had never been the only source of scholarship. Temples throughout Babylonia and Assyria also kept tablet collections and were centres of learning. The temple of Marduk in Babylon was another of the greatest, but we do not have as many of its tablets. Other libraries have been discovered in the cities of Sippar and Uruk in Babylonia, Kalhu in Assyria, and Me-Turnat in the Diyala region bordering the two. They contain many of the same texts as Ashurbanipal's library, attesting to a common scholarly culture across Mesopotamia, albeit with local variations and developments over time. Some of these libraries survived the Persian conquest and their scholars continued producing knowledge into the Hellenistic period and beyond.

Throughout the first millennium BC, cuneiform culture became increasingly the preserve of the elite, as Akkadian was gradually replaced by Aramaic as the most spoken language in both Assyria and Babylonia. The Assyrians started to use Aramaic in their imperial administration in the ninth century BC after they absorbed the western provinces into the empire, where Aramaic was widely spoken. By the middle of the eighth century Aramaic was being used as a lingua franca throughout the empire, and scribes are depicted on palace reliefs keeping records in both Aramaic and Akkadian, counting piles of enemy heads on the battlefield. These scribes always come in pairs, one writing cuneiform on a clay tablet or wax-covered writing board, the other holding a scroll of parchment or papyrus, the media for drawing Aramaic characters in ink. In Babylonia, Aramaic was also widely used in the Neo-Babylonian period following the fall of Nineveh, and it would go on to be the dominant language of the Persian empire.

The Persians had no desire to impose their culture on the lands that they ruled. They allowed the Mesopotamians to carry on worshipping their old gods and living as they had done before. It was business as usual – the Babylonian upper classes carried on keeping their accounts in cuneiform, writing contracts on clay tablets, and holding on to their identity under foreign rule. In fact, it was the Persians who took on aspects of Babylonian culture: Darius's palace at Persepolis is a treasure trove of Mesopotamian influences, from the winged bulls flanking the gateways to the cuneiform script used to record the king's accomplishments. Babylonian craftsmen worked on the palace at Susa, bringing their knowledge of making glazed bricks, a technology that was still being used in the Islamic period. The Persians left the structures underlying the empire's governance in place – the system of provinces and royal roads connecting them, which had been established by the Assyrians. But this does not mean the state of affairs was a happy one. A failed uprising against the Persian king Xerxes resulted in a harsh crackdown in northern Babylonia – all the archives of the families who supported it come to an end at the same time, indicating that they were severely punished and their power curbed. This in itself was not fatal to cuneiform culture, since pro-Persian families continued to thrive, but nevertheless the use of cuneiform dwindled. By the time of Alexander, it was only the priests in the temples keeping Mesopotamian traditions alive, worshipping the old gods and caring for their cults, which required them to be proficient in astronomy, ritual, and lamentation. These responsibilities were passed down in families of the old nobility, a tightly knit social class keeping to the traditional ways.

Though smaller and smaller in number, these priests made huge developments in advancing cuneiform knowledge, particularly in astronomy and mathematics. It was in the Persian period that Babylonian priests came up with the Zodiac, and under Greek rule that mathematical astronomy reached its peak. It is thanks to the astronomical diaries that we know the exact date of Alexander's death – 11 June 323 BC.

With Alexander's conquest, then, Babylon became part of the Greek world. Greeks and Macedonians settled there and brought their culture with them, but Alexander and his successors respected Babylonian traditions too. As befitted a good Babylonian king, Alexander started to clear the ground in preparation for rebuilding Marduk's temple, which had fallen into disrepair, though his early death prevented him from finishing the task. Half a century later, Antiochus I carried on the work and rebuilt both the main shrine of Marduk in Babylon and that of Marduk's son Nabu in the city of Borsippa. He commissioned a foundation cylinder commemorating his work, just as the native Babylonian kings had always done, claiming to have moulded bricks for the temple with his own hands.[3] Around eighty years after that, Antiochus III took up residence in Nebuchadnezzar's palace in Babylon and was present during the New Year festival in 205 BC. Even when other kings were less enthusiastic, the Babylonians kept this New Year ritual going, and continued to celebrate it in some form right up until 78 BC at least.

The first Greek ruler after Alexander, Seleucus I, took over from him as king of Babylon, but also founded a new city nearby, Seleucia on the Tigris. This new city attracted great wealth and resources and may have overshadowed Babylon in some ways, but ultimately complemented rather than displaced it. Later rulers built a gymnasium and even a theatre in Babylon which could have staged the classics of Greek tragedy or served as a place for citizens to gather for political assemblies. The Babylonian priests refer to it in the astronomical diaries as 'the house of watching' (E_2 IGI.DU_8.MEŠ), a literal translation of the Greek word for theatre, *theatron*, into the now ancient language of Sumerian. In the second century BC a substantial number of Greeks permanently settled in Babylon, which was granted the status of *polis*, becoming an official Greek city.[4] Around this time astronomical and astrological texts were translated from Babylonian into Greek and turn up in the cosmopolitan city of Alexandria in Egypt, providing invaluable data for Greek scientists and influencing their ideas. Despite their very different backgrounds, Greek and Babylonian scholars were now both part of a thoroughly interconnected world.

A Babylonian priest known to the Greeks as Berossus wrote, in Greek, the *Babyloniaca* – an introduction to Babylonian cosmology, culture, and history which he dedicated to Alexander's successor.[5] Berossus' works only survive today in fragments quoted by other writers, but even these extracts show that he was highly educated in cuneiform traditions and that the scholarship of Ashurbanipal's library was still thriving. Classical historians report that Berossus taught astrology to the Greeks and founded a school on the island of Cos. He was honoured so much that there was purportedly a statue of him in Athens with a golden tongue symbolising his wisdom. But it was not simply a matter of one culture teaching another: new ideas arose thanks to the interaction. The Greeks who made Babylonia their home were influenced by its traditions when developing their own theories. Greek philosophers were born and bred in Babylonia, such as Diogenes the Stoic from Seleucia. Diogenes was one of the founders of Stoicism, and his keen interest in grammar may well have been shaped by Babylonian ideas on the subject, which go back far longer than any recorded in Greece.

By the Hellenistic period nobody spoke Akkadian as a first language, but scribes still had to learn it during their training. They did this through the medium of Greek. An extraordinary group of tablets has been found inscribed with both cuneiform characters and Greek letters, showing how the students got to grips with the ancient signs by transcribing how they were pronounced in a more familiar alphabet. This approach could also have taught scribes to consistently render Akkadian terms in Greek letters and vice versa, which they would have needed when operating in both cultures and when referring to words and ideas from one language while writing in the other. Rather than Greeks learning cuneiform, it is more likely that these tablets represent the efforts of native Babylonians training to serve their traditional gods, but Babylonians who spoke Greek just as well as their native Aramaic. These bilingual tablets show how Babylon was increasingly influenced by Greek culture, and yet they also show cuneiform still being learned in the same traditional manner as it had been two thousand years before – starting with syllables and lists of words, progressing to simple bilingual incantations in both Akkadian and Sumerian, and moving on to the classics of literature. The old traditions carried on.

Although this cultural exchange intensified during the Hellenistic period, it had been taking place for centuries. Some individuals had already travelled directly between Greece and the heart of Mesopotamia – the archaic poet Alcaeus had a brother who fought as a mercenary in the Babylonian army at the end of the seventh century BC, and the Athenian historian Xenophon led an army of Greek mercenaries marching on Babylon in 401 BC, this time fighting for the Persian king Cyrus the Younger as he attempted to seize the throne from his brother.[6] From the other side, Sennacherib tells us that Ionian sailors were part of the crew manning his fleet in his expedition to Elam,[7] and Ionians had been bothering Assyrian kings with skirmishes in their territory for decades before that.[8]

The ancient world was a much more internationally connected place than we often acknowledge. As far back as the eighth century BC the Greeks were trading with the Near East via their colonies in Anatolia, resulting in cultural influences that have given the era the name 'the Orientalising period'. The effects can be seen in art, literature, religion, and philosophy. The famous Gorgon – the monster killed by Perseus whose gaze turned all who met it to stone, and whose severed head Perseus then carried with him into battle – appears on pottery and is likely indebted to depictions of the monster Humbaba slain by Gilgamesh and Enkidu. As we've seen, there are many similarities between Greek and Near Eastern myths, suggesting at the very least a shared culture where similar stories were spun in slightly different ways. But the sharing of ideas may have gone even further. In the sixth century BC some early Greek philosophers were promoting theories that sound distinctly Babylonian, such as Thales of Miletus, who believed the world emerged from water, or Heraclitus, who reasoned that opposite concepts were fundamentally connected. Mesopotamian divination, too, reached the Mediterranean at an early stage, with Etruscan diviners taking up the practice of extispicy in the ninth or eighth century BC and passing it on to the Romans, while Greek papyri on liver divination show striking resemblances to the Mesopotamian technical manuals.

Mesopotamian knowledge did not only move west towards the Greeks, but in the opposite direction as well, through long-standing contacts to the east. The Sumerians were trading precious materials with Afghanistan and the Indus Valley as early as the third millennium BC. The board game pack of dogs has also been found in the Indus Valley, and may have originated there. In the other direction, astronomical knowledge seems to have moved from Mesopotamia to India in the first millennium BC, most likely transmitted through

Iran. Along with similarities in astronomical texts, we find similarities in the interpretation of omens, both in the heavens and in daily life, and, most strikingly, detailed similarities in the omens of physiognomy that predicted the fortunes and character of a person from their physical features.

It seems that Mesopotamian omens were adopted by Indian sages and that even the Buddha had encountered them, though he did not approve. The Buddha lived in the mid-fifth century BC when the Persians ruled both the Indus and Mesopotamia, and the fact that the empire united these distant lands would have made it easier for ideas to travel between them. One of the Buddha's sermons condemns wandering sages for a whole host of 'debased arts' and 'wrong means of livelihood', which include prophesying based on marks on a person's body, predicting eclipses and other celestial portents, interpreting dreams, using charms to cure people possessed by ghosts, and all kinds of other means of making predictions.[9] His description of their astrological predictions in particular sounds like these sages traded in the same knowledge contained in the great Mesopotamian series *Enuma Anu Enlil* – lunar and solar eclipses, the properly timed appearances of the constellations, the sighting of meteors, earthquakes, the rising and setting of stars, and the meaning of all such occurrences.[10] The Buddha in his complaints also lists the terrestrial omens, which cover the same ground and are almost in the same order as their Mesopotamian counterparts in *Shumma alu* – omens involving the construction of houses, sightings of ghosts and demons, snakes, scorpions, mice, birds, and other animals.

Despite the Buddha's criticism, by the first century AD both mathematical astronomy and omen lore had become respected parts of higher learning in Buddhist culture, spreading to Central Asia along with the religion. It seems they were just too useful to be ignored. At the turn of the second to the first century BC the Chinese *Records of the Grand Historian* record celestial omens that work with a similar logic as those in *Enuma Anu Enlil*, raising the question of whether even Chinese scholarship might have been influenced by Mesopotamian precedent. Omens like those found in the library were known to the Sogdians in modern-day Uzbekistan, who could have carried them to China. More work is needed to determine the true extent of Mesopotamian influence on these omen traditions, versus how much they developed independently, but it seems that the library's knowledge travelled many miles east of Nineveh and inspired scholars at least as far as India, and potentially even beyond.

⁂

To the west of Mesopotamia lay the kingdoms of Israel and Judah, and the most obvious influence of its culture is on the Bible. I had never really picked up the Old Testament until well after I had become an Assyriologist and what strikes me again and again is just how Mesopotamian it is. The book of Lamentations which mourns the destruction of Jerusalem recalls the Sumerian laments over destroyed cities; the creation stories in Genesis echo those of the Babylonian tradition; and the laws in Exodus and Deuteronomy have direct parallels in Hammurabi's law code, including the famous 'an eye for an eye, a tooth for a tooth' principle of retribution. The primeval history in Genesis which attributes life spans of hundreds of years to the descendants of Adam and Noah recalls Mesopotamian traditions of the rulers who lived before the flood, who ruled for hundreds or thousands of years.[11] The stories of the writing on the wall (Daniel 5) and Jonah and the whale take place in Babylon and Nineveh respectively, the two great capitals of the Mesopotamian world.

This is no coincidence. The biblical lands were part of the ancient Near East and interacted with their powerful eastern neighbours over the millennia, sharing many aspects of their culture, and reacting against others. Abraham himself is said to have been born in the city of Ur,[12] probably in the early second millennium BC, and all manner of cuneiform texts have been discovered in Palestine and Israel from this period, showing that local scribes were trained in the Mesopotamian tradition. In the first millennium BC these contacts became more intense and the stakes higher, as Israel and

Judah frequently clashed with their powerful eastern neighbours. The Assyrian kings expanded their empire into the Levant from the ninth century onwards, first demanding tribute, then seizing the territory when the kings refused to pay. These clashes are narrated in the historical books of the Bible (specifically 2 Kings and 2 Chronicles) and made a deep impact upon them. When the Israelite king Hosea stopped paying his tribute, the Assyrians crushed the rebellion and took control of Israel in its entirety, turning it into an Assyrian province in 720 BC. Not long afterwards, in 701, King Hezekiah of Judah managed to fend off Sennacherib from taking Jerusalem, but still ended up paying tribute, an altercation that both sides claim as a victory.[13] Mostly the Bible depicts the Assyrian kings as the instrument of God, punishing the Israelites for their idolatry and disloyalty to him. It is with glee that the Old Testament prophets predict the fall of Nineveh, and the writers of 2 Kings are sure to mention Sennacherib's murder by his two sons.[14] The Assyrians would get their comeuppance in the end.

After conquering territory in the Levant, the Assyrian kings deported large swathes of the population, which had a profound impact on ethnic diversity in the Near East, and resulted in a multicultural empire. The Babylonian kings later followed the same strategy, most famously with Nebuchadnezzar's destruction of Jerusalem in 587/6 BC.[15] Large numbers of Judaeans were resettled in and around Babylon itself, where they worked the land as farmers and took part in commerce as merchants, and where members of the royal family were kept captive at Nebuchadnezzar's court. Some Judaeans took Babylonian names, a few even took Babylonian wives, but most held on to their religion and gave their children names like 'Yahweh saves'. Nevertheless, they were living in the very midst of Babylonian culture, interacting daily with its people and traditions.

Perhaps it was inevitable that Babylon would make its mark on the Hebrew Bible given the huge upheaval the Babylonians forced upon the Judaeans, destroying their temples and moving the people to a foreign land for many generations. Although there are many similarities between the Hebrew scriptures and Babylonian texts, it is the differences that are most illuminating, as they are very often polemical, intending to show just how different the Hebrew God was from the gods that the Babylonians worshipped. The story of the tower of Babel is a particularly good illustration of this. In the biblical tale, the people of Sumer (there called Shinar) decide to build 'a city with a tower that reaches to the heavens'.[16] God becomes angry with their arrogance and mixes up their language so that they cannot understand each other – whereas formerly there was only one language in the whole world, now there are many, and God scatters their speakers across the world. The Bible proclaims that this is why the city is called Babel, because God confused their language – this is a pun on the Hebrew word *balal*, which means 'to confuse', which explains the 'real' meaning of the name of the city of Babylon, as the Hebrew writers would have seen it. Interpretation by pun is exactly the kind of technique that Babylonian scholars themselves used; here the Hebrew Bible turns it against them.

The tower of Babel story was likely inspired by the ziggurats built throughout Mesopotamian history, perhaps especially the ziggurat of Marduk in Babylon – a tower-like pyramidal structure of seven stages in the centre of the city, Babylon's most spectacular monument. The temple was called 'bond of heaven and underworld' and was located in the precinct 'house that raises its head to heaven', names that are echoed by the ambitions of the builders of Babel. In the Bible the tower is built by speakers of many different languages, and in Nebuchadnezzar's inscriptions he describes how he brought labourers from all over his empire to build Marduk's temple, which of course is as much a monument to his own greatness as it is a gift to the god.[17] The biblical story can therefore be read as a direct attack on Babylonian kingship and beliefs, flipping them to show that self-aggrandising projects that attempt to put humans on the same level as God are futile and end in confusion.

After decades of exile, the Judaeans' captivity in Babylon finally ended when the Persian king Cyrus conquered Babylon and let them go home. The Hebrew Bible remembers Cyrus as a great liberator, speaking of how he not only let the Judaeans go back to their homeland but even returned all the treasure that Nebuchadnezzar had stolen from the great temple in Jerusalem.[18] It tells of how he issued a proclamation, sent to all parts of his kingdom, declaring that the Lord God of the heavens, who was also the Lord God of Israel, had chosen him to restore the temple in Jerusalem and would watch over anyone who wished to return and join in the rebuilding. It is likely that Cyrus did in fact make such an announcement, although the biblical writers have reinterpreted his words through the lens of their own theology. Once again, cuneiform texts can corroborate the biblical account and show us what is behind it. A famous document known today as the Cyrus cylinder gives the Babylonian side of the story. It is a clay cylinder found in Babylon that would have been buried in the foundations of a temple as it was being rebuilt, a message from the king to the gods and the future detailing his good deeds. Here Cyrus describes how the Babylonian god Marduk had commanded him to march into Babylon and allowed him to enter the city peacefully, welcomed joyfully by the people.[19] The cylinder is written in the first person, as if these are the words of Cyrus himself, but Cyrus would not have been able to write in Babylonian cuneiform, and it is more than likely that the Babylonian scribes who produced the cylinder had a hand in its message. The Cyrus cylinder does not mention the Judaeans specifically, but it does say that Cyrus allowed deities from all over the region, from Ashur in the north to Babylon in the south, from Susa in the east to the sanctuaries on the other side of the Tigris in the west, to return to their temples, and allowed their people to return with them.[20] This must be the event that the Bible remembers so fondly, though naturally the sources disagree about which god was behind Cyrus's benevolent actions.

After the death of Alexander the Great, his former generals fought over his empire, eventually fracturing it into three separate kingdoms.

Alexander's successors ruled Mesopotamia until 141 BC when they were defeated by the Parthians, an Iranian empire led by King Mithridates. The Romans established a province of Mesopotamia in AD 116 and frequently clashed with the Parthians, and the Sassanians who succeeded them over the next centuries, but parts of Syria and Iraq remained under Roman/Byzantine control until the Islamic conquests in the seventh century AD.

Even under the Parthians the temples were still going strong in Babylon and Uruk. Scribes in those two cities, the last bastions of cuneiform culture, continued to train their sons in the traditional scholarship, both the practical knowledge needed to calculate the positions of the stars and the old stories about Mesopotamia's traditional gods and heroes, from the *Epic of Creation* to the *Epic of Gilgamesh*. The very last datable cuneiform tablet known to us is an astronomical almanac predicting celestial phenomena for the year AD 79/80, when the Parthians ruled Mesopotamia.[21]

Yet the decline of cuneiform did not mean the death of Mesopotamian culture. Temples in other cities may have long abandoned cuneiform but they continued to worship the same Mesopotamian gods. Under the Parthians the inhabitants of Ashur rebuilt the temple of their traditional god and even the special temple outside the city walls used for the New Year festival. The city of Harran in Syria continued to be an important centre for worship of the moon god well into the Roman period, even when the surrounding people had become Christian. As late as AD 384 a nun on a pilgrimage to the Holy Land visited Harran and scathingly commented that it was full of heathens with hardly a Christian to be seen.[22] In the seventh century AD Islamic authors record stories of pagans worshipping the Babylonian gods and practising Babylonian-style magic across Iraq. And long after the old gods had been forgotten their legacies lived on. Even after the Islamic conquest people still used magic as part of medicine; still believed that demons caused illness and that the movements of the stars held meaning for human destiny – all core Babylonian principles.

The history of the influence of Mesopotamia on the Middle East has yet to be written. We know far more about the legacy of cuneiform knowledge in the west than in the lands where it originated, but it undoubtedly continued to shape traditions there too. After the destruction of the libraries, the knowledge of Mesopotamia lived on in the Aramaic language used by ordinary people and by new generations of intellectuals. We find it reflected in Aramaic Jewish texts, which record omens very similar to the Mesopotamian omens of daily life, and in the names of Mesopotamian gods written on magic bowls used to protect people against evil. Not all the Judaeans returned to their homeland after Cyrus conquered Babylon and let them leave; many continued to live in Babylon. The rabbis who wrote the Babylonian Talmud display knowledge of Babylonian medicine, numerology, and magic stones, all tools used by Mesopotamian exorcists. Jews and later even Christians wore amulets to protect themselves against the demon Lilith, who was Sumerian in origin, just as the Mesopotamians had done. To this day the Jewish calendar is structured similarly to the Babylonian one, and its months have the same names.

In the realm of literature too the old stories continued to be told in other tongues. The debate poems popular in cuneiform scribal schools were passed down into Syriac and later Middle Persian. Stories about an Assyrian court sage named Ahiqar were written in Aramaic but turn up in a whole host of traditions in far-flung countries from Ethiopia to Russia. As we've seen, echoes of the *Epic of Gilgamesh* may be heard in the *Iliad* and *Odyssey*, and copies of *Gilgamesh* made their way into the great libraries of Ugarit in Syria, Megiddo in Israel, and the Hittite capital in Turkey. The culture diffused, its traditions were translated, and it lived on in new forms.

The Babylonian *Epic of Creation* had a particularly long afterlife and was still known in southern Iraq as late as the sixth century AD. Remarkably, its preservation was at least partly thanks to the Greeks and Romans. In 529 the Christian emperor of Rome Justinian closed the great Academy at Athens, and the pagan philosophers left. They ended up founding a school in the notoriously pagan city of Harran, in Syria. There the philosopher Damascius wrote about creation stories in different cultures and summarised the Babylonian version. But he did not learn about it from his new home in the east – he was already familiar with this Babylonian tradition from the work of Athenian philosophers at the Academy. Eudemus of Rhodes, a colleague of Aristotle, had translated the *Epic of Creation* into Greek eight hundred years earlier, and Damascius' summary shows he had probably read it. Babylonian knowledge had spread far abroad, and was being brought home again.

⁂

The substitute king ritual is a good example of the extraordinary longevity and diffusion of Mesopotamian culture. The ritual was adopted by the Hittites in what is now Turkey, theirs being an empire that also adapted the cuneiform writing system to their own language, as well as borrowing classic Mesopotamian prayers and rituals for their own gods. That they performed the substitute king ritual shows how far they went in appropriating Babylonian scholarly knowledge, even its most esoteric rites. The Greek historian Dio Chrysostom records that the Persians also used the substitute king ritual, saying that Alexander the Great first heard of it from them when he enquired about their customs, and the ritual probably inspired the story of 'The Sleeper Awakened' in the *Arabian Nights*. But the substitute king ritual survived into much more recent times. Shah Abbas of Persia was advised by his astrologers to abdicate the throne while 'an unbeliever' was crowned for three days and then put to death, fulfilling the portents and allowing the shah to ascend his throne again and enjoy a long and glorious reign.[23] This took place in AD 1591, just over four hundred years ago, and 1,500 years after the death of cuneiform.

The influence of Mesopotamia on the modern world is pervasive, but often invisible to us. This civilisation that flourished four thousand years before our own has sown the seeds of many of our modern institutions and beliefs. In that time the kernels have grown into something often quite unrecognisable from the original germ, but nevertheless owe their existence to it. Yet the traces are clearly there if only we can read them. Just as the Mesopotamian gods placed signs in the natural world as messages to be decoded, so the Mesopotamians have left their signs upon our culture.

The Mesopotamian kings buried cylinder accounts of their deeds in the ground, leaving them for future rulers to read. They knew that their words would stand the test of time, even if they were buried for many centuries before being unearthed again. It would be easy to assume that they would have been surprised at just how well their inscriptions have been preserved – that it would have surpassed their wildest dreams to know that we are still reading them in the third millennium AD. But to do so would be a fallacy of modern thinking. In the sixth century BC the Babylonian king Nabonidus excavated the inscriptions of several already ancient figures, including King Nebuchadnezzar I of Babylon (r. 1124–1103); Hammurabi, who founded the first Babylonian empire (r. 1792–1750); the sister of Rim-Sin, who ruled the city state of Larsa in southern Mesopotamia (r. 1822–1763); and even Naram-Sin of Akkad (r. 2254–2218), who ruled more than 1,600 years before him.[24] That is an incredibly long time span, and during that millennium-and-a-half cuneiform had always been the default – perhaps Nabonidus too would have expected his own cylinders to last another 1,600 years or more. In fact, Nabonidus probably had an even longer perspective since the Babylonian kings saw themselves as part of a line of ancient rulers stretching back hundreds of thousands of years. What is another three millennia when the sages had first taught cuneiform to the Mesopotamians 430,000 years before the flood?[25]

That we can still read their words today is of course all thanks to the incredible durability of cuneiform tablets, a technology so simple yet with profound implications, as it ensured the survival of the world's very first written records and literature. The achievements of the twenty-first century are far more vulnerable. Our technology moves so rapidly that our means of storing information quickly become obsolete, and it is all too easy for hard drives to degrade or be wiped. In response to this, clay tablets have been resurrected as the ultimate medium of data storage. In a salt mine in Austria, two thousand metres underground, the Memory of Mankind Project is depositing one thousand of the most important books from our era to keep them safe in case of a global technological failure. They are printed on microfilm tablets made of ceramic, the only material deemed durable enough to survive the test of time. It is a curated library, a selection of works deemed important to preserve, the knowledge of the twentieth and twenty-first centuries AD microscopically printed on clay. This is the ultimate time capsule, and like those left by the Mesopotamian kings, is addressed to a future civilisation at least as advanced as we are, giving them a snapshot of our era. The project was directly inspired by cuneiform and the astonishing longevity of its writing materials but is enhanced by modern technology. No fire can turn these tablets to glass, as they are made to withstand temperatures of up to 1,500 degrees, and can resist water damage and even acid. We have come full circle, from writing on clay tablets at the very beginning of history to returning to them now to ensure the survival of the information age. This is one of the most fundamental lessons of all that we can learn from Mesopotamia: that the way we record knowledge matters and can have a real impact on the preservation of our culture. Drawing on the past can directly shape the future and cut across vast swathes of time to highlight the common issues we still face today. The legacy of Mesopotamia will be with us for millennia more to come. We can only hope our own civilisation will survive as well.

Bibliographical Essay

The main sources for this book – the texts preserved on tablets in Ashurbanipal's library, and other relevant cuneiform texts – are referenced where appropriate in the endnotes. More and more are now available online – see the Guide to the Primary Sources for information on how to access them.

Naturally there is also an ever-increasing body of secondary literature, which it would be impossible to survey here. Accordingly, the following suggestions do not claim to be exhaustive. They include the works that I found most helpful, and provide guidance for readers wanting to explore topics more deeply.

General Further Recommended Reading

On the political history of Assyria aimed at a general audience see Frahm (2023). The articles in Frahm ed. (2017) introduce further topics in depth. The catalogue to the British Museum exhibition on Ashurbanipal, Brereton ed. (2018), has articles on a range of aspects and is fantastically illustrated.

For an introduction to the Sumerians and their rediscovery see Collins (2021), and the articles in Crawford ed. (2013a).

Several introductory books on the history of Babylon are now available: Beaulieu (2018), Radner (2020), and Dalley (2021). Further aspects of the culture are unpacked in Leick ed. (2007).

An excellent history of the ancient Near East in general is Podany (2022). Lassen et al. (2019) illustrates Mesopotamian history with the Yale Babylonian Collection. Many introductory articles to different aspects of Mesopotamian culture are available in Radner and Robson eds (2011), all with more suggestions for further reading.

Preface

The number of cuneiform tablets known today is estimated by Streck (2010). For a critique of the 'cradle of civilisation' see Bahrani (1998).

Introduction

An excellent summary of the archaeology of Nineveh is Reade (2000). A highly readable account of the early excavations and rediscovery of the library can be found in Damrosch (2007), while more academic summaries can be found in Reade (1986) and Fincke (2004). On the looting of the tablets from the palace see Fincke (2004, pages 114–15). A description of the Sippar library is given in 'Excavations in Iraq 1985–86' (*Iraq*, 1987, pages 248–9), also discussed in Maul (2010, page 218). For the latest discussion of the Sippar collection see Robson (2019, pages 210–13), who does not believe it was in active use. A treatment of cuneiform archives and libraries more widely is given by Veenhof (1986), see page 13 for the other Assyrian examples mentioned here. The labels for omen collections are mentioned by Weidner (1941, page 179), and Maul (1994, page 191).

The artificial intelligence project is the Electronic Babylonian Library hosted at LMU Munich: https://www.ebl.lmu.de/. The new tablets I refer to that appeared during the writing of this book are primarily Tablets II and III of the poem of *Erra and Ishum*, which are due to be published by Enrique Jiménez on eBL in 2025. A British Museum project analysing Ashurbanipal's library collection has recently concluded, and a monograph with the results by Jon Taylor is forthcoming. For an analysis of its Babylonian tablets, with many useful insights into the collection as a whole, see Fincke (2004), especially pages 124–9 for the inventories, which are published and discussed by Parpola (1983; for the writing board see page 8). For the Borsippan scholars sending writing boards instead of tablets see Frame and George (2005), who published the letters concerning this episode. See now also Frazer (2021) for the memory of this event.

For the transition between Sennacherib and Esarhaddon I have followed Esarhaddon's version of events. There has been some debate about the identity of Sennacherib's murderer: Parpola (1980, pages 174–5) suggested that it was Urad-Mulissu on the basis of SAA 18 100, but some propose the killer was Esarhaddon (e.g. Dalley 2007, pages 38–46; Knapp 2015, pages 320–24; Dalley and Siddall 2021). Parpola's interpretation still seems to me to be the most coherent explanation of the evidence, and recently has been strongly backed up by Jones (2023). The events surrounding the conspiracies of the year 671/70 were reconstructed by Radner (2003) and Frahm (2010); for a readable synthesis see Frahm (2017, chapter 11).

The exact date of the end of Ashurbanipal's reign is unknown – for the latest discussion see RINAP 5/3, pages 26–31 (Novotny et al. 2023). For tablets written in Ashurbanipal's own hand see Livingstone (2007), especially pages 106–7, plus page 113 for the connection with Ashurbanipal's own claims. Ashurbanipal's tablet-collecting is discussed by Fincke (2004, pages 1–3) and Frame and George (2005). For the proportion of divination texts in the library compared with other Mesopotamian collections see Robson (2019, pages 113–16), and Oppenheim (1977, page 20) for its emphasis on magic and ritual. That even the literature was 'useful' is argued by Wisnom (2024). For precursors to Ashurbanipal's collection see Reade (2001, page 44) and Frame and George (2005, pages 278–80). For divination as 'wisdom' see Parpola (1993b).

Paul the octopus has his own Wikipedia page, inspired a Chinese film called *Kill Octopus Paul*, and was followed by a Japanese octopus, Rabio, who was put to work as an oracle for the 2018 World Cup. See Jones (2024) and Fermie (2024).

Recommended Further Reading

Damrosch (2007) is a good introduction to the discoveries of the nineteenth century. Robson (2019) is an easily accessible study of

Assyrian and Babylonian scholarly tablet collections, as is the website Geographies of Knowledge in Assyria and Babylonia (https://oracc.museum.upenn.edu/cams/gkab/), which has many introductory articles as well as publications of texts found in each location.

1. The Scribal Art

For what is known about Ashurbanipal's sister Sherua-etirat see Novotny and Singletary (2009, pages 172–3). The theory that writing developed from tokens was advanced by Schmandt-Besserat (1992). See Woods (2010) for a discussion of the nuances. Nissen et al. (1993) describe the development of proto-cuneiform (see especially pages 11–13 and 19–24 for points raised here). For the population estimate of Uruk see Algaze (2008, page 103). Van De Mieroop (2016) discusses the increasing complexity of the writing system (page 198), the influence of cuneiform on Derrida (pages 77–9), and puns constructing the nature of reality (throughout, but summarised on pages 9–10).

For the connections between 'dark', 'to be well', and 'to be stable' see Veldhuis (2010, pages 83–4). For the translation of Sumerian 'essences' as Akkadian 'battles' see Seminara (2002, page 249). Cooper (1996, page 53) points out that divination texts can be made up of up to 85 per cent logograms. The number of signs a person had to know for everyday use is estimated by Wilcke (2000) and Charpin (2010, pages 61–5): it is sixty-eight in the Old Assyrian period (1600–1200 BC), eighty-two in the Old Babylonian period (2004–1595 BC), and 112 in the Neo-Assyrian period (911–609 BC). For the history of Ea-nasir as an internet meme see Hamilton (2024).

The confusion between pots and straw is discussed by Worthington (2012, page 92). 'Overlook it if a woman has written it' is discussed by Svärd (2015, page 125), Stol (2016, page 370), and Frahm (2023, page 252), who suggests that it was Ashurbanipal's wife asking on this occasion. An introduction to Enheduanna and new translation of her works are provided by Helle (2023), excluding two works attributed to her whose authorship is not certain: *Inanna and Ebih*, and a *balbale* to *Inanna B*. For discussion of these see Konstantopoulos (2021, pages 59–62).

Scribal education in the first millennium has been studied by Gesche (2001); for the summary here see pages 210–18, for Sumerian literature still being studied in this period see pages 18, 20, 251–3. The tablet with bite marks was taken to the dentist by Guinan and Leichty (2010). Ashurbanipal's literacy and education are discussed by Livingstone (2007). Tablets dedicated to Nabu and deposited in his temple are published by Cavigneaux (1981).

The sage that Berossus calls Oannes was called Adapa in Akkadian, who is the subject of other mythical tales such as *Adapa and the South Wind* (see Izre'el 2001). For discussion of the sages as 'pure carp' see Lenzi (2008b, pages 106–20). The Ugaritic cuneiform alphabet is discussed by Boyes (2021). For the decipherment of Old Persian see Daniels (1994, pages 33–8). For Hincks' decipherment of Akkadian see Cathcart (2011). Rawlinson's probable plagiarism is noted by Daniels (1994, pages 51–3).

Recommended Further Reading

Especially accessible are Nissen et al. (1993) on early writing, and Van De Mieroop (2016) on the philosophy of the cuneiform writing system. For literacy and scribal culture see Charpin (2010). The most readable accounts of the decipherment of cuneiform are given by Daniels (1994) and Bottéro (1992, chapter 3, pages 41–54).

2. *The Power of the Gods*

An account of Sennacherib's religious reforms is given by Pongratz-Leisten (2015, pages 416–26). Sennacherib's destruction of Babylon may not have been as total as he claims – for arguments against see Frame (1992, pages 55–6) and George (2005, page 79), though as Frahm notes there is evidence for considerable damage and disruption (2023, pages 224–5). On the Assyrian version of the *Epic of Creation* see Lambert (1997, especially pages 78–9). For the practice of 'godnapping' see Zaia (2015).

For the rise of Marduk in connection with the power of Babylon see Lambert (2013, especially pages 199–201). The name Enlil means 'Lord wind' but despite this he does not have much to do with the weather – for discussion and references see Hays (2020, pages 226–7). On Dumuzi's hazy origins see Klein (2010). Competition between the *Epic of Creation* and earlier poems is treated by Wisnom (2020). The editing-out of the birth goddess is noted by Foster (2005, page 469; 2016, page 95) and Seri (2006, page 515). 'A text that tolerates no rivals' is Lambert's phrase (2010, page 24). For discussion of the list of gods equated with Marduk ending 'Marduk of everything' (CT 24 50, translated by Lambert 1975, page 198) see now Beaulieu (2020). For this characterisation of Ashur see Maul (2017, especially pages 339 and 352). Worship of Ashur outside Assyria was probably political – see Beaulieu (1997).

For discussion of Mesopotamian deities assuming multiple powers see Hundley (2013). On the demotion of female deities see Frymer-Kensky (1992, pages 70–80). That the third-millennium pantheon was based on the household while in the second and first it was based on the state was proposed by Sallaberger (2004, page 307). For further information on the rock relief showing a procession of gods see the archaeological project The Archaeological Complex of Faida's website, link given in note 16.

Similarities between Enlil's sleep-deprived rage and Apsu's are no coincidence – see Wisnom (2020, page 201). For the Mesopotamian source of the Greek names of the planets see Pingree (1998, page 133). The classic account of Sumerian religion is given by Jacobsen (1976, pages 20–21 and 134–5 for points noted here), yet to be replaced. That the lesson of the poem of the righteous sufferer is that everything depends on the will of Marduk was put forward by Lenzi (2012). That people had closer relationships with their personal gods than those of the higher pantheon is also argued by Lenzi (2010). The ritual for cleansing a person of their sin with long lists of offences is treated in detail by Simons (2019). One guess for the meaning of 'the curse of bellows and stove' is that it might be a misuse of cultic equipment (van der Toorn 1985, page 54).

The latest analysis of the Babylonian New Year festival is by Debourse (2022). That the slapping of the king might be a response to the aggression of Sennacherib was suggested by Michalowski (1990, page 393); that it might be an even later response to the Persian and Greek kings was proposed by Smith (1976); the interpretations of this episode are discussed by Debourse (2022, pages 277–81). The song 'Come out like the sun!' was sung to Enlil in the Old Babylonian period, treated by Löhnert (2009). The initiation of Babylonian priests is described by Waerzeggers and Jursa (2008, page 4 for the eligibility criteria here). For the documentary evidence for the installation of priests in Assyria see Löhnert (2007). A thorough study of the Nabu temple in Borsippa is conducted by Waerzeggers (2010): for the offerings boasted by Nebuchadnezzar II see page 114; for the professions that the temple employed in the order discussed here see pages 38–9, 49, 6, and 454. For sacrifices and redistribution of meat in the Ishtar temple of Uruk see Kozuh (2014 and 2010). Temples acting as banks in the Old Babylonian period is discussed by Harris (1960, page 128). The mouth-washing ritual is published and analysed by Walker and Dick (2001). For cultic objects treated as divine see Porter (2009), and for the cultural dilemma posed by moving a god's bed see Porter (2006). The literature on the relationship between Mesopotamia and the Hebrew Bible is voluminous, but as a starting point see Chavalas (2011) for a guide, and Hays (2014) and Walton (2018) for comparative perspectives, the latter especially aimed at a Christian audience.

Recommended Further Reading

Pongratz-Leisten (2015) is especially recommended on Assyrian religion. Another good summary is provided by Maul (2017). For a comprehensive introduction to the Babylonian *Epic of Creation* see Haubold et al. (2024), also available open access on the Bloomsbury website. An introduction to Mesopotamian religion more generally is Hrůša (2015).

3. Magic and Witchcraft

For discussion of the female witches in *Enmerkar and Ensuhgirana* see Konstantopoulos (2020). For the gendered conception of the witch as female see Van Buylaere (2019). The *Exorcist's Manual* is discussed alongside the edition by Geller (2018, pages 292–312). A study of the education and practice of exorcists in the city of Ashur is provided by Arbøll (2020).

For the treatment of figurines of witches see Abusch and Schwemer (2011, page 23). The bell known as 'mighty copper' is identified as a gong by Simons (2024). On how the exorcist had to be an all-rounder see Geller (2010, page 124). For the making of the figurines see Parpola (1983, page 166). That witch crazes never spiralled out of control like they did in medieval Europe is observed by Schwemer (2014). For documented accusations of witchcraft see Schwemer (2007, pages 119–26). For 'cutting of the throat magic' see Abusch and Schwemer (2011, page 8). On manipulative magic (though from the Old Babylonian period) see Mertens-Wagschal (2018).

On royal women in Assyria see MacGregor (2012) and Svärd (2015). Frahm gives a readable summary of what is known of the main protagonists (2023, chapter 10). Not much is known about the armies of queens apart from the names of the commanders; for these see Radner (2008, page 510). A charioteer belonging to Ashurbanipal's wife's household took part in the war against Babylon – see Svärd (2015, page 164) and Baker (2001, page 79). The ghost that appeared to the young Ashurbanipal is unnamed in the letter and that she is Ashurbanipal's mother Esharra-hamat is conjecture – on her identity see Novotny and Singletary (2009, pages 174–6). This letter which is assumed to be by Adad-shumu-utsur is not signed by him, but it spells words in the same way that he does (Parpola 1983, page 120). For a full account of what is known about Naqia during the reign of Sennacherib see Melville (1999, pages 13–29). Melville portrays Naqia's role at court as symbolic (see also 2004 on the status of Assyrian royal women), but Svärd argues that she had a more active role and very real authority (2012, 2015).

For a thorough study of *namburbi* rituals see Maul (1999, in German, see page 129 for the length of the series), while a summary in English is available in Maul (1999). Some namburbi texts are published in English by Caplice (1974). For studies of Pazuzu see Heeßel (2002, in German, pages 9–11 for the description here; 2011 in English summary). The last published count identified 119 different demons in Mesopotamia (Wiggermann 2011, page 307; for the *alu* demon see page 309). Frahm (2014) proposes that Sennacherib's encounter with the *alu* may have reflected a kind of post-traumatic stress (especially pages 203–4). More Freudian interpretations of Mesopotamian magic are provided by Geller (1997a).

The troubles of Urad-Gula are pieced together by Parpola (1987). The suggestion that he may have been one of Ashurbanipal's tutors was made by Jean (2006, page 118), while Geller (2010, pages 78–9) notes the confidence in the tone of his letters. The letter about the royal childbirth gone wrong (SAA 10 293) is fragmentary and we don't know what happened exactly. It could have been miscarriage, injury to the mother, or death of the child, possibilities which are proposed by Parpola (1983, page 355 and 1987, page 271). It is also Parpola who points out there is no mention of Adad-shumu-utsur's son in Ashurbanipal's response (1987, page 270).

Recommended Further Reading

A large number of anti-witchcraft ritual texts are available online, including *Maqlu* (see CMAwR), and the website is provided with introductory articles (https://www.phil.uni-wuerzburg.de/cmawro/magic-witchcraft/maqlu/). Incantations are too numerous to list here in full, but see Geller (2016) for a long series against demons. Especially good overviews of Mesopotamian magic are available in Schwemer (2011), which also suggests more further reading, and (2015). An accessible book on ghosts and the netherworld in Mesopotamia is Finkel (2022).

4. *The Treatment of Disease*

For some reflections on the relationship between ritual and medical efficacy see Zisa (2021, pages 201–13). That tying magical stones on to the head may activate pressure points is proposed by Mateuszewska (2018, page 170). The significance of the statement 'the King executed a large number of his nobles' in two *Babylonian Chronicle* texts (Glassner 2004, no. 16, line 29, pages 202–3; no. 18, line 30, pages 208–9) is unpacked by Radner (2003, pages 174–5).

Academics have been arguing about the respective roles and responsibilities of the physician and exorcist for sixty years (beginning with Ritter 1965, for an overview see Scurlock 1999), though what all the overlaps show is just how holistic Mesopotamian medicine was. Any healing practitioner had to be acquainted with both plants and spells, and had a range of tools they could call upon, some of which were used by both professions. For a recent discussion of the curricula and core expertise of each and where they overlap see Steinert (2018b, page 178–81). Urad-Nanaya's advice to Esarhaddon is analysed and compared with that of Adad-shumu-utsur by Geller (2010, pages 79–88, especially pages 79 and 85–6 for points noted here).

For the debates concerning the relationship between the treatments in the *Nineveh Medical Compendium* and those used by Esarhaddon's doctors see e.g. Geller and Panayotov (2020, pages 10–12). For the relationship between early Greek and Babylonian medicine see Geller (2001). That the codes of divination affect the prognoses in the *Diagnostic Handbook* is shown by Heeßel (2004, pages 107–10) and was made especially clear to me by the PhD thesis of Lynette Talbot (University of Cambridge, as yet unpublished). For the empirical dimensions of medicine mixing with these codes see also Heeßel (2004, page 110). For physicians using fossilised writings of e.g. 'hand of Ishtar' see Johnson (2018, page 79), building on Heeßel (2007, pages 122–5). That the therapeutic text on stomach ailments parodies the style of exorcists is suggested by Johnson (2018, pages 75–7), while the eye disease text with the physician garbling his Sumerian is discussed by Geller and Panayotov (2020, pages 41–2). For symptoms caused by the hands of various gods see Heeßel (2004, page 109).

An overview of Lamashtu is given by Wiggermann (2000) – see pages 236-8 for her medical effects, as well as Bácskay (2019) for treatments against them. The texts are edited by Farber (2014). The comparison between diseases caused by spiritual entities and microorganisms is made by Geller (2010, page 14). Scurlock and Andersen (2005) discuss knowledge of contagion (pages 18–19) and hygiene (page 16), while information about toilets and sanitation can be found in George (2015, especially pages 77–9).

For the physician's understanding of disease caused by the body malfunctioning see Steinert (2020, page 149). Steinert (2017) discusses bodily functions described in terms of cooking and brewing (pages 223–4) and the birth goddesses connected with crafts such as carpentry (page 303). The womb functioning like an oven or a kiln is discussed by Couto-Ferreira (2013). For the influence of the environment and comparison with other traditions see Steinert (2020, pages 168–70). Prescriptions for ghost-induced ear-ringing are given by Scurlock and Andersen (2005, pages 377–424 and 2014, pages 380–82). The summary of treatments for eyes 'under pressure' is given by Geller and Panayotov (2020, pages 124–6), and liver for night blindness is noted by Scurlock (2014, page 361). For turtles in Chinese medicine see Hempen and Fischer (2009, page 812).

For the alarming secret names of plants see Köcher (1995). That some ingredients referred to as dung occur only in rectal disease texts is noted by Geller (2005, page 7). The same page also gives references to where some of the other unpleasantly named ingredients are found, while more are listed in the plant list extract published by Scurlock (2014, page 290, lines 26–30).

For cryptic plant names in other cultures see Rumor (2020, page 40). A new presentation of Mesopotamian herbal medicine has recently become available in Böck (2023), who discusses plant identifications (summarising methods on page 51). For the *ninu* plant see Kinnier-Wilson (2005, page 50). The Assyrian plant list grouping together different plant names is currently only available in cuneiform copy (Fincke 2021) but the translations are forthcoming. For the passage cited here see Böck (2011, page 693), who also discusses Ashurbanipal's editing of the text (pages 692–3).

There is a long-running debate about Ashurbanipal's proficiency in cuneiform scholarship. It has been argued that his advisers had to explain to him some of the basic terms of the omen texts, as they gloss some of the logograms which are not especially difficult (Fincke 2004, page 121), but these could just as well have been for the benefit of the scribes who read the letters out loud to the king (as argued by Oppenheim 1969, page 119).

That Esarhaddon's illness was lupus was suggested by Parpola (1983, pages 230–35). For the non-specific terminology for the human body compared with the highly specific terminology for sheep entrails see Geller (2010, page 22). That Esarhaddon may have been afflicted by the hand of Sin was suggested by Radner (2003, pages 172–3). Sennacherib's suspiciously pious enquiries about the sins of his father are discussed by Weaver (2004).

The king's letter concerning the 'fall of the heavens' (SAA 10 295) is listed as undatable by Parpola (1983, page 413). Fincke (2004, page 121) ascribes it to Ashurbanipal and cites it as evidence for his lack of understanding of scholarly language, but I believe Esarhaddon is more likely given that the letter is addressed to Urad-Gula, who was more active under his reign.

For the red-plastered room of the exorcist's house in Ashur see Pedersén (1986, pages 41–3). For apprentices practising on animals see Arbøll (2020, pages 86–7, 90, and 110–12). For female physicians, healing goddesses, and herbalists see May (2019, pages 152–7), though note we can't always extrapolate from goddesses to humans: Ishtar is a goddess of war but we do not find women on the battlefield.

The point about the relative safety of Mesopotamian medicine is made by Geller (2010, page 3). Geller also compares Mesopotamian medicine with the Greek Methodists (2001, pages 53–6), and prognosis in the Hippocratic corpus (pages 63–7); for specific comparisons in Greek and Roman eye disease texts see Geller and Panayotov (2020, pages 33–4 and 27), and for medieval Syria see pages 25, 28–31. It is Geller who has argued throughout his publications that the technical knowledge of Mesopotamia had the most impact beyond its borders.

Recommended Further Reading

Translations of the *Diagnostic Handbook* and a selection of therapeutic recipes are available in Scurlock (2014). Many editions are also available online through the Babylonian medicine project that ran in Berlin from 2013 until 2018 (https://www.geschkult.fu-berlin.de/e/babmed/). An accessible introduction to Babylonian medicine that also draws on evidence from Assyria is Geller (2010). Böck (2024) presents the uses of a selection of medicinal plants.

5. Reading the Signs

For an account of the growing tensions between the two brothers see Brinkman (1984, pages 85–92). For a reconstruction of the events of the war see Frame (1992, pages 102–30). A thorough description of the extispicy ritual is given by Maul (2018, chapter 3). See also chapter 4 on formulating the questions.

Many insights about the practice of extispicy can be found in Robson (2011), who observes that the more junior Dannaya corrected his superior (page 614), and that entrail diviners did not collaborate with scholars of other disciplines (pages 610–11). That Mesopotamian divination should be treated as part of the history of science is vigorously argued by e.g. Pingree (1992). Rationality in Assyrian and Babylonian scholarship is discussed in the works of Rochberg (e.g. 2016).

The text that has Sennacherib recommend splitting diviners into groups (SAA 3 33) is thought to have been written during the reign of Esarhaddon – see Weaver (2004). For the academic context of omens in general see Rochberg (2004, pages 52 ff.). The terms for the anatomy of the sheep liver have been well studied by Leiderer (1990), who provides plenty of images to show what they correspond to (see page 76 for a discussion of 'the design'). See also Meyer (1989) for a study based on liver models. For the meanings of the zones and marks see the introduction to the edition of the extispicy omen series published by Koch-Westenholz (2000, pages 43–70). The comparison between creases on the liver and modern palmistry is made by Jeyes (1980, page 25).

Robson calculates the percentage of omens from the compendia that are quoted in reports to the king (2011, pages 620–21). For omens as a type of Babylonian philosophy see Van De Mieroop (2016). On impossible omens see Rochberg (2016, pages 106–7). The scholars found a way to make omens like 'If the sun comes out at midnight' possible by interpreting the sun as the planet Saturn – for similar examples see Koch-Westenholz (1995, pages 122–3). That the diviners always travelled with the king is pointed out by Robson (2011, pages 611–12). For the requirements of the ritual see Maul (2018, pages 20–24). For eunuchs at the Assyrian court see Deller (1999, pages 306–7 for the benefits they received). Radner (2011) points out the scarcity of eunuch diviners (page 363).

The Sealand was a region between Babylonia and Elam that had been loyal to Ashurbanipal thus far but had a history of opposition to Assyria – see Frame (1992, page 175). Frame puts the extispicy reports into the context of the war as a whole; for the question about the Elamites joining the war see page 146 note 56. For the calculation of the time period that the extispicy was valid for according to the omen series see Heeßel (2010). The time spans relevant to each extispicy in the Assyrian records are summarised by Starr (1990, page XVI). For the transmission of extispicy between Mesopotamia and Greece see e.g. Furley and Gysembergh (2015, especially pages 78–80).

Recommended Further Reading

The extispicy omens are most easily readable in the three chapters published by Koch-Westenholz (2000), who also introduces the history, content, and structure of the series. Maul (2018) gives a comprehensive overview of both extispicy and astrology. A shorter introduction is provided by Koch (2011) with more suggestions for further reading. A guide to divination texts of all kinds in Mesopotamia can be found in Koch (2015).

6. *Messages in the Stars*

That astrologers are responsible for one-third of the correspondence in the royal archive was calculated by Radner (2011, page 369). This figure includes the reports in SAA 8 as well as the letters in SAA 10. For astrology as one of the least understood types of Mesopotamian science see Koch (2019). 'The heavenly writing' is the subject of a book by Rochberg (2004), which is an excellent introduction to Mesopotamian celestial divination in general. That the Sumerian word for 'star' can also refer to a cuneiform sign is noted by Roaf and Zgoll (2001, page 289 note 68). For the concept of fate in Mesopotamia see the book of the same name by Lawson (1994) and Rochberg (2010, pages 19–28 and 411–24). For the workings of calendars see Steele (2011a).

The 'inner circle' of advisers close to the king was defined by Parpola (1993a, pages XXV–VI). All but one are Assyrian, whereas letters from Babylonian scholars are mostly straightforward reports and petitions for help. The Assyrian advisers are also more likely to report negative omens than their Babylonian counterparts, which may reflect a greater security in their position (see e.g. Koch-Westenholz 1995, pages 71 and 144–5).

For the role of the Venus tablet of Ammisaduqa in establishing Babylonian chronology see Nahm (2013), though problems remain – see Gasche (1998, pages 72–4) and Gurzadyan (2000) for further details. The miscommunications between the scholars over Venus and Mercury were reconstructed by Parpola (1983) in his commentary to LAS 65–6 (= SAA 10 72 and 51) and LAS 12 (SAA 10 23) – see pages 14–15 and 70.

The length of the series *Enuma Anu Enlil* varies between cities. At Nineveh it is seventy tablets long, whereas in other places it ranges from sixty-three to sixty-nine tablets. For this and the content of the series tablet by tablet see Koch (2015, pages 165–78).

That half of the astrological reports are concerned with the moon was observed by Koch-Westenholz (1995, page 99). For metaphorical descriptions of the moon see Rochberg (2004, pages 167–70). The main commentary the scholars used to understand *Enuma Anu Enlil* is called *Shumma Sin ina tamartishu*, edited and analysed by Wainer (2016, see especially page 432). The codes of interpretation for the meanings of the omens are given by Brown (2000, pages 140–53). The analogical principles and binary codes of opposition are further set out by Rochberg (2004, pages 54–8), who also discusses their applicability across other omen series. The reversing of 'false star' to make 'Cancer' is discussed by Frahm (2011, pages 39 and 148).

For various manipulations of the meaning of Mars see Brown (2000, page 79). That the omens are gloomy but astrologers optimistic is noted by Koch-Westenholz (1995, pages 144–5). The quadrants of the moon in eclipse omens are discussed by Rochberg-Halton (1988, pages 53–5). The scholars reminding the king about future predictions coming true was noticed by Koch (2011, pages 454–5 and 460). For Assyrian knowledge of eclipse forecasting see Koch-Westenholz (1995, pages 110–11). That mathematical astronomy was a breakthrough that established the concept of mathematical models is pointed out by Britton and Walker (1996, page 67), which is a useful introduction to Babylonian astronomy in general. On this point see now also Rochberg (2018a).

The smallest unit of time used to predict eclipses is known as an *ush* (four minutes) – see Britton and Walker (1996, page 48). For the names of the constellations see Rochberg (2010, page 36); those given here are from MUL.APIN.

On the background of the zodiac see Verderame (2009); on its transmission to Greece see originally van der Waerden (1953). Influence between Mesopotamia and Greece could go both ways. For instance the 'hired man' is described as the 'hired sheep' in the Hellenistic text from Uruk MLC 1866, Section A i 13–16 (for edition see Beaulieu et al. 2017, page 46), and whether this is Mesopotamian in origin or influence from the Greeks is an open question (see Beaulieu et al. 2017, page 46; Beaulieu 2019). For further discussions of these dynamics see Stevens (2019). For the various names and depictions of Pisces see Beaulieu et al. (2017, pages 44–5) and Ossendrijver (2021, page 236).

That the astronomical diaries are the longest-running scientific project in history was pointed out by Campion (2009, pages 75–6). The latest series of studies on them is Haubold et al. eds (2019). The article in this volume by Ossendrijver (2019) discusses tablets with rules predicting market rates (especially pages 65 ff.). For nativity omens see Koch-Westenholz (1995, page 172). All known Babylonian horoscopes are published by Rochberg (1998), who discusses their development in her 2004 book (chapters 3–5, with a note that calculating positions of the planets is especially useful for this purpose on page 101). That Anu-belshunu in this horoscope is the same individual who owned the tablet illustrating the constellations was identified by Beaulieu and Rochberg (1996, pages 93–4), who also calculate the length of his career. For relationships between the scholars in Uruk see Robson (2008, pages 240–60) and Ossendrijver (2011 and 2021).

The description of System A and System B draws on Britton and Walker (1996). See also Ossendrijver (2014) for a more recent summary. That there must have been direct contact between Babylonian and Greek astronomers is claimed by Toomer (1988, pages 357–60, specifically referencing the Greek astronomer Hipparchus), and Steele (2011b, pages 453–5). See also Jones (1991) for a discussion of the transmission of mathematical methods. Babylonian influence on Greek mathematics is only documented during the Hellenistic period, making the Babylonian version of Pythagoras' theorem unlikely to be the result of direct transmission. For discussion of this see Robson (2008, pages 284–8). That the Babylonians were the first to use a graph to understand motion or speed over time is established by Ossendrijver (2016), who publishes the tablet proving it.

The analysis of the number of astronomical tablets in Seleucid Uruk is given by Robson (2019, pages 230–31, figure 6.4, and table 6c), taking together the proportions of those found in the Resh temple itself and those of unknown origin excavated illicitly from Uruk in general. For some relevant points of comparison between divination and economics see Koch (2016).

Recommended Further Reading

Koch-Westenholz (1995) is a good introduction to Mesopotamian astrology. Rochberg (2004) places it in its scholarly context and discusses its development over time. See again those recommended for extispicy, Maul (2018) and Koch (2015) as above. For science in Mesopotamia see Rochberg (2018b). For a discussion of the history of Babylonian astronomy, see Steele (2018).

7. Literature

Nabu-zuqup-kenu copying *Gilgamesh* Tablet 12 in response to the death of Sargon was proposed by Frahm (1999). It may also have been copied for a specific purpose – George (2003) has suggested it might have been used in a memorial ritual for the dead king (pages 53–4). Building on this, Frahm (2005) pointed out that 27 Du'uzu falls in the middle of the festival for the dead, suggesting it is possible the epic was recited during a ritual for Sargon's spirit. For the rituals surrounding care of the dead, see Tsukimoto (1985, especially pages 230–31) and MacDougal (2014, for the libation pipes pages 203–4).

The comparison between tablets and TV episodes is made by Helle (2023). An analysis of the distribution of the manuscripts of *Gilgamesh* is given by George (2003, pages 380–91); that only Ashurbanipal had a copy of every tablet in the series is noted on page

391, that he had five 'sets' of *Gilgamesh* is brought out by Robson (2004). The colophon stating that Ashurbanipal copied and checked the tablet himself, although in first person, might just mean that he ordered scribes to do it on his behalf (George 2003, page 382 note 11), though I like to think it at least shows a special interest in the poem.

For the height of Gilgamesh see Annus (2012). The type of creature that the gardener was changed into cannot be identified for certain, but George (2003, pages 835–8) suggests it may be a dwarf. The similarities between the Bull of Heaven episode in *Gilgamesh* and the *Iliad* were first proposed by Burkert (1992, pages 96–9). The issue is hotly debated – for a recent critique see Ballesteros (2021), though I side with Currie (2016, pages 173–9).

For a large catalogue of other parallels between Greek and Near Eastern literature and religion see West (1997). A recent set of reflections on the relationship between the two is provided in the essays in Kelley and Metcalf eds (2021). On the love between Gilgamesh and Enkidu see Nissinen (2010), Walls (2001, pages 9–92), and Helle (2021, pages 171–8). That 'everyone needs a friend' was suggested by my student Robbie Moore. That Babylonian poetry appeals to the imagination instead of describing outright is proposed by Haubold (2013, pages 37–9).

For interpretations of Gilgamesh as a business tycoon see Terry (2018), as a queer icon see Cohen (2021), for superhero see LoCicero (2008, pages 7–17) and Turri (2020). The reception of *Gilgamesh* by modern poets is discussed by Schmidt (2019). For the theme of the need to take advice, see Sonik (2020, page 404 for Gilgamesh abandoning his kingly responsibilities). Urad-Gula's allusion to the advice to a prince was noticed by Parpola (1987, pages 272–3). For Sargon's portrayal of himself as Gilgamesh see Bach (2019, pages 245–6), and for Esarhaddon's Gilgamesh allusions see pages 340–41.

For women in *Gilgamesh* see Harris (1990), who is more pessimistic, and Sonik (2021). The roles of women in the poem may not necessarily be a celebration of their influence but may reflect an anxiety about it, as argued by Helle (2021, pages 208–13).

For birds flying into the house as the souls of dead ancestors see the rituals in Maul (1999, pages 233–69). Although the death of Gilgamesh himself does not feature in the Standard Babylonian epic, it has been argued that the death of Enkidu alludes to the death of Gilgamesh (see Currie 2012). For the change in tone between Old Babylonian and Standard Babylonian versions see George (2003, pages 32–3).

The debate over the first line of *Atrahasis* started when the edition by Lambert and Millard was published in 1969, and raged for forty-seven years. It is summarised by Ziegler (2016), who provides conclusive evidence that the gods were never human after all. The vast bibliography on this poem is surveyed by Shehata (2001). The puns on the Babylonian words for 'man', 'god', and the name of the rebel leader are discussed by Alster (2002). Lambert and Millard (1969, page 28) draw attention to the exorcist's letter that cites *Atrahasis*, and the logic behind it.

The scribal school in Nippur is discussed by Robson (2001, page 44 for tablets built into the fabric of the building), and the excavation report is published by McCown and Haines (1967, see page 64 for the bench). On the relationship between the curriculum and the values of the scribal profession see Robson (2008, pages 118–23).

For the king acting as Ninurta see Maul (1998); for this in the lion hunt in particular see Watanabe (1998, pages 444–5). For Esarhaddon's portrayal of himself as being like Ninurta see Parpola (2001, pages 185–6 note 26) and Bach (2019, pages 338–42). Ninurta as a model for the king is discussed more fully in Pongratz-Leisten (2015, chapter 6). See also the monograph on Ninurta by Annus (2002, pages 138–45 for Ninurta's role in medical texts). The usefulness of *Ninurta's Exploits* to exorcists is further discussed by Wisnom (2024). For omens in the poems foreshadowing events later in the narrative see Cooley (2013) on the poem of *Erra and Ishum* (pages 95–110).

Recommended Further Reading

Accessible translations of *Gilgamesh* are George (2020) and Helle (2021). George's translation is also available online at eBL, which will be updated as new fragments appear. Ultimately all of the classics of Babylonian literature will be available on this website. Helle's book on *Gilgamesh* contains excellent essays on its interpretation. A wide-ranging anthology of Akkadian literature in translation is Foster (2005). A useful introduction to Akkadian literature with full references to further reading can be found in Lenzi (2019). A companion series to eBL, The Library of Babylonian Literature, has just been launched that will provide interpretive essays on each of the major works of Akkadian poetry, starting with Haubold et al. (2024) on the *Epic of Creation*, and with more volumes to follow.

8. *War*

Ashurbanipal's palace reliefs are beautifully presented and discussed in Brereton ed. (2018). The volume gives succinct accounts of the king's campaigns (Novotny 2018, pages 196–211), and analyses Til-Tuba in particular (Nadali 2018; Goldstein and Weisert 2018). For the flow of the narrative on the reliefs see Watanabe (2008 and 2018). For the comparison between the inscriptions and historical novels see Grayson (1992, page 142). On deportations see Oded (1979). For details of Ashurbanipal's war against his brother I have drawn on Brinkman (1984, page 86 for escalating tensions in the run-up). On the dynamics between the brothers see now also Zaia (2018).

The inscription of Naram-Sin that Nabonidus dug up may have been a fake – see Powell (1991). Nabonidus also thought that Naram-Sin ruled 3,200 years before him, a good 1,500 years out. For Nabonidus as the first archaeologist see Winter (2000). For a summary of intended audiences of Assyrian royal inscriptions see Tadmor (1997, pages 331–2), though he is cautious about public performance.

The Assyrian strategy at Til-Tuba is discussed by Nadali (2018, pages 240–41). For the portrayal of Elamites and the lions in the reliefs see Collins (2006) and Miller (2021). The allusions to omens in the Til-Tuba relief were spotted by Goldstein and Weissert (2018, pages 248–50), who also discuss the literary resonances (pages 256–67). For the allusion to *Gilgamesh* see Bonatz (2004, page 100), also on the taking of Teumman's head in general. For the possible apotropaic function of Teumman's head see Goldstein and Weissert (2018, pages 260–61). Ashurbanipal's Elamite campaigns are discussed by Gerardi (1987). A summary can be found in Novotny and Jeffers (2018, pages 20–25, see especially page 23 note 149 for discussion of motives).

That the narrative of Ashurbanipal staying in Arbela was used to justify the fact that the king of Elam was accidentally killed by a common soldier is suggested in an unpublished paper by Novotny and Watanabe presented at the Marburg Rencontre Assyriologique Internationale in 2017. That Bel-ushezib's advice was unconventional is noted by Koch-Westenholz (1995, pages 148–9). For discussion of the letter to the scholars of Borsippa see Frame and George (2005, page 265 for the intercity rivalry) and now Frazer (2021). For the stories about Sardanapalus see Frahm (2003, page 39 for discussion of Ctesias).

Recommended Further Reading

Brereton ed. (2018) is the recommended starting point. The campaigns are summarised also by Novotny and Jeffers (2018) in the introduction to their publication of Ashurbanipal's inscriptions (RINAP 5), which are also all published online. An account of Assyria's expansion and a survey of its interaction with other states of the Near East are given by Novotny (2023, pages 352–424). In the same volume (Radner et al. 2023) surveys can be found of the histories of these regions in their own right as well as their encounters with Assyria – see especially Bartelmus for Elam and Sergi for Israel and Judah. Another resource for the Elamite side is Potts (2016). For a survey of Assyrian warfare see Dalley (2017). For Assyrian imperialism in general see Liverani (2017).

9. Lamentation

Nabu-zeru-iddina's family history is reconstructed by Gabbay (2014a), which I have drawn on extensively for this chapter. See especially pages 118–19 for an analysis of the ranking of lamenters, and pages 121–2 for their outsider status and accusations made against them. We don't know when exactly they moved to Assyria, and it is possible that Nabu-zeru-iddina had already been born there. Nevertheless his cultural connection to Babylon must have remained strong.

The executions at the site of Sennacherib's murder probably took place in Nineveh rather than Babylon – see von Soden (1990). The Assyrians had earlier experimented with adapted Babylonian laments, as evidenced by a *balag* to Ashur called *Zibu zibum* dating from about 1100 BC which had originally been addressed to Enlil, but it did not catch on. At some point between the Middle and Neo-Assyrian periods the Babylonian tradition was imported wholesale and became a regular part of the Assyrian cult – see Gabbay (2014a, pages 129–30), and for *Zibu zibum* see Cohen (1988, pages 43 and 342–6). For the inner circle of the king's advisers see Parpola (1993a, pages XXV–XXVII).

Whether Sargon II of Assyria is named after Sargon of Agade is disputed – for discussion see Novotny et al. (2023, pages 19–21). A study of this is forthcoming by Worthington, whom I follow here. For the composition of the Sumerian city laments see Michalowski (1989, pages 6–8) in his introduction to the *Lamentation over the Destruction of Sumer and Ur*. The memory of the fall of the Ur III dynasty is the subject of a book by Schaudig (2019). That the *Lamentation over the Destruction of Sumer and Ur* was still known in the first millennium is proposed by Wisnom (2020, chapter 7).

For performance instructions in the form of vocal ornaments see Mirelman (2010) and Gabbay (2011). A book-length study of 'Come out like the sun!' is available in Löhnert (2009). For the performance schedule of temple laments in Ashur see Cohen (1988, page 22). On Alexander's demolition of the temple of Marduk in Babylon see George (2005, page 91).

The other genre of Sumerian texts in the library of which there are many examples is incantations (e.g. *Udug-hul*, see Geller 2016). For the connection between *Erra and Ishum* and ritual lament see

Wisnom (2020, pages 238–42). The amulets containing the text have been most recently discussed by Heeßel (2014, pages 59–61).

The ritual that likely would have accompanied Ashurbanipal's lament is reconstructed from ritual number 9 in Maul (1988, page 54), who edited the *ershahungas*. For the feelings produced by ritual laments in performers and audience see Delnero (2020). Gabbay (2022) has independently come to similar conclusions about the psychology of lament.

Recommended Further Reading

A selection of *balags* is presented in Cohen (1988), while *ershemmas* are available in Gabbay (2015). Löhnert (2011) is a good introduction with further recommended reading. An important study of lament in Mesopotamia is Gabbay (2014b).

10. *A Day in the Life of Ashurbanipal*

For studies of dreams in Mesopotamia see Oppenheim (1956) and Butler (1998). A new edition of the dream omens will soon be published by Zomer. For the Assyrian lion hunt see Watanabe (1998 and 2018). For hunting with Elamite princes in tow see Reade (2018, page 71). That the lion hunt may have been part of other victory celebrations is suggested by Weissert (1997, pages 348 ff.), who also compares the campaign against the lions with the campaign against Teumman (pages 352–3).

The hemerologies are edited and discussed by Livingstone (2013), who analyses the dates of real-life extispicies and legal transactions on pages 269–72 and 275–6 respectively, and talks about the chief scribe's manoeuvres for the oath of allegiance on page 270.

Ashurbanipal's correspondence is published by Parpola (2018) and Frame and Parpola (2023) in SAA 21 and 22. An analysis of the relationship between the king and priest is given by Zaia (2019). For the letter from Ashurbanipal's 'baby brother' see Novotny and

Singletary (2009, pages 173–4). For an introduction to the logic of omens in *Shumma alu* see Guinan (1990). Snake catchers are discussed by Sibbing-Plantholt (2022, pages 177–84).

Assyrian banquets have recently been studied by Ermidoro (2015). For more on food and drink in Babylonia see Bottéro (1995), who publishes the recipe tablets, and Reynolds (2007). Music is discussed by Ziegler (2011). That *Anzu* has the structure of a song is proposed by Wisnom (2023). For board games in Mesopotamia see Finkel (2007, see page 25 for the letter from Shamash-shum-ukin and page 17 for the number of boards and their distribution). Wee (2018) gives a further in-depth analysis of 'pack of dogs'. The sex omens are discussed by Guinan (1997). For *Shumma alu* in Assyrian palace reliefs see Zamazalová (2018, pages 185–9). I thank Sophus Helle for the interpretation of two women having sex leading to civil war. Sexual potency remedies and rituals have been studied by Zisa (2021, see pages 202–3 for the role of women in these incantations).

See *Daily Telegraph* (2010) for an example of a malformed sheep born in Turkey. Also, Campbell (2012) for a two-faced cat born in the United States. For an example of this phenomenon in Zimbabwe see Ncube (2009). Likewise in Australia a five-legged lamb caused a stir in local media, see Keane (2021).

Recommended Further Reading

For daily life in Mesopotamia, drawing on various periods, see Nemet-Nejat (2002).

Epilogue: The Afterlife of Cuneiform Culture

For Marduk's temple in Babylon in the fourth century BC see Beaulieu (2018, page 258). The evidence for the substitute king ritual is presented by Parpola (1983, pages XXII–XXXII) and is also discussed by Bottéro (1995, pages 138–55). A substitute was enthroned once during the reign of Ashurbanipal but by mistake – in that particular eclipse the planet Jupiter was present, meaning the king was safe, and one of the scholars vigorously complains about his colleague's error in SAA 10 90. For discussion see Parpola (1983, pages 304–6). For lamentations during eclipses see Linssen (2004, pages 109–17).

Though most of the correspondence of Ashurbanipal's successors has not been found, see Jursa (2007) for an important exception from the reign of Sin-shar-ishkun. For the looting of the library by invading armies see Fincke (2004, page 112). For other libraries in Mesopotamia see Robson (2013 and 2019). For what is known of the tablets from the temple of Marduk in Babylon see Clancier (2009). The use of Aramaic in Assyrian imperial administration is discussed by Radner (2014, page 84) and Parpola (2004, page 9). See Reade (2012) for the scribes in the reliefs. The rise of Aramaic as a lingua franca is discussed by Folmer (2020). For Babylonian craftsmen working on the palace in Susa see Dalley (1998a, page 37). Xerxes's crackdown is discussed by Waerzeggers (2003); for its effect on scholarship in particular see Robson (2019, chapter 6). For the old nobility of Uruk see Clancier (2011).

On Alexander's preparations for rebuilding the temple see Downey (1988, pages 7–14). The Antiochus cylinder is discussed by Stevens (2014). On the continued performance of the Babylonian New Year festival see Debourse (2022, pages 73–89 and 423–4). For the relative importance of Babylon and Seleucia on the Tigris see Dalley (2021, pages 298–300). On the theatre in Babylon see van der Spek (2001) and Potts (2011). The settlement of Greeks in Babylon and its status of *polis* are discussed in van der Spek's (2004) commentary to BCHP 14.

A detailed study of Greek and Babylonian scholarship in the Hellenistic period is provided by Stevens (2019) – for both Berossus and the tablets with Greek letters (known as the *Graeco-Babyloniaca*) see chapter 3 (page 109 for his reputation among classical historians, and pages 132–3 for the argument that these bilingual tablets helped teach scribes to render Akkadian and Greek terms in both scripts). A series of articles on Berossus is available in Haubold et al. eds (2013), while earlier studies of the *Graeco-Babyloniaca* include Geller (1997b) and Westenholz (2007, pages 276–7 for the traditional curriculum carrying on). For Diogenes the Stoic see e.g. Dalley (1998a, page 46).

The classic study of the Orientalising period is Burkert (1992). For the Gorgon's debts to Humbaba see Graff (2012, page 119). Thales of Miletus is discussed by Van De Mieroop (2016, page 5), and Heraclitus by Viano (2021, especially pages 231–44). For the diffusion of extispicy see Burkert (1992, pages 47–53), Turfa (2012, pages 255–8), and Furley and Gysembergh (2015), who publish the Greek extispicy texts (see pages 78–80 for a summary of the transmission).

Trade between Sumer, Afghanistan, and the Indus Valley is discussed by Crawford (2013b, pages 454–6). That the board game 'pack of dogs' may have originated in the Indus Valley is suggested by Reade (2003, page 101). For a summary of the proposed influences of Mesopotamian astronomical knowledge on India, Central Asia, and China see Pingree (1998), though for a critique of the proposed borrowing of the water clock and sundial see Falk (2000). Similarities between Mesopotamian and Indian physiognomy traditions are discussed by Zysk (2020). The argument that the Buddha preached against Mesopotamian-style omens is made by Dalley (1997 and 1998a, page 39). That his description of astrological predictions follows the same order as *Enuma Anu Enlil* is noted by Pingree (1998, page 131), and for the similarities in terrestrial omens see also Pingree (1992). On transmission of omens into Central Asia see Pingree (1963) and Sims-Williams (1996). Mesopotamian influence on astrology in China was originally proposed by Bezold (1919), but his specific ideas have been refuted by Steele (2013 and 2022) and Pankanier (2014). However, there are other similarities between the two systems that these authors do not address, which may or may not have developed independently. The Chinese treatise on the celestial offices in the *Grand Scribe's Records* (translated by Pankanier 2014) does represent a 'major reformulation of astral divination theory and practice' (Pankanier 2013, page 452), which does not exclude external influence on the interpretation of the signs even if methods of observing them were indigenous.

On biblical history and the Near East see e.g. the essays within

Stökl and Waerzeggers eds (2015), especially Grabbe (2015). For a study of Judaeans in Babylonia see Alstola (2020, pages 267–72 for points noted here in the summary). The cuneiform documents belonging to these Judaean exiles are published by Pearce and Wunsch (2014, see pages 10–17 for an analysis of their names) and now also Wunsch (2022). For cuneiform in Canaan see Horowitz (2018). A comparison of the tower of Babel story with Babylonian traditions is made by Frahm (2010). For the connection with the ziggurat of Marduk in Babylon see George (2005). On both of these see also Finkel et al. (2008, pages 124 ff.). On the length of the exile see Walker (page 146 in Finkel et al. 2008). Babylonian kingship in the Persian period is discussed by Waerzeggers (2015). That many of the motifs in the Cyrus cylinder follow established Babylonian traditions is noted by Kuhrt (2007, pages 174–5).

Temples under the Parthians have been studied by Dirven (2014). For Harran as a centre of moon god worship into the Roman period see Green (1992, especially pages 47–59) and Pingree (2002). That Babylonian-style magic was still being practised in the Islamic period is discussed by Morony (2015, pages 397–9 and 429–30). For omens in Aramaic Jewish texts see Geller (2000). Other influence on Aramaic sources is summarised by Salvesen (1998, especially pages 156 and 146–8 for the points about magic in the Talmud and literature respectively). For debate poems see Jiménez (2017, page 133).

For Greek philosophers founding a school in Harran see Athanassiadi (1993, pages 24–9) and Pingree (2002, pages 9–11). On Damascius' summary of the *Epic of Creation* see Ahbel-Rappe (2010, page 418). Nabonidus' antiquarianism is discussed by Reiner (1985, pages 1–16) and Winter (2000). For the Memory of Mankind Project see https://www.memory-of-mankind.com/.

Recommended Further Reading

Articles summarising various aspects of the legacy of Mesopotamia are available in Dalley (1998b). Interactions between the ancient Near East and the West are discussed throughout Quinn (2024).

A Guide to the Primary Sources

Translations are those of the authors of the cited editions except when noted. Roman numerals in capitals usually refer to the Tablet number, while non-capitals refer to the column number.

I have referred to editions available online wherever possible so that the non-specialist reader can access them easily. There are three main electronic sources: ORACC, eBL, and ETCSL.

ORACC
https://oracc.museum.upenn.edu/projectlist.html

The ORACC website (Open Richly Annotated Cuneiform Corpus) is an umbrella project that gathers together many different collections of texts.

Texts with abbreviations listed here can be found as sub-projects on ORACC as well as in associated print editions.

ADART or ADsD: Astronomical Diaries and Related Texts from Babylonia or Astronomical Diaries Digital. This project combines six volumes of texts. The print volume cited within this book is ADART 1 or Sachs and Hunger (1988).

CMAwR or CMAwRo: Corpus of Mesopotamian Anti-witchcraft Rituals online. This project combines three volumes of anti-witchcraft rituals. For print publications see Abusch and Schwemer (2011); Abusch et al. (2016); Abusch et al. (2019).

GKAB: The Geography of Knowledge in Assyria and Babylonia. This project combines the holdings of four other scholarly tablet collections that can be explored online. An extensive bibliography is available within the project.

DCCLT: Digital Corpus of Cuneiform Lexical Texts. This project endeavours to publish cuneiform lexical texts from all periods of Mesopotamian history. An extensive bibliography is available within the project.

RINAP or RIAo: The Royal Inscriptions of the Neo-Assyrian Period or Royal Inscriptions of Assyria online. These five volumes collect together royal inscriptions of the Neo-Assyrian kings. All are available online on ORACC under the RIAo project title.

The print volumes cited within this book include: RINAP 3/1 = Grayson and Novotny (2012); RINAP 4 = Leichty (2011); RINAP 5/1 = Novotny and Jeffers (2018); RINAP 5/2 = Jeffers and Novotny (2023); RINAP 5/3 = Novotny et al. (2023).

While on RIAo all RINAP texts are grouped together, they are broken up in the print volumes. RINAP 5/1 has Ashurbanipal nos. 1–71; 5/2 has Ashurbanipal nos. 72–240; and 5/3 has Ashurbanipal nos. 241–70.

RINBE or RIBo: Royal Inscriptions of the Neo-Babylonian Empire or Royal Inscriptions of Babylonia online. This project brings together publications of Neo-Babylonian and later royal inscriptions. Of particular relevance here is Babylon 7 (Neo-Babylonian) and Babylon 8 (Cyrus). There are three print volumes that cover Babylon 7: Novotny and Weiershäuser (2020); Novotny and Weiershäuser (2024); Novotny and Weiershäuser (2025).

RLAsb: Reading the Library of Ashurbanipal Project. This project digitises the colophons of the tablets in the library.

SAA or SAAo: State Archives of Assyria or State Archives of Assyria online. This project brings together twenty-two volumes of texts pertaining to the state archives of Assyria and all can be found online at ORACC under the SAAo project.

The print volumes cited in this book include: SAA 2 = Parpola and Watanabe (1988); SAA 3 = Livingstone (1989); SAA 4 = Starr (1990); SAA 7 = Fales and Postgate (1992); SAA 8 = Hunger (1992); SAA 9 = Parpola (1997); SAA 10 = Parpola (1993a); SAA 13 = Cole and Machinist (1998); SAA 14 = Mattila (2002); SAA 16 = Luukko and Van Buylaere (2002); SAA 18 = Reynolds (2003);

SAA 19 = Luukko (2012); SAA 20 = Parpola (2017); SAA 21 = Parpola (2018); SAA 22 = Frame and Parpola (2023).

See also the commentary by Parpola (1983) to the letters when he published them as *Letters from Assyrian Scholars to the Kings Esarhaddon and Ashurbanipal* (LAS). A concordance of LAS numbers and SAA numbers can be found in the back of Parpola's print edition of SAA 10 (1993a), as well as alongside each online publication on ORACC (SAAo).

eBL
https://www.ebl.lmu.de/

The electronic Babylonian Library (eBL) website, like ORACC, brings together many different texts. Primarily, they are concerned with Akkadian literary texts, but are slowly adding other genres such as divination, medicine, and magic. Akkadian–English translations are provided. When a piece of Akkadian literature is cited, an eBL number is also provided if available at the time of writing. This number can be used to locate the piece of literature on the website, (e.g. 1.1 for *Atrahasis*).

ETCSL
https://etcsl.orinst.ox.ac.uk/

The Electronic Text Corpus of Sumerian Literature (ETCSL) comprises nearly 400 Sumerian literary compositions. It has both Sumerian text transliterations and English translations, as well as an extensive bibliography for each composition. Additionally, each composition has an associated three-to-five-digit tag which this book uses to reference a particular story. For example, 1.8.1.3 refers to the Sumerian narrative *The Death of Gilgamesh*. Many of the translations on this website can be found in the print edition Black et al. (2004).

Sumerian literature is difficult to access in the original language as up-to-date editions are often not available, and publications are in multiple modern languages. I have also provided references to the most complete print editions that ETCSL bases its editions on, and to newer versions where they exist, but in some cases ETCSL is still the most recently and comprehensively edited source.

Other Abbreviations

Additional abbreviations that appear in the book but are not online sources are as follows:

AO: Museum siglum of Musées du Louvre, Paris (Antiquités orientales).
BAM (aka Köcher Medizin): F. Köcher, *Die babylonisch-assyrische Medizin in Texten und Untersuchungen* (Berlin 1963 ff.).
BM: Museum siglum of the British Museum, London.
DPS: Diagnostic and Prognostic Series; published with an English translation by Scurlock (2014).
KUB: Keilschrifturkunden aus Boghazköi; a long-running (1921–1990) journal with tablets related to the Bogazköy Archive found in modern-day Turkey.
SpTU: Spätbabylonische Texte aus Uruk. A series of tablets from late Babylonian and Seleucid Uruk published by Hunger and von Weiher from 1968 until 1998. See Hunger (1976); von Weiher (1983; 1988; 1993; 1998).
TCL: Textes cuneiforms from Musées du Louvre; TCL 6 refers to Thureau-Dangin (1922).
VAT: Museum siglum of the Vorderasiatisches Museum, Berlin.
YOS: Yale Oriental Series, Babylonian Texts (New Haven 1915 ff.).

Another list of Assyriological abbreviations that is continually updated can be found here: https://cdli.ox.ac.uk/wiki/abbreviations_for_assyriology.

Other print sources are referenced using the Author-Date format and can be found in the bibliography.

Bibliography

Abusch, T. 2015. *The Magical Ceremony Maqlû: A Critical Edition*. Leiden; Boston: Brill.

Abusch, T., and D. Schwemer. 2011. *Corpus of Mesopotamian Anti-Witchcraft Rituals*. Vol. 1. Boston; Leiden: Brill.

Abusch, T., D. Schwemer, M. Luukko, and G. Van Buylaere. 2016. *Corpus of Mesopotamian Anti-Witchcraft Rituals*. Vol. 2. Boston; Leiden: Brill.

Abusch, T., D. Schwemer, M. Luukko, and G. Van Buylaere. 2019. *Corpus of Mesopotamian Anti-Witchcraft Rituals*. Vol. 3. Boston; Leiden: Brill.

Ahbel-Rappe, S. 2010. *Damascius' Problems and Solutions Concerning First Principles*. Oxford; New York: Oxford University Press.

Alster, B. 1974. *The Instructions of Suruppak*. Copenhagen: Akademisk Forlag.

———. 2002. 'Ilū Awīlum: We-e i-La, "Gods : Men" versus "Man : God", Punning and the Reversal of Patterns in the Atrahasis Epic.' In *Riches Hidden in Secret Places: Ancient Near Eastern Studies in Memory of Thorkild Jacobsen*, edited by Tzvi Abusch, 35–40. Winona Lake, Indiana: Eisenbrauns.

Alstola, T. 2020. *Judeans in Babylonia: A Study of Deportees in the Sixth and Fifth Centuries* BCE. Boston; Leiden: Brill.

Annus, A. 2001. *The Standard Babylonian Epic of Anzu*. Helsinki: Neo-Assyrian Text Corpus Project.

———. 2002. *The God Ninurta in the Mythology and Ideology of Ancient Mesopotamia*. Helsinki: Neo-Assyrian Text Corpus Project.

———. 2012. 'Louvre Gilgamesh (AO 19862) Is Depicted in Life Size.' *NABU* 2012 (2): 44–45.

Anor, N. 2015. 'The Babylonian Extispicy Ritual: Theory and Practice.' PhD thesis. Freie Universität Berlin.

Arbøll, T.P. 2020. *Medicine in Ancient Assur: A Microhistorical Study of the Neo-Assyrian Healer Kiṣir-Aššur*. Boston; Leiden: Brill.

Athanassiadi, P. 1993. 'Persecution and Response in Late Paganism: The Evidence of Damascius.' *The Journal of Hellenic Studies* 113: 1–29.

Attinger, P. 1998. 'Inana et Ebiḫ.' *Zeitschrift für Assyriologie und Vorderasiatische Archäologie*, 88 (2), 164–195.

———. 'Enki et Ninhursaga (1.1.1)', 2011, actualisé en 2015.

———. 'Enlil et Ninlil (1.2.1)', 2015, actualisé en 2019. DOI: https://doi.org/10.5281/zenodo.2667748.

———. 'Innana et Ebiḫ (1.3.2)', 2011, actualisé en 2019. DOI: https://doi.org/10.5281/zenodo.2667753.

Bach, J. 2019. *Untersuchungen zur Transtextuellen Poetik. Assyrischer Herrschaftlich- Narrativer Texte*. Helsinki: Neo-Assyrian Text Corpus Project.

Bácskay, A. 2019. 'Incantations and Healing Treatments against Lamaštu in Mesopotamian Therapeutic Prescriptions.' *Current Debates on Social Sciences* 2: 5–13.

Bahrani, Z. 1998. 'Conjuring Mesopotamia: Imaginative Geography and a World Past.' In *Archaeology Under Fire*, edited by L. Meskell, 159–74. London: Routledge.

Baker, H.D. 2001. 'Marduk-Šarru-Uṣur.' In *The Prosopography of the Neo-Assyrian Empire, Volume 2, Part II: L–N*, 727–31. Helsinki: Neo-Assyrian Text Corpus Project, Institute for Asian and African Studies, University of Helsinki.

Ballesteros, B. 2021. 'On Gilgamesh and Homer: Ishtar, Aphrodite and the Meaning of a Parallel.' *The Classical Quarterly* 71 (1): 1–21.

Beaulieu, P.A. 1997. 'The Cult of AN.ŠAR/Aššur in Babylonia after the Fall of the Assyrian Empire.' *State Archives of Assyria. Bulletin* 11: 55–73.

———. 2018. *A History of Babylon, 2200 BC–AD 75*. Chichester, West Sussex: Wiley Blackwell.

———. 2019. 'Interactions between Greek and Babylonian Thought in Seleucid Uruk.' In *Scholars and Scholarship in Late Babylonian Uruk*, edited by Christine Proust and John Steele, 235–54. Cham: Springer International Publishing.

———. 2020. 'The God List CT 24 50 as Theological Postscript to Enūma Eliš.' In *Des Polythéismes Aux Monothéismes: Mélanges d'assyriologie Offerts à Marcel Sigrist*, edited by Uri Gabbay and J.J. Pérennès, 109–26. Leuven: Peeters.

Beaulieu, P.A., E. Frahm, W. Horowitz, and J. Steele. 2017. 'The Cuneiform Uranology Texts: Drawing the Constellations.' *Transactions of the American Philosophical Society* 107 (2): i–121.

Beaulieu, P.A., and F. Rochberg. 1996. 'The Horoscope of Anu-Bēlšunu.' *Journal of Cuneiform Studies* 48: 89–94.

Bezold, C. 1919. 'Sze-Ma Ts'ien und die Babylonische Astrologie.' *Ostasiatische Zeitschrift* 8: 42–9.

Black, J., G. Cunningham, E. Robson, and G. Zólyomi, eds. 2004. *The Literature of Ancient Sumer.* New York: Oxford University Press.

Böck, B. 2000. *Die Babylonische-Assyrische Morphoskopie*. Vienna: Institut für Orientalistik.

———. 2011. 'Sourcing, Organizing, and Administering Medicinal Ingredients.' In *The Oxford Handbook of Cuneiform Culture*, edited by Karen Radner and Eleanor Robson, 690–705. Oxford: Oxford University Press.

Böck, B., S. Ghazanfar, and M. Nesbitt. 2024. *An Ancient Mesopotamian Herbal*. Kew, Richmond, Surrey: Kew Publishing; Royal Botanic Gardens.

Boddy, K., and C. Mittermayer. 2023. 'Chapter 104, If a Man Approaches an Old Woman (for Sex): He Will Quarrel Daily.' https://www.ebl.lmu.de/corpus/D/2/6/SB/104.

Bonatz, D. 2004. 'Ashurbanipal's Headhunt: An Anthropological Perspective.' *Iraq* 66: 93.

Borger, R. 1971. 'Gott Marduk und Gott-König Šulgi als Propheten.' *Bibliotheca Orientalis* 26: 3–24.

———. 1973. 'Die Weihe eines Enlil-Priesters.' *Bibliotheca Orientalis* 30: 163–76.

Bottéro, J. 1992. 'A Century of Assyriology.' In *Mesopotamia: Writing, Reasoning, and the Gods*. Chicago; London: University of Chicago Press.

———. 1995. *Mesopotamia: Writing, Reasoning, and the Gods*. Chicago: University of Chicago Press.

———. 1995. *Textes Culinaires Mesopotamiens: Mesopotamian Culinary Texts*. Mesopotamian Civilizations Vol. 6. Winona Lake, Indiana: Eisenbrauns.

Boyes, P.J. 2021. *Script and Society: The Social Context of Writing Practices in Late Bronze Age Ugarit*. Oxford; Philadelphia: Oxbow.

Brereton, G., ed. 2018. *I Am Ashurbanipal: King of the World, King of Assyria*. London: British Museum; Thames & Hudson.

Breucker, G. de. 2010. 'Berossos (680).' In *Brill's New Jacoby*, edited by Ian Worthington. Leiden: Brill.

Brinkman, J.A. 1984. *Prelude to Empire: Babylonian Society and Politics, 747–626 B.C.* Philadelphia, PA: University of Pennsylvania Museum of Archaeology and Anthropology.

Britton, J., and C. Walker. 1996. 'Astronomy and Astrology in Mesopotamia.' In *Astronomy before the Telescope*, edited by Christopher Walker, 42–67. London: British Museum.

Brown, D. 2000. *Mesopotamian Astronomy-Astrology*. Groningen: Styx.

Brownson, C.L. 2014. *Xenophon Anabasis*. Edited by John Dillery. Revised edn. Cambridge, Mass.; London: Harvard University Press.

Burkert, W. 1992. *The Orientalizing Revolution*. Cambridge, Mass.: Harvard University Press.

Butler, S.A.L. 1998. *Mesopotamian Conceptions of Dreams and Dream Rituals*. Alter Orient und Altes Testament. Münster: Ugarit-Verlag.

Buylaere, G. Van. 2019. 'The Decline of Female Professionals – and the Rise of the Witch – in the Second and Early First Millennium BCE.' *Magic, Ritual, and Witchcraft* 14 (1): 37–61.

Cagni, L. 1969. *L'epopea di Erra*. Rome: Istituto di studi del Vicino Oriente dell'Università.

Campbell, A. 2012. 'Two-Faced Kitten Born Healthy in Port Charlotte, Florida.' Accessed 6 June 2024. https://www.huffpost.com/entry/two-faced-cat-born_n_1246835.

Campbell, D.A. 1990. *Greek Lyric, Vol I: Sappho and Alcaeus*, LCL 142. Cambridge, Mass.; London: Harvard University Press.

Campbell, T.R. 1904. *The Devils and Evil Spirits of Babylonia*. Vol. 2. London: Luzac and Co.

Campion, N. 2009. *A History of Western Astrology. Volume I: The Ancient World*. London: Bloomsbury.

Caplice, R. 1965. 'Namburbi Texts in the British Museum. I.' *Orientalia Nova Series* 34 (2): 105–31.

———. 1974. *The Akkadian Namburbi Texts: An Introduction*. Los Angeles: Undena Publications.

Cavigneaux, A. 1981. *Textes Scolaires du Temple de Nabû ša Harê*. Baghdad: Ministry of Culture & Information, State Organization of Antiquities & Heritage.

Chapman, C., and M. Coogan. 2018. *The Old Testament: A Historical and Literary Introduction to the Hebrew Scriptures*. 4th edn. New York; Oxford: Oxford University Press.

Charpin, D. 2010. *Reading and Writing in Babylon*. Cambridge, Mass. Harvard University Press.

Chavalas, M.W. 2011. 'The Comparative Use of Ancient Near Eastern Texts in the Study of the Hebrew Bible.' *Religion Compass* 5 (5): 150–65.

Chinnock, E.J. 2014. Translation of Arrian of Nicomedia's *The Anabasis of Alexander*. London: Hodder and Stoughton.

Clancier, P. 2009. *Les Bibliothèques en Babylonie dans la Deuxième Moitié du Ier Millénaire av. J.-C.* Münster: Ugarit-Verlag.

———. 2011. 'Cuneiform Culture's Last Guardians: The Old Urban Notability of Hellenistic Uruk.' In *The Oxford Handbook of Cuneiform Culture*, edited by K. Radner and E. Robson, 752–73. Oxford: Oxford University Press.

Cohen, L. 2021. 'A Lacuna Follows.' *Post45*. 2 February 2021. https://post45.org/2021/02/a-lacuna-follows/.

Cohen, M.E. 1988. *The Canonical Lamentations of Ancient Mesopotamia*. Potomac, MD: Capital Decisions.

Collins, P. 2006. 'The Development of the Individual Enemy in Assyrian Art.' *Source: Notes in the History of Art* 25 (3): 1–8. http://www.jstor.org/stable/23207999.

———. 2021. *The Sumerians*. Lost Civilizations. London: Reaktion Books.

Cooley, J.L. 2013. *Poetic Astronomy in the Ancient Near East*. Winona Lake: Eisenbrauns.

Cooper, J.S. 1978. *The Return of Ninurta to Nippur*. Rome: Pontificium Institutum Biblicum.

———. 1983. *The Curse of Agade*. Baltimore: Johns Hopkins University Press.

———. 1996. 'Sumerian and Akkadian.' In *The World's Writing Systems*, edited by P.T. Daniels and W. Bright, 37–57. New York: Oxford University Press.

Couto-Ferreira, E. 2013. 'The River, the Oven, the Garden: The Female Body and Fertility in a Late Babylonian Ritual Text.' In *Approaching Rituals in Ancient Cultures*, edited by C. Ambos and L. Veredame, 97–116. Pisa; Rome: Fabrizio Serra Editore.

Crawford, H., ed. 2013a. *The Sumerian World*. London and New York: Routledge.

———. 2013b. 'Trade in the Sumerian World.' In *The Sumerian World*, edited by H. Crawford, 447–98. London and New York: Routledge.

Currie, B. 2016. *Homer's Allusive Art*. Oxford: Oxford University Press.

Daily Telegraph. 2010. 'Sheep Gives Birth to Human-Faced Lamb.' Accessed 6 June 2024. https://www.dailytelegraph.com.au/sheep-gives-birth-to-human-faced-lamb/news-story/c93e1bc5d032889f3b5e44cec6ab686b.

Dalley, S.M. 1997. 'Babylonian Influence in the Far East through the Buddha and Mani.' *Journal of Ancient Civilisations* 12: 25–36.

———. 2000. *Myths from Mesopotamia*. Oxford: Oxford University Press.

———. 2017. 'Assyrian Warfare.' In *A Companion to Assyria*, edited by E. Frahm, 522–33. Hoboken: Wiley.

———. 2021. *The City of Babylon*. Cambridge: Cambridge University Press.

Dalley, S.M., and L.R. Siddall. 2021. 'A Conspiracy to Murder Sennacherib? A Revision of SAA 18 100 in the Light of a Recent Join.' *Iraq* 83: 45–56.

Dalley, S., A.T. Reyes, D. Pingree, A. Salvesen, and H. McCall. 1998. *The Legacy of Mesopotamia*. Edited by Stephanie Dalley. Oxford: Oxford University Press.

Damrosch, D. 2007. *The Buried Book: The Loss and Rediscovery of the Epic of Gilgamesh*. New York: Macmillan.

Daniels, P.T. 1994. 'Edward Hincks's Decipherment of Mesopotamian Cuneiform.' In *The Edward Hincks Bicentenary Lectures*, edited by Kevin J. Cathcart, 30–57. Dublin: Department of Near Eastern Languages, University College Dublin.

Debourse, C. 2022. *Of Priests and Kings: The Babylonian New Year Festival in the Last Age of Cuneiform Culture*. Boston; Leiden: Brill.

Deller, K. 1999. 'The Assyrian Eunuchs and Their Predecessors.' In *Priests and Officials in the Ancient Near East*, edited by K. Watanabe, 303–11. Heidelberg: Universitatsverlag C. Winter.

Delnero, P. 2020. *How to Do Things with Tears: Ritual Lamenting in Ancient Mesopotamia*. Berlin; Boston: De Gruyter.

Dijk, J. van. 1983. *LUGAL UD ME-LÁM-bi NIR-G̃ÁL: Le Récit Épique et Didactique des Travaux de Ninurta, du Déluge et de la Nouvelle Création*. Leiden: Brill.

Dirven, L. 2014. 'Religious Continuity and Change in Parthian Mesopotamia: A Note on the Survival of Babylonian Traditions.' *Journal of Ancient Near Eastern History* 1 (2): 201–29.

Dossin, G. 1978. *Correspondance Féminine: Transcrite et Traduite*. Paris: Librairie Orientaliste Paul Geuthner.

Downey, S. 1988. *Mesopotamian Religious Architecture: Alexander through the Parthians*. Princeton: Princeton University Press.

Ebeling, E. 1931. *Tod und Leben nach den Vorstellungen der Babylonier. Teil 1: Texte*. Berlin and Leipzig: De Gruyter.

Ermidoro, S. 2015. *Commensality and Ceremonial Meals in the Neo-Assyrian Period*. Venice: Edizioni Ca' Foscari – Digital Publishing.

Fales , F. M., and J. N. Postgate. 1992. Postgate. *Imperial Administrative Records, Part I: Palace and Temple Administration*. Helsinki: Helsinki University Press.

Falk, H. 2000. 'Measuring Time in Mesopotamia and Ancient India.' *Zeitschrift der Deutschen Morgenländischen Gesellschaft* 150 (1): 107–32.

Farber, W. 1990. 'Mannam Lušpur Ana Enkidu: Some New Thoughts about an Old Motif.' *Journal of Near Eastern Studies* 49 (4): 299–321.

———. 2014. *Lamaštu: An Edition of the Canonical Series of Lamaštu Incantations and Rituals and Related Texts from the Second and First Millennia* B.C. Winona Lake: Eisenbrauns.

Fermie, E. 2024. 'SEASICK The Grim Fate of "Psychic Octopus" that Perfectly Predicted World Cup Results.' *The Sun*. 11 June 2024. https://www.thesun.co.uk/sport/28430673/world-cup-rabio-psychic-octopus/.

Fincke, J.C. 2004. 'The Babylonian Texts of Nineveh.' *Archiv für Orientforschung* 50: 111–49.

———. 2021. *An Ancient Mesopotamian Herbal Handbook: The Series URU.AN.NA and MÚD-UR.MAH*. Leuven; Paris; Bristol: Peeters.

Finkel, I.L. 2007. 'On the Rules for the Royal Game of Ur.' In *Ancient Board Games in Perspective*, edited by I.L. Finkel, 16–32. London: British Museum.

———. 2022. *The First Ghosts: A Rich History of Ancient Ghosts and Ghost Stories from the British Museum Curator*. London: Hodder and Stoughton.

Finkel, I., and M.J. Seymour, eds. 2008. *Babylon: Myth and Reality*. London: The British Museum Press.

Földi, Z.J. 2022a. 'From the eBL Lab 30. New Fragments of *Bullussa-rabi's Hymn to Gula*.' *Kaskal* 19, January.

———. 2022b. 'From the eBL Lab 31. *Bullussa-rabi's Hymn to Gula* as Part of a Series.' *Kaskal* 19, January.

Folmer, M. 2020. 'Aramaic as Lingua Franca.' In *A Companion to Ancient Near Eastern Languages*, edited by R. Hasselbach-Andee, 373–99. Hoboken: John Wiley & Sons.

Foster, B.R. 2005. *Before the Muses: An Anthology of Akkadian Literature*. Bethesda: Pennsylvania State University Press.

Frahm, E. 1999. 'Nabû-zuqup-kēnu, das Gilgameš-Epos, und der Tod Sargons II.' *Journal of Cuneiform Studies* 51: 73–90.

———. 2005. 'Nabû-Zuqup-Kenu, Gilgamesh XII, and the Rites of Du'uzu.' *N.A.B.U.* 1 (5): 4–5.

———. 2010. 'Counter-Texts, Commentaries, and Adaptations: Politically Motivated Responses to the Babylonian Epic of Creation in Mesopotamia, the Biblical World, and Elsewhere.' *Orient: Reports of the Society for Near Eastern Studies in Japan* 45: 3–33.

———. 2011. 'Keeping Company with Men of Learning: The King as Scholar.' In *The Oxford Handbook of Cuneiform Culture*, edited by E. Robson and K. Radner, 508–32. Oxford: Oxford University Press.

———, ed. 2017. *A Companion to Assyria*. New Haven: Wiley Blackwell.

———. 2023. *Assyria: The Rise and Fall of the World's First Empire*. Bloomsbury Publishing.

Frame, G. 1992. *Babylonia 689–627 B.C. A Political History*. Leiden: Nederlands Instituut voor het Nabije Oosten.

———. 2021. *The Royal Inscriptions of Sargon II, King of Assyria (721–705 BC)*. Vol. 2. University Park: Penn State University Press.

Frame, G, and A.R. George. 2005. 'The Royal Libraries of Nineveh: New Evidence for King Ashurbanipal's Tablet Collecting.' *Iraq* 67 (1): 265–84.

Frame, G., and S. Parpola. 2023. *The Correspondence of Assurbanipal, Part II: Letters from Southern Babylonia*. Helsinki: Neo-Assyrian Text Corpus Project.

Frazer, M. 2021. 'From Clay to Stone and Back Again: The Unusual Biography of a Babylonian Letter.' In *Sprechende Objekte: Materielle Kultur und Stadt Zwischen Antike und Früher Neuzeit*, edited by Babett Edelmann-Singer and Susanne Ehrich, 17:37–58. Regensburg: Schnell and Steiner. www.schnell-und-steiner.de.

Freedman, S.M. 1998. *If a City Is Set on a Height: The Akkadian Omen Series Šumma Alu Ina Mēlê Šakin. Volume 1*. Philadelphia.

———. 2006. *If a City Is Set on a Height: The Akkadian Omen Series Šumma Alu Ina Mēlê Šakin: Volume 2: Tablets 22–40*. Philadelphia, PA: University of Pennsylvania Museum.

———. 2017. *If a City Is Set on a Height, Volume 3*. Winona Lake: Eisenbrauns.

Frymer-Kensky, T. 1992. *In the Wake of the Goddesses: Women, Culture, and the Biblical Transformation of Pagan Myth*. New York: The Free Press.

Furley, W., and V. Gysembergh. 2015. *Reading the Liver: Papyrological Texts on Ancient Greek Extispicy*. Tübingen: Mohr Siebeck.

Gabbay, U. 2011. 'Two Summary Tablets of Balag Compositions with Performative Indications from Late-Babylonian Ur.' *Zeitschrift für Assyriologie* 101: 274–93.

———. 2014a. 'The Kalû Priest and Kalûtu Literature in Assyria.' *Orient* 49: 115–44.

———. 2014b. *Pacifying the Hearts of the Gods: Sumerian Emesal Prayers of the First Millennium* BC. Wiesbaden: Harrassowitz Verlag.

———. 2015. *The Eršema Prayers of the First Millennium* BC. Heidelberg: Harrassowitz Verlag.

———. 2022. *Emotions and Emesal Laments: Motivations, Performance, and Management*. Edited by Karen Sonik and Ulrike Steinert. London: Routledge.

Gadotti, A. 2014. *Gilgamesh, Enkidu, and the Netherworld and the Sumerian Gilgamesh Cycle*. Boston; Berlin: De Gruyter.

Gasche, H., J.A. Armstrong, S.W. Cole, and V.G. Gurzadyan. 1998. *Dating the Fall of Babylon: A Reappraisal of Second-Millennium Chronology*. Chicago; Ghent: Oriental Institute / University of Ghent.

Gehlken, E. 2012. *Weather Omens of Enūma Anu Enlil: Thunderstorms, Wind and Rain (Tablets 44–49)*. Leiden; Boston: Brill.

Geller, M.J. 1997a. 'Freud, Magic and Mesopotamia: How the Magic Works.' *Folklore* 108: 1–7. http://www.jstor.org/stable/1260701.

———. 1997b. 'The Last Wedge.' *Zeitschrift für Assyriologie und Vorderasiatische Archäologie* 87 (1): 43–95.

———. 2000. 'The Survival of Babylonian Wissenschaft in Later Tradition.' In *Melammu Symposia 1: The Heirs of Assyria. Proceedings of the Opening Symposium of the Assyrian and Babylonian Intellectual Heritage Project. Held in Tvärminne, Finland, October 8–11, 1998*, edited by Sanno Aro and R.M. Whiting, 1–6. Helsinki: The Neo-Assyrian Text Corpus Project.

———. 2001. 'West Meets East: Early Greek and Babylonian Diagnosis.' *Archiv für Orientforschung* 48/49: 50–75.

———. 2005. *Renal and Rectal Disease Texts*. Berlin; New York: De Gruyter.

———. 2010. *Ancient Babylonian Medicine, Theory and Practice*. Chichester, England: Wiley Blackwell.

———. 2016. *Healing Magic and Evil Demons: Canonical Udug-Hul Incantations*. Boston; Berlin: De Gruyter.

———. 2018. 'The Exorcist's Manual (KAR 44).' In *Assyrian and Babylonian Scholarly Text Catalogues: Medicine, Magic and Divination*, edited by U. Steinert, 292–312. Berlin; Boston: De Gruyter.

Geller, M.J., and S. V. Panayotov. 2020. *Mesopotamian Eye Disease Texts: The Niniveh [sic] Treatise*. Berlin; Boston: De Gruyter.

George, A.R. 1991. 'Babylonian Texts from the Folios of Sidney Smith: Part Two, Prognostic and Diagnostic Omens, Tablet I.' *Revue d'Assyriologie et d'archéologie Orientale* 85 (2): 137–67.

———. 1993. 'Ninurta-Pāqidāt's Dog Bite, and Notes on Other Comic Tales.' *Iraq* 55: 63–75.

———. 2003. *The Epic of Gilgamesh: The Babylonian Epic Poem and Other Texts in Akkadian and Sumerian*. London: Penguin.

———. 2005. 'The Tower of Babel: Archaeology, History and Cuneiform Texts.' *Archiv für Orientforschung* 51: 75–95.

———. 2015. 'On Babylonian Lavatories and Sewers.' *Iraq* 77: 75–106.

———. 2018. 'Enkidu and the Harlot: Another Fragment of Old Babylonian Gilgameš.' *Zeitschrift für Assyriologie Und Vorderasiatische Archäologie* 108 (1): 10–21.

———. 2020. *The Epic of Gilgamesh: The Babylonian Poem and Other Texts in Akkadian and Sumerian*. 2nd edn. London: Penguin Books.

George, A.R., G. Rozzi, and E. Jiménez. 2022. 'Poem of Gilgameš Chapter Standard Babylonian I.' *Electronic Babylonian Library*.

Gerardi, P. 1987. 'Assurbanipal's Elamite Campaigns: A Literary and Political Study.' Philadelphia.

Gesche, P. D. 2001. *Schulunterricht in Babylonien im Ersten Jahrtausend v. Chr.* Münster: Ugarit-Verlag.

Glassner, J. 2004. *Mesopotamian Chronicles*. Edited by Benjamin R. Foster. Atlanta, GA: Society of Biblical Literature. (Original work published: 1993.)

Goetze, A. 1947. *Old Babylonian Omen Texts*. New Haven and London: Yale University Press.

———. 1968. 'An Old Babylonian Prayer of the Divination Priest.' *Journal of Cuneiform Studies* 22 (2): 25–29.

Goldstein, R., and E. Weissert. 2018. 'The Battle of Til-Tuba Cycle and the Documentary Evidence.' In *I Am Ashurbanipal: King of the World, King of Assyria*, edited by G. Brereton, 244–73. London: British Museum/Thames & Hudson.

Grabbe, L. 2015. 'The Reality of the Return: The Biblical Picture versus Historical Reconstruction.' In *Exile and Return: The Babylonian Context*, edited by J. Stökl and C. Waerzeggers, volume 478: 292–307. Berlin: De Gruyter.

Graff, S.B. 2012. 'Humbaba/Huwawa.' PhD thesis. New York University. New York.

Grayson, A.K. 1992. 'Assyria 668–635 B.C.: The Reign of Ashurbanipal.' In *The Cambridge Ancient History*, edited by J. Boardman, I. Edwards, E. Sollberger, and N. Hammond, 142–61. Cambridge: Cambridge University Press.

Grayson, K.A., and J. Novotny. 2012. *The Royal Inscriptions of Sennacherib, King of Assyria (704–681 BC), Part 1, RINAP 3/1*. Vol. 3/1. Winona Lake, Indiana: Eisenbrauns.

Green, M.W. 1978. 'The Eridu Lament.' *JCS* 30 (3): 127–67.

———. 1984. 'The Uruk Lament.' *JAOS* 104 (2): 253–79.

Green, T.M. 1992. *The City of the Moon God: Religious Traditions of Harran.* Religions in the Graeco-Roman World, v. 114. Leiden; E.J. Brill.

Guinan, A. 1990. 'The Perils of High Living: Divinatory Rhetoric in Summa Alu.' In *DUMU-E-DUB-BA: Studies Presented to Ake Sjöberg*, 227–35.

———. 1997. 'Auguries of Hegemony: The Sex Omens of Mesopotamia.' *Gender & History* 9 (3): 462–79.

Guinan, A., and E. Leichty. 2010. 'Tasteless Tablets.' In *Gazing on the Deep: Ancient Near Eastern and Other Studies in Honour of Tsvi Abusch*, edited by Jeffrey Stackert, Barbara Nevling Porter, and David P. Wright. Bethesda, MD: CDL Press.

Gurney, O.R. 1956. 'The Sultantepe Tablets (Continued). V. The Tale of the Poor Man of Nippur.' *Anatolian Studies* 6: 145–64.

———. 1957. 'The Sultantepe Tablets (Continued). VI. A Letter of Gilgamesh.' *Anatolian Studies* 7: 127–36.

Gurzadyan, V.G. 2000. 'On the Astronomical Records and Babylonian Chronology.' *Akkadica* 119–120: 175–84.

Hackl, J., and M. Jursa. 2015. 'Egyptians in Babylonia in the Neo-Babylonian and Achaemenid Periods.' In *Exile and Return: The Babylonian Context*, edited by J. Stökl and C. Waerzeggers, volume 478: 157–80. Berlin: De Gruyter.

Hallo, W.W., and J.J.A. van Dijk. 1968. *The Exaltation of Inanna.* Yale Near Eastern Researches 3. New Haven/London: Yale University Press.

Hamilton, P. 2024. 'Complaint Tablet to Ea-Nasir | Know Your Meme.' Accessed 24 April 2024. https://knowyourmeme.com/memes/complaint-tablet-to-ea-nasir.

Harris, R. 1960. 'Old Babylonian Temple Loans.' *Journal of Cuneiform Studies* 14 (4): 126–37.

———. 1990. 'Images of Women in the Gilgamesh Epic.' Edited by Tzvi Abusch and William L. Moran. *Harvard Semitic Studies*, no. 37: 219–30.

Haubold, J. 2013. *Greece and Mesopotamia Dialogues in Literature*. New York: Cambridge University Press.

Haubold, J., S. Helle, E. Jimenéz, and S. Wisnom, eds. 2024. *Enuma Elish: The Babylonian Epic of Creation*. London: Bloomsbury Publishing.

Haubold, J., G.B. Lanfranchi, R. Rollinger, and J.M. Steele, eds. 2013. *The World of Berossos: Proceedings of the 4th International Colloquium on 'The Ancient Near East between Classical and Ancient Oriental Traditions', Hatfield College, Durham 7th–9th July 2010*. Wiesbaden: Harrassowitz Verlag.

Haubold, J., J.M. Steele, and K. Stevens, eds. 2019. *Keeping Watch in Babylon: The Astronomical Diaries in Context*. Culture and History of the Ancient Near East. Vol. 100. Boston; Leiden: Brill.

Hays, C. 2014. *Hidden Riches: A Sourcebook for the Comparative Study of the Hebrew Bible and the Ancient Near East*. Louisville, KY: Westminster John Knox Press.

———. 2020. 'Enlil, Isaiah, and the Origins of the 'ĕlîlîm: A Reassessment.' *Zeitschrift für die Alttestamentliche Wissenschaft* 132 (2): 224–35.

Heeßel, N.P. 2002. *Pazuzu: Archäologische und Philologische Studien zu einem Altorientalischen Dämon*. Leiden; Boston; Köln: Styx.

———. 2007. 'The Hands of the Gods: Disease Names, and Divine Anger.' In *Disease in Babylonia*, edited by Irving L. Finkel and Markham J. Geller, 120–30. Leiden: Brill.

———. 2011. 'Evil against Evil, the Demon Pazuzu.' In *Demoni Mesopotamici, Studi e Materiali di Storia delle Religioni 77/2*, edited by Lorenzo Verderame, 357–68. Brescia: Morcelliana.

———. 2014. 'Amulette und "Amulettform": Zum Zusammenhang von Form, Funktion und Text von Amuletten im Alten Mesopotamien.' In *Erscheinungsformen und Handhabungen Heiliger Schriften*, Materiale Textkulturen 5, edited by J.F. Quack and D.C. Luft, 53–77. Berlin; Boston; München: De Gruyter.

Heimpel, W. 2002. 'The Lady of Girsu.' In *Riches Hidden in Secret Places*, edited by Tzvi Abusch, 155–60. Ancient Near Eastern Studies in Memory of Thorkild Jacobsen. University Park: Penn State University Press.

Heinrich, A.C. 2021. 'Poem of Creation (Enūma Eliš).' Electronic Babylonian Library. 2021.

Helle, S. 2021. *Gilgamesh: A New Translation of the Ancient Epic*. New Haven: Yale University Press.

———. 2023. *Enheduana: The Complete Poems of the World's First Author*. New Haven; London: Yale University Press.

Hempen, C.H., and T. Fischer. 2009. *A Materia Medica for Chinese Medicine: Plants, Minerals, and Animal Products*. 1st edn in English. Edinburgh: Churchill Livingstone.

Horowitz, W., T. Oshima, and S. Sanders. 2018. *Cuneiform in Canaan: The Next Generation*. 2nd edn. University Park, PA: Eisenbrauns.

Hrůša, I. 2015. *Ancient Mesopotamian Religion. A Descriptive Introduction.* Munster: Ugarit-Verlag.

Hundley, M.B. 2013. 'Here a God, There a God: An Examination of the Divine in Ancient Mesopotamia.' *Altorientalische Forschungen* 40 (1): 68–107.

Hunger, H. 1968. *Babylonische und Assyrische Kolophone*. Neukirchen-Vluyn: Butzon & Bercker Kevelaer.

———. 1976. *Spätbabylonische Texte aus Uruk Teil I*. Berlin: Gebr. Mann Verlag.

Hunger, H., and T. de Jong. 2014. 'Almanac W22340a from Uruk: The Latest Datable Cuneiform Tablet.' *Zeitschrift für Assyriologie und Vorderasiatische Archäologie* 104 (2): 182–94.

Hunger, H., and H. Steele. 2019. *The Babylonian Astronomical Compendium MUL.APIN*. New York: Routledge.

Izre'el, S. 2001. *Adapa and the South Wind – Language Has the Power of Life and Death*. Winona Lake, Ind.: Eisenbrauns.

Jacobsen, T. 1976. *The Treasures of Darkness*. New Haven: Yale University Press.

Jean, C. 2006. *La Magie Néo-Assyrienne en Contexte: Recherches sur le Métier d'exorciste et le Concept d'āšipūtu*. Helsinki: Neo-Assyrian Text Corpus Project, Institute for Asian and African Studies, University of Helsinki.

Jeffers, J., and J. Novotny. 2023. *The Royal Inscriptions of Ashurbanipal (668–631 BC), Aššur-Etel-Ilāni (630–627 BC), and Sîn-Šarra-Iškun (626–612 BC), Kings of Assyria, Part 2*. Philadelphia, PA: Pennsylvania University Press.

Jeyes, U. 1980. 'The Act of Extispicy in Ancient Mesopotamia: An Outline.' *Assyriological Miscellanies*, 13–32.

Jiménez, E. 2017. *The Babylonian Disputation Poems*. Leiden; Boston: Brill.

———. 2019: 'From the Electronic Babylonian Literature Lab 1–7.' *Kaskal: Rivista di Storia, Ambiente e Culture del Vicino Oriente Antico* 16: 75–94.

Johnson, J.C. 2018. 'Towards a New Perspective on Babylonian Medicine.' In *Assyrian and Babylonian Scholarly Text Catalogues*, edited by Ulrike Steinert, 55–88. Berlin: De Gruyter.

Jones, A. 1991. 'The Adaptation of Babylonian Methods in Greek Numerical Astronomy.' *Isis* 82 (3): 440–53.

Jones C.W. 2023. 'Failed Coup: The Assassination of Sennacherib and Esarhaddon's Struggle for the Throne, 681–680 B.C.' *Journal of Ancient Near Eastern History* 10 (2): 293–369.

Jones, J. 2024. 'Crazy Life and Death of Paul the Octopus Who Became Honorary Citizen of Town and Was at Centre of Conspiracy Theories.' *The Sun*. Accessed 6 June 2024. https://www.the-sun.com/sport/11641430/life-death-paul-octopus-conspiracy-theories-world-cup/.

Jursa, M. 2007. 'Die Söhne Kudurrus und Die Herkunft der Neubabylonischen Dynastie.' *Revue d'assyriologie et d'archéologie Orientale* 101 (1): 125–36.

Keane, D. 2021. 'Sheep with Five Legs Spotted among Orroroo Lamb Flock, with "Intrigued" Farmer to Raise It as a Pet.' 2021. https://www.abc.net.au/news/2021-10-14/sheep-with-five-legs-found-among-orroroo-lamb-flock/100530244.

Kelly, A., and C. Metcalf, eds. 2021. *Gods and Mortals in Early Greek and Near Eastern Mythology*. Cambridge: Cambridge University Press.

Keynes, J.M. 1956. 'Newton, the Man.' In *The World of Mathematics: A Small Library of the Literature of Mathematics from A'h-Mosé the Scribe to Albert Einstein*, edited by J.R. Newman, 277–85. New York: Simon and Schuster.

Kinnier Wilson, J. 2005. 'Notes on the Assyrian Pharmaceutical Series URU.AN.NA: MAŠTAKAL.' *Journal of Near Eastern Studies* 64 (1): 45–51.

Klein, J. 2010. 'The Assumed Human Origin of Divine Dumuzi: A Reconsideration.' In *Proceedings of the 53th Rencontre Assyriologique Internationale*, edited by S. Tishchenko, S. Loesov, N. Koslova, and L. Kogan, 1:1121–34. Penn State University Press.

Knapp, A. 2015. *Royal Apologetic in the Ancient Near East*. Atlanta, Georgia: SBL Press.

Koch, U. 2011. 'Sheep and Sky: Systems of Divinatory Interpretation.' In *The Oxford Handbook of Cuneiform Culture*, edited by K. Radner and E. Robson, 447–69. Oxford: Oxford University Press.

———. 2015. *Mesopotamian Divination Texts: Conversing with the Gods. Sources from the First Millennium* BCE. Münster: Ugarit Verlag.

———. 2016. 'Bias in Observations of Natural Phenomena Made for Divinatory Purposes.' In *Divination as Science*, edited by J.C. Fincke, 11–46. Philadelphia, PA: Penn State University Press.

———. 2019. 'Principles of Astrological Omen Composition – Some Challenges of Reverse Engineering the Astrological Hermeneutics.' *Kaskal: Rivista di Storia, Ambiente e Culture del Vicino Oriente Antico* 16: 221–35.

Köcher, F. 1957. 'The Old-Babylonian Omen Text VAT 7525.' *Archiv für Orientforschung* 18: 62–80.

———. 1995. 'Ein Text Medizinischen Inhalts aus dem Neubabylonischen Grab.' In *Uruk: Die Gräber, Ausgrabungen in Uruk-Warka 10*, edited by R. Boehmer, F. Pedde, and B. Salje, 203–17. Mainz am Rhein: von Zabern.

Koch-Westenholz, U. 1995. *Mesopotamian Astrology: An Introduction to Babylonian and Assyrian Celestial Divination*. Cophenhagen: Museum Tusculanum Press, University of Copenhagen, Carsten Niebuhr Institute of Near Eastern Studies.

———. 2000. *Babylonian Liver Omens: The Chapters Manzāzu, Padānu, and Pān Takālti of the Babylonian Extispicy Series Mainly from Aššurbanipal's Library*. Cophenhagen: Carsten Niebuhr Institute Publications.

Konstantopoulos, G. 2020. 'Looking for Glinda: Wise Women and Benevolent Magic in Old Babylonian Literary Texts.' In *Cult Practices in Ancient Literatures: Egyptian, Near Eastern and Graeco-Roman Narratives in a Cross-Cultural Perspective. Proceedings of a Workshop at the Institute for the Study of the Ancient World, New York, May 16–17, 2016*, edited by F. Naether. ISAW Papers 18.

———. 2021. 'The Many Lives of Enheduana: Identity, Authorship, and the "World's First Poet".' In *Powerful Women in the Ancient World: Perception and (Self) Presentation. Proceedings of the 8th Melammu Workshop, Kassel, 30 January–1 February 2019*, edited by K. Droß-Krüpe and S. Fink, 57–76. Münster: Zaphon.

Kozuh, M. 2010. 'Lamb, Mutton, and Goat in the Babylonian Temple Economy.' *Journal of the Economic and Social History of the Orient* 53 (4): 531–78.

———. 2014. *The Sacrificial Economy: Assessors, Contractors, and Thieves in the Management of Sacrificial Sheep at the Eanna Temple of Uruk (ca. 625–520 B.C.)*. Winona Lake, IN: Eisenbrauns.

Kuhrt, A. 2007. 'Cyrus the Great of Persia: Images and Realities.' In *Representations of Political Power: Case Histories from Times of Change and Dissolving Order in the Ancient Near East*, 169–91. Winona Lake, Indiana: Eisenbrauns.

Lamb, W.R. 1955. *Plato: Charmides, Alcibiades I and II, Hipparchus, The Lovers, Theages, Minos, Epinomis*. Cambridge, Massachusetts; London: Harvard University Press.

Lambert, W.G. 1974a. 'Dingir. Šà. Dib. Ba Incantations.' *JNES* 33 (3): 267–70+272–322.

———. 1974b. 'Review of W. von Soden (Ed.), Akkadisches Handwörterbuch: Unter Benutzung des Lexikalischen Nachlasses von Bruno Meissner (1868–1947).' *JSS* 19 (1): 82–7.

———. 1975. 'The Historical Development of the Mesopotamian Pantheon: A Study in Sophisticated Polytheism.' In *Unity and Diversity*, edited by H. Goedicke and J.M.M. Roberts, 191–99. Baltimore: Johns Hopkins University Press.

———. 1996. *Babylonian Wisdom Literature*. Winona Lake, Indiana: Eisenbrauns.

———. 1997. 'The Assyrian Recension of Enūma Eliš.' *CRRAI* 39: 77–9.

———. 1998. 'The Qualifications of Babylonian Diviners.' In *Tikip Santakki Mala Bašmu. Festschrift für Rykle Borger zu Seinem 65. Geburtstag am 24. Mai 1994*, 141–48. Groningen.

———. 2010. 'Mesopotamian Creation Stories.' In *Imagining Creation*, edited by M. Geller, 15–59. Leiden: Brill.

———. 2013. *Babylonian Creation Myths*. Winona Lake, Ind.: Eisenbrauns.

Lambert, W.G., and A.R. Millard. 1969. *Atra-Ḫasīs: The Babylonian Story of the Flood*. Oxford: Clarendon Press.

Lambert, W.G., A.R. Millard, with M. Civil. 1999. *Atra-Hasis: The Babylonian Story of the Flood, with the Sumerian Flood Story*. 2nd edn. University Park, Pennsylvania: Eisenbrauns.

Lambert, W.G., and R.D. Winters. 2023. *An = Anum and Related Lists*. Edited by A. George and M. Krebernik. Tübingen: Mohr Siebeck.

Lapinkivi, P. 2010. *Ištar's Descent and Resurrection*. Helsinki: Neo-Assyrian Text Corpus Project.

Lassen, A., E. Frahm, and K. Wagensonner, eds. 2019. *Ancient Mesopotamia Speaks: Highlights of the Yale Babylonian Collection*. The Yale Peabody Museum.

Lawson, J. 1994. *The Concept of Fate in Ancient Mesopotamia of the First Millennium: Toward an Understanding of Shīmtu*. Wiesbaden: Harrassowitz.

Layard, A.H. 1853. *Discoveries in Nineveh and Babylon*. London.

Leemans, W.F. 1960. *Foreign Trade in the Old Babylonian Period as Revealed by Texts from Southern Mesopotamia*. Studia et Documenta ad Iura Orientis Antiqui Pertinentia. Leiden: Brill.

Leichty, E. 1970. *The Omen Series Šumma Izbu*. Locust Valley, NY.

———. 2011. *The Royal Inscriptions of Esarhaddon, King of Assyria (680–669 BC)*. Royal Inscriptions of the Neo-Assyrian Period. Winona Lake, IN: Eisenbrauns.

Leick, G., ed. 2007. *The Babylonian World*. London; New York: Routledge.

Leiderer, R. 1990. *Anatomie der Schafsleber im Babylonischen Leberorakel. Eine Makroskopisch-Analytische Studie*. Munich: W. Zuckschwerdt Verlag.

Lenzi, A. 2008. *Secrecy and the Gods: Secret Knowledge in Ancient Mesopotamia and Biblical Israel*. Winona Lake, IN: Eisenbrauns.

———. 2010. 'Invoking the God: Interpreting Invocations in Mesopotamian Prayers and Biblical Laments of the Individual.' *Journal of Biblical Literature* 129 (2): 303–15.

———. 2012. 'The Curious Case of Failed Revelation in Ludlul Bēl Nēmeqi: A New Suggestion for the Poem's Scholarly Purpose.' In *Between Heaven and Earth: Communication with the Divine in the Ancient Near East*, edited by C.L. Crouch, J. Stökl, and A.E. Zernecke, 36–66. New York.

———. 2019. *An Introduction to Akkadian Literature: Contexts and Content*. University Park, PA: Eisenbrauns.

Linssen, M.J.H. 2004. *The Cults of Uruk and Babylon: The Temple Ritual Texts as Evidence for Hellenistic Cult Practice*. Leiden; Boston: Brill.

Liverani, M. 2017. *Assyria: The Imperial Mission*. University Park, PA: Eisenbrauns.

Livingstone, A. 1989. *Court Poetry and Literary Miscellanea*. State Archives of Assyria Vol. III. Winona Lake: Eisenbrauns.

———. 2007. 'Ashurbanipal: Literate or Not?' *Zeitschrift für Assyriologie und Vorderasiatische Archäologie* 97 (1): 98–118.

———. 2013. *Hemerologies of Assyrian and Babylonian Scholars*. Bethesda, MD: Eisenbrauns.

LoCicero, D. 2007. *Superheroes and Gods: A Comparative Study from Babylonia to Batman*. Jefferson: McFarland & Company.

Löhnert, A. 2007. 'The Installation of Priests According to Neo-Assyrian Documents.' *State Archives of Assyria Bulletin* 16: 273–86.

———. 2009. *Wie die Sonne Tritt Heraus!* Alter Orient und Altes Testament. Münster: Blackwell.

———. 2011. 'Manipulating the Gods: Lamenting in Context.' In *The Oxford Handbook of Cuneiform Culture*, 402–17. Oxford: Oxford University Press.

MacDougal, R. 2014. 'Remembrance and the Dead in Second Millennium BC Mesopotamia.'

MacGregor, S. 2012. *Beyond Hearth and Home: Women in the Public Sphere in Neo-Assyrian Society*. University Park, PA: Eisenbrauns.

Malcolm, J. 1829. *The History of Persia*. Revised Edition. Vol. 1. London: John Murray; Longman and Co.

Matuszewska, N. 2018. 'Why Could Magical Stones Have Relieved Headaches?' *Nouvelles Assyriologiques Brèves et Utilitaires*, no. 4: 170.

Maul, S.M. 1988. *'Herzberuhigungsklagen': Die Sumerisch-Akkadischen Ershahunga-Gebete*. Wiesbaden.

———. 1994. *Zukunftsbewältigung: Eine Untersuchung Altorientalischen Denkens Anhand der Babylonisch-Assyrischen Löserituale (Namburbi)*. Mainz am Rhein: von Zabern.

———. 1998. 'Der Assyrische König – Hüter der Weltordnung.' In *Gerechtigkeit. Richten und Retten in der Abendländischen Tradition und Ihren Altorientalischen Ursprüngen*, edited by J. Assmann, B. Janowski, and M. Welker, 65–77. Munich: Wilhelm Fink Verlag.

———. 1999. 'How the Babylonians Protected Themselves against Calamities Announced by Omens.' In *Mesopotamian Magic: Textual, Historical, and Interpretative Perspectives*, edited by T. Abusch and K. van der Toorn, 123–29. Leiden; Boston: Brill.

———. 2010. 'Die Tontafelbibliothek aus dem Sogenannten "Haus Des Beschwörungspriesters".' In *Assur-Forschungen. Arbeiten aus der Forschungsstelle 'Edition Literarischer Keilschrifttexte aus Assur' der Heidelberger Akademie der Wissenschaften*, edited by S.M. Maul and N.P. Heeßel, 189–228. Wiesbaden: Harrassowitz.

———. 2017. 'Assyrian Religion.' In *A Companion to Assyria*, edited by E. Frahm, 336–58. Hoboken: Wiley Blackwell.

———. 2018. *The Art of Divination in the Ancient Near East*. Waco, Texas: Baylor University Press.

Maul, S.M., and R. Strauß. 2011. *Ritualbeschreibungen und Gebete 1: Mit Beiträgen von Daniel Schwemer*. Wiesbaden: Harrassowitz Verlag.

May, N. 2018. 'Female Scholars in Mesopotamia?' In *Gender and Methodology in the Ancient Near East*, edited by S. Budin, M. Cifarelli, A. Garcia-Ventura, and A. Millet Albà, 149–62. Barcelona: Universitat de Barcelona.

McClure, M.L., and C.L. Feltoe. 1919. *The Pilgrimage of Etheria*. London: Society for Promoting Christian Knowledge.

McCown, D.E., and R.C. Haines. 1967. *Nippur I, Temple of Enlil, Scribal Quarter, and Soundings: Excavations of the Joint Expedition to Nippur of the University Museum of Philadelphia and the Oriental Institute of the University of Chicago*. Chicago: The University of Chicago Press.

Meek, T.J. 1920. 'Some Explanatory Lists and Grammatical Tests.' *Revue d'assyriologie et d'archéologie Orientale* 18 (3–4): 117–206.

Melville, S.C. 1999. *The Role of Naqia/Zakutu in Sargonid Politics*. Helsinki: Neo-Assyrian Text Corpus Project, Institute for Asian and African Studies, University of Helsinki.

———. 2004. 'Neo-Assyrian Royal Women and Male Identity: Status as a Social Tool.' *Journal of the American Oriental Society* 124 (1): 37–57.

Mertens-Wagschal, A. 2018. 'The Lion, the Witch, and the Wolf: Aggressive Magic and Witchcraft in the Old Babylonian Period.' In *Sources of Evil: Studies in Mesopotamian Exorcistic Lore*, edited by G. Van Buylaere, M. Luukko, D. Schwemer, and A. Mertens-Wagschal, 158–69. Leiden; Boston: Brill.

Meyer, J.-W. 1987. *Untersuchungen zu den Tonlebermodellen aus dem Alten Orient*. Kevelaer: Neukirchener Verlag.

Michalowski, P. 1989. *The Lamentation over the Destruction of Sumer and Ur*. Winona Lake, Indiana.

———. 1990. 'Presence at the Creation.' In *Lingering over Words: Studies in Ancient Near Eastern Literature in Honor of William W. Moran*, edited by T. Abusch, J. Huehnergard, and P. Steinkeller, 381–96. Leiden: Brill.

Mieroop, M. van de. 2016. *Philosophy before the Greeks: The Pursuit of Truth in Ancient Babylonia*. Princeton: Princeton University Press.

Miller, E. 2021. 'Drawing Distinctions: Assyrians and Others in the Art of the Neo-Assyrian Empire.' *Studia Orientalia Electronica* 9 (2): 82–107.

Mirelman, S. 2010. 'Performative Indications in Late Babylonian Texts.' In *Musicians and the Tradition of Literature in the Ancient Near East*, edited by R. Pruzsinszky and D. Shehata, 241–64. Vienna: Wiener Offene Orientalistik 8.

Mitto, T., A. Hätinen, A.C. Heinrich, and E. Jiménez. 2024. 'Catalogue of Texts and Authors Chapter Neo-Assyrian.' *Electronic Babylonian Library*.

Mitto, T., E. Jiménez, A. Hätinen, G. Rozzi, and Z. Földi. 2022. 'From the Electronic Babylonian Literature Lab 25–35.' *Kaskal : Rivista di Storia, Ambiente e Culture del Vicino Oriente Antico*. 19, 2022, 105–202.

Morony, M. 2015. *Iraq after the Muslim Conquest*. Piscataway, NJ: Gorgias Press.

Nadali, D. 2018. 'The Battle of Til-Tuba in the South-West Palace: Context and Iconography.' In *I Am Ashurbanipal: King of the World, King of Assyria*, edited by G. Brereton, 234–73. London: British Museum/Thames & Hudson.

Nahm, W. 2013. 'The Case for the Lower Middle Chronology.' *Altorientalische Forschungen* 40 (2) , 350–72.

Ncube, T. 2009. 'Gweru Goat Gives Birth to Human Being.' Accessed 7 June 2024. https://nehandaradio.com/2009/09/03/gweru-goat-gives-birth-to-human-being/.

Nemet-Nejat, K. 2002. *Daily Life in Ancient Mesopotamia*. Peabody, MA: Hendrickson Publishers.

Nissen, H., P. Damerow, and R.K. Englund. 1993. *Archaic Bookkeeping: Early Writing and Techniques of Economic Administration in the Ancient Near East*. Chicago; London: University of Chicago Press.

Nissinen, M. 2010. 'Are There Homosexuals in Mesopotamian Literature?' *Journal of the American Oriental Society* 130 (1): 73–77. http://www.jstor.org/stable/25766947.

Novotny, J. 2018. 'Ashurbanipal's Campaigns.' In *I Am Ashurbanipal: King of the World, King of Assyria*, edited by G. Brereton, 196–211. London: British Museum/Thames & Hudson.

———. 2023. 'The Assyrian Empire in Contact with the World.' In *The Oxford History of the Ancient Near East: The Age of Assyria*, edited by K. Radner, N. Moeller, and D.T. Potts, 4:352–424. Oxford: Oxford University Press.

Novotny, J., and J. Jeffers. 2018. *The Royal Inscriptions of Ashurbanipal (668–631 BC), Aššur-Etel-Ilāni (630–627 BC), and Sîn-Šarra-Iškun (626–612 BC), Kings of Assyria, Part 1*. Royal Inscriptions of the Neo-Assyrian Period. University Park, Pennsylvania: Eisenbrauns.

Novotny, J., J. Jeffers, and G. Frame. 2023. *The Royal Inscriptions of Ashurbanipal (668–631 BC), Aššur-Etel-Ilāni (630–627 BC), and Sîn-Šarra-Iškun (626–612 BC), Kings of Assyria, Part 3*. University Park, PA: Eisenbrauns.

Novotny, J., and J. Singletary. 2009. 'Family Ties: Assurbanipal's Family Revisited.' *Studia Orientalia Electronica* 106: 167–78.

Novotny, J., and F. Weiershäuser. 2020. *The Royal Inscriptions of Amēl-Marduk (561–560 BC), Neriglissar (559–556 BC), and Nabonidus (555–539 BC), Kings of Babylon*. University Park, PA: Eisenbrauns.

———. 2024. *The Royal Inscriptions of Nabopolassar (625–605 BC) and Nebuchadnezzar II (604–562 BC), Kings of Babylon, Part 1*. University Park, PA: Eisenbrauns.

———. 2025. *The Royal Inscriptions of Nabopolassar (625–605 BC) and Nebuchadnezzar II (604–562 BC), Kings of Babylon, Part 2*. University Park, PA: Eisenbraun.

Oded, B. 1979. *Mass Deportations and Deportees in the Neo-Assyrian Empire*. Wiesbaden: Ludwig Reichert Verlag.

Oldfather, C.H. 1933. Translation of Diodorus Siculus, *The Library of History*. Harvard: Harvard University Press.

Oppenheim, L. 1956. 'The Interpretation of Dreams in the Ancient Near East. With a Translation of an Assyrian Dream-Book.' *Transactions of the American Philosophical Society New Series* 46 (3): 179–373.

———. 1969. 'Divination and Celestial Observation in the Last Assyrian Empire.' *Centaurus* 14: 97–135.

———. 1974. 'A Babylonian Diviner's Manual.' *Journal of Near Eastern Studies* 33 (2): 197–220.

———. 1977. *Ancient Mesopotamia: Portrait of a Dead Civilization*. Revised edn. Chicago: University of Chicago Press.

Oshima, T. 2013. *The Babylonian Theodicy*. Helsinki: The Neo-Assyrian Text Corpus Project.

———. 2014. *Babylonian Poems of Pious Sufferers*. Tübingen: Mohr Siebeck.

Ossendrijver, M. 2011. 'Science in Action: Networks in Babylonian Astronomy.' In *Babylon*, edited by E. Cancik-Kirschbaum, M. van Ess, and J. Marzahn, 213–21. Berlin, Boston: De Gruyter.

———. 2014. 'Babylonian Mathematical Astronomy.' In *Handbook of Archaeoastronomy and Ethnoastronomy*, edited by C.L. Ruggles, 1863–70. New York: Springer.

———. 2016. 'Ancient Babylonian Astronomers Calculated Jupiter's Position from the Area under a Time-Velocity Graph.' *Science* 351 (6272): 482–4.

———. 2019. 'Babylonian Market Prediction.' In *Keeping Watch in Babylon: The Astronomical Diaries in Context*. Culture and History of the Ancient Near East, Vol. 100, edited by J. Haubold, J. Steele, and K. Stevens. Leiden; Boston: Brill.

———. 2021. 'Astral Science in Uruk during the First Millennium BCE: Libraries, Communities and Transfer of Knowledge.' In *Uruk – Altorientalische Metropole und Kulturzentrum 8. Internationales Colloquium der Deutschen Orient-Gesellschaft 25. und 26. April 2013, Berlin*, 319–41. Wiesbaden: Harrassowitz Verlag.

Ottervanger, B. 2016, *The Tale of the Poor Man of Nippur*. Helsinki: The Neo-Assyrian Text Corpus Project.

Panayotov, S. 2013. 'A Ritual for a Flourishing Bordello.' *Bibliotheca Orientalis* 70: 285–309.

———. 2018. 'Notes on the Assur Medical Catalogue with Comparison to the Nineveh Medical Encyclopaedia.' In *Assyrian and Babylonian*

Scholarly Text Catalogues, edited by U. Steinert, 89–120. Medicine, Magic and Divination. De Gruyter.

Pankenier, David W. 2013. *Astrology and Cosmology in Early China: Conforming Earth to Heaven*. Cambridge and New York: Cambridge University Press.

———. 2014. 'Did Babylonian Astrology Influence Early Chinese Astral Prognostication "Xing Zhan Shu" "星占術"?' *Early China* 37: 1–13.

Parpola, S. 1980. 'The Murderer of Sennacherib.' In *Death in Mesopotamia: Papers Read at the XXVIe Rencontre Assyriologique Internationale*, edited by B. Alster, 171–82. Copenhagen: Akademisk Forlag.

———. 1983. *Letters from Assyrian Scholars to the Kings Esarhaddon and Assurbanipal, Part II: Commentary and Appendices*. Kevelaer: Verlag Butzon & Bercker; Neukirchen-Vluyn: Neukirchener Verlag.

———. 1987. 'The Forlorn Scholar.' In *Language, Literature, and History: Philological and Historical Studies Presented to Erica Reiner*, edited by F. Rochberg-Halton, 257–78. New Haven: American Oriental Society.

———. 1993a. *Letters from Assyrian and Babylonian Scholars, Part II: Commentary and Appendices*. State Archives of Assyria. Helsinki: Helsinki University Press.

———. 1993b. 'Mesopotamian Astrology and Astronomy as Domains of the Mesopotamian "Wisdom".' In *Die Rolle der Astronomie in den Kulturen Mesopotamiens: Beiträge zum 3. Grazer Morgenländischen Symposion (23.–27. September 1991)*, edited by H.D. Galter, 47–59. Graz: Druck & Verlagsgesellschaft.

———. 2001. 'Mesopotamian Precursors of the Hymn of the Pearl.' In *Mythology and Mythologies*, 181–93. Melammu Symposia. Helsinki: The Neo-Assyrian Text Corpus Project.

———. 2004. 'National and Ethnic Identity in the Neo-Assyrian Empire and Assyrian Identity in Post-Empire Times.' *Journal of Assyrian Academic Studies* 18: 5–22.

———. 2018. *The Correspondence of Assurbanipal: Part I, Letters from Assyria, Babylonia and Vassal States*. State Archives of Assyria. Helsinki: The Neo-Assyrian Text Corpus Project.

Parpola, S., and K. Watanabe. 1988. *Neo-Assyrian Treaties and Loyalty Oaths*. Helsinki: Helsinki University Press.

Pearce, L.E., and C. Wunsch. 2014. *Documents of Judean Exiles and West Semites in Babylonia in the Collection of David Sofer*. Bethesda, MD: CDL Press.

Pedersén, O. 1986. *Archives and Libraries in the City of Assur: A Survey of the Material from the German Excavations, Part II*. Uppsala: Uppsala University.

Pingree, D. 1963. 'Astronomy and Astrology in India and Iran.' *Isis* 54 (2): 229–46.

———. 1992. 'Hellenophilia versus the History of Science.' *Isis* 83 (4): 554–63.

———. 1998. 'Legacies in Astronomy and Celestial Omens.' In *The Legacy of Mesopotamia*, edited by S. Dalley, 125–37. Oxford: Oxford University Press.

———. 2002. 'The Ṣābians of Ḥarrān and the Classical Tradition.' *International Journal of the Classical Tradition* 9 (1): 8–35.

Podany, A. 2022. *Weavers, Scribes, and Kings: A New History of the Ancient Near East*. Oxford: Oxford University Press.

Pongratz-Leisten, Beate. 1994. *Ina Šulmi Īrub: Die Kulttopographische und Ideologische Programmatik der Akītu-Prozession in Babylonien und Assyrien im I. Jahrtausend v. Chr.* Mainz: von Zabern.

———. 2015. *Religion and Ideology in Assyria*. Boston; Berlin: De Gruyter.

Porter, B.N. 2006. 'Feeding Dinner to a Bed, Reflections on the Nature of Gods in Ancient Mesopotamia.' *State Archives of Assyria Bulletin* XV: 307–31.

———. 2009. 'Blessings from a Crown, Offerings to a Drum: Were There Non-Anthropomorphic Deities in Ancient Mesopotamia?' In *What Is a God? Anthropomorphic and Non-Anthropomorphic Aspects of Deity in Ancient Mesopotamia*, edited by B.N. Porter, 153–94. Winona Lake, Indiana: Eisenbrauns.

Potts, D.T. 2011. 'The Politai and the Bīt Tāmartu: The Seleucid and Parthian Theatres of the Greek Citizens of Babylon.' In *Babylon: Wissenskultur in Orient und Okzident*, edited by E. Cancik-Kirschbaum, M. van Ess, and J. Marzahn, 239–52. Berlin; Boston: De Gruyter.

———. 2016. *The Archaeology of Elam: Formation and Transformation of an Ancient Iranian State*. Cambridge: Cambridge University Press.

Powell, M.A. 1991. 'Naram-Sin, Son of Sargon: Ancient History, Famous Names, and a Famous Babylonian Forgery.' *Zeitschrift für Assyriologie* 81: 20–30.

Quinn, J. 2024. *How the World Made the West: A 4,000-Year History*. London: Bloomsbury Publishing.

Radau, H. 1908. *Letters to Cassite Kings from the Temple Archives of Nippur*. Pennsylvania: The Department of Archaeology, University of Pennsylvania.

Radner, K. 2003. 'The Trials of Esarhaddon: The Conspiracy of 670 BC.' In *Assur und Sein Umland. Isimu: Revista sobre Oriente Próximo y Egipto en la Antigüedad* 6, edited by P. Miglus and J.M. Córdoba Zoilo: 165–84.

———. 2008. 'The Delegation of Power: Neo-Assyrian Bureau Seals.' In *L'archive des Fortifications de Persépolis. État des Questions et Perspectives de Recherches (Persika 12)*, edited by P. Briant, W. Henkelman, and M. Stolper, 481–515. Paris: De Boccard.

———. 2014. 'An Imperial Communication Network: The State Correspondence of the Neo-Assyrian Empire.' In *State Correspondence in the Ancient World: From New Kingdom Egypt to the Roman Empire*, edited by K. Radner, 64–93. Oxford: Oxford University Press.

———. 2020. *A Short History of Babylon*. London: Bloomsbury Publishing.

Radner, K., N. Moeller, and D.T. Potts, eds. 2023. *The Assyrian Empire in Contact with the World. The Oxford History of the Ancient Near East: The Age of Assyria*. Vol. 4. Oxford: Oxford University Press.

Radner, K., and E. Robson, eds. 2011. *The Oxford Handbook of Cuneiform Culture*. Oxford: Oxford University Press.

Reade, J. 1986. 'Archaeology and the Kuyunjik Archives.' *CRRAI* 30: 213–22.

———. 1998–2001. 'Ninive (Nineveh).' In *Reallexikon der Assyriologie und Vorderasiatischen Archäologie*, edited by D.O. Edzard, 9: 388–433. Berlin: De Gruyter.

———. 2003. 'The Royal Tombs of Ur.' In *Art of the First Cities: The Third Millennium B.C. from the Mediterranean to the Indus*, edited by J. Aruz and R. Wallenfels, 93–107. New York; New Haven: Metropolitan Museum of Art; Yale University Press.

———. 2012. 'Visual Evidence for the Status and Activities of Assyrian Scribes.' In *Leggo! Studies Presented to Frederick Mario Fales on the*

Occasion of His 65th Birthday, edited by G. Lanfranchi, D.M. Bonacossi, C. Pappi, and S. Ponchia, 699–718. Wiesbaden: Harrassowitz Verlag.

———. 2018. 'The Assyrian Royal Hunt.' In *I Am Ashurbanipal: King of the World, King of Assyria*. Edited by G. Brereton, 52–79. London: British Museum / Thames & Hudson.

Reiner, E. 1958. *Šurpu: A Collection of Sumerian and Akkadian Incantations*. Graz: Im Selbstverlage des Herausgebers.

Reiner, E., and D. Pingree. 1975. *Babylonian Planetary Omens, Part One, Enūma Anu Enlil Tablet 63: The Venus Tablet of Ammiṣaduqa*. Malibu: Undena Publications.

———. 1981. *Babylonian Planetary Omens, Part Two: Enūma Anu Enlil, Tablets 50–51*. Malibu: Undena Publications.

Reynolds, F. 2007. 'Food and Drink in Babylonia.' In *The Babylonian World*, edited by G. Leick, 171–186. London: Routledge.

Ritter, E. 1965. 'Magical-Expert (= Ašipu) and Physician (= Asû): Notes on Two Complementary Professions in Babylonian Medicine.' In *Studies in Honor of Benno Landsberger*, edited by H.G. Güterbock and T. Jacobsen, 299–321. Chicago: The University of Chicago Press.

Roaf, M., and A. Zgoll. 2001. 'Assyrian Astroglyphs: Lord Aberdeen's Black Stone and the Prisms of Esarhaddon.' *ZA* 91 (2): 264–95.

Robson, E. 2001. 'The Tablet House: A Scribal School in Old Babylonian Nippur.' *RA* 93: 39–66.

———. 2004. 'Review of: A.R. George, The Babylonian Gilgamesh Epic: Introduction, Critical Edition and Cuneiform Texts, 2 Vols. Oxford: Oxford University Press, 2003. Pp. xxxv, 986; Pls. 147. ISBN 0-19-814922-0.' *Bryn Mawr Classical Review*, April.

———. 2008. *Mathematics in Ancient Iraq: A Social History*. Princeton; Oxford: Princeton University Press.

———. 2011. 'The Production and Dissemination of Scholarly Knowledge.' In *The Oxford Handbook of Cuneiform Culture*, edited by K. Radner and E. Robson, 557–76. Oxford: Oxford University Press.

———. 2013. 'Reading the Libraries of Assyria and Babylonia.' In *Ancient Libraries*, edited by J. König and A. Oikonomopoulou, 38–56. Cambridge: Cambridge University Press.

———. 2019. *Ancient Knowledge Networks: A Social Geography of Cuneiform Scholarship in First-Millennium Assyria and Babylonia*. London: UCL Press.

Rochberg, Francesca. 1998. 'Babylonian Horoscopes.' *Transactions of the American Philosophical Society* 88 (1): i–164.

———. 2004. *The Heavenly Writing*. Cambridge: Cambridge University Press.

———. 2010. *In the Path of the Moon: Babylonian Celestial Divination and Its Legacy*. Boston: Brill.

———. 2016. *Before Nature: Cuneiform Knowledge and the History of Science*. Chicago: University of Chicago Press.

———. 2018a. 'Reasoning, Representing, and Modeling in Babylonian Astronomy.' *Journal of Ancient Near Eastern History* 5 (1–2): 131–47.

———. 2018b. 'Science and Ancient Mesopotamia.' In *The Cambridge History of Science*, edited by A. Jones and L. Taub, 7–28. Cambridge: Cambridge University Press.

Rochberg-Halton, F. 1988. *Aspects of Babylonian Celestial Divination: The Lunar Eclipse Tablets of Enūma Anu Enlil*. Horn, Austria: Ferdinand Berger & Söhne.

Roth, M.T. 1997. *Law Collections from Mesopotamia and Asia Minor*. 2nd edn. Writings from the Ancient World, Vol. 6. Atlanta: Scholars Press.

Rumor, M. 2020. 'Dreck-, Deck-, or What the Heck?' *Le Journal des Médecines Cunéiformes* 36: 37–53.

Sachs, A. 1976. 'The Latest Datable Cuneiform Tablets.' In *Kramer Anniversary Volume: Cuneiform Studies in Honour of Samuel Noah Kramer*, edited by B.L. Eichler, 379–98. Kevelaer: Butzon & Bercker.

Sachs, A., and H. Hunger. 1988. *Astronomical Diaries and Related Texts from Babylonia, Vol. 1: Diaries from 652 B.C. to 262 B.C.* Vienna: Verlag der Osterreichischen Akademie der Wissenschaften.

Sallaberger, W. 2004. 'Pantheon. A.I. in Mesopotamien.' In *Reallexikon der Assyriologie* X: 294–308. Berlin: De Gruyter.

Salvesen, A. 1998. 'The Legacy of Babylon and Nineveh in Aramaic Sources.' In *The Legacy of Mesopotamia*, edited by S. Dalley, 139–62. Oxford; New York: Oxford University Press.

Samet, N. 2014. *The Lamentation over the Destruction of Ur*. Winona Lake, Indiana: Eisenbrauns.

Schaudig, H. 2019. *Explaining Disaster. Tradition and Transformation of the 'Catastrophe of Ibbi-Sîn' in Babylonian Literature*. Münster: Zaphon.

Schmandt-Besserat, D. 1992. *Before Writing, Vol. 1. From Counting to Cuneiform*. Vol. 1. Austin: University of Texas Press.

Schmidt, M. 2019. Gilgamesh: *The Life of a Poem*. Princeton: Princeton University Press.

Schmidtchen, E. 2018. 'Esagil-Kīn-Apli's Catalogue of Sakikkû and Alamdimmû.' In *Assyrian and Babylonian Scholarly Text Catalogues*, edited by U. Steinert, 137–57. Berlin, Boston: De Gruyter.

Schwemer, D. 2007. *Abwehrzauber und Behexung. Studien zum Schadenzauberglauben im Alten Mesopotamien*. Wiesbaden: Harrassowitz.

———. 2011. 'Magic Rituals: Conceptualization and Performance.' In *The Oxford Handbook of Cuneiform Culture*, edited by E. Robson and K. Radner. Oxford: Oxford University Press.

———. 2014. 'Corpus of Mesopotamian Anti-Witchcraft Rituals Online.' Accessed 24 April 2024. https://www.phil.uni-wuerzburg.de/cmawro/magic-witchcraft/maqlu/.

———. 2015. 'The Ancient Near East.' In *The Cambridge History of Magic and Witchcraft in the West: From Antiquity to the Present*, edited by S.J. Collins and J. David, 17–51. Cambridge: Cambridge University Press.

Scurlock, J. 1999. 'Physician, Exorcist, Conjurer, Magician: A Tale of Two Healing Professionals.' In *Mesopotamian Magic*, edited by T. Abusch and K. van der Toorn, 69–79. Groningen: Styx.

———. 2014. *Sourcebook for Ancient Mesopotamian Medicine*. Atlanta, Georgia: SBL Press.

Scurlock, J., and B.R. Andersen. 2005. *Diagnoses in Assyrian and Babylonian Medicine: Ancient Sources, Translations, and Modern Medical Analyses*. Urbana; Chicago: University of Illinois Press.

Seminara, S. 2002. 'The Babylonian Science of the Translation and the Ideological Adjustment of the Sumerian Text to the "Target Culture".' In *Ideologies as Intercultural Phenomena. Proceedings of the Third Annual Symposium of the Assyrian and Babylonian Intellectual Heritage Project. Held in Chicago, USA, October 27–31, 2000*, edited by A. Panaino and G. Pettinato, 245–55. Milan: Università di Bologna & IsIAO.

Seri, A. 2006. 'The Fifty Names of Marduk in "Enūma Eliš".' *JAOS* 126 (4): 507–19.

Shakespeare, W. *Macbeth*. Edited by B. Mowat, P. Werstine, M. Poston, and R. Niles. Washington DC: Folger Shakespeare Library. Accessed 2 May 2024. https://www.folger.edu/explore/shakespeares-works/macbeth/read/4/1/.

Shehata, D. 2001. *Annotierte Bibliographie zum Altbabylonischen Atramḫasīs-Mythos*. Göttingen: Seminar für Keilschriftforschung der Universität Göttingen.

Sibbing-Plantholt, I. 2022. *The Image of Mesopotamian Divine Healers Healing Goddesses and the Legitimization of Professional Asûs in the Mesopotamian Medical Marketplace*. Cuneiform Monographs 53. Leiden; Boston: Brill.

Simons, F. 2019. 'Burn Your Way to Success: Studies in the Mesopotamian Ritual and Incantation Series Šurpu.' PhD thesis. University of Birmingham.

———. 2024. 'Bang a Gong (Demons Gone): The Mighty Copper and Magic with Automatic Consent.' In *Legitimising Magic Strategies and Practices in Ancient Mesopotamia*, edited by N.P. Heeßel and E. Zomer, 77–90.

Sims-Williams, N. 1996. 'From Babylon to China, Astrological and Epistolary Formulae across Two Millennia.' In *Convegno Internazionale sul Tema: La Persia e l'Asia Centrale de Alessandro al X Secolo*, 77–84. Rome: Accademia nazionale dei Lincei.

Sjöberg, Åke W. 1975. 'in-nin šà-gur$_4$-ra: A Hymn to the Goddess Inanna by the en-Priestess Enḫeduanna'. In *Zeitschrift für Assyriologie* 65: 161–253.

Sjöberg, Åke W., and E. Bergmann. 1969. 'The Collection of the Sumerian Temple Hymns'. In *The Collection of the Sumerian Temple Hymns*. Texts from Cuneiform Sources III, edited by Åke W. Sjöberg, E. Bergmann, and G. B. Gragg. 3–154. Locust Valley, New York: J.J. Augustin.

Smith, J.Z. 1976. 'A Pearl of Great Price and a Cargo of Yams: A Study in Situational Incongruity.' *History of Religions* 16 (1): 1–19. http://www.jstor.org/stable/1062294.

Soden, W. von. 1969. 'Zur Wiederherstellung der Marduk-Gebete BMS 11 und 12.' *Iraq* 31: 82–9.

———. 1990. 'Gibt es Hinweise auf die Ermordung Sanheribs im Ninurta-Temple (Wohl) in Kalaḫ in Texten aus Assyrien?' *N.A.B.U.* 1 (22): 16–17.

Soldt, W.H. van. 1995. *Solar Omens of Enuma Anu Enlil: Tablets 23 (24)–29 (30)*. Leiden: Nederlands Instituut voor het Nabije Oosten.

Sonik, K. 2020. 'Gilgamesh and Emotional Excess: The King without Counsel in the SB Gilgamesh Epic.' In *The Expression of Emotions in Ancient Egypt and Mesopotamia*, edited by S.W. Hsu and R. J. Llop, 390–409. Leiden; Boston: Brill.

———. 2021. 'Minor and Marginal(ized)? Rethinking Women as Minor Characters in the *Epic of Gilgamesh*.' *Journal of the American Oriental Society* 141 (4): 779–801.

Spek, R. J. van der. 2001. 'The Theatre of Babylon in Cuneiform.' In *Veenhof Anniversary Volume: Studies Presented to Klaas R. Veenhof on the Occasion of His Sixty-Fifth Birthday*, edited by W.H. van Soldt, J.G. Dercksen, N.J.C. Kouwenberg, and J.H. Krispijn, 445–56. Nederlands Instituut voor het Nabije Oosten.

———. 2004. 'BCHP 14 (Greek Community Chronicle).' In *Livius*. https://www.livius.org/sources/content/mesopotamian-chronicles-content/bchp-14-greek-community-chronicle/.

———. 2022. 'The Challenge of the Astronomical Diaries from Babylon.' *Journal of the American Oriental Society* 142 (4): 975–81.

Stadhouders, H. 2018. 'The Unfortunate Frog: On Animal and Human Bondage in K 2581 and Related Fragments with Excursuses on BM 64526 ad YOS XI, 3.' *Revue d'assyriologie et d'archéologie Orientale* 112: 159–76.

Starr, I. 1983. *The Rituals of the Diviner*. Malibu: Undena Publications.

———. 1990. *Queries to the Sun God: Divination and Politics in Sargonid Assyria*. Helsinki: Helsinki University Press.

Steele, J. 2011a. 'Making Sense of Time: Observational and Theoretical Calendars.' In *The Oxford Handbook of Cuneiform Culture*, edited by K. Radner and E. Robson, 470–85. Oxford: Oxford University Press.

———. 2011b. 'Visual Aspects of the Transmission of Babylonian Astronomy and Its Reception into Greek Astronomy.' *Annals of Science* 68 (4): 453–65.

———. 2013. 'A Comparison of Astronomical Terminology, Methods and Concepts in China and Mesopotamia, with some Comments on Claims for the Transmission of Mesopotamian Astronomy to China.' *Journal of Astronomical History and Heritage* 16 (3): 250–60.

———. 2018. 'Babylonian and Assyrian Astral Science.' In *The Cambridge History of Science*, edited by A. Jones and L. Taub, 73–98. Cambridge: Cambridge University Press.

———. 2022. 'The Influence of Assyriology on the Study of Chinese Astronomy in the Late Nineteenth and Early Twentieth Centuries.' In *Overlapping Cosmologies in Asia: Transcultural and Interdisciplinary Approaches*, edited by B. Mak and E. Huntington. Leiden and Boston: Brill.

Steinert, U. 2012. 'K. 263+10934: A Tablet with Recipes against the Abnormal Flow of a Woman's Blood.' *Sudhoffs Archiv* 96 (1): 64–94.

———. 2017. 'Cows, Women and Wombs: Interrelations between Texts and Images from the Ancient Near East.' In *From the Four Corners of the Earth: Studies in Iconography and Cultures of the Ancient Near East in Honour of F.A.M. Wiggermann*, edited by D. Kertai and O. Nieuwenhuyse, 205–58. Münster: Ugarit-Verlag.

———. 2018a. *Assyrian and Babylonian Scholarly Text Catalogues*. Boston; Berlin: De Gruyter.

———. 2018b. 'Catalogues, Texts and Specialists: Some Thoughts on the Assur Medical Catalogue, Mesopotamian Medical Texts and Healing Professions.' In *Assyrian and Babylonian Scholarly Text Catalogues: Medicine, Magic and Divination*, edited by U. Steinert, 158–203. Berlin; Boston: De Gruyter.

———. 2020. 'Disease Concepts and Classifications in Ancient Mesopotamian Medicine.' In *Systems of Classification in Premodern Medical Cultures*, edited by U. Steinert, 140–94. Oxon: Routledge.

Steinert, U., S.V. Panayotov, M.J. Geller, E. Schmidtchen, and J.C. Johnson. 2018. 'The Assur Medical Catalogue (AMC).' In *Assyrian and Babylonian Scholarly Text Catalogues*, edited by U. Steinert, 203–91. Boston; Berlin: De Gruyter.

Stevens, K. 2014. 'The Antiochus Cylinder, Babylonian Scholarship and Seleucid Imperial Ideology.' *Journal of Hellenic Studies* 134: 66–88.

———. 2019. *Between Greece and Babylonia: Hellenistic Intellectual History in Cross-Cultural Perspective*. Cambridge: Cambridge University Press.

Stökl, J., and C. Waerzeggers, eds. 2015. *Exile and Return: The Babylonian Context*. Beihefte zur Zeitschrift für die alttestamentliche Wissenschaft, Vol. 478. Berlin: De Gruyter.

Stol, M. 2016. *Women in the Ancient Near East*. Berlin; Boston: De Gruyter.

Streck, M.P. 2010 'Großes Fach Altorientalistik. Der Umfang des keilschriftlichen Textkorpus.' In M. Hilgert (ed.), *Altorientalistik im 21. Jahrhundert: Selbstverständnis, Herausforderungen, Ziele.* Mitteilungen der Deutschen Orient-Gesellschaft 142 35–58.

Svärd, S. 2012. 'Women, Power, and Heterarchy in the Neo-Assyrian Palaces.' In *Organization, Representation, and Symbols of Power in the Ancient Near East: Proceedings of the 54th Rencontre Assyriologique Internationale at Würzburg 20–25 July 2008*, edited by G. Wilhelm, 507–18. Winona Lake: Eisenbrauns.

———. 2015. *Women and Power in Neo-Assyrian Palaces*. State Archives of Assyria Studies, Vol. 23. Helsinki: Neo-Assyrian Text Corpus Project.

Tadmor, H. 1997. 'Propaganda, Literature, Historiography: Cracking the Code of the Assyrian Royal Inscriptions.' In *Assyria 1995*, edited by S. Parpola and R. Whiting, 325–38. Helsinki: The Neo-Assyrian Text Corpus Project.

Talbot, L. 2019. 'Language Use, Entry Composition and Tablet Structure in Babylonian Medicine: A Sample-Based Comparison of the Diagnostic and Therapeutic Corpora.' PhD thesis submitted to the University of Cambridge.

Tanret, M. 2011. 'Learned, Rich, Famous and Unhappy: Ur-Utu of Sippar.' In *The Oxford Handbook of Cuneiform Culture*, edited by K. Radner and E. Robson, 270–87. Oxford University Press.

Terry, P. 2018. *Dictator, a New Version of the Epic of Gilgamesh*. Manchester: Carcanet.

Thureau-Dangin, F. 1922. *Tablettes d'Uruk*. Paris: Geuthner.

Tinney, S. 1996. *The Nippur Lament: Royal Rhetoric and Divine Legitimation in the Reign of Išme-Dagan of Isin (1953–1935 B.C.)*. Occasional publications of the Samuel Noah Kramer Fund 16. Philadelphia: University of Pennsylvania Museum of Archaeology and Anthropology.

Toomer, G.J. 1984. *Ptolemy's Almagest*. London: Duckworth.

———. 1988. 'Hipparchus and Babylonian Astronomy.' In *A Scientific Humanist: Studies in Memory of Abraham Sachs*, edited by E. Leichty, M. Ellis, and

P. Gerardi. Philadelphia: Occasional Publications of the Samuel Noah Kramer Fund 9.

Toorn, K. van der. 1985. *Sin and Sanction in Israel and Mesopotamia: A Comparative Study*. Assen: Van Gorcum.

———. 2018. *Papyrus Amherst 63*. Münster: Ugarit-Verlag.

Tsukimoto, A. 1985. *Untersuchungen zur Totenpflege (Kispum) im Alten Mesopotamien*. Kevelaer: Neukirchener Verlag.

Turfa, J.M. 2012. *Divining the Etruscan World: The Brontoscopic Calendar and Religious Practice*. Cambridge: Cambridge University Press.

Turri, L. 2020. 'Gilgamesh, the (Super)Hero.' In *Receptions of the Ancient Near East in Popular Culture and Beyond*, edited by L. Verderame and A. Garcia-Ventura, 197–216. Atlanta: Lockwood Press.

Vanstiphout, H. 2003. *Epics of Sumerian Kings: The Matter of Aratta*. Atlanta: Society of Biblical Literature.

Veenhof, K.R. 1986. 'Cuneiform Archives: An Introduction.' In *Cuneiform Archives and Libraries: Papers Read at the 30e Rencontre Assyriologique Internationale, Leiden, 4–8 July 1983*, edited by K. R. Veenhof, 1–36. Leiden: Nederlands Instituut voor het Nabije Oosten.

Veldhuis, N. 2010. 'The Theory of Knowledge and the Practice of Celestial Divination.' In *Divination and Interpretation of Signs in the Ancient World*, edited by A. Annus, 77–91. Chicago: University of Chicago.

Verbrugghe, G.P., and J.M. Wickersham. 1996. *Berossos and Manetho, Introduced and Translated*. Ann Arbor: The University of Michigan Press.

Verderame, L. 2002. *Le Tavole 1-VI della Serie Astrologica Enūma Anu Enlil*. Messina: Di.Sc.A.M.

———. 2009. 'The Primeval Zodiac: Its Social, Religious, and Mythological Background.' In *Cosmology across Cultures*, edited by J.A. Rubiño-Martín, J.A. Belmonte, F. Prada, and A. Albert, 309: 151–56. San Francisco: ASP Conference Series.

Viano, M. 2021. 'Babylonian Hermeneutics and Heraclitus.' *Journal of Near Eastern Studies* 80 (2).

Virolleand, C. 1909. L'Astrologie chaldéenne: le livre intitulé 'Enuma (Anu ilu) Bel': Supplement. Paris: P. Geuthner.

Waerden, B.L. van der. 1953. 'History of the Zodiac.' *Archiv für Orientforschung* 26 (20): 216–30.

Waerzeggers, C. 2003. 'The Babylonian Revolts against Xerxes and the "End of Archives".' *Archiv für Orientforschung* 50: 150–73.

———. 2010. *The Ezida Temple of Borsippa: Priesthood, Cult, Archives*. Achaemenid History. Leiden: Nederlands Instituut voor het Nabije Oosten.

———. 2015. 'Babylonian Kingship in the Persian Period: Performance and Reception.' In *Exile and Return: The Babylonian Context*, edited by J. Stökl and C. Waerzeggers, 181–222. Berlin; Boston: De Gruyter.

Waerzeggers, C., and M. Jursa. 2008. 'On the Initiation of Babylonian Priests.' *Zeitschrift für Altorientalische und Biblische Rechtsgeschichte* 14: 1–38.

Walker, C., and M. Dick. 2001. *The Induction of the Cult Image in Ancient Mesopotamia: The Mesopotamian Mīs Pî Ritual*. Helsinki: Neo-Assyrian Text Corpus Project, Institute for Asian and African Studies, University of Helsinki.

Walls, N. 2001. *Desire, Discord, and Death: Approaches to Ancient Near Eastern Myth*. Boston: American Schools of Oriental Research.

Walton, J. 2018. *Ancient Near Eastern Thought and the Old Testament: Introducing the Conceptual World of the Hebrew Bible*. 2nd edn. Grand Rapids, MI: Baker Academic.

Wasserman, N. 2016. *Akkadian Love Literature of the Third and Second Millennium* BCE. 1st edn. Wiesbaden: Harrassowitz Verlag.

Watanabe, C.E. 1998. 'Symbolism of the Royal Lion Hunt in Assyria.' In *Intellectual Life of the Ancient Near East: Papers Presented at the 43rd RAI, Prague, July 1–5, 1996*, edited by J. Prosecky, 439–50. Prague: Academy of Sciences of the Czech Republic.

———. 2018. 'Composite Animals in Mesopotamia as Cultural Symbols.' In *Composite Artefacts in the Ancient Near East: Exhibiting an Imaginative Materiality, Showing a Genealogical Nature*, edited by S. di Paolo. Oxford: Archaeopress.

Waterfield, R., and A. Erskine. 2016. *Plutarch: Hellenistic, lives including Alexander the Great*. Oxford: Oxford University Press.

Weaver, A.M. 2004. 'The "Sin of Sargon" and Esarhaddon's Reconception of Sennacherib: A Study in Divine Will, Human Politics and Royal Ideology.' *Iraq* 66: 61–6.

Wee, J. 2018. 'Five Birds, Twelve Rooms, and the Seleucid Game of Twenty Squares.' In *Mesopotamian Medicine and Magic: Studies in Honor of Markham J. Geller*, edited by S. Panayotov and L. Vacín, 14:833–76. Leiden; Boston: Brill.

Weidner, E.F. 1941. 'Die Astrologische Serie Enûma Anu Enlil.' *Archiv für Orientforschung* 1941–1944: 172–95.

———. 1967. *Gestirn-Darstellungen auf babylonischen Tontafeln*, Vienna.

Weiher, E von. 1983. *Spätbabylonische Texte aus Uruk. Teil II*. Gebr. Mann Verlag

———. 1988. *Spätbabylonische Texte aus Uruk. Teil III*. Berlin.

———. 1993. *Spätbabylonische Texte aus Uruk. Teil IV*. Mainz am Rhein.

———. 1998. *Spätbabylonische Texte aus Uruk. Teil V*. Mainz am Rhein.

West, M.L. 1997. *The East Face of Helicon*. Oxford: Oxford University Press.

Westenholz, A. 2007. 'The Graeco-Babyloniaca Once Again.' *Zeitschrift für Assyriologie* 97: 262–313.

Westenholz, J.G. 1989. 'Enḫeduanna, En-priestess, Hen of Nanna, Spouse of Nanna'. In *DUMU-E$_2$-DUB-BA-A. Studies in Honor of Åke W. Sjöberg*. Occasional Publications of the Samuel Noah Kramer Fund 11, ed. Hermann Behrens, Darlene M. Loding, and Martha T. Roth, 539–56. Philadelphia: University Museum.

Wiggermann, F.A.M. 2000. 'Lamashtu, Daughter of Anu: A Profile.' In *Birth in Babylonia and the Bible: Its Mediterranean Setting*, edited by M. Stol, 217–52. Groningen: Styx Publications.

———. 2011. 'The Mesopotamian Pandemonium: A Provisional Census.' In *Demoni Mesopotamici, Studi e Materiali di Storia delle Religioni 77/2*, edited by L. Verderame, 298–322. Brescia: Morcelliana.

Wilcke, C. 2000. *Wer Las und Schrieb in Babylonien und Assyrien: Überlegungen zur Literalität im Alten Zweistromland: Vorgetragen in der Sitzung vom 4. Februar 2000:* Munich: Verlagder Bayerischen Akademie der Wissenschaften.

Winter, I. 2000. 'Babylonian Archaeologists of the(ir) Mesopotamian Past.' In *Proceedings of the First International Congress of the Archaeology of the Ancient Near East. Rome, May 18th–23rd 1998*, edited by P. Mattihiae, A. Enea, L. Peyronel, and F. Pinnock, 2:1785–1800. Rome: La Sapienza.

Wisnom, S. 2020. *Weapons of Words: Intertextual Competition in Babylonian Poetry. A Study of Anzû, Enūma Eliš, and Erra and Išum*. Leiden; Boston: Brill.

———. 2023. 'Dynamics of Repetition in Akkadian Literature.' In *The Shape of Stories: Narrative Structures in Cuneiform Literature*, edited by G. Konstantopoulos and S. Helle, 112–43. Leiden: Brill.

———. 2024. 'The Art of the Āšipu in Narrative Poetry.' In *Legitmising Magic: Strategies and Practices in Ancient Mesopotamia*, edited by N. Heeßel and E. Zomer, 146–75. Leiden: Brill.

Woods, C. 2010. 'The Earliest Mesopotamian Writing.' In *Visible Language: The Earliest Writing Systems*, 15–25. Chicago: Oriental Institute Museum Publications.

Worthington, M. 2012. *Principles of Akkadian Textual Criticism*. Berlin; Boston: De Gruyter.

Wunsch, C. 2022. *Judaeans by the Waters of Babylon: New Historical Evidence in Cuneiform Sources from Rural Babylonia*. Dresden: ISLET.

Zaia, S. 2015. 'State-Sponsored Sacrilege: "Godnapping" and Omission in Neo-Assyrian Inscriptions.' *Journal of Ancient Near Eastern History* 2 (1): 19–54.

———. 2018. 'My Brother's Keeper: Assurbanipal versus Šamaš-Šuma-Ukīn.' *Journal of Ancient Near Eastern History* 6: 19–52.

———. 2019. 'Kings, Priests, and Power in the Neo-Assyrian Period.' *Journal of Ancient Near Eastern Religions* 19 (1–2): 152–69.

Zamazalová, S. 2018. 'Mountains as Heroic Space in the Reign of Sargon II.' In *Neo-Assyrian Sources in Context: Thematic Studies on Texts, History, and Culture*, edited by S. Yamada, 185–213. Helsinki: Neo-Assyrian Text Corpus Project.

Zgoll, Annette. 1997. *Der Rechtsfall der En-ḫedu-Ana im Lied nin-me-šara*. Alter Orient und Altes Testament 246. Münster: Ugarit-Verlag.

Ziegler, N. 2011. 'Music, the Work of Professionals.' In *The Oxford Handbook of Cuneiform Culture*, edited by K. Radner and E. Robson, 288–312. Oxford: Oxford University Press.

———. 2016. 'Aqba-Hammu et le Début du Mythe d'Atram-Hasis.' *Revue d'assyriologie et d'archéologie Orientale* 110 (1): 107–26.

Zimmern, H. 1925. 'Assyrische Chemisch-Technische Rezepte, insbesondere für Herstellung Farbiger Glasierter Ziegel, in Umschrift und Übersetzung.' *Zeitschrift für Assyriologie* 36: 177–208.

Zisa, G. 2021. *The Loss of Male Sexual Desire in Ancient Mesopotamia: Niš Libbi Therapies*. Berlin: De Gruyter.

Zorzi, N. De. 2014. *La Serie Teratomantica Šumma Izbu: Testo, Tradizione, Orizzonti Culturali*. Vol. 2. Padua: S.A.R.G.O.N. Editrice e Libreria.

Zysk, K. 2020. 'Mesopotamian and Indian Physiognomy.' In *Visualizing the Invisible with the Human Body*, edited by J.C. Johnson and A. Stavru, 41–60. Boston: De Gruyter.

Notes

Preface

1 This description is inspired by the account of the destruction of Nineveh in the biblical book of Nahum (2: 1-7).

Introduction

1 State Archives of Assyria (henceforth SAA) 3 33.
2 This is according to Esarhaddon's interpretation of events, as given in his inscriptions (RINAP 4 Esarhaddon 1, col. i, line 8–col. ii, line 11; 6, col. i, lines 9b'–i 15'), and in the Bible (2 Kings 19:37; Isaiah 37:38).
3 Layard (1853, pp. 344–5).
4 RINAP 5 Ashurbanipal 220, col. i, line 5'.
5 Ibid., col. i, lines 10'–12'.
6 Ibid., col. i, lines 13'–18'.
7 RINAP 5 Ashurbanipal 2, col. v, lines 5–10.
8 RINAP 5 Ashurbanipal 11, col. viii, lines 10–14.
9 Ibid., col. i, line 120. For similar complaints about Shamash-shumu-ukin, see RINAP 5 Ashurbanipal 23, lines 108–9.
10 Ibid., col. iv, lines 133–7.
11 Ashurbanipal Library Colophon b, Hunger (1968, n. 318. pp. 97–8), RLAsb
12 SAA 16 19; Livingstone (2007, pp. 106–7).
13 Fincke (2021, plate CXCII); Oppenheim (1970, pp. 55–56) and Hunger (1968 n. 338, pp. 105–6).
14 SAA 10 101.
15 SAA 10 103, lines r. 1–4.
16 SAA 10 373, lines r. 11–r.e. 13.
17 Frame and George (2005, pp. 267–9), lines 8–13.

18 'Ninurta-gimilli, the son of the chief accountant, has completed the series and has been put (back) in irons. He is assigned to Banunu in the Succession Palace [=North Palace] and there is no work for him at present' – SAA 11 156, lines 8–13.
19 CT 22 1, see Frame and George (2005, pp. 280–81), lines 25 and 37.
20 SAA 10 177.
21 SAA 10 160, lines 36–43.
22 SAA 10 164.
23 SAA 10 161.
24 SAA 10 167.
25 SAA 10 180.
26 SAA 10 171.
27 SAA 10 58.
28 SAA 10 289.
29 SAA 10 143.
30 SAA 10 320.

1. *The Scribal Art*

1 SAA 16 28, lines 3–r. 4.
2 SAA 10 155.
3 ETCSL 1.8.2.3. For a print edition and translation see Vanstiphout (2003).
4 Ibid., lines 502–4.
5 Ibid., line 540.
6 Ibid., lines 569 and 577.
7 *Shumma Sin ina tamartishu*, Tablet 1, lines 68–71; SAA 8 304, lines 3–r. 4.
8 Also quoted in SAA 8 107, lines 6–9.
9 Leemans (1960, pp. 39–40).
10 Radau (1908, pp. 142, xvii).
11 SAA 7 24, lines r. 2, r. 1, 20, r.6, r.5.
12 SAA 14 8–14, lines 174–7.
13 SAA 4 321, lines r. 4–5; SAA 4 322, lines r. 6–7.
14 The works of Enheduanna comprise: the *Exaltation of Inanna* (ETCSL 4.07.2), the hymn known as *Inanna C* (ETCSL 4.07.3), the collection

of *Temple Hymns* (ETCSL 4.80.1), and potentially also *Inanna and Ebih* (ETCSL 1.3.2) and the hymn known as a *balbale to Inanna* B (ETCSL 4.13.02), though these are debated. See Helle (2023) for a print translation of the first three. For print editions of the others see Zgoll (1997, in German) and Hallo and van Dijk (1968, in English) for the *Exaltation*, Sjöberg (1975) for *Inanna C*, Sjöberg and Bergmann (1969) for the *Temple Hymns*, Attinger (1998 and 2011/2019) for *Inanna and Ebih*, and Westenholz (1989) for the *balbale to Inanna* B.

15 Known by its incipit *Ura* = *Hubullu* OB (Old Babylonian) and MB (Middle Babylonian) versions can be found on DCCLT under thematic word lists (OB Nippur *Ura* 1–6 and MB *Ura* 1–15).

16 SAA 10 374. Which king is unclear, it could be either Ashurbanipal or Esarhaddon.

17 SAA 16 19 lines 1–5.

18 Fincke (2021, plate CXCII); Oppenheim (1970, pp. 55–6 and Hunger (1968 n. 338, pp. 105–6).

19 K8005+, transliterated and translated by Livingstone (2007, pp. 115–18).

20 K143, published as ms. A by Lambert (1974a).

21 See for example the texts in Cavigneaux (1981).

22 Hunger (1968, pp. 105–6 n. 338), translation following Livingstone (2007, p. 113).

23 Mitto et al. (2022), 0.0 on eBL, lines 1–4.

24 The *Sumerian King List*, ETCSL 2.1.1, lines 1–39 and 430. Thanks to the tablet being broken, one of the numbers is missing from the final tally. For print edition see Glassner (2004, pp. 117–26).

25 Verbrugghe and Wickersham (1996, p. 44), F1.

26 Mitto et al. (2022), 0.0 on eBL, line 6.

27 For example in *Erra and Ishum* I 162, see Cagni (1969, pp. 76–7).

2. *The Power of the Gods*

1 For the inscription describing this event see Pongratz-Leisten (1994, pp. 207–8).

2 RINAP 3 Sennacherib 223, lines 43–54.

3 SAA 20 1–11.

4 Lambert (1997).

5 The *Marduk Prophecy*, Foster (2005, pp. 388–91) for English translation, and Borger (1971, pp. 5–20) for original edition.

6 *Atrahasis*, lines 11–12, Lambert and Millard (1999, p. 43).

7 *Enlil and Ninlil*, ETCSL 1.2.1. For an updated edition see Attinger (2015/2019).

8 *Enki and Ninhursaga*, ETCSL 1.1.1. For an updated edition see Attinger (2011/2015).

9 Online edition Heinrich (2021), 1.1 on eBL. For print translation, Foster (2005, pp. 436–86) and print edition Lambert (2013, pp. 45–134).

10 *Enuma Elish*, Tablet VII, lines 146–7, Heinrich (2021), 1.1 on eBL.

11 CT 24 50, translated in Lambert (1975, pp. 197–8).

12 The god list *An* = *Anum*, Lambert and Winters (2023).

13 SAA 3 3, lines r. 14, r. 13, and o. 13; SAA 3 13, lines r. 6–8.

14 SAA 9 7, lines r. 7–9.

15 SAA 9 1, col. i, lines 18–19, 8'–10; SAA 9 2, col. ii, lines 15–16.

16 See the Archaeological Complex of Faida project website: https://www.terradininive.com/projects/the-archaeological-complex-of-faida/?lang=en.

17 For translation of *Atrahasis*, see Foster (2005, pp. 227–80); for edition see Lambert and Millard (1999); Dalley (2000, pp. 1–38).

18 *Inanna and Enki*, ETCSL 1.3.1.

19 Foster (2005, pp. 555–78) or Dalley (2000, pp. 205–27) for translation, for edition see Annus (2001).

20 *Atrahasis*, Tablet III, col. viii, lines 15–16. Translation Foster (2005, p. 253), edition Lambert and Millard (1999, pp. 104–5).

21 Based on the pseudo-Platonic text *Epinomis* by Philip of Opus, 986E–987D, Lamb (1955, pp. 464–9), who discusses their origins in Egypt and Syria.

22 For Enlil see e.g. Cohen (1988, p. 138, line 71). Ashur 'whose heart is inscrutable', *Hymn to Ashur*, line 17. Translation Foster (2005, p. 817), originally published as SAA 3 1.

23 *Ludlul Bel Nemeqi*, Tablet I, lines 29–32, translation Foster (2005, p. 395); edition Oshima (2014, p. 81). See now eBL 2.2.

24 Ibid., Tablet II, lines 34–37, translation following Jiménez (2019, pp. 79–81).
25 *Babylonian Theodicy*, lines 72–5 translation Foster (2005, p. 917), edition Oshima (2014, p. 155). See now eBL 2.1.
26 *Shurpu*, Tablet II, lines 5–128, Reiner (1958, pp. 13–16).
27 Ibid., Tablet II, line 6.
28 Ibid., Tablet III, line 15.
29 Ibid., Tablet III, lines 3–175.
30 NYF 3, r. col. vi, lines 9–12 in Debourse (2022, p. 133).
31 SAA 13 175.
32 SAA 13 6.
33 See e.g. SAA 10 96 lines r.1–s. 3.
34 Borger (1973, p. 164), col. i, lines 13–14.
35 SAA 13 25 and 13 26.
36 SAA 13 138.
37 SAA 13 128, lines 13–14, r. 4–8.
38 SAA 13 157.
39 For the text of this ritual see Walker and Dick (2001).
40 Lines 181–4 (Walker and Dick 2001, p. 66). The whole passage spans lines 179–86.
41 SAA 1 54 and 55.

3. Magic and Witchcraft

1 SAA 10 200, line r. 5'. The tablet is broken and 'loss of flesh' is restored by Parpola in LAS 167 (1983, p. 156) but we will never know for sure.
2 Ibid., lines r. 6'–7'.
3 SAA 10 201.
4 ETCSL 1.8.2.4, *Enmerkar and Ensuhgirana*. For print edition see Vanstiphout (2003).
5 Geller (2018, pp. 292–312).
6 SAA 10 227, lines r. 15–16.
7 Corpus of Mesopotamian Anti-witchcraft Rituals online (CMAwRo henceforth), 11.3.1, line 3.

8 Ibid., lines 13–16.
9 Ibid., lines 21–25.
10 Leviticus 16:21–2
11 CMAwRo 11.1.1, lines 1–8.
12 Ibid., lines 9–17.
13 CMAwRo 11.3.2 MS E = Maul and Strauß (2011, pp. 34–55, line 6'). The text is from the city of Ashur rather than Ashurbanipal's library.
14 SAA 10 258.
15 SAA 10 263.
16 SAA 10 202, lines 5–12.
17 Ibid., lines r. 9–11.
18 SAA 10 228, lines r. 10–15.
19 SAA 10 255, lines 8–13.
20 CMAwRo 8.3, lines 103–111.
21 *Maqlu*, Tablet 1, lines 75–86. See Abusch (2015) for a print edition. An online edition is also available on ORACC.
22 SAA 16 63, lines r. 26–7.
23 *Middle Assyrian Laws* §47, Roth (1997, pp. 172–3).
24 One intriguing exception is a ritual for ensuring flourishing trade at a tavern, see Panayotov (2013).
25 SAA 10 15, lines 7–r. 3.
26 SAA 10 188, lines r. 3–4.
27 SAA 18 85.
28 SAA 10 244, lines r. 7–9.
29 SAA 10 17, lines r. 1–5.
30 SAA 9 1, col. v, lines 3–7.
31 SAA 2 6, §75, lines 568–9, §64, lines 532–3, §87, lines 603–5.
32 SAA 10 199.
33 SAA 2 8, lines 9–11.
34 *Maqlu*, Tablet 1, lines 1–19.
35 See the texts in Caplice (1974).
36 Caplice (1974, p. 14, no. 1).
37 Caplice (1974, p. 15, no. 4).
38 Heeßel (2002, pp. 55–69, lines 106–9.).
39 *Utukku Lemnutu*, Tablet 13, line 8, Geller (2016, p. 437).

40 SAA 3 32, lines r. 6, 3.
41 *Utukku Lemnutu*, Tablet 8, lines 5–9, Geller (2016, p.289).
42 Ibid. Tablet 8, line 3, Geller (2016, p. 288)
43 Ibid. Tablet 8, lines 4, Geller (2016, p. 288).
44 *The Diagnostic Handbook*, lines 20-3, Scurlock (2014, pp. 207 and 209).
45 SAA 10 109, lines r. 1–4.
46 Ibid., lines r. 6–7.
47 SAA 10 238, lines 10–r. 12.
48 SAA 10 309.
49 *Utukku Lemnutu*, Tablet 8, lines 27–51, Geller (2016, pp. 295–301).
50 Ibid., Tablet 8, lines 10–23 Geller (2016, pp. 289-93).
51 Ibid., Tablet 3, lines 59–60, Geller (2016, p. 102).
52 SAA 10 187, lines 10–15.
53 SAA 10 293.
54 SAA 10 224, lines r. 4–6.
55 SAA 10 226, lines 16–21.
56 SAA 10 226, lines 16–20.
57 SAA 10 227, lines r. 15–16.

4. *The Treatment of Disease*

1 SAA 10 315, lines 7–19.
2 SAA 10 196, lines 14–r. 6.
3 Ibid. lines r. 14–e.1
4 SAA 10 43, lines 7–15.
5 The *Chronicle* texts tell us simply 'the king executed a large number of his nobles' – Glassner (2004, pp. 202–3, no. 16, line 29; pp. 208–9, no. 18, line 30).
6 SAA 10 316, lines r. 7–8.
7 Ibid., lines 16–20. Translation modified.
8 SAA 10 215, lines 8–10.
9 SAA 10 320, lines r. 9–e. 2.
10 SAA 10 321.
11 SAA 10 326; 10 217.
12 SAA 10 217, lines 12–r. 2.

13 SAA 10 314, lines b.e. 10'–11'.

14 http://oracc.museum.upenn.edu/asbp/ninmed/.

15 Steinert (2018, pp. 209–91).

16 SAA 10 320, lines r. 1–5.

17 See Scurlock for edition (2014, pp. 7–271), henceforth DPS.

18 Schmidtchen (2018, p. 317), line 52.

19 Lenzi (2008, pp. 141–2), line r. 17.

20 George (1991, pp. 142–3), line 2.

21 Ibid., lines 21 and 14.

22 Ibid., (pp. 144–5), line 50. A creaking door could also signify witchcraft, as discussed in Chapter 3.

23 DPS 9, line 46.

24 DPS 22, lines 10–11.

25 *Shumma alu*, 12.73, in Freedman (1998, p. 197); DPS 3.97.

26 DPS 33, line 114.

27 DPS 26 lines 18', 20'–21', and 75'.

28 DPS 26, line 30'.

29 *Atrahasis*, Tablet III, col. vii, lines 3–4, for translation Foster (2005, p. 253), and for edition Lambert and Millard (1999, pp. 102–3).

30 Farber (2014, p. 147), lines 23–31.

31 Ibid., lines 32–6.

32 Dossin (1978, pp. 188–9, no. 129), lines 11–20.

33 Stadhouders (2018, p. 166), lines r. 9–14.

34 YOS 10.56, col. iii, lines 3–5; DPS 22, line 65.

35 SpTU 1.47, lines 3–5, Scurlock and Andersen (2005, p. 16).

36 *Shurpu*, Tablet II, lines 98–103, Reiner (1958, pp. 16–17).

37 Farber (1990, pp. 320–21), translation by author.

38 SAA 10 323; 10 324.

39 Scurlock (2014, pp. 380–82).

40 Ibid., col. ii, line 53'.

41 SAA 10 328, lines 15–18.

42 Laws 215–217, see Roth (1997, p. 123).

43 See recent edition of IGI 1–3 and BAM 520 in Geller and Panayotov (2020, pp. 56–205).

44 IGI 2, line 56', Geller and Panayotov (2020, p. 122).
45 Scurlock (2014, pp. 417–21), lines 27–35.
46 IGI 2, line 118', Geller and Panayotov (2020, p. 135).
47 SAA 10 315, lines 20–r.e. 18.
48 Ibid., lines 8–9.
49 SAA 10 241, lines r. 1–2.
50 Ibid., lines r. 6–13.
51 For example see BAM 107 and 106, Scurlock (2014, pp. 421–2).
52 DPS 33, line 24.
53 DPS 33, line 103.
54 DPS 33, lines 53–4.
55 DPS 33, line 55.
56 SAA 10 318.
57 BAM 318, col. iii, line 19; BAM 311, line 68.
58 Geller and Panayotov (2020, pp. 147–8), lines 196'-8'.
59 SpTU 2.50, Scurlock (2014, p. 363), lines 1–4.
60 Scurlock (2014, p. 290), lines 30, 26.
61 *Aluzinnu*, lines 40'–41'. For translation see Foster (2005, pp. 939–41). For edition see Ebeling (1931, pp. 9–19).
62 *Macbeth*, Act IV, Scene 1, lines 14–15, from the Folger Shakespeare (p. 120).
63 Böck (2011, p. 693), lines 1–7.
64 Hunger (1968, pp. 98–9); translation Böck (2011, pp. 692–3).
65 RINAP 5 Ashurbanipal 3, col. vi, lines 34–5.
66 SAA 10 212, line 12.
67 SAA 10 277.
68 DPS 18, line 1.
69 DPS 23, line 1.
70 SAA 3 33.
71 SAA 10 295.
72 Ibid., lines 11–12.
73 Laws 215–17, Roth (1997, p. 123).
74 Ibid., Law 218.
75 Ibid., Law 219.
76 SAA 7 24, lines r. 8–9.

77 Steinert (2012).

78 DPS 36–9.

5. Reading the Signs

1 Adapted from SAA 4 282.

2 Adapted from SAA 4 262, line 7.

3 The Amherst Papyrus 63, van der Toorn (2018, pp. 217–39).

4 RINAP 5 Ashurbanipal 11, col. iii, lines 72–81.

5 RINAP 5 Ashurbanipal 242, lines 24–5; 244, lines 19–20; 245, lines 19–20; 254, lines 46–8; 262, lines 21–2; 263, line 27.

6 They can be found in SAA 4.

7 SAA 4 18 lists eleven diviners.

8 SAA 4 308, lines r. 5'–7'.

9 SAA 3 33.

10 RINAP 5 Ashurbanipal 220, col. i, line 15'.

11 *Pan takalti*, Tablet 5, omens 35, 38, and 40, Koch-Westenholz (2000, pp. 332–3).

12 SAA 10 177, lines 15–r. 5.

13 YOS 10 42, line 16. Goetze (1947, pls. LXXVI–LXXVII).

14 Foster (2005, p. 209), lines 14–16 and Goetze (1968, p. 26), lines 1–16. For the importance of cedar see also Lambert (1998, p. 145), line 17; Anor (2015, vol. 2, pp. 15–16), line 18.

15 BBR 1, lines 4–5, Lambert (1998, p. 144) and Anor (2015, pp. 11–12).

16 The following description of the interpretation of the entrails is based on the report of the extispicy SAA 4 282.

17 *Prayer to the gods of extispicy*, Starr (1983, pp. 30 and 37), line 16.

18 SAA 4 280 and 281.

19 SAA 4 283.

20 SAA 4 285, 287, 288, and 290.

21 SAA 4 280, 281, 282, 283, 286, and 291.

22 SAA 4 283.

23 SAA 4 84–7.

24 SAA 4 299.

6. Messages in the Stars

1 SAA 10 51, lines 10–r. 11, r. 21–s. 2.

2 SAA 7 1 lists seven astrologers (col. i, lines 1–8), nine exorcists (col. i, lines 9–18), five diviners (col. ii, lines 1–6), nine physicians (col. ii, lines 7–16), six lamentation priests (col. i, lines r. 1–7), three augurs (col. i, lines r. 8–11), three Egyptian scholars (col. i, line r. 12–col. ii, line 2), and three Egyptian scribes (col. ii, lines r. 3–6).

3 Oppenheim (1974).

4 Ibid., lines 12, 35, and 11 respectively.

5 Ibid., lines 38–42.

6 *Shumma izbu*, recent edition by de Zorzi (2014, in Italian), see Leichty (1970) for an older English edition.

7 SAA 8 287, lines 1–4.

8 SAA 8 238, line 1; 237, lines 1–3.

9 e.g. SAA 8 349, and many others.

10 SAA 8 27, lines 1–5.

11 SAA 10 72, lines 9–10, r. 13–17, r. 18–19.

12 For the difficulty of observing Mercury see also SAA 10 50.

13 Reiner and Pingree (1975, p. 29, omen 1).

14 Ibid. (p. 33, omen 10).

15 For another text describing the cycles of Venus in the library, MUL.APIN, Tablet II, lines 44–8, see Hunger and Steele (2019, pp. 79–80).

16 SAA 8 83, line r.3.

17 Reiner and Pingree (1975, p. 34, omen 11). This is the reading of Ms. C - other tablets predict quarrels!

18 See Verderame (2002, p. 9) for edition.

19 SAA 8 69, lines 3–5.

20 van Soldt (1995, pp. 31, III 39).

21 Gehlken (2012, pp. 18-19), lines 21–5.

22 Ibid., (p. 19), line 26.

23 Ibid. (p. 44), lines 19'–21'.

24 Ibid., (p. 147), lines r. 23'–5'.

25 SAA 8 82, lines r. 3–4; 95, lines r. 1–7.

26 Reiner and Pingree (1981, pp. 40–41, III 8). 'The fox' is another name for Mars.

27 Reiner and Pingree (1975, p. 39, omen 22).

28 *Enuma Anu Enlil* 50, III 7a, Reiner (1981, pp. 40–1).

29 SAA 10 104, lines r. 2–13.

30 Ibid., line s.2.

31 SAA 10 206, lines r. 4'–10'.

32 SAA 10 262.

33 *The Eclipse Hemerology*, edition Livingstone (2013, pp. 195-198), lines 7–8.

34 SAA 8 82, line 10.

35 SAA 8 316, lines 3–4.

36 SAA 8 300, line r. 15; 336, line r. 11.

37 SAA 8 300, lines r. 8–10; 336, lines r. 4–8. Another letter from nine years later quotes the same prediction, SAA 8 4 lines 4–7. SAA 8 535 also reports a decision for Ur for an eclipse in Sivan (line r. 13), though it cannot be dated, and quotes omens for the fifteenth day instead of the fourteenth (line r.9).

38 SAA 8 316, lines r. 4–5;

39 Ibid., lines r. 1–3.

40 SAA 10.90, lines r. 10'–11'.

41 Ibid., lines r. 13'-14'.

42 SAA 8 250, lines r. 5–8.

43 Keynes (1956, p. 277).

44 See Hunger and Steele (2019) for edition.

45 Ibid., Tablet II, col. iii, line 42.

46 e.g. SAA 8 382, line 7 and SAA 10 45, lines r. 11–15.

47 Ptolemy, *Almagest* III.7, Toomer (1984, p. 166).

48 ADsD, AD-567, line r. 21' and AD-322D, line 4.

49 SpTU 1 94 (Hunger 1976), also available on ORACC within the GKAB project (http://oracc.org/cams/gkab/P348515).

50 ADsD, AD-330A, line r. 11'.

51 SAA 10 104, lines 1–2, quoting the omen series (Virolleaud, 1909, p. 63, IV line 22).

52 KUB VIII 35, lines r. 9–10, quoted in Koch-Westenholz (1995, p. 172).

53 BM 3224, col. ii, lines 13'–15', quoted in Rochberg (2004, p. 62).

54 Rochberg (1998, pp. 51–5, text 1).
55 Ibid., (pp. 79–81, text 9).
56 VAT 7847 + AO 6448, published in Weidner (1967, pp. 33–4) and Thureau-Dangin (1922, plate XXV).
57 Ossendrijver (2016).
58 SpTU 3, 91, von Weiher (1988, pp. 152–60), and online at GKAB as P348695.
59 SpTU 2, 33, von Weiher (1983, pp. 146–8), and online at GKAB as P348638.
60 SpTU 2, 45, lines 47 and 156–8, von Weiher (1983, pp. 185–9). TCL 6, 2, Thureau-Dangin (1922), also available online at GKAB as P363675.
61 Dropsie College text, line 1 (Sachs 1976, p. 393). The very last one we know of dates from AD 79/80 and is from Uruk (Hunger and de Jong, 2014).

7. Literature

1 *Gilgamesh*, Tablet XII, lines 148–53. Translations of Gilgamesh are based on Andrew George's edition, online with updates at eBL, with modifications by the present author. The print critical edition and commentary is George (2003). Other accessible translations include George's Penguin translation (2020) and Helle (2021).
2 *Gilgamesh*, Tablet XII, lines 146–47.
3 ETCSL 1.8.1.4., *Gilgamesh, Enkidu, and the Netherworld*, lines 302–3. In the updated edition by Gadotti (2014) it is lines 305–6.
4 George (2018).
5 *Gilgamesh*, Tablet V, line 303.
6 Ibid., Tablet VI, lines 46–79.
7 Ibid., Tablet I, line 269.
8 Ibid., Tablet VIII, line 59.
9 Ibid., Tablet XI, lines 207–8.
10 Ibid., Tablet X, lines 304–15.
11 This is the composition known as 'Advice to a Prince', lines 2–3 and 5. See Foster (2005, p. 867) for translation and Lambert (1996, pp. 112–13) for edition.
12 Parpola (1987, pp. 260–1, line 13).

13 *The Gilgamesh Letter*, lines 20–22, Foster (2005, pp. 1017–19) for translation and Gurney (1957) for edition.

14 Ms JJ of Tablet IX in George's edition (2003, pp. 409–10) bears the last five lines of the Ashurbanipal colophon type d (Hunger 1968, pp. 97–8, no. 319).

15 ETCSL 1.8.1.4, *Gilgamesh, Enkidu and the Netherworld*. See Gadotti (2014) for a print edition.

16 *Descent of Ishtar*, lines 5–11. For translation, Foster (2005, pp. 498–505). For edition, Lapinkivi (2010).

17 ETCSL 1.8.1.5. All versions including the OB and Sumerian versions can be found in George (2020).

18 The story can be read in Dalley (2000, pp. 1–38) and Foster (2005, pp. 227–80). See Lambert and Millard (1999) for a full edition.

19 *Atrahasis*, Tablet III, col. vi, lines 7–8.

20 SAA 8 461, lines r. 1–4. From Lambert and Millard (1999, p. 28).

21 ETCSL 5.6.1. See Alster (1974) for print edition.

22 Ibid., lines 126, 243, and 220.

23 *School Days*, edition Kramer (1949, p. 211).

24 ETCSL 1.6.2. For a print edition see van Dijk (1983).

25 ETCSL 1.6.1. For a print edition see Cooper (1978).

26 ETCSL 1.6.2, lines 96–108.

27 Ibid. lines 168–81.

28 Ibid., lines 292–5.

29 Ibid., line 304.

30 These stories can be found in Foster (2005, pp. 931–6 and 939–41). For full editions see Ottervanger (2016) and Ebeling (1931, pp. 9–19).

31 'Why Do You Curse Me?', Foster (2005, pp. 937–8) and George (1993, pp. 63–72).

8. *The Waging of War*

1 This is all portrayed in relief BM 124801,c.

2 RINAP 3 Sennacherib 15, col. iv, lines 1'–14'; 16, col. iv, lines 22–37; 17, col. iii, lines 66–81; 22, col. iii, lines 37b–49; 23, col. iii, lines 33–42; 140, lines r. 19–21.

3 RINAP 2 Sargon II 65, lines 42–50.

4 The *Marduk Prophecy*, translation Foster (2005, pp. 388–91), edition Borger (1971, pp. 5–20).

5 For the claim to have found an inscription of Hammurabi, see RIBo 7 Nabonidus 16, col. ii, lines 20–27, col. iii, lines 27–31. For Naram-Sin, see RIBo 7 Nabonidus 23, col. ii, lines 2'–12'. See also RIBo 7 Nabonidus 32, col. i, lines 11–15 where he claims to have read inscriptions by the Ur III period kings Ur-Namma and Shulgi.

6 Published in Novotny and Jeffers (2018), Jeffers and Novotny (2023), Jeffers, Novotny, and Frame (2023), and online at RINAP 5.

7 RINAP 5 Ashurbanipal 3. The events were first written down much closer to the time, however, as they were inscribed on objects dedicated to the goddess Ishtar (RINAP 200–206) – for instance, copies of these inscriptions tell us that thirty lines were inscribed on a golden bow given to Ishtar in her city of Arbela (RINAP 5/2, text no. 203), and these accounts were copied on later prisms.

8 RINAP 5 Ashurbanipal 3, col. iv, lines 68–79.

9 Ibid., col. iv, line 88–col. v, line 15.

10 Ibid., col. v, lines 62–4.

11 Ibid., col. v, lines 79–86.

12 Ibid., col. v, lines 87–96, translation modified.

13 For the omens see Freedman (2017, p. 27), line 23.

14 Freedman (2017, p. 27), line 29.

15 These are captions written for reliefs that no longer survive – see RINAP 5 Ashurbanipal 161, col. i, lines 1'–3' for spitting on Teumman's head and col. iii, lines 18'–23' for the New Year festival events.

16 The relief in question is BM 124920.

17 See SAA 3, 31, lines 12'–13', where Livingstone restores 'I will not [sleep until] I have come and din[ed] in the centre of Nineveh!'

18 Novotny and Jeffers (2018), RINAP 5/1, text no. 50 with figure 19.

19 And in the annals – RINAP 5 Ashurbanipal 3, col. vi, lines 79–85.

20 Also described in RINAP 5 Ashurbanipal 3, col. vi, lines 71–4.

21 Ibid., col. vi, lines 75–6.

22 RINAP 5 Ashurbanipal 94, col. iii, lines 16'–19'.

23 RINAP 5 Ashurbanipal 11, col. iii, lines 100b–106.

24 Ibid., col. iii, line 105 for the quote, col. vi, lines 11–15 for the bribes.

25 Ibid., col. iii, lines 130–35.
26 Ibid., col. iv, lines 41–5.
27 Ibid., col. iv, lines 46–63.
28 RINAP 5 Ashurbanipal 244, line 20; Ashurbanipal 245, line 20.
29 RINAP 5 Ashurbanipal 11, col. iv, lines 135–7.
30 Ibid., col. v, lines 1–14.
31 Ibid., col. v, lines 104–12.
32 Ibid., col. v, line 113–col. vi, line 26.
33 Ibid., col. vi, lines 71–2.
34 Ibid., col. vi, lines 74–6.
35 Ibid., col. vi, lines 77–96; col. vii, lines 9–15.
36 Ibid., col. vii, lines 32–3.
37 Ibid., col. vii, line 35.
38 Ibid., col. vii, lines 28–37 for the whole episode.
39 Ibid., col. vii, lines 38–50, for the quote see line 46.
40 Ibid., col. x, lines 6–16, for the quote see lines 15–16.
41 SAA 21 65.
42 Ibid., lines 16–17.
43 Ibid., lines r. 5'–13'.
44 Ibid., lines r. 18'–20'.
45 SAA 21 122.
46 e.g. SAA 21 59; 60.
47 SAA 21 120, lines 14–16.
48 SAA 21 4.
49 SAA 21 3.
50 SAA 21 5; 7; 8.
51 SAA 4 281; 270,.
52 e.g. SAA 4 4; 5; 18; 23.
53 SAA 4 24; 57.
54 SAA 4 31; 43; 48–51.
55 SAA 4 77.
56 SAA 10 111, lines 5–8.
57 Ibid., lines 15–16.
58 e.g. RINAP 4 Esarhaddon 1, col. iii, lines 59–61; SAA 10 112, lines 8–11.

59 SAA 10 112, line 12.
60 Ibid., lines 7–8.
61 Ibid., lines 13–18.
62 e.g. RINAP 5 Ashurbanipal 3, col. i, lines 6–14.
63 RINAP 5 Ashurbanipal 9, col. i, lines 24–6; 11, col. i, lines 31–4; cf. 220, col. i, lines 10'–11'.
64 RINAP 5 Ashurbanipal 9, col. i, lines 30–31.
65 Frame and George (2005, pp. 267–9), line 9.
66 Diodorus Siculus II 21.8; 23.1–28.8.

9. *Lamentation*

1 RINAP 5 Ashurbanipal 11, col. iv, lines 77–91.
2 Ibid., col. iv, lines 70–76.
3 SAA 7 1, lines r. i. 1–7.
4 SAA 13 128.
5 SAA 13 138.
6 SAA 13 134.
7 SAA 10 338, lines r. 3–7.
8 ETCSL 2.1.5. For print edition see Cooper (1983).
9 Ibid., lines 196–206.
10 The laments for Ur, Sumer and Ur, Nippur, Eridu, and Uruk. See ETCSL 2.2.2–6. For print editions see Samet (2014), Michalowski (1989), Tinney (1996), Green (1978), and Green (1984).
11 ETCSL 2.2.3.
12 ETCSL 2.2.3, line 64.
13 As is the refrain sung in and after the first verse: ibid., lines 2, 113.
14 ETCSL 2.2.3, line 86; RINAP 5 Ashurbanipal 11, col. vi, lines 70–76.
15 ETCSL 2.2.3, lines 364–70. Translation by author.
16 Ibid., line 457.
17 Ibid., lines 493–511. Rather than acting as a collective, various individual gods are named.
18 e.g. 'The bull in his fold', see Cohen (1988, pp. 157 and 167), lines 84–92.

19 Editions and translations of many of these can be found in Cohen (1988).

20 Cohen (1988, pp. 101 and 111), lines 143–57.

21 SAA 10 338 and 339.

22 A good English translation can be found in Foster (2005, pp. 880–911). For full edition, see Cagni (1969).

23 *Erra and Ishum*, Tablet II, Pericope C2 lines 52'–59'. Translations are from Foster (2005, pp. 880–911).

24 Ibid., Tablet III, line 36.

25 Ibid., Tablet IV, lines 76–86.

26 Ibid., Tablet IV, lines 121–4.

27 Ibid., Tablet IV, line 129.

28 Ibid., Tablet V, lines 53–6.

29 Ibid., Tablet V, lines 57–8.

30 Part of an anti-witchcraft ritual. Translation Foster (2005, p. 684), lines 33–43. For the whole ritual see Abusch et. al. (2016, pp. 230–46, text 8.28) where this passage is lines 49–58.

31 SAA 10 180.

32 SAA 10 294, lines r. 11–12.

33 RINAP 5 Ashurbanipal 185, line r. 3.

34 Ibid., lines r. 7–13.

35 *Babylonian Theodicy*, lines 256–7, Foster (2005, pp. 914–22, quoted section is from p. 920), for edition and another translation see Oshima (2013). See now eBL 2.1.

36 RINAP 5 Ashurbanipal 11, col. iv, lines 77–91.

37 From ritual 9 in Maul (1988, p. 53–4).

38 The line (15.f) reads 'He stood before my lifted hands, hear my prayer!', which is likely to be an error (Maul 1988, pp. 175–6).

39 *Ershahunga* no. 26, lines 1'f–17'f, Maul (1988, p. 176). Translation by author.

10. *A Day in the Life of Ashurbanipal*

1 The remnants of the dream come from an extispicy report SAA 4 316, but its fragmentary nature is due to the state of the tablet rather than Ashurbanipal's memory.

2 e.g. SAA 4 202, another extispicy report which may concern one of Ashurbanipal's dreams while he was crown prince.

3 Butler (1998, pp. 253 and 291), lines 7–12.

4 SAA 21 124, lines 6–8.

5 Oppenheim (1956, p. 271).

6 Ibid., pp. 265–6.

7 Ibid., p. 289

8 Ibid., p. 273.

9 Ibid., pp. 280, 279.

10 Ibid., p. 287.

11 Ibid., p. 277.

12 Ibid., p. 275.

13 Ibid., p. 287.

14 Translated in Foster (2005, pp. 751–2). See also Butler (1998, pp. 274–6, 298).

15 SAA 10 298.

16 RINAP 5 Ashurbanipal 14, line 8'; RINAP 5 Ashurbanipal 187, line 6'.

17 RINAP 5 Ashurbanipal 58, line 2.

18 SAA 20 18.

19 Livingstone (2013, p. 36), line 20.

20 Ibid., p. 35, line 9.

21 Ibid., p. 169, lines 69–71.

22 SAA 10 61, lines r. 2–13.

23 Livingstone (2013, p. 111), line 16.

24 SAA 10 6, lines r. 11–19.

25 SAA 20 9–11.

26 Livingstone (2013, pp. 204–5), lines 39–44.

27 SAA 13 19–22.

28 SAA 21 111.

29 SAA 21 101.

30 SAA 21 124, lines 18–21.

31 Ibid., lines r. 1–11.

32 SAA 21 66; 43, lines 5–11; 53; 55.

33 SAA 10 270. It is not specified what has appeared in the palace, but an infestation is perhaps the most likely.

34 Ibid., lines r. 5-6. Probably the king addressed is Esarhaddon.

35 Caplice (1965, 1, 2, 6; 1970, 38, Colophon A).
36 SAA 13 166.
37 *Alamdimmu*, edited by Böck (2000).
38 *Alamdimmu*, Tablet 2, line 90, Böck (2000, pp. 80–81). Translation Cale Johnson, BabMed primary source reader from the Physiognomy and Ekphrasis conference (16–17 February 2016; Berlin).
39 Ibid., Tablet 2, line 117, Böck (2000, p. 83). Translation Cale Johnson.
40 VAT 7525, col. iii, line 11. Translation Cale Johnson, edition Köcher (1957–8, p. 66).
41 VAT 7525, col. i, lines 15–16. Translation Cale Johnson, edition Köcher (1957, p. 63).
42 *Shumma alu*, Tablet 44, lines 4', 14', 16'–17', 21', Freedman (2017, pp. 34–35).
43 e.g. ibid., Tablet 59, line 2, Freedman (2017, p. 125).
44 Ibid., Tablet 60, line 1, Freedman (2017, p. 135).
45 Ibid., Tablet 58, line 26' and alternative excerpt line 25, Freedman (2017, pp. 113 and 117).
46 SAA 10 127.
47 *Shumma alu*, Tablet 44, lines 43'–44', Freedman (2017, p. 36).
48 *Shumma izbu*, Tablet XI, lines 97'-139', edition de Zorzi (2014, pp. 655–64), an older edition with English translation is Leichty (1970, pp. 138–41).
49 *Shumma izbu*, Tablet XXI, lines 14-19, de Zorzi (2014, pp. 845-6); Leichty (1970, p. 186).
50 *Shumma izbu*, Tablet VI, de Zorzi (2014, pp. 503–21); Leichty (1970, pp. 84–90).
51 *Shumma izbu*, Tablet X, line 82: de Zorzi (2014, p. 624), Leichty (1970, p. 128), line 73'.
52 SAA 10 120.
53 *Shumma izbu*, Tablet IX, lines 33', 24' and 25': de Zorzi (2014, pp. 795–6, 599), Leichty (1970, pp. 178, lines 13', 14', and 24', but the tablets were not yet fully reconstructed).
54 *Shumma izbu*, Tablet II, line 1: de Zorzi (2014, p. 393); Leichty (1970, p. 44).
55 *Shumma izbu*, Tablet II, lines 2–4: de Zorzi (2014, pp. 393–4), Leichty (1970, p. 46).
56 *Shumma izbu*, Tablet IV, line 56: de Zorzi (2014, p. 449), Leichty (1970, p. 71).

57 *Shumma izbu*, Tablet IV, line 57: de Zorzi (2014, p. 449), Leichty (1970, p. 71).

58 *Shumma alu*, Tablet 45, lines 27' and 30', Freedman (2017, p. 44). These omens describe cats being seen in a man's house.

59 Ibid., Tablet 44, lines 53', 52', 57', Freedman (2017, p. 36).

60 Ibid., Tablet 47, lines 42'–43', Freedman (2017, p. 62), concerning yellow and red dogs.

61 Ibid., Tablet 47, lines 45'–6', Freedman (2017, p. 63).

62 Ibid., Tablet 47, lines 50', 52', 53', Freedman (2017, p. 63). As usual with the omens, it is not so straightforward, however, since despite these positive associations one omen says 'if a dog enters a temple there will be no gods in the land' (Tablet 47, line 49', Freedman, 2017, p. 63), while a black dog was also bad: 'that temple's foundation will not be secure' (Tablet 47, line 51', Freedman, 2017, p. 63).

63 Ibid., Tablet 49, lines 19, 2, Freedman (2017, p. 76).

64 SAA 10 33, lines r. 8–10. Cf. *Shumma alu*, Tablet 34, Freedman (2006, pp. 224–9).

65 SAA 20 33.

66 Ibid., col. i, lines r. 48–9.

67 SAA 7 154, col. i, lines 1'–2'.

68 SAA 7 154.

69 SAA 7 148 and 149.

70 SAA 7 132.

71 Bottéro (1995).

72 SAA 7 24, line 27.

73 Erra and Ishum, Tablet V, lines 53–4, Foster (2005, pp. 880–911). For full edition, see also Cagni (1969) and pages 128–9 for this recommendation.

74 SAA 3 20–22.

75 Wee (2018, pp. 839–41), §IV and §IX,.

76 *Shumma alu*, Tablets 103 and 104 on eBL, for Tablet 104 see D.2.6 Boddy and Mittermayer (2023), Tablet 103 Boddy and Mittermayer (forthcoming).

77 Sex omen 1, Guinan (1997, p. 473); *Shumma alu* Tablet 104, line 17, Boddy and Mittermayer (2023).

78 *Shumma alu*, Tablet 104, line 36, Boddy and Mittermayer (2023).

79 Sex omen 5, Guinan (1997, p. 473), *Shumma alu* Tablet 104, line 20, Boddy and Mittermayer (2023).

80 Sex omen 4, Guinan (1997, p. 473).

81 Sex omen 12, Guinan (1997, p. 474), *Shumma alu* Tablet 104, line 18, Boddy and Mittermayer (2023).

82 Sex omen 16, Guinan (1997, p. 474), *Shumma alu* Tablet 104, line 13, Boddy and Mittermayer (2023).

83 *Middle Assyrian Laws* A 19 (Roth, 1997, p. 159). Another law (A 20 – Roth, 1997, p. 160) concerning sex between men punishes the instigator by forcing him to be penetrated in turn and castrating him, but whether this refers to consensual sex or only rape is not clear.

84 Sex omen 10, Guinan (1997, p. 474), *Shumma alu* Tablet 104, line 29, Boddy and Mittermayer (2023).

85 Zisa (2021, pp. 130, 165, 174–5 and *passim*). The texts are: *Nis libbi E*, lines 55–7 (Zisa 2021, pp. 319–20), *Nis libbi F*, lines 36–8, 42–3 (Zisa 2021, p. 345), and *Nis libbi N*, lines 1–22 (Zisa 2021, p. 445), though the last text comes from Anatolia.

86 Foster (2005, p. 1002), for edition see Zisa (2021, pp. 314–15).

87 Foster (2005, p. 1000), see also Zisa (2021, pp. 238–9).

88 e.g. Foster (2005, p. 975). See also von Weiher (1988, pp. 43–4).

89 Wasserman (2016, pp. 271-2, no. 33, line 106; p. 266, no. 31, line 69; pp.257-60, no. 27, line 22)

90 Maul and Strauß (2011, p. 42), col. ii, lines i–24'.

Epilogue

1 Plutarch, *Life of Alexander*, 73–5 (Waterfield and Erskine 2016).

2 Diodorus Siculus, *Library of History*, 17. 116.1–4 (Oldfather 1933); Arrian, *Anabasis* 7.24 (Chinnock 2014).

3 Antiochus I 1, lines 8–11, Stevens (2014, p. 68).

4 BCHP 14, see commentary by van der Spek (2004), https://www.livius.org/sources/content/mesopotamian-chronicles-content/bchp-14-greek-community-chronicle/.

5 For a recent edition see de Breucker (2010).

6 Alcaeus, fragment 350, see Campbell (1990, pp. 386–7); Xenophon, *Anabasis*, Brownson (2014).
7 RINAP 3 Sennacherib 46, lines 59–61 and Sennacherib 20, lines i' 6–11.
8 SAA 19 25; RINAP 2 Sargon 1, lines 117–19; 43, line 21.
9 The sermon is translated by Bodhi (2007) and is also available online at https://suttacentral.net/.
10 Bodhi (2007, p. 60).
11 Genesis 5, 9:28–9, 11:10–24. For the Sumerian king list see ETCSL 2.1.1 and Glassner (2004, pp. 117–26).
12 Genesis 11:31.
13 2 Kings 18–19; RINAP 3 Sennacherib 4, lines 55–60.
14 2 Kings 19:37 see also Isaiah 37: 38.
15 2 Kings 25.
16 Genesis 11:4.
17 RIBo 7 Nebuchadnezzar II 27, col. ii, lines 19–44.
18 Ezra 1:1–11.
19 RIBo 8 Cyrus II 1.
20 Ibid., lines 30–32.
21 Hunger and de Jong (2014).
22 McClure and Feltoe (1919, p. 38).
23 Malcolm (1829, p. 346).
24 RIBo 7 Nabonidus 34, col. i, lines 28–33 for Nebuchadnezzar and col. i, line 44–col. ii, line 5 in the same text for the priestess Enanedu sister of Rim-Sin. For Hammurabi, see RIBo 7 Nabonidus 16, col. ii, lines 20–27 and col. iii, lines 27–31. For Naram-Sin, see RIBo 7 Nabdonidus 23, col. ii, lines 2'–12'.
25 According to Berossus, fragment 3, Verbrugghe and Wickersham (1996, p. 47).

Acknowledgements

My first thanks go to my agent Jonathan Conway, for asking me to write this book and finding it such an excellent home at Penguin. Jonathan's sound advice has been invaluable in shaping the manuscript. My editors at Penguin Tom Penn, Eva Hodgkin and Olivia Kumar have been stellar in helping polish it to completion, as has Robert Sharman with his exceptionally sharp-eyed copy editing. Thanks also to my wonderful publicists, Annabel Huxley and Gavin Reade, whose enthusiasm has been invigorating.

Several institutions have supported me at various stages on this journey. Plans began to take shape while I was lecturing at Cambridge, where Pembroke college took me into their community, as did Selwyn when they offered me a Bye-Fellowship. The proposal and sample chapter were written during a Junior Research Fellowship at The Queen's College, Oxford, where I also later returned for a sabbatical as I was addressing peer review feedback. My fantastic colleagues at the University of Leicester have been extremely supportive of this project as part of my role as Lecturer in the Heritage of the Middle East, with particular thanks to Jo Appleby, Huw Barton, Ingrid Dyson, Oliver Harris, Jan Haywood, Andy Merrills, Sarah Scott, Graham Shipley and Ruth Young. The last round of edits was carried out during a visit to Tyndale House, Cambridge.

To write a book as wide-ranging as this has required me to expand into new fields of expertise, and the manuscript has benefitted from the comments of a number of scholars. Those who reviewed early drafts of chapters include: Nicholas Postgate, Alan Lenzi, Frank Simons, Ulrike Steinert, Ulla Koch, Martin Worthington, Jamie Novotny, Uri Gabbay, Gina Konstantopolou, and Kathryn Stevens. Alan Lenzi and Jamie Novotny both took extra time to discuss particular issues with me. Jamie also kindly shared his unpublished paper co-authored with Chikako Watanabe from the Marburg Rencontre Assyriologique Internationale 2017, while Martin Worthington shared parts of his forthcoming works on Sargon and the Sumerian sign list. Sophus Helle and Eli Tadmor both read the manuscript and gave valuable comments. Discussions with Sophus were also useful when I was planning the structure. The book has been further improved by the comments of four peer reviewers: Fran Reynolds and Gina Konstantopoulos acting for Penguin, and two further anonymous reviewers commissioned by University of Chicago Press. Other colleagues who have been generous with their time include Julian Reade, who answered questions about the archaeology of Kuyunjik, Auday Hussein, who sent me photographs of the modern site, and Neil Erskine, who produced drafts of the map. I have been fortunate to have assistants working with me to retrieve references and format the manuscript: Eleanor Home, Georgia Vance, Joe Barber, Philip Boyes, Camryn Good and Aga Arcisz, who made the process all the more enjoyable with their company. Eli Tadmor and Johannes Bach helped with last minute reference checking when time was ticking on the proofs. Any remaining errors are of course my responsibility.

I am proud to be a member of the Ancient World Cluster at Wolfson College, Oxford, where I did my DPhil, and an alumna of St Hilda's College, Oxford, where my undergraduate Classics tutor Emily Kearns encouraged my leanings towards the Near East. During my Assyriological education Jacob Dahl's classes introduced me to the idea of omens as part of the history of science, which greatly influenced my thinking, as did the mentorship of Fran Reynolds. Ultimately I owe my love of ancient languages to my Classics teacher at school, Barbara Bell, who was a great inspiration, and whose lessons I will always remember.

This book has its unlikely roots in the theatre. I first got to know Ashurbanipal, his family, and scholars through writing a trilogy of stage plays about them. I thank the creative team, cast, and crew of the National Theatre of Akkad for the heavy metal / Noh production of *Ashurbanipal: The Last Great King of Assyria* – Thomas Stell, Andrew Garner, Tom Clucas, Alex Woolley, Anahita Hoose, Timothy Foot, Rebecca Daley, Ante Qu, Abigail Adams, Claudia Freemantle, William Bolton, Francesca Whalen, Darya Shchepanovska, Antonio Mateiro, Tess Colley, Dòmhnall-Iain MacDonald, Francesca Balestrieri, Trudy Lynn, Sami Ibrahim, Felix Pollock and Valentine Kozin; all who worked on the naturalistic *Esarhaddon: The Substitute King* – Lucy Wood, Andrew Garner, Rebecca Wilkin, Laura Cull, Catherine O'Leary, Rose Azad Khan, Hannah Street, Olivia Lalude-Haworth, Francesca Balestrieri and Elyn Vandenwyngaert; and all behind the immersive version of *Ashurbanipal* staged at the Crypt Gallery in 2019 – Justin Murray, Victoria Jones, Charlotte Potter, Laurence Varda, Michal Banai, Wayne Wilson, Melissa Taydon, John Lutula, George Chaffey, Hakan Hafizoglu, Rachel Wise and Davide Vox. They all helped me explore how ancient Assyria can be dramatized in immediate and vivid ways, which has informed the writing of this book.

Thanks to my trusty band of Failed Novelists for reading and commenting on a whole draft – Morgan Davies, Martin Goodhead, James Harding, Anahita Hoose and Rosie McKeown – and to my friends at Leicester Writers Club for feedback that helped me rewrite the opening pages.

Some friends are due special thanks. Martin Worthington has cheered me on from the start, and helped maintain my sanity on many occasions with discussions on strategy and perspective – *ina ibrūtīka ma'diš ḫadâku*. John Blair has helped in more ways than I can count, from offering suggestions on the manuscript to giving advice on a whole range of practical matters, from taking photographs of books in libraries to sharing his wisdom on dealing with proofs. John has been an amazing source of moral support and intellectual encouragement, and I am lucky to count him as such a good friend. Thanks also to Kanerva, Edward and Ida Blair-Heikkinen, whose friendship has meant a great deal throughout the development of this book.

Finally, this book is dedicated to my parents, Tatiana and Michael

Wisnom, who made it possible in so many ways, and who both would have made excellent Mesopotamian scholars. I thank them for their love, encouragement and support over the years that has enabled me to flourish. That I ended up as a writer and academic is in large part down to them.

Index